MW00582911

Love
in
Marriage

DELITIÆ SAPIENTIÆ

DE

AMORE CONJUGIALI;

POST QUAS SEQUUNTUR

VOLUPTATES INSANIÆ

DE

AMORE SCORTATORIO.

A B

EMANUELE SWEDENBORG,

SUECO.

AMSTELODAMI,

MDCCLXVIII

Love in Marriage

A Translation of
Emanuel Swedenborg's

The Sensible Joy in Married Love

and

The Foolish Pleasures of Illicit Love

by
David F. Gladish

With an Introduction by
George F. Dole

SWEDENBORG FOUNDATION
NEW YORK

First published in Latin, Amsterdam, 1768
First English translation by John Clowes, Manchester, England, 1794
Second English Translation by Theophilus Parsons and
Warren Goddard, Boston, Massachusetts, 1833
Third English Translation by A. H. Searle, London, England, 1891
Fourth English translation by S. M. Warren, Boston, Massachusetts, 1907
Fifth English translation by William H. Alden, Bryn Athyn, Pennsylvania, 1915
Sixth English translation by William H. Wunsch, New York City, 1938
Seventh English translation by A. Acton, London, England, 1953

Emanuel Swedenborg's original work *Delitiae Sapientiae de Amore Conjugiali; Post Quas Sequuntur Voluptates Insaniae de Amore Scortatorio* when first translated into English carried the title *The Delights of Wisdom Pertaining to Conjugial Love, After Which Follow the Pleasures of Insanity Pertaining to Scortatory Love*. Subsequent translators used the titles *Conjugial Love, Marital Love*, and *Marriage Love*. Although bibliographic records remain obscure or contradictory, it appears that counting all translations, editions, and printings, English language versions of this work have been published some thirty times under these various titles.

The Swedenborg Foundation
139 East 23rd Street
New York 10010
© 1992 by The Swedenborg Foundation. All rights reserved
Printed in the United States of America

Library of Congress Catalog Card Number: 92-060085
ISBN 0-87785-141-7

Cover and book design, Paul Germain

The basis for the illustration used throughout this book is a drawing by George Baine (taken from an old Celtic design), which appeared in *Celtic Art: The Methods of Construction*, originally published in 1951 by MacLellian & Co., Ltd., Glasgow, and republished by Dover Publications, Inc., in 1973. This illustration source is used by permission of the publisher.

Dedicated
to the people who
hope there is marriage

— D. F. G.

Translator's Notes

Foreword
We tend to think of love—especially sexual love—as something you do. We even speak of it as something you make. But according to Swedenborg, love is actually something that you *are*. Or, to put it more accurately, love is something that comes through you. In marriage, this is just as true of love on its most physical plane as it is of love on its highest spiritual plane.

Love originates in the Lord God, who *is* love. It is wise love in the Lord—love that knows all time and space and can fathom the perfect balance of all the infinite forces in our spiritual and worldly environment. Divine love and its wisdom radiate from the Lord and shine throughout all that He created, the way the love and wisdom of two parents shine throughout their family life, or the way the sun's heat and light bathe its solar system, as a kind of reiteration of the love and wisdom that created it.

When married people love each other, and especially when married people who love each other "make" love together, they, too, are precisely a reiteration of the marriage of divine love and wisdom that created them. In fact, when *any* man and woman "make" love, or when any other sexual creatures do, for that matter, it reflects the effort of divine love and wisdom to unite and to create. But unless the whole creature is involved in the lovemaking, body, mind, and soul, the lovemaking is just copulation, on a material plane, with the smallest, most disconnected relationship imaginable to its spiritual impetus. So the genuine love in marriage is only to be had by people, and by people who *are* married, and who believe in marriage, and who believe that marriage is a deeply spiritual union that sounds their profoundest reaches and "plays," as Swedenborg put it, all the way to their outermost bodily parts, with joy. Most of us taste this miracle only rarely in its completeness. Some never do. But all of us can, if we want it enc ugh to make it a goal in life, and if we know about its beauty.

The operative word here is *know*. At the beginning of Chapter 13 (p. 295 below), there is the statement that

> the purpose of . . . this book is for the reader to agree as a result of seeing the truths by his rationality. This is how his spirit is convinced. Things that your spirit is convinced of take precedence over things that come through faith in authority without the counsel of reason. These things go no further into your head than your memory . . . so they are inferior to rational intellectual convictions.

Rational intellectual convictions. *Love in Marriage* is neither *pro*scriptive nor *pre*scriptive. It is *de*scriptive. The book's author, Emanuel Swedenborg, was a Swedish scientist and philosopher, prominent in eighteenth-century Europe. In his fifties he turned his scientifically trained mind from extensive examination of the natural environment to an examination of humanity's spiritual environment, and his virtually journalistic reportage makes spiritual life after death if anything less mysterious than the life we are familiar with in our natural environment. In fact, as the reader of this book will come to see, waking up to spiritual life after "death" is as easy as waking up in the morning here, feeling yourself all over and finding that, yes, you are all there. You eat, you drink, you marry (or continue to be married), and you make love in that life. You have a job, you go to church if you like church, you have recreation, you have friends, and you learn new things every day. In a word, you might not even know you died— or think to ask.

The occult elements of today's Christianity turn out to be a smoke screen. For example, *angels*, as Swedenborg uses the term, means people who have lived in this world and are now continuing to live in *heaven*, which means in love and mental clarity. *Devil* and *Satan* are terms for people who thoroughly involved themselves in selfishness during life in the world and therefore reject heaven in their life after death, or, to put it another way, choose to be in their own presence rather than the Lord's. *The Lord, God, Jesus Christ,* and *Holy Spirit* are all names for the one Creator, who in this theology is the only deity there ever was.

The word *charity,* in this book, means love for mankind, really. Instead of being a gratuitous and often perfunctory kindness, charity is loving to do what the Lord made you for. The implications are marvelous. If you love your work, that's charity. If you love to keep your body in shape and be good at some sport, that's charity, too. To enjoy a good meal in good company is charity. Charity is a love for fulfilling your potential on all planes. And, especially, a love for helping others to fulfill theirs.

Faith is an understanding of the truth—again, an intellectual conviction. Faith does not have to grope in the dark. It does not "leap." Faith is your recognition of the truth, and your acceptance of it, when the truth comes your way. Reason does not seek God through faith. It works the other way around. God seeks you through His gift of your rationality, and when you see why, that's faith.

The terms *church* and *religion* have earned a tainted reputation these days. People associate church and religion with institutions manufactured by humans for human power. Churches and religions already had that reputation in Swedenborg's time. He uses the terms, but when he talks about "the church" he means the Christian religion, and when he speaks of religion he means worship of the Lord.

The *will* of a human being, in *Love in Marriage,* means the deep-down motivation in our thoughts and actions. It is actually a person's essential life. Even our intellect is the servant of our will, for it justifies the things our will demands. If our will (our love) reaches for heaven, our intellect helps to show us how and why. If it reaches for the hell of self-interest and materialism, intellect rationalizes the folly.

How Swedenborg knows these refreshing Christian concepts, he himself explains in the first paragraph of Chapter 1. The Lord made it possible. Sometimes the explanation of the most perplexing mystery is right under our noses. In any case, having access to the spiritual range of human existence enabled Swedenborg to cut through the whole buildup of human-made Christian belief and reaffirm Christianity's true premises, that there is a God, that He is the Lord Jesus Christ, and that there is an even better life after this one.

Swedenborg was methodical. In this book he worked from the top down, so to speak. He begins by establishing through firsthand experience that spiritual life exists and that it includes all the human and environmental qualities of earthly life. His first chapter of exposition establishes that marriage is a heavenly thing—is, in fact, an essential quality in the Lord God. The rest of the book traces marriage down step by step through its more finite forms, clear to the mere travesties of marriage that have sprung up on earth, and, in the second part, even the downright inversions of marriage that spring from a will to destroy it.

Swedenborg's methodical paragraph numbers have been retained in the present translation, even though his actual paragraphs have been broken down into shorter ones. An effort has been made to keep these paragraph numbers relatively inconspicuous—less obtrusive, it is hoped, than line numbers in a translation of the *Iliad*. The considerable corpus of scholarship on Swedenborg's voluminous writings is traditionally indexed and referenced according to these paragraph numbers.

Texts and Translation

Swedenborg first published this book, in Latin, at Amsterdam, in 1786, under the title *Delitiae Sapientiae de Amore Conjugiali; Post Quas Sequuunter Voluptates Insaniae de Amore Scortatorio*. A translation into English was made in the nineteenth century by Samuel M. Warren and revised by Louis H. Tafel. It was also translated, more recently, by William Frederic Wunsch and by Dr. Alfred Acton, in the twentieth century. These three translations were constantly consulted in the preparation of the present translation. The Latin text that this translation follows is the Swedenborg Society's reprint of the Swedenborg Foundation's text, edited by S. Worcester, 1889.

There is no such thing as the ultimate translation of any important book. Too many things change too rapidly. The text of the original book gets edited and improved. Scholarship improves our knowledge of the subject matter. Most of all, our own language changes, as does the demography of the readership. The translator himself learns more as he goes, no matter how much he knew to start with. It is hard to hit a moving target, especially when you yourself are moving. You have to let fly your best shot. If the book is important, and I am dead sure that this one is, the next translator will soon be ready with his own best shot.

I have attempted to render both the meaning and the tone of Swedenborg's book, as I myself sense it and feel it. But translation is not like interpreting Morse code, where a certain symbol always represents a certain letter, or like building with dimensional lumber or bricks, where a certain piece of material will always fill a certain corresponding gap. Translation is more like stone work, where you strive for a dimensional and aesthetic structure, but with nondimensional materials. Language is funny that way.

The easiest part of translating Latin is to find out what your Latin text says. You have dictionaries, grammars, commentarias, other translations, and colleagues to help you if you get stuck. The hard part is to determine what the English should say in order to carry the author's meaning to the reader without causing him to stumble, flounder, wince, or scratch his head. Ideally, a book should seem to say just what the reader thought it would, phrase by phrase and sentence by sentence. Reading it should be as easy as watching the scenery go by through the window of a train.

It never is. I only hope that this translation makes it easier than it used to be.

Acknowledgements

Without the much-appreciated backing of the Swedenborg Foundation, this translation might still be lying dormant in a file. Mr. Lee Woofenden's input as Latin consultant for the Foundation has on virtually every page saved me from some obscurity, inaccuracy, or awkwardness. Those that remain are my fault, not his. Dr. George Dole, the Reverend D. L. Rose, and John R. Seekamp have given advice and help from the outset. The Swedenborg Library has been especially helpful. And I particularly wish to express my own and the Swedenborg Foundation's appreciation to the people who have lent encouragement and support both out of friendship and out of interest in seeing this translation published: Mr. Lavar Howard, Patrick and Gillian Mayer, Ian and Frea Woofenden, Dolores and Allan Soderberg, Gabrielle and Thomas Gladish, Endrede and Donald P. Gladish, the Reverend Kent Junge, and Margaret and Robert Merrill.

Introduction

by George Dole

Love in Marriage is perhaps the most distinctive of Swedenborg's theological publications. It was the first of these works to bear his name on its title page, even though the secret of his authorship had been out for at least eight years, during which time he had published seven works. He himself defended *Love in Marriage* as "not a theological work, but mostly a book of morals,"[1] and in no other work does he pay so much attention, in the expository sections, to human behavior and circumstances. No other work of Swedenborg's has such a high proportion of narrative to exposition. It is significant that Swedenborg chose the title "The Sensible Joy in Married Love" in preference to "The Angelic Wisdom in Married Love." Further, the device of opening with an extended story, especially one with strong comic elements, is quite without precedent in his works.

In particular, the focus on human behavior and circumstances may create problems for the contemporary reader, because the circumstances Swedenborg was addressing were those of his own times. Marriage was a civil ceremony, preceded by careful legal arrangements of property rights. The role of the church was simply to bless the marriage after it had taken place, and to urge the practice of Christian love and virtue in the home. Girls were trained primarily for the task of managing a household, and might well begin doing so in their early teens. Household management was

---

[1]   Rudolph L. Tafel, ed., comp., trans., *Documents Concerning the Life and Character of Emanuel Swedenborg*, 2 vols., (London: Swedenborg Society, 1875, 1877), 306. This should probably be taken to mean that the work did not deal with matters treated in official Lutheran dogma.

not simply the routine of modern "housekeeping." In an era when the necessities of life itself could not be taken for granted, it was a vital and difficult task, requiring careful calculation and fore-thought. Travel was physically demanding, and travel abroad particularly dangerous. In the long Swedish winter, even travel from house to house could be fatal—especially after dark, and the daylight hours were few. It was by no means inconsiderate for the husband to leave the wife at home. Unless the need were urgent, it would be irresponsible to risk her health and life.

This distinction of functions was literally a *modus vivendi*, a way of surviving in a hostile climate. The unanswerable arguments for it were not found on the theoretical level, but on the pragmatic level. Whatever one might think about inherent differences be-tween masculine and feminine natures, the system worked.

When Swedenborg sat down to write *Love in Marriage*, though, such considerations were peripheral. For him, the essence of mar-riage was the union of souls. The critical issues to be addressed were not how the tasks were divided, but how married partners understood and cared for each other. If his recommendations were to be at all practicable to his readers, they had to remain within the bounds set by circumstance.

The contemporary reader, then, needs two sets of standards to evaluate the book. When the subject is what men and women do—their physical behavior—this can be fully understood only within its eighteenth-century, Swedish context. When the subject is the motivation of the behavior, the human relationship of the partners, we are dealing with principles that transcend culture. They must express themselves differently in different times and places—one would not expect a Bantu husband to bring home a salary check, or a Bantu wife to stay in the house and cultivate embroidery—but the essence of thoughtfulness is still the same, and still central. Any will to dominate or manipulate the other is always and everywhere destructive of a marriage or of any human relationship. Any effort to understand lovingly is always and everywhere constructive.

It is at this level that Swedenborg's spiritual experience qualifies him uniquely. What we infer from behavior he saw face to face, in a spiritual world where "the internals appear." The cultural specifics remind us that this spiritual view is not simply romantic or hopelessly idealistic. It presents ideals, yes, but ideals designed to work in a very problematic world.

There is one further potential benefit to this approach. Our world is still problematic, and we are often blind to our embeddedness in our own culture. It is all too easy to become so absorbed in our necessary efforts to change unjust practices that we ourselves become domineering or manipulative—"in a good cause," of course. Looking at the eighteenth century from the vantage point of the twentieth, we may perhaps have an inkling of what the twentieth century will look like from the vantage point of the twenty-second. We may hope that the enlightened researchers of that era will recognize that we were doing the best we could with what we had to work with, and that they will find in our efforts some things whose value has not diminished with the years.

Contents

xviii ◇ Contents

and live by His teachings.—So real married love is available only
for Christians.—This is why a Christian may take only one wife.—
If he takes more, he commits worldly and spiritual adultery.—The
Israelites were allowed more wives, because they did not have
Christianity.—Mohammedans are allowed more wives, because
they do not recognize the Lord Jesus Christ as one with Jehovah
the Father.—The Mohammedan heaven is outside the Christian
heaven.—Polygamy is lascivious.—For polygamists, the chastity,
purity, and holiness of marriage are not possible.—Polygamists
cannot become spiritual.—Polygamy is not a sin for those who do
it from religion.—Nor for those who do not know about the
Lord.—Mohammedan polygamists are saved if they acknowledge
God and live by the law.—But in heaven they are not with
Christians.

Love flares up in zeal.—Zeal is spiritual.—Zeal is as good or bad
as the love it comes from.—But the outward appearance is the
same.—The zeal of a good love harbors love, but that of a bad love
harbors hate.—The zeal of married love is called jealousy.—
Jealousy is like a fire flaring out and a fear of loss.—Spiritual
jealousy and worldly jealousy.—Jealousy is anguish lest married
love become divided and perish.—Partners who do not love each
other have jealousy, too.—Some people have no jealousy.—
Jealousy for mistresses is not the same as jealousy for wives.—
Animals and birds also have jealousy.—Jealousy is different in
husbands than in wives.

An aura of having offspring and an aura of protecting them
radiate from the Lord.—They converge with the aura of married
love.—They influence everything in heaven and on earth—The
aura of love for children is an aura of protecting and nourishing.—It affects good and bad people alike.—It affects mothers,
and through them, fathers.—It is an aura of innocence and peace
from the Lord.—It influences children, and through them,
parents.—It influences the parents' souls, especially through

touch.—As children grow less innocent, the affection diminishes.—Parents are conscious of innocence and peace in their
children.—This aura progresses step by step.—Love for children
reaches downward, not upward.—Wives' love before conception
is different than after.—Married love is connected with love for
children for spiritual, and therefore for natural, reasons.—Love for
children is different in spiritual partners than in earthly ones.—In
spiritual partners it is from inner things, in earthly partners it is
from outer things.—So it is in partners who love each other and in
those who do not.—Love for children remains after death,
especially in women.—They bring up children under the Lord's
guidance, as in the world.—The Lord sees to it that the children
become angels.

Story:

Everything in the natural world comes through the spiritual
world from the Lord

Part 2 : The Foolish Pleasures of Illicit Love

18. Illicit Love and Married Love Are Opposite

Without knowing what married love is, you cannot know what
illicit love is.—It is opposite to married love.—It is opposite as a
worldly person is opposite to a spiritual person.—Or as a "marriage" of evil and lies is opposite to a marriage of good and
truth.—Or as hell is opposite to heaven.—The filthiness of hell
comes from illicit love, the cleanness of heaven from married
love.—The same goes for uncleanness and cleanness in the
church.—Illicit love makes a person less a person and less a man,
but married love makes a person more a person and more a
man.—There is an aura of illicit love and an aura of married
love.—That of illicit love comes from hell, and that of married love
from heaven.—These two auras meet but do not mingle.—People
are in a balance between these two auras.—They can turn to
whichever they choose.—Each aura brings delight.—The delights
of illicit love are physical, the delights of married love spiritual,
even in the body.—Illicit love's delights are foolish, married love's
sensible.

Story:

An attempt to discuss illicit love with angels

19. Fornication

Fornication relates to sexual love.—It begins when a boy starts to
think and act from his own intellect.—It belongs to the worldly

side of a person.—It is a desire, but not for adultery.—In some
people, love for the other sex cannot be restrained.—This is why
brothels are tolerated.—A desire for fornication is a small matter if
married love is preferred.—It is serious if it has adultery in
view.—It is worse if it desires promiscuity and defloration.—In its
beginning it is neutral between illicit love and married love.—
Watch out that married love is not lost.—Marriage is the treasure
of human life and of Christianity.—Marriage can be protected.—A
mistress is preferable to roving passions.

Two types of concubinage.—Having a concubine and a wife is
impermissible for Christians.—It is polygamy.—It destroys
marriage.—It is permissible when separated from a wife.—
Legitimate reasons for divorce are reasons for concubinage.—As
are just reasons for separation.—Some reasons are valid, some
specious.—Valid, serious reasons are the just reasons.—Specious
reasons only seem just.—Those who have a concubine for
legitimate, just, and important reasons may still have love for
marriage.—While concubinage continues, sexual union with a
wife is not permissible.

There is a simple, double, and triple adultery.—Simple adultery is
between a single person and another person's spouse.—Double
adultery involves a husband and another's wife, or vice versa.—
Triple adultery is adultery with blood relations.—There are four
levels of adultery.—Adulteries of the first level do not involve
intellect.—These are mild.—Adulteries of the second level involve
passion and intellect.—These are blameworthy precisely as
intellect favors them afterwards.—Adulteries rationalized as not
being sinful are of the third level.—They are serious in the
measure that they are confirmed.—Adulteries of the fourth level
are committed with intention and represented as lawful.—These
are the most serious.—Adulteries of the third and fourth level are
sinful to the extent that they involve intellect and will.—They
make people worldly, sense-oriented and physical-minded.—

PART 1

The Sensible Joy in Married Love

Chapter 1

Introduction:
The Joys of Heaven
and a Wedding There

1   I foresee that many people who read the following chapters and the remarkable stories after each chapter, are going to think that the stories are imaginative inventions. But I assert, in truth, that they are not invented but really done and seen—and not when my mind was in a trance, but when I was wide awake. In fact, the Lord Himself saw fit to let me see Him and has sent me to teach things about the new church that the Book of Revelation refers to as the "New Jerusalem." To do this He opened the inner levels of my mind for me, and this enables me to be in the spiritual world with angels and in the natural world with people at the same time—and this for twenty-five years now.

2   Once I noticed an angel flying under the eastern sky, holding a trumpet to his mouth. He sounded it north, west, and south. The robe he wore fluttered behind him, and was cinched with a band of rubies and sapphires that seemed to flash and sparkle. He swooped down and glided slowly to the earth near me. On landing he walked here and there and came up to me when he saw me. It was a spiritual experience, in which I was standing on a hill toward the south.

And when he was close, I spoke to him and asked, "What's happening now? I heard the sound of your trumpet and saw you come down through the air."

"I was sent to summon the most famous in learning, the

most insightful talents, and those of highest reputation for wisdom, from all the countries of the Christian world, who are in this continent," the angel answered, "to meet on this hill where you're standing, and from within their souls to express their minds as to what they thought, knew, and sensed while in the world, about the joy of heaven and about eternal happiness.

"I was sent on this errand because our community in the eastern part of heaven has received some new arrivals from the world who say that not even one person in the whole Christian world knows what the joy of heaven is, or eternal happiness, nor therefore what heaven is.

"My brothers and friends were really amazed at this and said to me, 'Go down, give a call and summon the wisest in the world of spirits, where all human beings first gather after leaving the natural world, to get definite information from the mouths of many whether it is true that Christians have such a befogged, dark ignorance about the future life.'"

Then he said, "Wait a while and you will see crowds of wise people flocking this way. The Lord will get a hall ready for them to meet in."

I waited, and in a half hour I saw two groups from the north, two from the west, and two from the south! And as they arrived the angel with the trumpet ushered them into the hall that was ready, where they took their places according to their quarter of the compass. There were six groups or companies. A seventh, which the others could not see for the light, was from the east.

After they assembled, the angel explained the reason for the meeting and asked the groups to take turns presenting their wisdom about the joy of heaven and eternal happiness. And then each group formed a circle, each person facing another, to recall the ideas they had formed on this subject in their previous life, to clarify them, and after clarification, to speak out about them.

3 After considering it, the first group—from the north—said, "The joy of heaven and eternal happiness are the same thing as heavenly life, and so everyone who goes to heaven to live enters its festivities—the way someone who goes to a wedding goes to its festivities. Isn't heaven in plain sight up above us, and therefore in a place? That is where blessings upon blessings are, and pleasures

upon pleasures, and not somewhere else. A person is swept into these with all mental perception and all bodily sensation, thanks to the overflowing joys of the place, when he is swept up to heaven. So the happiness of heaven, which is eternal, is nothing but getting into heaven—getting in by Divine Grace."

After these words, the other group from the north expressed this interpretation: "Heavenly joy and eternal happiness are nothing but a most delightful companionship with angels and the sweetest conversations with them. This keeps every delighted face wide open forever and every mouth in the crowd laughing with pleasure in the charming talk and wit. What are the joys of heaven but a variety of conversations like that to eternity?"

The third group, the first group of wise people from the western quarter, fetched this from the meditations they loved: "What is the joy of heaven and eternal happiness but feasts with Abraham, Isaac, and Jacob? On their tables will be plenty of delicacies and rich food to eat and lots of fine, noble wine, and after the feasts shows and dances by young women and men moving to rhythmic harmonies and flutes, alternating with the sweetest songs. And then in the evening there will be stage plays with actors. And after all this, feasts again—every day to eternity."

After this statement the fourth group—the second from the western quarter—announced their opinion, saying, "We have cherished many ideas about the joy of heaven and eternal happiness, have considered various joys and have compared them, and we conclude that the joys of heaven are the joys of Paradise. What is heaven but a paradise stretching from east to west and south to north? In it are fruit trees and delightful flowers, with the magnificent Tree of Life in the middle, and the blessed sitting around it, enjoying delicately flavored fruits and festooned with wreaths of the sweetest smelling flowers. And the breath of spring is perpetual, so the flowers bloom again and again in endless variety. And their constant growth and blossoming, with the constant spring temperature, keeps these souls continually refreshed, so they cannot help inhaling new joys and breathing them back out every day. It brings them into the flower of youth and thus to the primeval state in which Adam and his wife were created. So they are brought back to their Paradise, transferred from earth to heaven."

The fifth group—the first group of intellectuals from the southern quarter—declared this: "The joy of heaven and eternal happiness are nothing but supereminent dominion and richest treasures, which means more-than-regal magnificence and more-than-illustrious splendor. From people who had acquired these things in the previous world we can tell that they are the joys of heaven—and the perpetual enjoyment of them, which is eternal happiness. And besides, the blessed in heaven are to reign with the Lord and be kings and princes, because they are sons of the One who is King of kings and Lord of lords, and they will sit upon thrones, and angels will serve them.

"We have ascertained the magnificence of heaven from the New Jerusalem, which describes its glory. Each of its gates is a pearl, its streets are pure gold, and the foundations of its wall are precious stones. Consequently, anyone accepted into heaven gets his palace, glittering with gold and costliness, and dominion over one another according to rank. And since we have found out that joys and deep-down happiness are inherent in things like that, and that they are God's unbreakable promise, we cannot trace the very happy condition of heavenly life to anything else."

After this the sixth group—the second from the southern quarter—raised their voice and said, "The joy of heaven and its eternal happiness are nothing other than perpetual glorification of God, one eternal religious holiday, and most blessed worship, with songs and jubilation. This means continually lifting one's heart to God with full trust that He accepts one's prayers and praises for the divine bounty of one's blessings."

Some of this group added that this festivity would include magnificent lighting and the most fragrant incense, and majestic processions led by a pope with a great big trumpet, greater and lesser bishops and key bearers next, and after them men with palms, and women with golden icons in their hands.

4   The seventh group, which the rest could not see for the light, were from the eastern part of heaven. They were angels from the same community as the angel with the trumpet. When they heard in their heaven that not one person in the Christian world knew what the joy of heaven and eternal happiness are, they said to each other, "This can't be true. There can't be such thick darkness

and such mental stupidity among Christians. We should go down, too, and hear if it is the truth. And if it is, it is a real omen."

Then these angels spoke to the angel with the trumpet. "Every person, as you know, who had wanted heaven and had some particular idea of the joys there, is brought, after death, into the joys he imagined, and after finding out what those joys are like—that they are based on their groundless mental notions and confused fantasies—they are brought out again and instructed. This happens in the world of spirits to most people who used to think about heaven in their previous life, and have concluded something about the joys there—enough to want them."

The angel with the trumpet heard these words and said to the six groups of wise people from the Christian world who had been called together, "Follow me, and I'll lead you to your joys, or heaven."

5   After he said this the angel went ahead, accompanied first by the group persuaded that heavenly joys just consist of pleasant company and most agreeable conversations. The angel led them to crowds in the northern parts who in the former world had the same idea of heavenly joys. There was a spacious house there, where they were gathered. There were more than fifty rooms in the house, specified for different kinds of conversation. In one room they talked about things they saw and heard in public places and in the streets, in another they were telling various stories about the fair sex, throwing in more and more witticisms, until the faces of all the crowd were spread with cheerful laughter.

In other rooms they told news about the court, about the ministries, state policy, various things that had leaked out of secret councils, and they reasoned about the events and made conjectures. In others they talked about business. In others literary subjects. In others about things having to do with civic prudence and the moral life. In others about churches and sects. And so on.

I was able to investigate this house, and I saw them wandering from room to room looking for others who shared their interests and therefore their joys. And among the clusters I noticed three types—some catching their breath to speak, some eager to find out something, and some listening insatiably.

The house had four doors, one for each direction. I noticed

that many detached themselves from the company, in a hurry to go. I followed some of them to the east door and saw several sitting by it with sad faces. I approached and asked why they were sitting there so depressed.

"The doors of this house are kept shut against escapees," they answered. "It is now the third day since we came, and we have tried living out our expectations of company and conversation, and we are so tired of the ceaseless yammering that we can hardly stand to hear the drone of its sound. So we came to this door in disgust and knocked, but the response was, 'The doors of this house are not exits but entrances. Stay and reap the joys of heaven.' From this response we gather that we have to stay here forever, so gloom has invaded our minds, and now our chests are starting to tighten up, and we're getting desperate."

Then the angel spoke to them. "Your condition is that your joys are dying," he said. "You thought they were the only heavenly joys, when really they only accompany heavenly joys."

"So what *is* heavenly joy?" they asked the angel.

The angel answered in these few words. "It is the pleasure of doing something that is useful to yourself and to others. And the pleasure of usefulness gets its essence from love, and its outward expression from wisdom. The pleasure of usefulness that grows out of love through wisdom is the soul and life of all heavenly joys. In the heavens there are very happy parties that cheer the minds of angels, raise their spirits, delight their hearts, and refresh their bodies, but they have them after they have done useful things in their occupations or whatever they do. This is how all their joys and pleasures gain soul and life. But if that soul and life are missing, the accompanying joys become not joyful but incidental at first, then trivial, and finally dreary and troublesome."

Once he had said these words the door opened. The people sitting there escaped from the house and ran home, each to his occupation and work, and they recovered.

6   After that the angel spoke to the ones who had decided that for them heavenly joys and eternal happiness would be feasts with Abraham, Isaac, and Jacob, and after the feasts shows and games, and then more feasts, and so on to eternity.

"Follow me," he said, "and I will lead you into the pleasures of your joys." And he led them through a grove to a level place with a floor, which had tables placed on it—fifteen on one side and fifteen on the other.

"Why so many tables?" they asked.

"The first table is Abraham's, the second Isaac's, the third Jacob's," said the angel, "and next to them are lined up the tables of the twelve Apostles. On the other side is the same number of tables, for their wives. The first three tables are for Sarah, Abraham's wife; Rebecca, Isaac's wife; and Leah and Rachel, Jacob's wives. The other twelve are for the twelve Apostles' wives."

After a while, we saw all the tables loaded with platters placed between little ornamental pyramids of delicacies. The guests stood around them waiting to see the heads of the tables. In a while they arrived as expected, filing in, from Abraham to the last Apostle. Soon each approached his own table and settled onto a couch at the head of it. And then they told the standing group, "Settle back like us."

They did—the men with the Fathers and the women with their wives—and ate and drank in happiness, and with reverence.

After dinner the Fathers went away, and then began the sports, the dances of young women and men, and after them the performances.

When it was over, they were invited to feast again. It was set up so that the first day one ate with Abraham, the next with Isaac, the third with Jacob, the fourth with Peter, the fifth with James, the sixth with John, the seventh with Paul, and with the rest in order until the fifteenth day, when the feasting would start over again in the same order, and so on to eternity.

After this the angel called together the men in the group and told them, "All the people you saw at the tables had the same unreal concept as you about the joys of heaven and the eternal happiness one gains from those joys. To let them see how unreal their ideas were and to lead them away from those notions, mock revelries like that were provided and permitted by the Lord.

"Those leaders you saw at the heads of the tables were aged impersonators—mostly unsophisticated—who were prouder than others because they had beards and some wealth, which induced the fantasy that they were the ancient Fathers.

"But follow me. I'll show you the way out of this training room."

They followed and saw fifty people here and fifty there who had stuffed their bellies with food to the point of nausea and badly wanted to return to familiar home surroundings—some to their duties, some to their businesses, and some to their work. But the attendants in the grove detained many of them and asked about their days of feasting, and whether they had eaten at the table with Peter and Paul yet, saying that if they were leaving before they did so, it would be improper and shameful.

But most of them answered, "We are stuffed full with our joys. Food has lost its flavor for us. Our pleasure in it has burned out. Our stomachs loathe it. We can't bear to taste it. We have dragged ourselves through several days and nights of this indulgence, and we earnestly beg to be let out." And when they were turned loose they fled home, gasping for breath, at a dead run.

After these events the angel called together the men in the group, and on the way he taught them these things about heaven: "There is food and drink in heaven just as in the world. There are parties and feasts. And for the leaders there, there are tables with splendid meals on them, delicacies and luxuries, which exhilarate and refresh their spirits. And there are also games and performances, and musicals and sings—all in the highest perfection. These things are delightful for them, too, but they are not happiness. They are within the joys and therefore come from joys. The happiness behind the pleasures makes them pleasant, enriches them, and keeps them from fading and becoming distasteful. And this happiness comes to everyone from the usefulness in what he does. In the dispositions of every angel's will there is a natural bent that attracts his mind to something that needs to be done, and it soothes and satisfies his mind. This serenity and satisfaction produce a mental state that can receive from the Lord a love of being useful. From receiving this comes heavenly happiness— which is the vital element in those joys that were mentioned before.

"Heavenly food in essence is nothing but love, wisdom, and usefulness together! In other words, a use carried on, with wisdom, and springing from love. On account of this, a person in heaven gets food for his body according to the useful things he does—magnificent food for people who are useful on a large scale, plain but very delicious for those engaged in average usefulness, common food for those who do common work, and none for the inactive."

7   After this he called to him the group of so-called wise people who had placed the joys of heaven and the eternal happiness from them in supreme power, richest treasures, more prestige than royalty, and more brilliant glory, because in the Word it says they will be kings and princes, that they will reign with Christ to eternity, and that angels will serve them—among other things. The angel said to them, "Follow me, and I will lead you into your joys."

He led the way into a portico built of columns and pyramids. In front of it was a low palace with an entrance open to the portico. He led them in through the arcade. Twenty people were waiting here and twenty there! And then suddenly someone came along impersonating an angel and told them, "The way to heaven is through this portico. Wait a while and get ready, because the older ones of you are going to be kings and the younger ones princes."

When he said this, a throne appeared by each column, with a silk robe on the throne and a scepter and crown on the robe. And by each pyramid an official seat appeared, elevated four and one-half feet above the ground, and on the seat a chain of gold links and the ribbon of an order of knighthood joined at the ends with diamond circlets. And then came an announcement: "Now go enrobe yourselves, be seated, and wait." And immediately the older men scrambled to the thrones, and the younger to the official seats, and they put the robes on and sat down.

Then something mistlike appeared to rise up from below, and under its influence the ones seated on the thrones and seats began to swell in their faces, puff their chests out, and fill up with the assurance that now they were kings and princes. The mist was an airy form of the fantasy that inspired them. And suddenly, young men flew down as if from the sky and stood, two behind each throne and one behind each seat, to serve them. And then, from time to time, a herald would announce, "You kings and princes, wait a little longer. Your palaces are now being prepared in heaven. Courtiers with attendants will come right away and lead you in." They waited and waited until they were yawning and worn out with anticipation.

After three hours the sky opened up over their heads, and angels looked down at them. In pity for them they said, "Why are you sitting there playacting so foolishly? They have played tricks on you and changed you from men to idols, because you have persuaded yourselves that you will reign with Christ like kings and princes and that angels will serve you. Have you forgotten the Lord's words, that whoever wants to be great in heaven should be a servant? So you have to learn what 'kings and princes and reigning with Christ' means. It means being wise and doing useful things, for the kingdom of Christ, which is heaven, is the kingdom of usefulness. For the Lord loves everyone, so He wants what is good for everyone, and good is usefulness. Since the Lord does good, or useful, things indirectly through angels and through people in the world, He gives a love of usefulness to those who are faithfully useful, and its reward is inward blessedness—which is eternal happiness.

"In the heavens, just as on earth, there is preeminent dominion and boundless wealth, for there are governments and forms of government, so there are greater and lesser powers and dignities. And for those in the highest positions there are palaces and courts whose magnificence and splendor outdoes the palaces and courts of emperors and kings on earth. And due to the number of courtiers, ministers, and attendants, as well as their splendid clothing, they have overflowing honor and glory. But the highest ones of them are chosen from people whose hearts are in the public good. Only their bodily senses are involved in the abundance that goes with nobility—and only to command obedience.

"Anything anyone does that is useful contributes to the public good in society, which is like the public's body, and all the useful things that angels and people do as if on their own are from the Lord, so clearly this is reigning with the Lord."

When they heard these words come out of heaven, those pretended kings and princes climbed down from the thrones and official seats and threw away their scepters, crowns, and robes. The mist with its aura of fantasy left them, and a bright cloud veiled them over with an aura of wisdom, which brought sanity back to their minds.

8   After this the angel went back to the house where the wise from the Christian world were convened, and he gathered up the ones who had persuaded themselves that the joys of heaven and eternal happiness are the delights of Paradise. "Follow me," he said, "and I will lead you into Paradise—your heaven—to begin the blessings of your eternal happiness."

And he led them through a lofty gateway made from the limbs and branches of stately trees twined together. After entering he led them in a roundabout way from one place to another. It actually was a paradise in the first entrance to heaven, where they send people who had believed, while in the world, that heaven is all one paradise, because it is called that—people who had the notion impressed on them that after death comes total rest from labor and that this rest is nothing other than inhaling breezes of delight, walking on roses, cheered by the most delicious grape juice, and having festive banquets, and that this life is found only in a heavenly Paradise.

Led by the angel, they saw a great crowd of old and young men, boys, women, and girls, sitting three by three and ten by ten in rose gardens, weaving garlands to deck the heads of the old men and the arms of the young men and to twine around the chests of the boys. They saw others gathering fruit from the trees and taking it to their friends in osier baskets; others pressing the juice of grapes, cherries, and berries into cups and merrily drinking it; others sniffing the fragrances that the flowers, fruits, and odoriferous leaves gave off all around; others singing sweet songs to charm the ears of anyone around; others sitting at fountains making the water squirt from the ducts in various shapes; others walking around talking and tossing off pleasantries; others running, playing, and dancing, here in rhythm and there in circles; others going into little garden houses to relax on the couches. And there were many other paradisal delights.

After they saw these things, the angel led his group around here and there and at last to some people sitting in a very beautiful rose garden surrounded by olive, orange, and citron trees. They rocked back and forth with their hands to their cheeks, wailing and weeping. The angel's followers spoke to them and said, "Why are you sitting like that?"

"It is the seventh day now since we entered this Paradise," they answered. "When we came it looked as if our minds were raised to heaven and placed in the deepest happiness of its joys. But after three days the edge began to wear off this happiness. It faded from our minds and feelings, till it was no happiness at all. And when our imaginary joys ended like this we were afraid we had lost all pleasure from our life. We're becoming skeptical about eternal happiness—if there is such a thing.

"Then we wandered through paths and clearings looking for the gate where we came in, but we were wandering round and round in circles.

"We asked people we met. Some of them said, 'You won't find the gate, because this garden of Paradise is a great big labyrinth—the kind where anyone who wants to get out gets deeper in. So there's nothing to do but stay here forever. You are in the middle of it—the central point of all its delights.'"

And they further informed the angel's followers, "We have been sitting here for a day and a half now. We have no hope of finding the way out, so we sat down in this rose garden, and we see plenty of olives, grapes, oranges, and citrons around us. But the more we look at them the more tired our eyes are of seeing, our noses of smelling, and our mouths of tasting. This is why you see us weeping in grief and sorrow."

When the group's angel heard this he said, "This labyrinth of a paradise really is an entrance to heaven. I know the way and will lead you out."

When he said this, the people sitting there stood up and hugged the angel and followed him, together with his group. And the angel taught them on the way about the joy of heaven and the eternal happiness from it—that these are not the superficial delights of Paradise unless the inward delights of Paradise are there within them at the same time. "The outward delights of Paradise are only delights for the body's senses, but the inward delights of Paradise delight the feelings in your soul. The outward delights have no soul, so the life of heaven is not in them unless the inward delights are in them. And any delight without soul related to it gradually gets feeble and dull and is more tiring to the mind than work. There are garden paradises all over heaven, and the angels get pleasure from them, too, and they enjoy the pleasures just to the extent that the delight of their soul is in them."

"What is the delight of a soul?" everyone asked, when they heard this, "and where does it come from?"

"The delight of a soul is from the love and wisdom from the Lord," the angel replied. "Love is the motive force, and it acts through wisdom, so you find them both in their activity—which is something of use. This delight flows from the Lord into your soul and works down through the higher and lower levels of your mind into all your bodily senses, and there it is fulfilled. This is what makes joy really joy, and makes it eternal—from the Eternal, Whom it comes from. You have seen something of Paradise, and I assure you that not one thing is there—not even a leaf—that is not from a marriage of love and wisdom in usefulness. So if a person has this marriage in him he is in the paradise of heaven—in other words, in heaven."

9   After this the angel guide went back into the hall, to the people who had firmly persuaded themselves that the joy of heaven and eternal happiness are perpetual glorification of God and a religious holiday around the calendar to eternity, because in the world they had believed that then they would see God, and because the life of heaven is called a perpetual Sabbath because it is worship of God.

The angel told them, "Follow me, and I will take you to your joys," and he led them into a small city with a temple in the middle of it, and all the houses were known as sacred buildings.

In this city they saw people streaming in from every corner of the surrounding country, and among them a number of priests who received the new arrivals, greeted them, and led them by the hand to the doors of the temple and from there into some of the buildings around the temple and introduced them into the perpetual worship of God, saying, "This city is an entryway to heaven, and the temple of the city is the entrance to a magnificent and very spacious temple in heaven where the angels glorify God with prayers and praises to eternity. The regulations, both here and there, are that people who arrive have to go into the temple first and stay there three days and three nights, and after this initiation they must go into the city's houses, which are so many buildings consecrated by us, and pray, shout, and recite sermons from house to house together with the people gathered there.

"Be especially careful not to think to yourself, or say to your companions, anything but what is holy, pious, and religious."

Then the angel led his group into the temple, which was packed full with many who had enjoyed great honor in the world, and with many common people, too. There were guards posted at the doors to keep anyone from going out before the three-day stay was over.

The angel said, "Today is the second day since these people came in. Look at them! Look at their glorification of God!"

They looked around and saw most of them sleeping, and the ones that were awake yawned continually. Some looked like faces separated from their bodies from raising their thoughts continually to God and not letting them slip back to their bodies. In fact, they actually looked that way to themselves, and therefore to others. Some looked wild-eyed from being carried away without letup. In a word, all of them were tight-chested and sick at heart from boredom. They turned away from the pulpit, shouting, "Our ears are getting numb! End your sermon! The sound is starting to make us wince!"

And then they stood up and rushed en masse to the doors, broke them open, pushed the guards, and drove them away.

When the priests saw this, they followed after them and stuck close beside them, preaching on and on, praying, sighing, and saying, "Celebrate the festival! Glorify God! Sanctify yourselves! In this entry hall to heaven we are going to introduce you to eternal glorification of God in a huge, magnificent temple in heaven, so you will enjoy eternal happiness."

But they did not grasp these words and hardly heard them, due to the stupefaction resulting from two days of elevating their minds and being kept away from their domestic and public concerns. But when they tried to tear themselves away from the priests, the priests grabbed them by the arms and by the clothing, too, pushing them toward the buildings to read sermons there. But in vain. They shouted, "Let go of us! We feel like we're about to faint!"

When they said that, four men in white robes and miters appeared! One of them had been an archbishop in the world, and the other three were bishops. Now they were angels. They called the priests together and spoke to them. "We saw you from heaven with these sheep. How you feed them!" they said. "You feed them to insanity! You don't know what it means to glorify God. It means to produce things from love. In other words, to faithfully, sincerely, and diligently do whatever work you do. This, indeed, is love of God and love of your neighbor. This is the bond of society and the good of it. God is glorified by this, and then by worship at the appropriate times. Haven't you read the words of the Lord? 'My Father is glorified in the fact that you bear fruit, and you will become My disciples' (John 15:8). You, as priests, can glorify through worship as an occupation because it is your employment, and you get honor, fame, and pay for it. But if the honor, fame, and pay were not part and parcel of your employment, you couldn't make glorification through worship your occupation any more than they can."

After saying these things the bishops ordered the doorkeepers, "Let everyone go in and out, because a great many people cannot comprehend any heavenly joy other than perpetual worship of God, since they do not know anything about what heaven is like."

10   After this the angel and his group returned to the gathering place, which the groups of wise people had not yet gone away from, and there he gathered up those who thought that heavenly joy and eternal happiness were just getting into heaven—getting in by Divine grace—and that then they would have joy just the way people do in the world when they are invited to the palaces of kings on festival days, or to a wedding.

The angel said to them, "Stay here a while, and I'll blow my trumpet, and people will come this way who are famous for their wisdom about the spiritual aspects of the church."

Some hours later nine men approached, each wearing laurel, the mark of his fame. The angel led them into the meeting house where all the people were who had previously been called together. In their presence the angel addressed the nine laureates.

He said, "I know that at your request, pursuant to an idea of yours, you had a chance to go up to heaven, and that you have returned to this lower or subheavenly ground fully acquainted with the conditions in heaven. So tell us how heaven looked to you."

And they answered in turn. "My idea of heaven from early childhood until the end of my life in the world," said the first, "was that it would be a place of all blessedness, happiness, enjoyment, delightfulness, and pleasure, and that if I was admitted, an aura of those delights would surround me and I would breathe them in with all my heart, like a bridegroom when he celebrates his wedding and when he goes to the bedroom with his bride. I went up to heaven preoccupied with this idea, and I passed the first guards and the second ones, too. But when I came to the third ones, the officer of the guard spoke to me and said, 'Who are you, friend?'

"I answered, 'Isn't this heaven? I came up here to get my heart's desire. Please let me in.' And he did.

Then I saw angels in white clothes, and they walked around me, looked at me, and murmured, 'What? This new guest does not have heavenly clothes on.' And I heard it and thought, 'I seem like the guest the Lord said came to the wedding without a wedding garment,' and I said, 'Give me that kind of clothes.' They laughed. Then someone came running from the court with the command, 'Strip him naked, throw him out, and throw his clothes after him,' and so I was thrown out."

The second in turn said, "I believed as he did, that if I could just get into heaven, which is above my head, joys would surround me and give me life forever. I, too, got my wish. But the angels fled when they saw me and said among themselves, 'What is this monster? How did this bird of night get here?' And I actually felt changed from being human, although I was not changed. It came from breathing the atmosphere of heaven. Soon someone ran up from the court with an order for two servants to lead me out, and they led me back by the way I came up, all the way home. And when I came home I looked to others and to myself like a person."

The third said, "My idea of heaven always had to do with a place, and not love, so when I came to this world I had a great longing for heaven, and I saw some people going up and followed them. And I got in, but not more than a few steps. But when I wanted to consciously enjoy it according to my notion of the joys and blessings there, the light of heaven, which is white as snow (they say it is essentially wisdom), put my mind in a stupor, and my sight in darkness, and I became delirious. And soon, from the heat of heaven, which was in keeping with the dazzling light of the place (they say its essence is love), my heart throbbed, anxiety seized me, an inward pain racked me, and I threw myself on my back on the ground there. And as I lay there, an attendant from the court came with orders to carry me gently away into my own light and heat. Once I came back into them, my mind and heart returned."

The fourth said that he, too, had held the idea of heaven as a place and not a love, and said that "When I first came into the spiritual world I asked some wise people whether you could go up to heaven, and they said, 'Anyone can go, but you should be careful not to get thrown out.' I laughed at this and went up, believing like the others that anyone in the whole world can receive the joys there quite fully. But, honestly, as soon as I was in I nearly suffocated, and for the pain and torment it brought to my head and body I flung myself on the ground and writhed like a snake near a fire. And I crawled to a cliff and threw myself down. And afterwards some people standing below picked me up and carried me to an inn, where my health came back to me."

The other five also told surprising things about their going up to heaven and said the conditions of life changed up there the way they do for a fish lifted out of water into the air, or for a bird lifted up into space. And they said that after their hard luck they did not long for heaven any more—just the common lot of others like themselves, wherever they are. And they said, "We know that in the world of spirits, where we are, everyone is prepared first, the good for heaven and the bad for hell, and when they are ready they see pathways open for them to communities where there are people like them, whom they will stay with to eternity. And they cheerfully go their ways then, because the paths are the paths of their love."

When they heard these things everyone from the first convocation also admitted that they had no idea about heaven other than as a place where, with one's mouth wide open, one drinks in the joys that waft around one, to eternity.

After that the angel with the trumpet said to them, "Now you see that the joys of heaven and eternal happiness are not joys of a place, but are the joys of a person's state of life, and that a heavenly state of life comes from love and wisdom. And being useful is what brings the two together, so a heavenly state of life is when love and wisdom join in usefulness—which is the same as saying charity, faith, and good works, since charity is love, faith is truth, where wisdom comes from, and good works are usefulness. Furthermore, in our spiritual world there are places just as in the natural world. Otherwise there would not be places to live and separate houses. And yet place there is not place but an appearance of place, according to the state of your love and wisdom—or charity and faith.

"Everyone who becomes an angel has his own heaven within him, because his heaven is his love. For by creation every person is a tiny model, image, and pattern of heaven at large. The human form is nothing else. So everyone comes into the community of heaven of which he is an individual model. For that reason, he enters a form corresponding to himself when he enters that community, so he takes part in it as if putting himself in it and it in himself, and he is involved in its life as if it were his own and in his own life as if it were the community's. Each community is like something collective, and the angels there are like the similar parts that a whole emerges from.

"Now, this means that people who live by evils and therefore by falsehoods have formed a model of hell in themselves, and in heaven this is tormented under the surge and violent action of opposites against opposites. For hellish love is the opposite of heavenly love, and so the delights of the two loves clash with each other like enemies and kill each other when they meet."

11   When that was over a voice sounded from the sky to the angel with the trumpet, "Choose ten from the whole group and lead them to us. We have heard from the Lord that He will prepare them so that for three days the heat and light—or the love and wisdom—of our heaven will not harm them."

Ten were chosen and followed the angel, and they went up a certain hill by a steep path, and from there up a mountain where the heaven of those angels was. They had seen it before from a distance as if laid out in the clouds. The gates were opened before them, and when they passed the third gate the angel guide ran to the prince of that community of heaven and announced they were there.

And the prince answered, "Take some of my attendants, and report to the visitors that I acknowledge their arrival. Bring them into my outer court, and assign each one an apartment with a bedroom. And take some of my courtiers and servants to look after them and be on call."

This was done. But when the angel brought them in, they asked permission to go and see the prince. The angel answered, "Not before noon. It's morning now. They're all busy with their duties and work. But you're invited to lunch, and then you will sit at the table with our prince. Meantime, I'll take you into the palace, where you'll see magnificent and splendid things."

12   As he led them to the palace they saw the outside first. It was large, constructed of porphyry, with jasper foundations, and six tall columns of lapis lazuli outside the door. The roof had golden shingles, the tall windows were of the clearest crystal, and their frames were also gold.

Then they were led into the palace and all around from room to room, and they saw ornaments of indescribable beauty, under ceilings decorated with carvings that defied imitation. By the walls were silver tables inwrought with gold, and on them various utensils of precious stones and whole gems in heavenly forms— and many things that no eye in the world has seen, so no one could make himself believe that they exist in heaven.

They were stunned to see these magnificent things, so the angel said, "Don't be amazed, what you see was not made and fashioned by the hand of any angel. The Maker of the Universe made the things and gave them to our prince as gifts. So here you have the art of pure architecture, and all the rules of the art in the world come from this."

The angel went on, "You might think things like these would enchant our eyes and infatuate them until we thought they were the joys of our heaven. But since our hearts are not in them, they are only supplements to the joys of our hearts. So to the extent that we look on them as accessory and the workmanship of God, we see in them Divine omnipotence and mercy."

13   After this the angel said to them, "It's not noon yet. Come with me to our prince's garden by the palace." They went, and at the entrance he said, "Behold the most magnificent garden in this heavenly community!"

But they answered, "What are you saying? There's no garden here. All we see is one tree with fruit that looks gold on its branches and crown, and leaves like silver decorated at the edges with emeralds, and under the tree little children with their nurses."

At this the angel caught his breath and said, "This tree is in the middle of the garden, and we call it the tree of our heaven. Some call it the tree of life. But go ahead and get closer. Your eyes will be opened, and you'll see the garden."

They did, and their eyes were opened, and they saw trees with plenty of tasty fruits, twined around with vine tendrils, their tops bending with fruit toward the tree of life in the middle. These trees were planted in an unbroken row that went out and around in steady circles or spirals like an endless helix. It was a perfect helix of trees. Species after species followed one another according to the excellence of their fruits. The first sweep of the helix started at a considerable distance from the tree in the middle, and in the interval danced a sparkling of light, so the trees of the spiral gleamed with a steady, uninterrupted brightness from the first one to the last.

The first trees, called trees of paradise, were the finest of all, luxuriant with the plumpest fruits, and they have never been seen before, because they do not grow and cannot survive in the soil of the natural world. Next followed olive trees, then vine trees, then fragrant trees, and finally trees with good wood for woodwork. Here and there in the helix or spiral of trees were seats made by training and interlacing the young branches of the trees behind the seats, and they were enriched and ornamented by their fruits. In this perpetual cycle of trees were openings that led to flower gardens, and from there to lawns laid out in fields and terraces.

When the angel's party saw these they exclaimed, "Why, it's a model of heaven! Wherever we turn our eyes, in flows something heavenly and paradisal that defies description!"

The angel was glad to hear this. "All the gardens in our heaven are forms or images that represent heaven's blessings at their sources," he said, "and the influence of these blessings lifted up your minds, so you exclaimed, 'Why, it's a model of heaven!'" But people who do not receive that influence see these paradises as nothing but forests. Everyone who has a love of usefulness receives that influence, but people who are in love with fame—and not because of usefulness—don't receive it." Then he explained and taught what the different things in the garden represented and stood for.

14   While they were at this a messenger came from the prince, who invited them to eat bread with him, and at the same time two house attendants brought fine linen clothes and said, "Put these on, for no one is admitted to the prince's table without wearing the clothes of heaven."

They dressed and joined their angel, who led them into an open porch, a promenade of the palace, and they waited for the prince. The angel kept introducing them to eminent people and managers who were also waiting for the prince. Within an hour a double door opened, and sure enough, they saw him make his entrance through a wide door on the west in the order and pomp of a procession. Before him went the chief counselors, then the chamberlains, and after them the nobles of the court. Among them was the prince, and after him courtiers of various degrees, and last the attendants, numbering a hundred and twenty altogether.

Staying in front of the ten newcomers (now that they were dressed as guests), the angel approached the prince with them and reverently presented them. The prince did not linger in his procession, but said to them, "Come with me to bread," and they followed into the dining room and saw a splendidly prepared table. In the middle of it was a high pyramid of gold, with a hundred small dishes in a triple row on its trays. On the dishes were cakes, jellied wine, and other delicacies made of cake and wine. Through the center of the pyramid gushed a leaping fountain of wine, like nectar, and the stream divided, as it came out of the top of the pyramid, and filled the cups.

On either side of this high pyramid were various heavenly shapes of gold with dishes and plates of every kind of food on them. The heavenly shapes that held the dishes and plates were forms of art from wisdom that no worldly art could devise nor any words describe. The plates and dishes were of silver, engraved around the edges with designs like the ones on their supporting forms. The cups were clear gems. This is how the table was furnished.

15   The prince and his ministers were dressed as follows. The prince wore a purple robe embroidered with silver stars. Under the robe he was wrapped in a shining silk tunic colored blue. It was open at his chest, and you could see a sash with the medal of his community. The medal was an eagle brooding over her young in the top of a tree. It was of shining gold in a circle of diamonds. The chief counselors were clothed not much differently, but without the medal. Instead, carved sapphires hung from their necks on chains of gold. The courtiers had cloaks of chestnut brown with flowers woven on them encircling young eagles, and underneath, tunics of opal-colored silk, and the same for their breeches and stockings. This was what their clothing was like.

16   The chief counselors, privy counselors, and managers stood around the table and by the prince's command folded their hands and murmured a prayer of praise to the Lord together, and after that, at the prince's nod, they settled onto couches by the table.

The prince said to the ten visitors, "Recline with me, too. Look, your seats are there." They reclined, and the attendants whom the prince had sent earlier to look after them stood behind them. Then the prince said to them, "Everyone take a plate from its circle and a dish from the pyramid," and they did, and a new plate and dish instantly appeared where the other ones came from! Their cups were filled with wine from the fountain gushing from the great pyramid, and they ate and drank.

When they were comfortably satisfied the prince spoke to the ten guests. "I have heard that in the land down below this heaven," he said, "you were assembled to tell your thoughts about the joys of heaven and the eternal happiness from them, and you brought out your thoughts differently, each according to the pleasures of his physical senses. But what are physical pleasures without pleasures of the soul? The soul is what enjoys them. The delights of the soul are blessings you don't notice, but they become more and more apparent as they work down into the thoughts of your mind and from there into the sensations of your body. In mental thought they emerge as well-being, in bodily sensations as delights, and in the body itself as satisfaction. Eternal happiness comes from all these together. But the happiness from just the lower ones is not eternal, but temporary. It comes to an end and passes away and sometimes becomes unhappiness.

"Now you have seen that all your joys are also joys of heaven, and more excellent than you could ever have thought. But they do not affect our souls inwardly. Into our souls three things flow as one from the Lord, and these three as one, or this 'trine,' are love, wisdom, and use. But love and wisdom do not emerge except as an idea, because they only reside in affection and thoughts of the mind, but in use they become real, because then they are in the action and work of your body. And where they become real they also become substantial. And because love and wisdom emerge and become substantial in doing things, it is use that excites us, and use is doing the work of your calling faithfully, sincerely, and industriously.

"A love of use, and the devotion it brings to usefulness, keep the mind from branching out and wandering around soaking up all the desires that seep in enticingly from your body and the world through the senses, and that scatter to all the winds true religion and true morality, and the benefits of them. But a devotion to use wraps up religion and morality, binds them together, and puts the mind in a state to receive wisdom and its truth. And then it puts aside the illusions and mockeries of both falsities and aimlessness. But you will hear more about these things from the wise men of our community whom I'll send to you this afternoon."

When the prince said this he rose, and the guests with him, and he said, "Peace," and ordered their angel guide to take them back to their rooms and show them all honor and civilities, and also to invite cultivated and friendly men to entertain them with conversation about the various joys of this community.

17   When they returned they did just that. The men who were invited from the city to entertain them with talk about the various joys of their community came, and after greetings, they walked with them and talked politely.

But their angel guide said, "These ten men were invited to this heaven to see its joys, to get a new idea from them about eternal happiness. So tell them something about the joys that affect our bodily senses. After that, wise men will come and explain what makes these joys satisfying and happy."

When the men from the city heard this, here is what they said:

First: "The prince here designates holidays to relax our minds from the strain that wanting to do your best gives some people. On these days we have musical concerts and singing in the squares, and games and entertainment outside the town. Then, in the squares, bandstands are put up, surrounded by lattices thick with vines and clusters, and musicians sit inside on three levels with stringed and wind instruments, treble and bass, loud and soft. On either side are male and female singers. They entertain the people with very delightful music and singing, mixed and solo, with different kinds taking turns. On these holidays this goes on from morning till noon and after that till evening."

Second: "Another thing: Each morning we hear the sweetest songs of virgins and girls, coming from the houses around the squares. The whole town resounds with them. Each morning they sing some feeling of spiritual love. In other words, they express it by the intervals and rhythms of their singing voices, and the feeling comes out in the song as if the song were the feeling itself. It pours into the listeners' souls and awakens its echo in them. Heavenly song is like that. The singers say that the sound of their song seems to stir up and take life from within them, and rises up joyfully according to how the listeners receive it. When the singing stops, the windows and doors of the houses on the squares and streets close, and then the whole town is quiet, with no clamor anywhere, and no loiterers. Now everyone is ready for the duties of their occupations."

Third: "But at noon the doors open, and in the afternoon the windows open, too, in some places, and you see boys and girls playing in the streets while their nurses and tutors watch over them, sitting on the porches of the houses."

Fourth: "On the outskirts of town there are various games for boys and teenagers. There are running games, ball games, a game in which a ball is hit back and forth, called tennis. There are trials of skill among the boys as to which are quick and which are slow in speech, action, and perception, and the quickest get some laurel leaves as a prize. And there are many other things that bring out the latent abilities of the boys."

Fifth: "Also outside the city are stage shows by comedians representing various kinds of moral integrity and virtue, with actors among them who provide contrasts."

One of the ten said, "Provide contrasts?"

They answered, "No virtue can be represented in a lifelike way, with all its integrity and charm, except by comparisons from the highest degree of the virtue to the lowest. The actors present the lowest degree of the virtue all the way to where there is none of it left. But the law prohibits showing anything opposite—say, shameful or disgraceful—except by metaphor and as from a distance. This is established because nothing decent and good of any virtue passes over by stages into what is indecent and bad, but diminishes until it ceases, and when it ceases the opposite begins. So heaven, where everything is decent and good, has nothing in common with hell, where everything is indecent and bad."

18   During the conversation an attendant hurried up and announced that by the prince's order eight wise men were there and wanted to come in. When the angel heard this he went out, welcomed them, and led them in. And after the customary formalities and proprieties of introduction, the wise men were soon talking with them, first about the beginnings of wisdom and how it increases, adding various things about its progress. "With angels," they said, "wisdom never comes to an end and stops, but it grows and increases forever."

When the angel of the group heard this, he said to the wise men, "At lunch our prince spoke to these people about the seat of wisdom, saying that it is in usefulness. Would you speak to them about this, too?"

They said, "At first, people were created saturated with wisdom and its love, not for one's own sake but to communicate it from oneself to others, so it is attributed to the wisdom of the wise that no one is wise, or lives, for himself alone, but for others at the same time. This condition promoted society, which would not exist otherwise. To live for others is to perform uses. Uses are the bonds of society, and there are as many bonds as good uses, which is an infinite number. There are spiritual uses associated with love to God and love toward your neighbor. There are moral and civil uses associated with love for society and the community where the person is and for the companions and countrymen whom he is with. There are mundane uses having to do with love of the world and its necessities. And there are bodily uses associated with a love for keeping your body fit for the higher uses.

"All these uses are inscribed on the person and follow step-by-step, one after the other, and when two are together, one is within the other. People engaged in primary, or spiritual, uses are also engaged in the whole string of uses, and these people are wise. But those who are not engaged in the primary but the secondary ones, and therefore in the ones that follow, are not wise but only seem wise from outward morality and civility. Those not engaged in the primary or secondary, but in the third and fourth level, are nothing less than they are wise. In fact, they are satans, for they only love the world, and themselves because of the world. And those engaged only in the fourth level are the least wise of all. In fact, they are devils, for they live only for themselves, and if for others it is strictly for their own sakes.

"Furthermore, every love has its own delight, because love lives by delight, and the delight of loving usefulness is a heavenly delight. It goes into the lower delights in their order and exalts them according to their place on the scale, and makes them eternal."

Then they listed some heavenly delights that emerge from a love of usefulness and said, "There are thousands and thousands of them, and people who enter heaven enter them."

And they spent the day with them until evening in more wise conversations about the love of usefulness.

19   But around evening a runner dressed in linen came to the ten strangers accompanying the angel, and he invited them to a wedding, to be celebrated the following day. The visitors were extremely happy that they would see a wedding in heaven, too.

After that they were brought to one of the chief counselors and had dinner with him, and after dinner they went back one by one, and each retired to his own apartment, and they slept until morning.

They woke up hearing the singing of virgins and girls mentioned before, coming from the houses around the square. This time they were singing the feeling of married love. The sweetness of it deeply affected and stirred the guests, and they noticed that a happy pleasantness infused their joy, which uplifted it and renewed it.

When the time came the angel said, "Get ready, and put on the heavenly clothes that our prince sent you."

They put them on, and the clothing shone as if with a flaming light! They asked the angel, "What caused this?"

The angel answered, "It's because you're going to a wedding. At times like this around here our clothes shine and become wedding garments."

20   After that the angel led them to the house where the wedding was to be, and a doorman opened the doors. Once over the threshold they were received and greeted by an angel sent from the groom, brought inside, and led to seats that were for them. And presently they were invited into a room outside the bridal suite, where they saw a table in the middle, with a magnificent candle stand on it with seven branches and sconces of gold. Silver lamps hung on the walls. When they were lighted it made the air seem golden. Beside the candle stand they saw two tables with triple rows of bread on them, and in the four corners of the room were tables with crystal cups on them.

While they were looking at this a door opened from a room next to the bridal chamber, and they saw six virgins come out, and after them the bride and groom, holding hands and leading each other to a seat placed opposite the candle stand. They sat down there, the groom on the left and the bride on his right, and the six virgins stood beside the seat next to the bride.

The groom wore a radiant purple robe and a tunic of shining linen, with an ephod. It had on it a plate of gold set around with diamonds, and on the plate was engraved a young eagle, the wedding insignia of that community in heaven. The groom wore a miter on his head.

But the bride wore a scarlet mantle and underneath it an embroidered dress that reached from her neck to her feet, and under her chest a gold belt. And on her head was a crown of gold inset with rubies.

When they had sat down together like this, the groom turned to the bride and placed a gold ring on her finger. Then he pulled out bracelets and a necklace of large pearls. He fastened the bracelets on her wrists and the necklace around her neck, and said, "Accept these pledges," and as she accepted he kissed her and said, "Now you are mine," and called her his wife.

When this was done the guests cried, "Bless it!" Each cried this by himself, and then all together. The one the prince had sent to represent him also cried out. And in that instant an incense smoke that was a sign of a blessing from heaven filled the room. Then servants took bread from the two tables beside the candle stand and cups now full of wine from the tables in the corners, and they gave each guest his own bread and wine, and they ate and drank. After this the husband and his wife rose up, followed to the threshold by the six virgins with lamps in their hands, now lighted, and the married pair went into the bridal chamber, and the door was closed.

21   Afterwards the angel guide spoke with the wedding guests about his ten companions—how he brought them by command and showed them the splendor of the prince's palace and the wonders there, and how they had eaten at the table with him and afterwards had talked with their wise men. And he asked, "May they have some conversation with you, too?"

They came and spoke with them.

And one of the wedding guests, a wise man, asked, "Do you understand what the things you saw mean?"

"A little," they said, and asked him, "Why was the groom, now a husband, dressed in clothing like that?"

"The groom, now a husband, represented the Lord, and the

bride, now a wife, represented the church," he answered, "because in heaven a wedding represents the Lord's marriage with the church. This is why he had a miter on his head and was dressed like Aaron in a robe, a tunic, and an ephod. It is also why there was a crown on the head of the bride, now a wife, and she wore a mantle like a queen. But after this they will be dressed differently, because this representation lasts only for today."

They had another question. "Given the fact that he represented the Lord and she the church, why did she sit at his right?"

"Because the things that make the marriage of the Lord and the church are two: love and wisdom," the wise man answered, "and the Lord is love, and the church is wisdom, and wisdom is at love's right hand. For a person of the church discerns as if by his own resources, and as he develops wisdom he receives love from the Lord. The right hand also stands for power, and the power of love is through wisdom. But, once again, the representation changes after the wedding, for then the husband represents wisdom and the wife love for his wisdom—which love is not the primary love, certainly, but a secondary love that the wife gets from the Lord through her husband's wisdom. Love of the Lord—which is the primary love—is, for the husband, love of being wise. So after the wedding the husband and his wife both together represent the church."

They had another question. "How come you men didn't stand beside the groom, now the husband, the way the six virgins stood beside the bride, now the wife?"

"Because," the wise man answered, "we are numbered among the virgins today, and the number six stands for us all, and completeness."

But they said, "How so?"

He answered, "The virgins stand for the church, and the church includes both sexes, so we are also the virgins as far as the church goes. The truth of this is consistent with these words in Revelation: 'These are the ones who have not been contaminated by women, for they are virgins, and they follow the Lamb wherever He goes' (14:4). And because virgins do stand for the church the Lord compared the church to ten virgins invited to the wedding (Matt. 25:1–13). And because Israel, Zion, and Jerusalem stand for the church, the 'virgin and daughter' of Israel, Zion, and Jerusalem is often mentioned in the Word. The Lord also describes His marriage with the church in these words in David:

> The queen at your right, in the best gold of Ophir.... Her clothing is woven gold. She will be brought to the King in clothing of many colors, her virgin friends after her.... They will enter the King's palace. (Ps. 45:9, 13–15)

Afterwards they said, "Isn't it proper for a minister to be present and serve at these ceremonies?"

"On the earth it is," the wise man answered, "but not in the heavens, because the Lord and the church are represented. On earth they do not realize this. And even among us a minister serves at engagement ceremonies. He hears, receives, confirms, and consecrates the consent. Consent is the essential factor of a marriage, and the other things that follow are its formalities."

22   After this the angel guide went to the six virgins and told them, too, about his companions and asked them to favor his companions with their company. They approached, but when they came near they suddenly drew back and went into the women's quarters, where the other virgins, their friends, were.

When the angel guide saw this he followed them and asked why they withdrew so suddenly without speaking to them.

"We couldn't get near them," they answered.

He said, "Why not?"

"We don't know," they said, "but we could feel something that repelled us and drove us back. We hope they will excuse us."

The angel went back to his companions and told them the answer, and he added, "I surmise that you don't have a pure interest in their sex. In heaven we love virgins because of their beauty and the refinement of their ways, and we love them very much—but chastely."

His companions laughed at this and said, "You guessed right. Who can see such beauty near and not feel any desire?"

23   After this social celebration the wedding guests all left, and the ten men also, with their angel. It was late in the evening, and they went to bed.

At dawn they heard a proclamation, "Today is the Sabbath." And they got up, asking the angel, "What's that?"

He answered, "It is for the worship of God, which happens at regular times. The ministers proclaim it. We celebrate it in our temples, and it takes about two hours. So come with me if you like and I'll take you there."

So they got ready and joined the angel and went in. And that temple was big! It could hold about three thousand people. It was semicircular, with benches or seats running all the way around, following the shape of the temple, and the rear seats were higher than the ones in front. The pulpit in front of the seats was a little beyond the center. There was a door behind the pulpit to the left. The ten visiting men entered with their angel guide, and the angel led them to places where they could sit, saying to them, "Everyone who enters the temple knows his place. They know it intuitively and can't sit anywhere else. If they do, they hear nothing and feel nothing. It also creates a disturbance that does not inspire the minister."

24   After they all gathered, a minister mounted the pulpit and delivered a sermon full of the spirit of wisdom. The sermon was on the holiness of Sacred Scripture and how it joins the Lord both with the spiritual and with the natural world. In the enlightenment he enjoyed, he demonstrated fully that the holy Book was composed by Jehovah the Lord, and that therefore He Himself is in it to the point that He Himself is the wisdom in it. But he showed that the wisdom that is Himself in it lies concealed beneath the literal sense and appears only to those who have truths from religious instruction and at the same time have good in their lives, so that they are in the Lord and the Lord in them. He added to his talk a spoken prayer and stepped down.

After the listeners left, the angel asked the priest to say a few words of peace with his ten companions. He came up to them, and they talked together for half an hour and discussed the Divine Trinity, saying that it is in Jesus Christ, in whom the fullness of all divinity resides bodily, according to what the Apostle Paul said. Then they discussed the union of charity and faith—only he called it the union of charity and truth, because faith is truth.

25   After expressing thanks they went home, and there the angel

said to them, "Today is the third day since you came up to this community of heaven, and the Lord prepared you to stay three days, so the time has come for us to separate. So take off the clothes the prince sent and put on your own." And when they did put them on, something made them want to leave, and they left and went back down, with the angel accompanying them, to the place where they had met. And there they gave thanks to the Lord that He had seen fit to honor them with knowledge and therefore with an understanding of heavenly joys and eternal happiness.

26   Again I affirm in truth that I have told these things just the way they were done and said. The first part happened in the world of spirits, which is between heaven and hell, and the subsequent ones in a community of heaven where the angel with the trumpet, who was their guide, came from.

Who in the Christian world would have known anything about heaven and the joys and happiness there (knowledge of it is also knowledge of salvation) unless it had pleased the Lord to open the sight of someone's spirit for him and show and teach him?

It is clear from the things that the Apostle John saw and heard that things like this exist in the spiritual world. He described them in Revelation. For example, he saw the Son of man among the seven candlesticks; a tabernacle, a temple, an ark, and an altar in the sky; a book, sealed with seven seals, opened, and horses going out of it; four animals around a throne; twelve thousand people chosen from each tribe; locusts swarming out of an abyss; the dragon and his war with Michael; a woman who bore a male son fleeing into the wilderness because of the dragon; two beasts, one rising out of the sea, and the other out of the earth; a woman sitting upon a scarlet beast; a dragon thrown into a pool of fire and brimstone; a white horse and a big dinner; a new sky and a new earth, and the holy Jerusalem descending (he describes its gates, its wall, and its foundation); and a river of the water of life, and trees of life bearing fruit every month.

And there were other things. John saw all these things when he was in the spiritual world and in heaven, so far as his spirit was concerned.

In addition, there are the things the Apostles saw after the Lord's resurrection, and what Peter saw later (Acts 11), and what Paul saw and heard.

Besides these things, there are the things the prophets saw. Ezekiel, for example, saw four creatures that were cherubs (Ezek. 1 and 10); a new temple and a new land, and an angel measuring them (Ezek. 40–48). And he was carried away to Jerusalem and saw abominations there, and he was also taken into captivity, to Chaldea (Ezek. 8, 11).

The same happened to Zechariah. He saw a man riding among myrtle trees (Zech. 1:8ff.). He saw four horns, and then a man with a measuring line in his hand (1:18–21; 2:1f.). He saw a candlestick and two olive trees (4:2ff.). He saw a flying scroll and a measuring basket (5:1–6). He saw four chariots, and horses, coming out from between two mountains (6:1ff.).

The same for Daniel. He saw four beasts coming up out of the sea (Dan. 7:3ff.), and a fight between a ram and a he-goat (8:2ff.). He saw the angel Gabriel and spoke with him (9:20ff.).

Elisha's servant saw chariots and horses on fire around Elisha. He saw them with his eyes wide open (2 Kings 6:17).

These and many other things in the Word show that the things that exist in the spiritual world have appeared to many people before and after the Lord's advent. Why wonder that they should appear now, also, at the beginning of a church, or at the descent of the New Jerusalem from the Lord out of heaven?

Chapter 2

Marriages in Heaven

27   Those who think that people are souls or spirits after death
and cherish the idea that souls and spirits are a wisp of air or a
breath—these people cannot grasp the idea that there are marriages
in heaven. They also think that people will not be alive as people,
until after the day of the Last Judgment. In general they know
nothing about the spiritual world, where the angels and spirits
are, so they do not know where heaven and hell are. That world
was unknown until now, and no one at all knew that the angels
of heaven are people in a completely human form (so are the
spirits of hell, only deformed), so nothing could be revealed about
marriages there. For people would say, "How can a soul be joined
together with a soul, or a breath with a breath, the way married
partners join on earth?" And they would say many other things
that would snatch away any belief in marriages there and scatter
it the moment the words were spoken.

But now the books *Heaven and Hell* and *Apocalypse Revealed*
have made known many things about that world, and have described what it is like. So it can be established that there are
marriages there, through these points:

(1) A person lives on—still a person—after death.
(2) Then men are still male and women are female.
(3) Everyone's love remains with him after death.
(4) Love for the other sex, especially, continues, and so does
     married love, for people who come into heaven. They are
     the ones who became spiritual on earth.

(5) There is full confirmation of these things by my own experience.

(6) Consequently, there are marriages in heaven.

(7) The Lord's statement that there are no weddings after resurrection referred to spiritual weddings.

The explanation of these things one by one follows here.

28　　　(1) *A person lives on—still a person—after death.* For the reasons given just above, the world has not known until now that people live on as people after death. This is surprising, especially in the Christian world, which has the Word, and therefore enlightenment about eternal life, and in which the Lord Himself taught that all of the dead revive and that "God is not God of the dead but of the living" (Matt. 22:30–32; Luke 20:37–8).

Moreover, as to mental feelings and thoughts, people are among the angels and spirits and in their company in such a way that people cannot be separated from the angels and spirits without dying.

And it is even more surprising that this is unknown, when for all that, every person who has ever died since the first creation has come, and comes, to his own people, or as it says in the Word, has been gathered and is gathered.

And moreover, people share a general perception that coincides with the influence of heaven on their innermost minds. By this perception they sense truths within themselves and see them, so to speak, and especially this truth—that they live on as people after death, happy if they lived well and unhappy if they lived badly. Indeed, who does not feel this when he raises his mind a little above his body and away from the thoughts nearest his physical senses—which he does when deep in Divine worship and when he lies on his deathbed and waits for the end?

It is the same when he hears about the dead and what happens to them. I have reported a thousand things about them, such as what became of people's brothers, wives, and friends. I have also written about what happens to the English, Dutch, Catholics, Jews, and non-Christians, and what became of Luther, Calvin, and Melanchthon. And so far I have never heard anyone say, "How could these things happen to them, when they have not yet risen from their graves, because the Last Judgment hasn't happened yet? Aren't they souls in the meantime, which are breaths? And aren't they in some waiting place or other?" I still have never heard anyone say anything like that, which leads me to conclude that everyone senses within himself that he lives on as a person after death.

What man who has loved his wife and his babies and children does not tell himself that they are in God's hand when they are dying or have died, if his thought rises above his physical senses while considering it? And doesn't he think he will see them again after his death and join them again in a life of love and joy?

29   Who cannot see from reason, if he wants to, that after death people are not a breath? A breath cannot conceivably be anything but a puff of wind, or some airy, ethereal thing that is the soul of a person, or has the soul in it, hoping and waiting for a reunion with its body so it can enjoy its senses and their pleasures in the world as before. Who cannot see that if people were like that after death they would be worse off than the fish, birds, and animals on earth, whose souls do not live, and therefore are not so anxious from longing and waiting? If people were just a breath and a puff of wind like that after death, then they would either be fluttering around the universe or, according to some traditions, confined in some waiting place, or with the Fathers, in limbo until the Last Judgment.

Anyone can rationally conclude from this that those who have lived since the first creation, which is thought to be six thousand years ago, would still be in a state of anxiety like that, and becoming more anxious all the time, because all waiting and longing breed anxiety and intensify the anxiety from moment to moment. So they would still be fluttering around the universe or would be kept closed up somewhere and therefore in extreme misery. The same goes for Adam and his wife, for Abraham, Isaac, and Jacob, and for all the other people who have lived since that time. As a result, nothing would be more lamentable than to be born human.

But the Lord, who is Jehovah from eternity and Creator of the universe, has provided just the opposite—that people who have joined themselves together with Him by a life according to His directions have more blessed and happier circumstances after death than they had before it in the world. And what makes it more blessed and happier is that they are spiritual then, and a spiritual person feels and takes in spiritual pleasure, which is far greater than worldly pleasure because it is a thousand times as good.

30   You can see that angels and spirits are people from the ones Abraham, Gideon, Daniel, and the prophets saw—especially the ones John saw while he was writing Revelation and also the ones the women saw in the Lord's tomb. In fact, the disciples saw the Lord Himself after His resurrection. The reason they saw angels and spirits was that their spiritual eyes were opened, and when these eyes are opened you can see angels in their own form—which is human. But when those eyes are closed—that is, veiled over by the sight of the eyes that receive everything from the material world—spirits are not visible.

31   But note that after death people are not natural people but spiritual people. Yet to themselves they seem entirely the same—so much so that for all they know they are still in the natural world, with the same body, the same face, the same voice, and the same senses—because they have the same feelings and thoughts, or the same will and intellect.

As a matter of fact, a person is actually not the same, because he is a spiritual person and therefore an internal person. But he does not notice the difference, because he cannot compare his condition with his previous earthly one, since he left that one behind and is in the other state. So I have often heard spirits say that for all they know they are still in the previous world—the only difference being that they no longer see the people whom they left behind in the world, while they do see those who had gone away from the world, or in other words, had died.

Actually, the reason they now see these people and not the others is that they are not natural people but spiritual, or *substantial*, and a spiritual or substantial person sees spiritual or substantial people just the way a natural or material person sees natural or material people. But the two do not see each other because of the difference between substance and matter, which is just like the difference between a source and its result. And because the source in its own right is finer, it cannot appear to the result, which in its own right is coarser, nor can the result, because it is coarser, appear to the source, which in its own right is finer. So an angel cannot appear to a person in this world nor a person in this world to an angel.

After death people can be spiritual or substantial people because the spiritual part was there all the time, unseen within the natural or material person, which was like clothing or a skin that they shed, to come out spiritual or substantial and therefore purer, more profound, and more complete.

The spiritual person is a complete person all the while, though unseen by the natural person. This is obvious, because the Apostles saw the Lord after His resurrection. He appeared and disappeared. Still, He was the same Person whether seen or unseen. And they, too, said that when they saw Him their eyes were opened.

32   (2) *Then men are still male and women are female.* People live on as people after death, and people are male and female. Maleness is one thing and femaleness another in such a way that one cannot change into the other. Therefore, a man has to live on as a male and a woman as a female after death, each a spiritual person.

Having said that a male cannot change into a female nor a female into a male and that after death male is male and female female, I shall now tell briefly what essential maleness and femaleness depend on—because this is not known.

Here is what the essential difference consists in. The innermost thing in masculinity is love, and its covering is wisdom, or in other words, love enfolded in wisdom. The innermost thing in femininity is this masculine wisdom, and its covering is love. But this love is a feminine love, and the Lord gives it to a wife through the channel of her husband's wisdom. That other love is a masculine love and is love of becoming wise, and the Lord gives it to a husband according to his acceptance of wisdom. This is why masculinity is wisdom that belongs to love, while femininity is love of this wisdom. So from creation a love of joining together as one is implanted in each. But more about this later.

These words from Genesis show that femaleness is from maleness, or that woman is taken from man:

> The Lord God . . . took one of the man's ribs and closed up the flesh in its place. Then He made the rib which He had taken from man, into a woman, and He brought her to the man.

> And the man said: "This is bone of my bones and flesh of my flesh. She shall be called Woman [*'ishshah*] because she was taken out of man [*'ish*]." (Gen. 2:21–23)

The meaning of rib and flesh is explained in another place.

33   From this original formation springs the phenomenon that masculinity is born to be intellect discerning and femininity is born to be will, or in other words, masculinity is born into an inclination toward knowledge, intellect, and wisdom, while femininity is born into a love of joining itself with that inclination in masculinity. And since what is inner forms what is outer in its own likeness, and the form of masculinity is the form of intellect, while the form of femininity is the form of loving it, this is why a male has a different face, a different voice, and a different body than a female, as everybody knows—a harder face, a rougher voice, and a stronger body, and a bearded chin besides—a less beautiful appearance, by and large, than a female. Males and females also differ in behavior and habits. In a word, nothing about them is the same, but each and every particular offers conjunction.

    Certainly masculinity in a male is masculine in all parts of his body, even the tiniest, and also in every idea of his thinking and every scrap of his feelings. The same goes for femininity in a female. And because the one cannot change itself into the other on that account, it follows that after death men are still male and women are female.

34   (3) *Everyone's love remains with him after death.* People know that love exists, but they do not know what love is. They can tell that love exists from common expressions, for we say "he loves me," "the king loves his subjects," "subjects love the king," "a husband loves his wife and a mother her children," and vice versa, and

that this or that person loves his country, his countrymen, and his neighbors. The same goes for impersonal abstractions like "he loves this or that thing."

But although we mention love all the time, hardly anyone knows what love is. People cannot piece together any idea of it through study and therefore cannot place it in the light of knowledge, because it belongs to heat, not light. So when they think it over they pronounce it to be either not anything or else just something that flows in through sight, hearing, and social contact, and stirs you in that way. They are completely unaware that love is actually their life—not just the life that belongs to their whole body and all their thoughts in a general way, but also the life of every single part of them. The way a perceptive person can grasp this is to say, "If you take away the feeling of love can you think about anything, and can you do anything? Thought, speech, and action cool down as the feelings that go with them cool down and heat up as they heat up, don't they?" So love is the heat of a person's life, or his vital heat. The heat of blood and its red color are from nowhere else. What produces this is the fire of the angelic sun, which is pure love.

35   Everyone has his own love, or a love distinct from anyone else's. That is, no one has the same love as anyone else. You can tell this from the infinite variety of faces, which are images of loves—for we know that faces change and differ according to feelings of love. Desires, too, which belong to love, besides its joys and sorrows, shine out from the face. This makes it clear that a person is his love—in fact he is the living image of his love. But note that it is the inner person, which is the same as the person's spirit that lives after death, that is the image of his love, and not the outer person in the world, because the outer person has learned from infancy to hide the desires of his love—indeed to simulate and display different ones than its own.

36   It is because love is a person's life (see no. 34), and therefore is the person himself, that everyone's love continues after death. A person's thought, and therefore what he knows and his perception, are also the person, but they work together with his love, since the person thinks on account of love and according to it. In fact, he speaks and acts from it if he can. This shows that love is the being of

a person's life, or the essential reality of it, and that thinking from love is the visible existence or manifestation of his life. So the speech and action that spring from thinking do not really spring from thinking, but from love, and flow out through thought.

From many experiences I have found out that after death people are not their thoughts, but they are their feelings and the thought from them—in other words, they are their love and the understanding that comes from it. After death people reject everything not in harmony with their love. In fact, they gradually assume the face, voice, speech, gestures, and manners of their life's love. This is why all heaven is arranged according to all the varieties of dispositions that go with loving good, and all hell according to all the dispositions that go with loving evil.

37   (4) *Love for the other sex, especially, continues, and so does married love for people who come into heaven.* They are the ones who became spiritual on earth. Love for the other sex remains with people after death because then men are still male and women are female, and masculinity in a male is masculinity in all of him and in every part of him. The same goes for femininity in a female. And every particular—in fact every little detail—of them offers conjunction. Now, this disposition to unite has been implanted from creation, so it is always there, and that means that the one yearns and pants to unite with the other. Viewed in its own right, love is nothing other than a desire, and from it an effort, to join together— and in the case of married love, to join into one person.

After all, people were created male and female this way so that the two of them could become like one person, or one flesh, and when they do become one, taken together they are a complete person. Without this conjunction they are two, and each is like a divided or half person. Now, because this attraction hides deep within each particle of a male and each particle of a female, and because the ability and the drive to join together into one is in each particle, a mutual and reciprocal love for the other sex remains with people after death.

38   I use the terms *love for the other sex* and *married love* because love for the other sex is something other than love for marriage. Love for the other sex is found in worldly people, and love for

marriage is found in spiritual people. The worldly person loves and wants only external unions and the bodily pleasures that come out of them. But the spiritual person loves and wants an inner union and the kinds of happiness that his spirit gets from them. And he can tell that these are available with one wife whom he can join with as one, more and more. And the more they are united in this way, the higher he can see the happiness climbing, step by step, steadily, to eternity. But the worldly person does not think about this.

This is the reason for saying that love for marriage remains after death for people who enter heaven—the ones who became spiritual on earth.

39   (5) *There is full confirmation of these things by my own experience.* So far I have had my hands full showing by methods that are intellectual and are known as rational that people live on as people after death, and that then men are still male and women are female, and that everyone's love remains with him—particularly love for the other sex and love for marriage. But starting in infancy, from parents and teachers, and then from the learned and the clergy, one acquires the belief that he will not live on as a person after death until after the Last Judgment Day (they have waited for it for six thousand years now), and many have represented these as concepts that you get from faith, not intellect. Therefore I have had to demonstrate the ideas by the evidence of my own eyes. Otherwise a person who believes only his senses will say, from his ingrained faith, "If people lived on as people after death, I'd see and hear them. Besides, who has come down from heaven or up from hell to report?"

But it is not possible, and never has been possible, for any angel of heaven to come down or any spirit of hell to come up and speak with any human unless the Lord opened the interiors of the person's mind, which are spiritual. And this cannot happen fully except to those whom the Lord has prepared to accept what relates to spiritual wisdom. Therefore it pleased the Lord to do just that to me in order to keep the conditions in heaven and hell and the condition of people's life after death from being unknown, laid to rest in ignorance, and finally entombed in denial. But the firsthand evidence for what I have been saying is too extensive to bring in here. However, it is brought together in the book *Heaven and Hell*, and then in *The Continuation about the World of Spirits*, and afterwards in *Apocalypse Revealed*. The part that is specifically about marriages will be contained in the stories that follow the paragraphs or chapters of the present work.

40   (6) *Consequently, there are marriages in heaven.* This has now been confirmed by reason and at the same time by experience, so it does not need more demonstration.

41   (7) *The Lord's statement that there are no weddings after resurrection was about spiritual marriages.* We read this in the Gospels.

Certain Sadducees, who deny resurrection, questioned Jesus, saying: "Teacher, Moses wrote that if someone's brother, with a wife and no children, is dead, his brother should take his wife and raise children for his brother. There were seven brothers. One after the other they took the wife but died childless. In the end, the woman died, too. So which one's wife does she become in the resurrection?"

But in answer Jesus told them, "The children of this time celebrate weddings and give away in marriage. But those who will measure up to the next age and the resurrection from the dead will neither have weddings nor give away in marriage. For they can no longer die, for they are like the angels and are God's children. For they are the children of rebirth. But that the dead rise, even Moses showed, at the burning bush, when he called the Lord Abraham's God and Isaac's God and Jacob's God. For He is not the God of the dead, but of the living. For everyone lives in Him." (Luke 20:27–38; Matt. 22:23–32; Mark 12:18–27)

The Lord taught two things by these words—first, that people rise again after death, and second, that there are not marriages in heaven.

He taught that people rise again after death by saying that God is not the God of the dead but of the living and that Abraham, Isaac, and Jacob are alive. He teaches it again in the parable of the rich man in hell and Lazarus in heaven (Luke 16:22–31).

The second thing—that there are not marriages in heaven—
He taught by these words, "But those who will measure up to the
next age . . . will neither have weddings nor give away in marriage." The words that come next—that they cannot die any more
because they are like the angels and sons of God when they are
children of the rebirth—show clearly that He was referring to no
weddings other than spiritual weddings. "Spiritual weddings"
refers to conjunction with the Lord, and this is made on earth.
Once made on earth it is also made in heaven, so weddings are
not made again in heaven, nor "giving away in marriage." This is
also how to understand the words, "The children of this time
have weddings and give away in marriage. But those who will
measure up to the next age neither have weddings nor give away
in marriage." The Lord also calls them "children of weddings"
(Matt. 9:15; Mark 2:19). In this passage He calls them "angels,"
"children of God," and "children of rebirth."

Clearly in the following passages "to have a wedding" is to
be conjoined with the Lord, and "to go to a wedding" is to be
received in the kingdom of heaven by the Lord:

In Matthew (22:1–14) the kingdom of heaven is like a man, a
king, who held a wedding for his son and sent servants with
invitations to the wedding.

In Matthew (25:1ff.), the kingdom of heaven is like ten virgins
who went out to meet the bridegroom, and the five of them who
were ready went in to the wedding. It is clear from 25:13, where it
says, "Watch . . . for you know neither the day nor the hour in
which the Son of Man is coming," that this refers to the Lord.

And in Revelation (19:7, 9), the time "for the wedding of the
Lamb has come, and His wife has made herself ready. . . . Blessed
are those who have been called to the wedding supper of the
Lamb!"

*The Doctrine for the New Jerusalem Concerning the Sacred Scrip-
tures* (published in Amsterdam in the year 1763) fully explains
that there is a spiritual meaning in every single word that the
Lord spoke.

42   I add to this two stories from the spiritual world. First this one:
Once in the morning I looked up into the sky, and above me
I saw domed openings, one above another. And I noticed the first

and nearest opening fold away, then another higher one, and finally a third, which was highest. And in the light coming from there I could tell that on the first level were angels who make up the first, or lowest, heaven, and on the second level were angels who form the second, or middle heaven, and on the third level were angels who form the third, or highest heaven.

At first I wondered what it was, and why, and then a voice like a trumpet sounded out of the sky. "We could tell you were thinking about married love," it said, "and now we see that you are. And we know that, so far, no one on earth knows what real married love is, as far as its origin and essence go. But it does make a difference to know this! So the Lord decided to open the heavens for you so the light that illuminates can flow into your inner mind and you will understand. For us in the heavens, especially in the third heaven, heavenly joys come mainly from love for marriage, so we have permission to send down a married couple for you to see."

Then what did I see but a chariot coming down from the highest, or third, heaven, and there seemed to be one angel in it. But as it came closer I could tell there were two.

From a distance the chariot gleamed before my eyes like a diamond, and hitched to it were colts as white as snow. The couple sitting in the chariot had two turtledoves in their hands. They called to me, "You want us to come closer. But watch out that the fiery glare of our heaven, where we came down from, does not get very deep inside you. It will flood your higher mental perceptions with light—they are heavenly per se. But you'll never be able to describe them in the world where you are. So you'll have to take what you're going to hear rationally, and you'll have to express it the same way to be understood."

"I'll be careful," I answered. "Come nearer."

And they came closer, and they were a husband and his wife! "We are married partners," they said. "We have lived blessedly in heaven since the first Age, which you call the Golden Age, and always in the same flower of youth that you see us in today."

I looked closely at them both, because I could tell that they must represent married love in its life and in its outward splendor—in its life in their faces and in its outward splendor in their clothing. For all angels are feelings of love in a human form. Their most dominant feeling shines out from their faces, and they choose clothes by and according to their disposition. So in heaven the saying is that your disposition clothes you.

The husband's age seemed halfway between adolescence and young adulthood. In his eyes there flashed a sparkling light from his perceptiveness about love, which made his face seem to shine from within, and from its glow the surface of his skin fairly shone, so that his whole face was one bright elegance. He wore an ankle-length robe with a blue garment under it, and it was belted with a gold sash with three precious stones on it—two sapphires on the sides and a fiery stone in the middle. His stockings were shining linen with silver thread woven in, and his shoes were all silk. This was how the husband represented the form of married love.

But the wife represented it this way. I saw her face—and did not see it. I could see it as beauty itself, and I could not see it because this is inexpressible. For a flaming brightness was in her face—the kind of light that angels in the third heaven have—and it dulled my vision so I was somewhat dazzled.

Noticing this, she spoke to me and said, "What do you see?"

"All I see is married love and what it looks like," I said, "but I see and do not see!"

At this she turned partly away from her husband, and then I could look at her better. Her eyes sparkled with the light of her heaven, which, as I said, is flaming, and so it derives from a love of wisdom. In fact, wives in that heaven love their husbands on account of wisdom and in relation to their wisdom, and the husbands love their wives according to that love directed toward them and in relation to it, and this is the way they are united.

From this she had such beauty that no painter could try to capture the image of it, since his colors have no such vibrance nor his art the power to express such beauty. Her hair was done up becomingly to match her beauty, and flowers made of diamonds were stuck into it. Her necklace was of fiery stones with a rose drop of chrysolites, and her bracelets were of large pearls. She wore a scarlet gown with a purple blouse under it, buttoned in front with rubies. But what I admired was that the colors were variegated according to whether or not she was facing her husband and also were now more vibrant, now less, according to her glance—more when they faced each other and less when they looked aside.

After I saw these things they spoke to me again, and when it was the husband speaking it was just as if it came from the wife at the same time. When it was the wife it was just as if it came from the husband, for their speech sprang from such a unity of minds. And then I heard the speech of married love, too. It is inwardly simultaneous with the joy of their states of peace and innocence. And it comes from them, too.

In the end they said, "They're calling us back. We'll go now." And then they appeared to ride in a chariot again, as before, and it carried them along a paved road between flower gardens. From the beds sprang olives and laden orange trees. And when they approached near their heaven, girls came to meet them on the way, greeted them, and led them in.

43   After this I saw an angel from that heaven, holding a parchment in his hand, which he unrolled, saying, "I saw you meditating about married love. On this parchment is unknown lore about married love—things not discovered in the world until now. Now they are disclosed, because it is important. In our heaven there are more of these secrets than in the others because wisdom and married love are within us. But I predict that only those whom the Lord receives into the New Church which is the New Jerusalem will make that love a part of themselves."

After these words the angel dropped the unrolled parchment down. Then an angelic spirit caught it and laid it on a table in a certain room, which he closed at once, handing me the key, and saying, "Write."

44   Another story: Once I saw three spirits fresh from the world wandering around, looking, and finding things out. They were surprised that they were living people just as before and that the things they saw were the same. They did know that they had left the former or natural world and that there they had thought that they would not revive as people before the day of the Last Judgment, when they would be clothed by flesh and bones laid away in graves. So to remove all doubt about whether they were really people, by turns they examined and touched themselves and others

and felt objects, and by a thousand ways assured themselves that they were now people the same as in the world before, except that they saw each other in a brighter light and objects in more brilliance and therefore much more perfectly.

Then two angelic spirits happened to fall in with them and stopped them, saying, "Where are you from?"

They answered, "We came from the world, and we're alive in a world again, so we migrated from one world to another. We're amazed at this!"

Then the three newcomers asked the two angelic spirits about heaven, and because two of the three newcomers were adolescents and a spark of sexual eagerness glittered from their eyes, the angelic spirits said, "Maybe you saw some women."

They said, "We did!"

They had asked about heaven, so the spirits said, "In heaven everything is magnificent and splendid such as no eye has seen. Young women and men are there—young women of such beauty that they can be called beauty's own image, and young men of such morality that you could call them morality's own image. And the women's beauty and the men's morality suit each other like pieces in a puzzle."

The two newcomers asked, "Are human figures in heaven exactly like the ones in the natural world?"

The answer was, "Exactly the same. Nothing is taken away from a man and nothing from a woman. In a word, a man is a man and a woman is a woman in total perfection of the form that they were created in. Step aside and look at yourself if you want, and see if anything is missing—whether you are male as before."

Once again the newcomers spoke. "In the world we came from we have heard that there are no weddings in heaven because the people are angels. Then isn't there sexual love?"

"Your sexual love isn't found there," the angelic spirits answered, "but an angelic sexual love that is chaste, without any enticement of lust."

To this the newcomers said, "If there is sexual love without allurement, then what kind of sexual love is it?" And while they were thinking about this love they sighed and said, "Oh, what a dry heavenly joy! What young man can choose heaven, then? Love like that is sterile and without life, isn't it?"

These words made the angelic spirits laugh, and they replied, "Angelic sexual love, the kind in heaven, is still full of deep delights. It is the most pleasant opening of everything in the mind, and therefore everything in your chest, and in your chest it is as if your heart plays with your lungs, and your breath, voice, and words come out of this play, which makes fellowship between the sexes, or between young men and women, precisely the pleasantness of heaven—which is pure.

"All newcomers going up to heaven are tested out to see what their chastity is like, for they are put in the company of young women—heavenly beauties—who can tell, from their voice, their speech, their face, eyes, gestures, and the sphere they give off, what they are like as far as sexual love goes. If the love is unchaste the women run away and tell their friends they saw satyrs or lechers. And those newcomers undergo a change, besides, and to the eyes of angels they look hairy, with feet like cows or leopards, and pretty soon they get thrown out to keep their lust from polluting the air there."

When they heard these things the two newcomers said once more, "So then there is no sexual love in heaven. What is chaste sexual love but love emptied of its essential life? Companionships of young men and women there are dry pleasures, aren't they? We aren't stones and posts. We take in life and feel it!"

The angelic spirits resented this when they heard it and answered, "You definitely don't understand what chaste sexual love is, because so far you are not chaste. It's precisely the joy of your mind and therefore of your heart and not of the flesh below your heart at the same time. Angelic chastity, which both sexes have in common, does not let that love get past the confines of your heart, but within that and above it the joys of chaste sexual love, which are too deep and too rich in pleasure for words to describe, make a young man's morality delight in a young woman's beauty. But this sexual love is for angels, because they have only married love, and this love is incompatible with unchaste sexual love.

"Real married love is a chaste love and has nothing in common with unchaste love. It is love for just one of the other sex. All the others are out of the question. You see, it is a spiritual love and therefore bodily, not a bodily love and therefore spiritual. That is, not a love that annoys your spirit."

Hearing these things pleased the two adolescent newcomers, and they said, "Then there is sexual love there yet! What else is love that belongs to marriage?"

But the angelic spirits answered them, "Think deeper. Consider and you will see that your sexual love is extramarital love and married love is totally different—as different as wheat from chaff, or rather human from bestial! If you asked women in heaven what extramarital love is, I assure you that the response would be, 'What's this? What are you saying? How can you let a thing that hurts our ears this way come out of your mouth? How can a person invent a love that was not created?'

"If you asked them what real married love is, I know what the answer would be: that it isn't a love for the other sex but a love for one member of the other sex, which happens only one way—when the Lord arranges for a young man to notice a young woman and the woman the man, and they both feel marriage take fire in their hearts, and they can tell that she is his and he is hers. For love meets love and makes itself known and joins both souls together at once, and then their minds join, and from there it goes into their breasts, and farther after their wedding, and this is how it becomes a complete love. It joins them together more every day, to the point where they are not two any more, but just like one. I also know that they will swear that they know of no other sexual love. In fact, they say, 'How can there be sexual love without its being so responsive and mutual that it aims at an eternal union, which is that two become one flesh?'"

The angelic spirits added to this. "In heaven they absolutely do not know what fornication is, nor that it exists, nor that it can exist. An angel's whole body is cold to unchaste or extramarital love, and, vice versa, his whole body gets warm from chaste or married love. Among men, every cord goes slack at the sight of a prostitute, and tunes up at the sight of their wives."

The three newcomers listened to this and asked, "Is love between married partners the same in heaven as on earth?"

"It is just the same," the two angelic spirits answered. They could tell that the newcomers wanted to know if there was the same physical pleasure, so they said, "Completely the same, but much richer, because angelic perception and sensation is much more exquisite than a mortal's is. And what vitality does that love have unless it comes from a vein of potency? If this is missing, doesn't that love diminish and cool off? And isn't that strength the very measure, the very degree, and the very basis of that love? Isn't it the beginning, the foundation, and the capstone of it? It is a universal law that the highest things exist, subsist, and persist in relation with the lowest. The same goes for this love as well, so without the physical pleasure there would not be any married love."

Then the newcomers asked, "Are babies born there from the physical pleasure of this love, and if not, what good does the pleasure do?"

The angelic spirits answered, "There aren't any worldly off-spring, but there are spiritual offspring."

They asked what "spiritual offspring" are.

"The physical pleasure," they answered, "brings the partners closer together in a marriage of good and truth, and marriage of good and truth is a marriage of love and wisdom, and love and wisdom are the offspring that are born from this marriage. Since a husband in heaven is wisdom and a wife is its love, and since both are spiritual, it means that no offspring but spiritual offspring can be conceived and born there. This is why angels do not get depressed after the pleasure as some do on earth, but happy, and they get this from a constant fountain of resounding potency that refreshes and brightens them up as well. You see, everyone who comes to heaven returns to the springtime of his youth and the energy of that age, and stays that way forever."

When the three newcomers heard these things they said, "Don't we read in the Word that in heaven there are no weddings because they are angels?"

The angelic spirits answered this. "Look up to heaven and you will get the answer."

"Why look up to heaven?" they asked.

"Because all interpretations of the Word come to us from there," they said. "Inwardly the Word is spiritual, and angels, who are spiritual, will teach its spiritual meaning."

And pretty soon heaven opened over their heads, and two angels came into view for them and said, "There are weddings in heaven as on earth. But only for people there who have a marriage of good and truth—as all angels do—so this passage refers to spiritual marriages, which are marriages of good and truth. These take place on earth and not after death, so not in heaven. Thus it says of the five foolish virgins invited to the wedding that they could not go in. They had no marriage of good and truth, you see. They had no oil but only lamps. 'Oil' is a way of saying good and 'lamps' truth. And to 'get married' is to enter heaven, where that marriage is."

The three newcomers were glad to hear these things and they fully desired heaven and hoped to get married there, and they said, "We'll work on the morality and propriety of our life, to get our wish!"

Chapter 3

The Condition of
Married Partners
After Death

45   I have just demonstrated that there are marriages in heaven. Now for the marriage covenant made in the world—whether it will continue and hold fast after death or not.

This is not a matter of opinion but of experience, which I have had through association with angels and spirits, so it is up to me to pass it on, and in a way that reason accepts. It is one of the things married people hope and pray to know. For men who loved their wives, and whose wives have died, want to know if their wives are all right, and whether they and their wives will meet again, just as wives who loved their husbands do. And many married people want to know ahead of time whether they will be separated or will live together after death. Those with incompatible minds want to know if they will be separated, and those with compatible minds want to know if they will live together. Since this will be welcome information, I pass it on, arranged this way:

    (1) After death every person's sexual love stays the way it was inwardly in the world—that is, as it was in his inward desire and thought.

    (2) The same goes for marital love.

    (3) Married partners usually do meet after death, recognize each other, get together again and live together for a while. This happens in the first state, when they live, outwardly, as they had in the world.

(4) But gradually, as they shed the superficialities and settle into what they are like inwardly, they find out what their love and their attraction for each other was like, and whether or not they can live as one.

(5) If they can live as one they remain married, but if they cannot they separate, sometimes the man from the wife, sometimes the wife from the man, and sometimes mutually from each other.

(6) Then the man gets a suitable wife, and similarly the wife a suitable husband.

(7) Partners enjoy intercourse with each other just like intercourse in the world, only happier and richer, though without having children. Instead of that, or in place of it, they have spiritual offspring—loves and perceptions.

(8) This happens to those who enter heaven. It is different for those who go to hell.

Now an explanation follows that will illustrate and demonstrate these points.

46   (1) *After death every person's sexual love stays the way it was inwardly in the world—that is, as it was in his inward desire and thought.* Every love follows a person after death, because it is the essence of his life. The controlling love, which is the head of all the others, remains with the person forever, and so do the subordinate loves. They remain because a love belongs to a person's spirit and to his body from his spirit. And since a person becomes a spirit after death, he carries the love with him. Love is the essence of a person's life, so clearly whatever his life was like in the world, his condition after death is the same.

As for sexual love, it is the basic one of all loves, because by creation it is placed in the person's soul itself, where the person's whole essence comes from. Sexual love is there to enlarge the human race. The reason this love especially remains is that after death men are still male and women are female, and there is nothing in the soul, mind, and body that is not male in a man and female in a woman, and these two are created in such a way that they seek to be united—united into one person; in fact this urge is the sexual love that precedes the love for marriage. Now because the inclination to join is written all over each and every thing about men and women, this means that the inclination cannot be erased and die with your body.

47   Sexual love stays as it was inwardly while the person was in the world, because everyone has an inward and an outward side. These two are also called the inner and outer person. So there is an inner and an outer will and thought. A person leaves the outer part behind and keeps the inner part when he dies, because the outer things belong to his body and the inner ones belong to his spirit.

Now, a person is his love, and love resides in his spirit, so this means that sexual love stays with him after death the way it was, inwardly, in him. For example, if his inner love has been for marriage, or chaste, it continues to be a love for marriage and chaste after death. And if it has been inwardly a love for promiscuity, it remains that way after death, too. But note that sexual love is not the same with one person as it is with another. There are infinite varieties of it. But it absolutely stays the same as it was in each person's spirit.

48   (2) *Similarly, married love remains just as it was inwardly in the world—that is, as it was in the person's inner will and thought.* I mention both love for the other sex and love for marriage because they are two different things. I also say that after death married love remains with a person just as it was in his inner part while he lived in the world. But few people know the difference between love for the other sex and love for marriage, so here at the beginning of this treatise I shall sketch out something about it.

Love of the other sex is love for and with many of the other sex, but married love is only for one and with one of the other sex. Love for many and with many is a natural love, and in fact we have it in common with beasts and birds, which are natural. But love for marriage is a spiritual love, unique and appropriate to people, because people were created to become spiritual and are born for that reason. So a person sheds the love of the other sex and puts on the love in marriage to the extent that he becomes spiritual. At the beginning of a marriage a love for the other sex seems connected with the love in marriage, but these separate as the marriage goes on, and then for those who are spiritual the love for the other sex fades away and a love for marriage replaces it. For those who are worldly, the opposite happens.

Now it is clear from what I have said that love for the other sex has to do with many and is natural, even animal in its own right, so it is impure and unchaste. And since it wanders without limits it is fornication. But married love is completely different. It will be obvious in the things that follow that marriage is spiritual and appropriate to people.

47b   (3) *Two married partners usually do meet after death, recognize each other, get together again, and live together for a while. This happens in the first state, when they live outwardly as they had in the world.* The states that people enter after death are two—external and internal. First they enter their external state and then their internal. In the external state, if either has died earlier, spouse meets spouse, they recognize each other, and if they had lived together in the world they get together and live together for a while. While they are in this state one does not know the other's disposition toward himself, because this is hidden within. But later when they do come into their internal state their disposition makes itself obvious, and if both dispositions are of the same mind and are sympathetic they continue married life. But they dissolve it if they are in discord and feel different.

If a man had several wives he joins them one by one while in his external state. But when he enters his internal state and can tell the particular tendencies of love, he either chooses one or leaves them all, for in the spiritual world, just as in the natural world, they do not let any Christian have more than one wife, because this disturbs and profanes the religion.

It is the same with a woman who had several husbands. But women do not attach themselves to their husbands. They only appear on the scene, and the husbands take the wives to themselves.

Note that husbands rarely recognize their wives, but wives know their husbands well. The reason is that women have an inner grasp of love and men have only an outward one.

48b   (4) *But gradually, as they shed the superficialities and settle into what they are like inwardly, they find out what their love and attraction for each other was like, and whether or not they can live as one.* There is no need to explain these things further, because they follow from the things explained in the last article. Here I will just illustrate how people shed what they are outwardly and put on what they are inwardly.

After death everyone is first introduced to the world called the *world of spirits*, which is between heaven and hell. There they are prepared—the good for heaven and the bad for hell. The intent of the preparation there is for your internal and external parts to agree so you are integrated, not disagree so you are fragmented. In the natural world the external and internal parts are two things and unite only in people with sincere hearts. We know they are two from cunning and deceitful people, especially hypocrites, flatterers, frauds, and liars. In the spiritual world you are not allowed to have a divided mind like this, but the inwardly bad people will also be bad outwardly, and likewise, the good will be good both inwardly and outwardly. In fact, after death every person becomes what he was inwardly and not what he was outwardly. For this purpose he is made to live outwardly and inwardly by turns. Every person, even an evil one, is sensible while in his outward life—that is, he wants to appear sensible. But inwardly an evil person is a fool. By the changes back and forth the person can see his folly and come to his senses. But if he did not come to his senses in the world he cannot afterward, for he loves his irrationality and wants to stay that way, so he drives his outward self into the same insanities, as well. This integrates his internal and external self, and when that has been done he is ready for hell.

But a good man is the opposite. He looked to God in the world and became sensible, so he has better sense inwardly than outwardly, because outwardly the attractions and deceptions of the world sometimes made him act crazy, too. Therefore his outside also is brought into harmony with his inside, which I already said is sensible. When this is done he is ready for heaven. This explains how you shed your external qualities and put on your internal qualities after death.

49   (5) *If they can live as one they remain married, but if they cannot they separate, sometimes the man from the wife, sometimes the wife from the man, and sometimes mutually from each other.* Separations happen

after death because unions made on earth are rarely made from any inner sense of love, but from an outer one that hides what is inside. Our external concept of love has its cause and source in the kind of things that have to do with worldly and bodily love. Wealth and possessions particularly belong to worldly love, while status and honors go with bodily love. And in addition there are the different attractions that entice you, such as beauty and a facade of acting fashionably. Sometimes even lewdness is an attraction. Moreover, marriages are set up within your district, city, home town, or household with only a narrow choice, limited to familiar families and those of similar status. This is why marriages entered in the world are mostly external and not internal at the same time, and yet an internal union—a union of souls—makes marriage itself. That union goes unnoticed until a person sheds his external part and puts on his internal, which happens after death.

So, under the circumstances, separations do take place after death, and then new unions with those of likeness and similarity—unless it has already happened on earth. This does happen for people who from their youth have loved a legitimate and loving relationship with one, have longed for it and prayed to the Lord, and have kept away from roving desires, holding their noses.

50   (6) *Then the man gets a suitable wife and the wife a suitable husband.* The reason is that no married partners can be accepted into heaven to stay there unless they are are united inwardly, or can be united as if they are one. For they do not call two partners there two, but one angel. The Lord made this known in His words that they are "no longer two but one flesh."

The reason no others are accepted into heaven is that no others can live together there—that is, be together in the same house, and in the same bedroom and bed. For everybody in heaven associates according to relationships and kinships of love, and they have their homes according to these. For there is no distance in the spiritual world, but something that seems like distance, which depends on the condition of your life. The condition of your life depends on the condition of your love. So no one there can live anywhere but in the home provided and assigned him according to what his love is like. Anywhere else his chest heaves and he has trouble breathing. And two people cannot live to-gether in the same house unless they are alike—and certainly not married partners, unless they are mutually inclined. If there are external inclinations and not inner ones too, the house itself, and the very place, separates, rejects, and expels them.

This is why those who are ready and are accepted into heaven are able to marry a partner whose soul is so much inclined to unite with the other person that they do not want to be two lives but one. This is why, after separation, a man gets a suitable wife and a woman a suitable husband.

51   (7) *Partners enjoy intercourse with each other just like intercourse in the world, only happier and richer, though without having children. Instead of that, or in place of it, they have spiritual offspring—loves and perceptions.* Partners enjoy intercourse in the same way as they do in the world, because after death men are still male, and women are female, and from conception both have an implanted tendency to join together. This human tendency is in your body because of your spirit, so after death, when people are spirits, the same mutual inclination remains, which is not possible without the same inter-course. For people are people as before, with nothing missing from a man nor a woman. They stay the same in bodily form as well as in feelings and thoughts. So what else can follow but that they have the same intercourse? And because love for marriage is chaste, pure, and holy, the intercourse is complete. But more about this appears in the story in no. 44.

Intercourse is happier and richer then because when that love becomes spiritual it becomes deeper and purer and therefore more fully appreciated. All joy grows with awareness, and it grows to the point where you can feel the blessedness in the joy of it.

52   Marriages in heaven do not produce children, but spiritual offspring instead (loves and perceptions) because for those in the spiritual world an ingredient is missing—the material level. This provides the vessel for spiritual things, and without their con-taining vessel they do not take a physical form the way offspring conceived in the natural world do. And spiritual things, seen for what they are, trace back to love and perceptiveness, so these are the offspring that spiritual marriages conceive. I say conceive

because married love fulfills an angel. It unites him with his partner to make him more and more human, for, once again, two
married people in heaven are not two but one angel. So it is
through marital union that they fill themselves with humanity—
which is wanting to be wise and loving what belongs to wisdom.

53   (8) *This happens to those who enter heaven. It is different for those
who go to hell.* Those who are received into heaven and become
angels are spiritual, and marriages are spiritual in their own right
and therefore holy, so after death a man gets a suitable wife and
similarly a wife a suitable husband, and they enjoy happy and
rich intercourse, though without having children. This applies to
those who go to heaven.

However, those who enter hell are all worldly, and merely
worldly marriages are not marriages but liaisons derived from
unchaste desire. Later, where the subject is chastity and unchastity,
and further when love of fornication is discussed, I tell what these
liaisons are like.

54   The following things should be added to what I have mentioned so far about what happens to married people after death.

(a) All the couples who are merely worldly are separated
after death. The reason is that their love for marriage cools off
and their love of adultery warms up. Yet after separation they
sometimes still form relationships like marriages with others, but
after a short time they separate themselves from one another.
This often happens repeatedly. And finally the man is left to some
prostitute and the woman to some adulterer. This takes place in
prison in hell (see *Apocalypse Revealed,* no. 153 [10]). They are both
forbidden promiscuous lechery.

(b) When one partner is spiritual and the other worldly, they
too are separated after death, and the spiritual one gets a suitable
spouse, but the worldly one is banished among his own kind in
places of promiscuity.

(c) But those who were single in the world and kept marriage
completely out of their minds stay single, if they are spiritual. But
if they are worldly they become lechers. It is different for those
who longed for marriage while single, especially people who tried

unsuccessfully to marry. If they are spiritual they are provided with happy marriages, but not until they are in heaven.

(d) People who have been shut up in monasteries in the world, virgins and men, are released and set free after their monastic life ends (it goes on a while after death), and they gain the freedom to do things they wanted to, whether they wanted to be married or not. If they did, they do get married. If not, they are taken to the celibates, to one side of heaven. But those who constantly smoldered with lust are expelled.

(e) There is a reason why the celibates are to one side of heaven. The aura of complete celibacy disturbs the aura of marriage love, which is the very aura of heaven. It is the very aura of heaven because it comes down from the heavenly marriage of the Lord and the church.

55   I add to these things two stories. First this one:

Once I heard a very pleasant tune coming out of heaven. Wives and young women were there who were harmonizing to a simple melody. The sweetness of the singing was like some feeling of love flowing out in harmony. Heavenly songs are nothing other than affections resonating, or feelings expressed and modulated in sounds. For just the way words express thoughts, song expresses feelings. From the pattern of the rhythms and the flow, angels can tell what feelings a song has to do with.

There were many spirits around me at that time, and I heard from some of them that they had heard that very pleasant tune and that it was the tune of some lovely feeling that they did not get the gist of. So they made different guesses, but in vain. They thought the song might express the feelings of a bridegroom and bride when they are engaged. Some thought it was the feeling of a bride and a groom entering marriage, and some thought it was the first love of a husband and wife.

And then an angel from heaven appeared among them and said, "They are singing chaste love for the other sex."

But the group standing around asked, "What is chaste love for the other sex?"

The angel said, "It is a man's love for a maiden or wife with a beautiful figure and fine manners, and it is without any lewd thoughts. The same goes for the love of a woman for a man." When he had said this the angel vanished.

The song went on, and now that they knew what feeling it was about they heard it in many different ways, each according to the condition of his love. Those who looked chastely at women heard the song as harmonious and pleasant. But those who looked at women unchastely heard it as unharmonious and gloomy. And those who viewed women with disdain heard it as discordant and harsh.

Then suddenly the level place where they were standing turned into a theater, and they heard a voice say, "Investigate this love."

Then some spirits from various communities suddenly came up, with some angels in white among them. And the angels said, "In this spiritual world we have looked into all kinds of love—not only men's love toward men, women's toward women, and the reciprocal love of husbands and wives, but also love of men for women and women for men. We've had a chance to cover the communities and investigate, and so far the only place we found this general love for the other sex to be chaste is with people in a state of perennial potency thanks to their genuine love for marriage. They are in the highest heavens.

"And we also were able to observe this love's influence on the feelings of our hearts, and we felt clearly that it is sweeter than every other love but the love of two married partners whose hearts are one.

"But we beg you to investigate this love because it is new to you and unknown, and because it is pleasantness itself. In heaven we call it heavenly sweetness."

They talked it over. Then the first to speak were the ones who could not think chastely about marriages, and they gave this opinion: "What man, when he sees a beautiful and lovable young woman or wife, can restrain and purify the thoughts in his mind from desire enough to love her beauty and still have no wish at all to sample it if he could? Who can change the inborn desire of any man into such chastity—change it from what it is—and still love? When sexual love goes from your eyes into your thoughts can it be satisfied with a woman's face? Doesn't it immediately move down to her chest, and beyond? There's nothing in what the angels said—that this love can be chaste and yet is the sweetest love of all, and is only possible with husbands who have a true love for marriage and therefore have very strong potency with their wives. When they see beautiful women, could they, of all people, keep the thoughts in their minds on a high level and hang them up there securely enough not to come down and charge right on to the thing that makes that love?"

The next ones who spoke were both cold and hot—cold toward their wives and hot for the other sex—and they said, "What is chaste love of the other sex? Isn't 'chaste sexual love' a contradiction in terms? With this contradiction put in, what is it but something with its attributes taken away—which is not anything! How can a chaste love for the other sex be the sweetest of all loves when chastity takes away its sweetness? You all know where the sweetness of that love lies. Banish any idea connected with that, and where is the sweetness, and where does it come from?"

Some others took that up, saying, "We have been with the most beautiful women and felt no desire, so we know what a chaste love for the other sex is."

But their friends, who knew about their lewdness, answered, "You were impotent at the time so sex turned you off. That isn't chaste love for the other sex, but the end result of *un*chaste love!"

When they heard this the indignant angels begged the ones standing on the right, toward the south, to speak up. They said, "There is love between men, love between women, and love between men and women. These three kinds of love are quite different from each other. Love between men is like love between understanding and understanding, for a man is created, and therefore born, to become understanding. Love between women is like an affection for men's understanding loving an affection for men's understanding, for a woman is created, and therefore born, to become a love for a man's understanding. These loves—of men for other men and women for other women—do not penetrate deep into their hearts, but they stand outside and only touch each other, so they do not join the two together inwardly.

"This is also why two men argue on and on, 'sparring' with each other like two athletes. And two women sometimes do this to one another, matching desire with desire like two pantomimists in a fist fight.

"But love between men and women is the love of understanding and an attraction to understanding, and this does go deep and join them together. This conjunction is that love. But a union of minds and not of bodies at the same time—or an effort toward a union of minds alone—is a spiritual love and therefore a chaste love. This love is possible only for those who have a true love for marriage and have superior potency from it, because their chastity keeps each from letting in the influence of love from any woman's body other than his wife's.

"And because they have this outstanding potency they can't help loving the other sex and resisting unchastity at the same time! So love for the other sex is chaste for them. It is an inner spiritual friendship, in its own right, which takes its sweetness from their outstanding but chaste potency. Their potency is outstanding from their totally renouncing fornication, and chaste from loving only their wives.

"Now, this love is chaste for them because it is not activated by flesh but only by spirit, and it is sweet because feminine beauty enters the mind at the same time from an inborn tendency."

Many of the bystanders put their hands over their ears when they heard all this, saying, "Those words hurt our ears, and the things you said are worthless to us." They were unchaste.

And then we heard the song from heaven again, sweeter than before. But to the ones who were unchaste it grated so discordantly that they rushed out of the theater to escape the discord. Just a few stayed, who had the sensitivity to love marital chastity.

56   The second story: Talking with angels in the world of spirits one time, I was inspired with a happy wish to see the Temple of Wisdom, which I had seen once before, and I asked them how to get there. They said, "Follow the light and you will come to it."

I said, "What do you mean, 'Follow the light'?"

They said, "Our light shines brighter and brighter as you approach that temple, so head for where the light becomes brighter. Our light comes from the Lord as a Sun, seen for what it is. Therefore, it is wisdom."

Then, together with two angels, I walked on according to the increasing brightness of light and went up by a steep path all the way to the top of a hill in the southern quadrant, and there was a magnificent gate. The keeper saw the angels with me and opened it. Sure enough, we saw an avenue of palm and laurel trees, which we followed. The avenue curved around and ended in a garden with the Temple of Wisdom in the middle.

As I looked around I saw little chapels like the temple, with wise men in them. We went to one temple and spoke with the host there at the entrance, and told him why and how we came.

"Welcome!" he said. "Come in! Sit down! Let's visit and talk about wisdom."

I could see that the inside of the chapel was divided in two but was still one room. It was divided by a transparent wall, but it seemed like one room because of the transparency, which was like the purest crystal.

"Why is it like this?" I asked.

"I am not alone," he said. "My wife is with me, and we are two, but still we are not two but one flesh."

I said, "I know you are a wise man. What does a wise man, or wisdom, have to do with a woman?"

Some displeasure at this came over our host's face. He held his hand out, and we saw other wise men coming from the neighboring buildings. "Our guest here," he teased, "wants to know 'What does a wise man, or wisdom, have to do with a woman?'"

Everyone laughed at this and said, "What is a wise man or wisdom without a woman—or without love? A wife is love of a wise man's wisdom."

But the host said, "Now let's visit with some conversation about wisdom. Let's talk about reasons—right now, the reason for the feminine sex's beauty."

Then, one after the other, they spoke.

The first one said, "Here's why: The Lord created women to be an affection for men's wisdom, and an affection for wisdom is beauty itself."

The second said, "This is why: The Lord created woman through the wisdom of man because He created her from man, and therefore she is the embodiment of wisdom inspired with a feeling of love, and a feeling of love is life itself, so woman is the life of wisdom (though the male is wisdom), and the life of wisdom is beauty itself."

The third said, "Here's why: Women can feel the joys of love for marriage, and their whole body is an organ of this perception, so beauty is precisely home for the joys of married love, with its perception."

The fourth gave this reason: "The Lord took the beauty and refinement of life from man and assigned it to woman, so without a reunion with life's beauty and refinement in a woman, a man is wild, rigid, dry, and repulsive, and he is not wise except for his own benefit, which is stupidity. But when a man unites with his life's beauty and refinement in a wife, he becomes happy, friendly, lively, and lovable, and in this way wise."

The fifth gave this reason: "Women are not created beautiful for themselves but for men—to soften up men's own harshness, mellow their serious intellects, and warm their cold hearts. And this is what happens when men make one flesh with their wives."

The sixth gave this reason: "The universe the Lord created is a most perfect product. And nothing created is more perfect than a woman with a beautiful face and nice manners. This makes a man thank the Lord for His generosity and repay it by accepting wisdom from Him."

After these things and many more like them had been said, the man's wife appeared through the crystal partition and said to her husband, "Please say something." And when he spoke you could notice in his conversation the vitality of his wisdom from his wife, for her love was in the tone of his voice. This experience showed that those things were true.

After this we looked the Temple of Wisdom over, and also the garden paradise around it, and, filled with the happiness of it, we left, took the avenue to the gate, and went down by the path we came up on.

Chapter 4

The Real Love in Marriage

57   The love in marriage comes in endless variety. It is not the same for one person as for another. It does seem the same for everyone, but that is only if your body is the judge of it. The body's judgment does not show anyone the whole picture, because it is heavy and dull. Bodily judgment is a mental judgment based on the five senses.

But to people who approach it with spiritual judgment, the differences stand out. They stand out the more noticeably the higher these people lift the sight of this spiritual judgment by taking their eyes off the senses and looking up where the light is better. Eventually they can settle the question intellectually—and then they see that the love in marriage is not the same for one person as for another.

But no one at all—not even the highly intellectual—can see the endless varieties of this love with any intellectual clarity without first knowing what its very essence and purity is like—or what it was like when the Lord put it and life into man together. Without knowing this state of it, which was most perfect, any investigation of its differences is useless, because there is no fixed point that the differences come from, like warp threads, and that they depend on for alignment so as not to be seen deceptively, but clearly.

This is the reason I undertake to describe that love in its true essentials here (it was in these essentials when the Lord infused it into man together with life) and to describe it as it was in its primeval state. This chapter is called "The Real Love in Marriage" because it was the real love in marriage when in that state. This description of it comes in this order:

(1) There is a real married love that is so rare today that people do not know what it is, and they hardly even know it exists.

(2) The origin of this love is a marriage of good and truth.

(3) This love corresponds to the marriage of the Lord and the church.

(4) In view of its origin and correspondence, this love is heavenly, spiritual, holy, pure, and clean beyond every other love that angels of heaven or people on earth have from the Lord.

(5) It is also the basic love of all heavenly, spiritual and, therefore, earthly loves.

(6) And all joys and delights, from first to last, are gathered up in this love.

(7) But only those who approach the Lord, love the truths of the church, and do its good services, enter this love and can experience it.

(8) This love was the love of loves among the ancient people who lived in the Golden, Silver, and Copper ages, but afterwards it gradually went away.

Here is the explanation of these topics:

58   (1) *There is a real married love that is so rare today that people do not know what it is, and they hardly even know it exists.* There is such a marital love as the following articles describe. You can certainly tell it from the first state of that love when it wins its way and enters the heart of a young man and woman—in other words, you see it in men who are beginning to love only one woman of the whole sex and want to marry her, and even more during the period of engagement as it becomes longer and the wedding approaches, and finally at the wedding and the first days after it. At that time, who would not agree and consent to the fact that this love is basic to all loves, and that then all joys and delights, from first to last, are gathered together in it?

And who does not know that after this charming time those joys pass and go away one by one, until at last the couple hardly notice them? Then if someone says to them the same thing as before—that this love is the basic one of all loves, and that all joys and delights are gathered together in it—they do not consent and agree. And they might say the delights are a laugh, or that they are fleeting fancies. This shows that the first love in a marriage emulates the real love in marriage and sets it up as a kind of pattern to keep in view. This happens because at that time love of the other sex, which is unchaste, is discarded, and in its place a love for one person of the other sex, which is real married love, and is chaste, takes root. Who does not look upon other women without interest at that time, and look at his one and only with love?

59   Still, the real love in marriage is so rare that people do not know what it is like, and hardly that it exists, because the happy state before the wedding changes afterwards to a state of indifference due to apathy. The reasons for this change of state are too many to take up here, but they come up later where the reasons for coldness, separation, and divorce are examined in turn. This will show that for most people today the vision, and with it the knowledge, of this married love is so annihilated that they do not know what it is like and hardly that it exists.

We know that every person is physically oriented when newborn. And then he becomes oriented to the natural world on a deeper and deeper level and in this way becomes rational, and finally spiritual. It goes step by step this way because physicality is like the soil where the natural, rational, and spiritual qualities are planted one by one. In this way a person becomes more and more fully human. Practically the same thing happens when he enters marriage. He becomes more fully human, because he works together with a partner and acts as one person with her. But in the first state this comes in a sort of pattern, already mentioned. Then in married life he begins the same way—physically—and moves on to the natural world and from there to union into one.

From that point, those who love physically on a worldly plane and involve their reason only on those terms can only join together as one with a partner outwardly. And when the outward amenities fail, coldness invades the inner person, and this shatters the happiness of their love mentally and therefore physically—and then physically and therefore mentally. And this goes on until the person has no memory of the first state of his marriage, and consequently no recognition of it. Now, this happens to many people these days, so that people obviously do not know what the real love in marriage is like, and they hardly even know it exists.

It works differently for spiritual people. To them the first state is an introduction to perpetual happiness. This gradually expands as the spiritual dimensions of their rational minds, and therefore the natural dimensions of their bodily senses, join together and unite with one another. But these people are rare.

60   (2) *The origin of this love is a marriage of good and truth.* Every intelligent person recognizes that everything in the universe relates to good and to truth, because this is a universal fact. And he cannot fail to recognize that good is joined with truth and truth with good in each and every detail of the universe, because this is also a universal fact consistent with the other. The reason everything in the universe relates to good and truth, and good is joined with truth, and vice versa, is that both come from the Lord, and they come as a unit from Him. The two things that come from the Lord are love and wisdom. They are from Him because they are He. And everything having to do with love is called good, while everything having to do with wisdom is called truth. Because these two things come from Him as Creator, it means that they are both in created things. The warmth and light that radiate from the sun illustrate this. Everything on earth comes from them, for things sprout when warmth and light are there and according to their being there together. The heat in nature corresponds to spiritual heat, which is love, while the light in nature corresponds to spiritual light, which is wisdom.

61   The next chapter will show that the love in marriage comes from a marriage of good and truth. It is mentioned here only to show that the love in marriage is heavenly, spiritual, and holy because it comes from a heavenly, spiritual, and holy source. To show that the source of the love in marriage is a marriage of good and truth, it will be appropriate to take a short cut and say something about it here. I already said that there is a combination of good and truth in each and every created thing, and the combination does

not happen unless it is reciprocal, for a connection from one side and not the other dissolves itself.

Now, because the union of good and truth exists and is reciprocal, it means that there is truth belonging to good or truth that comes from good, and there is good belonging to truth, or good on account of truth. This truth that belongs to good, or comes from good, is in man and is masculinity itself. And the good that belongs to truth, or is there on account of truth, is in a woman and is femininity itself. There is a marital union between those two. This will be seen in the next chapter. I mention it here just to introduce the concept.

62   (3) *This love corresponds to the marriage of the Lord and the church.* In other words, a husband and wife love each other just as the Lord loves the church and wants the church to love Him. The Christian world knows about the correspondence between these things, but does not yet know what it is like, so a special chapter that follows will show what the correspondence is like. I mention it here to show that the love in marriage is heavenly, spiritual, and holy because it corresponds to the heavenly, spiritual, and holy marriage of the Lord and the church.

Moreover, this correspondence results from the source of married love being the marriage of good and truth (mentioned in the last article) because the marriage of good and truth is the church with mankind. For the marriage of good and truth is the same thing as a marriage of charity and faith, since good is charity, and truth is faith—a marriage that constitutes the church. It is impossible not to see this, because it is a universal truth, and all universal truths are recognizable as soon as they are heard. This is because of the Lord's influence and also his encouragement from heaven.

Now, since the church is the Lord's because it comes from the Lord, and since the love in marriage corresponds to the marriage of the Lord and the church, this means that this love is from the Lord.

63   However, the chapter mentioned above will clarify how the Lord forms a church for two married partners and through it forms married love. Here I just mention that the Lord makes a

church for the man and through the man for the wife, and when it is complete for both of them it is a complete church. For the conjunction of good and truth becomes complete at that time, and the conjunction of good and truth is a church. Later, in its place, I will show by a descriptive line of reasoning that the inclination to join together that is married love is in proportion to the conjunction of good and truth that is the church.

64   *(4) In view of its origin and correspondence, this love is heavenly, spiritual, holy, pure, and clean beyond every other love that angels of heaven or people on earth have from the Lord.* A little above it was partly explained that the love in marriage is like this due to its source, the marriage of good and truth, but that was just a foretaste. It was also explained that it is like this due to its correspondence with the marriage of the Lord and the church. These two marriages, which married love springs from like an offshoot, are holiness itself, so that if married love is received from its Author, Who is the Lord, holiness comes from Him with it. This holiness continually refines and purifies it. And then it makes the love clean and pure every day, perpetually, if the person's will wants it to and works toward it.

Married love is called heavenly and spiritual because angels in the heavens have it—heavenly for angels of the highest heaven because they are called heavenly, and spiritual for the angels below that heaven, because these angels are called spiritual. The reason they are called this is that the heavenly angels consist of loves and the wisdom that comes from it, while the spiritual ones are wisdom and the love that comes from it. The same goes for their marriage relationships.

Now, because angels of both the higher and lower heavens have married love, as the first chapter, about marriages in heaven, showed, this establishes that it is holy and pure.

In view of its essence and where it comes from, this love is more holy and pure than any other love that angels and mankind have, because it is like the head of all the other loves. The article that comes next says something about this precedence that it has.

65   *(5) It is also the basic love of all heavenly, spiritual and, therefore, earthly loves.* In view of its essence, the love in marriage is the

basic love of all loves in heaven and the church because its source is the marriage of good and truth, and all the loves that make a heaven and a church for people come from this marriage. The good in this marriage creates love, and its truth creates wisdom, and when love accepts wisdom, or joins with it, then love becomes love. When wisdom accepts love in return, or joins in with it, then wisdom becomes wisdom.

The real love in marriage is nothing other than love and wisdom uniting. Two partners who both at once have this love between them, or in them, are likenesses and patterns of it. And in heaven, where faces are genuine expressions of one's love, the people all resemble it. For it is in them everywhere and in each part, as I showed already. Now, because two partners are this love in likeness and pattern, it follows that every love that comes from the pattern of this love is a likeness of it. So if married love is heavenly and spiritual, so are the loves that come from it. The love in marriage itself is like a parent, and the other loves are like children. This is why marriages of angels in heaven produce spiritual offspring—which are loves and wisdoms, or goods and truths. (See no. 51, above, about this procreation.)

66   You can see that the same thing is confirmed by the fact that people are created for that love and later are formed by it. A man is created to become wisdom, motivated by a love of being wise, and a woman is created to become love of a man for his wisdom, which is to say according to his wisdom. It is clear from this that two partners are the very form and image of a marriage of love and wisdom, or of good and truth.

It is well to know that there is neither any good nor truth except in a substance, as its material form. Abstract good and truth do not exist, for they are nowhere, since they have nowhere to be. Why, they cannot even appear fleetingly, so they are just things that your mind thinks it is pondering abstractly, although it is quite incapable of thinking except in relation to objects. For all human ideas, even the sublime ones, are substantial—that is, attached to substance. Note, too, that there is no substance unless there is a form. A substance without form is not anything, either, because you cannot attribute anything to it, and a subject with no qualities is a theoretical nonentity.

I added these philosophical remarks to show in this way,

too, that two partners who enjoy real love in marriage are actually forms of the marriage of good and truth, or of love and wisdom.

67   Since earthly loves spring from spiritual loves and spiritual loves from heavenly ones, you can say that the love in marriage is the most basic of all heavenly and spiritual loves, and so it is the most basic of all earthly loves, too. Earthly loves have to do with self-love and worldly loves, spiritual loves have to do with love toward one's neighbor, and heavenly ones have to do with love for the Lord. And since the loves are in this relationship, the order they follow in, and are in for people, is obvious. When they are in this order, then earthly loves obtain their life from spiritual loves and spiritual loves from heavenly ones. And all are in this order from the Lord, whom they come from.

68   (6) *And all joys and delights, from first to last, are gathered up in this love.* Every pleasant thing that a person senses has to do with his love. Love discloses itself—even exists and lives—through those things. We know that pleasures intensify as love intensifies, and as the accompanying feelings touch a governing love more closely. Now, because the love in marriage is the basic one of all good loves, and because it is etched on the most special qualities of a person, as mentioned before, the consequence is that there is more pleasure in it than in any other love. Its pleasures are pleasant according to this love's presence, moreover, and according to its involvement in them at the same time. For it opens out the inner reaches of both mind and body as the delightful stream of its wellspring flows through them and emerges.

All joys from highest to lowest are gathered up in this love because it has a more important use than the others—propagation of the human race, and from the race, angels of heaven. This function was the whole purpose of creation, so the result is that all blessings, good times, happiness, friendliness, and enjoyments that the Lord could ever give to people are all gathered up in this love that they have.

The pleasures of the five senses—sight, hearing, smell, taste, and touch—demonstrate that joys follow function and that a person has pleasures according to his love of an activity. All senses have their pleasures, differing according to their particular functions.

All the other functions are wrapped up in the function of married love, so what sense does it not please?

69   I know that not many people are going to recognize that all joys and all pleasures from highest to lowest are gathered together in married love, because the real love in marriage where they are gathered is so rare today that people do not know what it is, and they hardly know that it exists (as was explained and demonstrated above, nos. 58–59), because the joys are only in a genuine love for marriage. And since this is so rare on earth the only way to describe its exceptional joys is from the mouths of angels, because they do have it.

They have said that its inner delights—of the soul, where the married relationship of love and wisdom or good and truth from the Lord first flows in—are beyond comprehension, so they defy description. They have to do with both peace and innocence. But they say the delights become more and more understandable as they filter down. In the higher levels of the mind they are like blessings, in the lower like good feelings, in the heart like the pleasures that blessings and good feelings bring. And from there they pour into each and every thing in your body and finally come together in your most outward parts, in the greatest delight of all.

Angels have mentioned other surprising things about the delights. They have said that the different kinds of delights in the souls of married partners—as well as the ones in their minds from those in their souls, and those in their hearts from those in their minds—are infinite, and also last forever, and the delights become more intense according to the husband's wisdom. This is because angel husbands live in the prime of life forever and because nothing is more blessed to them than to become wiser and wiser.

But more things that angels said about these delights appear in the stories in this book, especially in the ones after the next few chapters.

70   (7) *But only those who approach the Lord, love the truths of the church, and do its good services, enter this love and can experience it.* Only people who approach the Lord can enter that love, because monogamous marriages—of one man with one wife—correspond

to the marriage of the Lord and the church, and because their
source is the marriage of good and truth (see nos. 60 and 62 above).
The real love in marriage is from the Lord and is for those who
approach Him directly, because of this source and that correspondence. The only way to establish this fully is to discuss specifically
two things, as yet unrecognized. This is done in the chapters that
come next. One thing will be the origin of married love from the
marriage of good and truth and the other the marriage of the Lord
and the church, and how these correspond. You will also see there
that it follows from these ideas that a person's married love coincides with the condition of the church in him.

71   No one can be in love—not in true married love—except
those who receive it from the Lord. They are the ones who approach
Him directly and live religiously with Him in view. This is because
that love, with regard to its source and correspondence, is more
heavenly, spiritual, holy, pure, and clean than any other love that
angels of heaven and people in the church have (see no. 64 above),
and these qualities of it are only present in those who are joined
together with the Lord and whom He puts in the company of
angels of heaven. For these people flee extramarital loves, which
are relationships with others than your own wife or husband, like
their soul's damnation or the fens of hell. And the more a married
person does flee those relationships—even fantasies and the urges
they create—the more that love is purified for him and keeps
becoming more spiritual, first while he lives in the world and
afterwards when he lives in heaven.

No love can ever be purified within men, nor within angels,
so neither can this love. But the Lord regards the intention of your
will primarily, so the more a person has the intention and perse-
veres, the more he is introduced to the love's purity and holiness
and keeps making progress. Only those who get spiritual love for
marriage from the Lord can have it, because heaven is in it, and
for a worldly person that love only finds satisfaction in the flesh,
so he cannot approach heaven nor any angel, nor, for that matter,
any person with that love in him. For this love is the basic one of
all heavenly and spiritual loves (see nos. 65–67 above).

The truth of this has been established for me by experience. I
saw demons in the spiritual world who were in preparation for

hell approach a happy angel and his wife. At a distance, as they approached, they went crazy and threw themselves into caves and pits they found to hide in. Evil spirits love anything consistent with their own inclinations however unclean it is, and are turned away from spirits of heaven because heaven is pure and unlike them. You can draw this conclusion from the things recorded in Chapter 1 (no. 10).

72   The people who love the truths of the church and take part in its good activities achieve the love in marriage and can participate in it, because the Lord receives no others. These are the ones who are in agreement with Him, so He can keep them in that love. Two things make up the church and therefore heaven in a person: the truth of his faith and the good in his life. The truth of faith brings about the Lord's presence, and the goodness in one's life according to the truths of faith establishes a union with Him, and thus a connection with the church and heaven. The truth of faith brings the Lord near because it is light. Spiritual light is nothing else. The goodness of one's life establishes a union with Him because it is heat. Spiritual heat is nothing else, for it is love, and the good of life is love. Everyone knows that all light—even winter light—brings presence, and heat together with light brings union. For orchards and flower beds appear in every light, but they do not flower and fruit except when heat joins the light. These things lead to a conclusion—that the Lord cannot supply real married love for those who only know the church's truths, but for those who know them and take part in the good activities of the church.

73   (8) *This love was the love of loves among the ancient people who lived in the Golden, Silver, and Copper ages.* The histories do not teach that the love in marriage was the love of loves for the very ancient and the ancient peoples who lived in those early ages named as above, because their writings did not survive. Those that did survive come from later writers, who do mention them and also describe the purity and soundness of their life, as well as its gradual decline, figuratively, from gold to iron. But something of the last, or Iron, age, which began at the time of these writers, can be pieced together from the histories of the lives of some kings, judges,

and sages who were called *Sophi* in Greece and elsewhere. But Daniel (2:43) predicts that this age will not last the way iron lasts by itself, but that it will become like iron and clay mixed, which do not hold together.

Now, the ages called Gold, Silver, and Copper were over before the days of the writers, and therefore we lack knowledge about marriages in those ages, on earth. So it suited the Lord to open it up for me by a spiritual route, bringing me to the heavens where those people's homes are, to verbally learn from them what marriages among them were like when they were living during their epochs. For everyone who has ever left the natural world, since creation, is in the spiritual world, and as to their loves they are all still the same and stay that way forever. Since these things are worth knowing and telling about, and they will establish the holiness of marriages, I want to publish them the way they were shown to me while I was wide awake, in a spiritual state, and were later recalled to my mind by an angel, and in this way written down. And since they are from the spiritual world like the other accounts following the chapters, I will divide them into six stories, according to the progress of those ages.

74   These six stories about married love, which are from the spiritual world, show what that love was like in the first age, what it was like after that, and what it is like today. They establish that this love gradually receded from its holiness and purity to the point where it has become fornication. But there is hope of its restoration to its original or ancient holiness.

75   The first story: Once when I was thinking about married love I had a yearning to know what that love was like for those who had lived in the Golden Age and what it was like later in the following ages named from silver, copper, and iron. I knew that everyone who lived rightly in these ages is in heaven, so I prayed the Lord to let me talk with them and be informed.

And there beside me stood an angel! And he said, "The Lord sent me to guide you and keep you company, and first I'm going to guide and accompany you to those who lived in the first age or era, called Golden." He said, "The way there is difficult. It goes through a dark woods that no one can get through unless the Lord gives him a guide."

It was a spiritual experience. I got ready for the road, and we turned toward the east. And going along, I saw a mountain whose altitude reached above the clouds. We crossed a great desert and entered the forest the angel had mentioned, full of many different kinds of trees and so dense that it was dark. But many narrow paths ran through the forest, and the angel said they were all winding in mazes, and a traveler on them would be led astray into the underworld, which was around the edges of the forest, unless the Lord opened his eyes to see olive trees with grape vines twined around them and guide his steps from tree to tree. The forest is like this in order to guard the approach, for only the very first people live on the mountain.

After we entered the woods our vision cleared, and here and there we saw the olive trees entwined with grape vines. Clusters of dark blue grapes hung from them. The olive trees were arranged in continuous spirals, so that we went round and round, following them as they appeared.

At last we saw a grove of tall cedars with some eagles on their branches. When the angel saw them he said, "Now we are on the mountain, not far from its summit."

We went on, and there beyond the grove was a rolling meadow where rams and ewes were grazing. They were symbolic of the mountain people's innocence and peace. We crossed this meadow, and what did we see but tent after tent, and thousands more before us and on both sides as far as the eye could see.

The angel said, "Now we are in the camp where the Army of the Lord Jehovah lives. This is what they call themselves and their dwellings. These very ancient people lived in tents while in the world, so they live in them now, too. But let's head off to the south, where the wiser of them are, to meet someone to visit with."

As we went I saw at a distance three boys and three girls sitting at the door of one of the tents. But when we came closer they turned out to be men and women of medium height.

"All the inhabitants of this mountain look like little children from a distance," the angel said, "because they are in a state of innocence, and childhood is what innocence looks like."

The men ran up to us when they saw us and said, "Where are you from? And how did you get here? Your faces aren't faces from our mountain!"

But the angel answered and told all about our coming through the woods and the reason for our visit. When he heard that, one of the three men invited us into his tent and brought us in. The man wore a blue cloak and a tunic of white wool, and his wife wore a purple gown and an embroidered linen blouse under her tunic.

Since I had been thinking that I wanted to find out about the marriages of the earliest people, I looked closely at the husband and the wife, one at a time, and I noticed in their faces a sort of unity of their souls. I said, "You two are one!"

"We *are* one," the man replied. "Her life is in me and mine is in her. We are two bodies but one soul. The union between us is like the two tents in your chest called heart and lungs. She's my heart, and I'm her lungs. But here we mean love when we say 'heart' and wisdom when we say 'lungs,' so she is love of my wisdom and I'm the wisdom of her love. Because of this her love from outside veils my wisdom, and my wisdom from inside is in her love. This is why you can see the unity of our souls, as you said, in our faces."

Then I asked, "If you have this kind of unity, can you look at a woman other than your own?"

He said, "I can. But my wife is united with my soul, so we look together, and not a shred of sensuality can enter. For when I look at other wives I look at them through my wife, who is the only one I love. And my wife can tell all my inclinations, so she sets my thinking straight and weeds out everything discordant, and at the same time she puts in a coldness and horror toward anything unchaste. So for us here it is just as impossible to look at a friend's wife lustfully as it is to look at the light of our heaven from the gloom of the underworld. For this reason we have no notion of the attraction of lust, let alone any spoken words for it." He couldn't say "fornication." The chastity of their heaven prevented it.

My angel guide told me, "You hear now that the speech of the angels in this heaven is the speech of wisdom. They speak from the reasons for things."

After this I looked around and saw that their tent seemed enveloped in gold. I asked, "How come?"

He answered, "It is a flaming light that sparkles like gold. It brightens and tints the curtains of our tent when we are talking about the love in marriage. You see, the heat from our sun, which in its essence is love, unveils itself then and colors the light, which in its essence is wisdom, with its color—which is gold. And this happens because married love originates in wisdom and love playing together. For a man is born to become wisdom and a woman to be love for the man's wisdom. So the joy of this play is in the married love between us and our wives. The joy comes from our love.

"For thousands of years here we have noted that this joy is excellent and outstanding in abundance, degree, and strength according to our worship of the Lord Jehovah. The heavenly union or heavenly marriage between love and wisdom flows in from Him."

When he had said this I saw a bright light on a central hill among the tents and asked, "What is that light from?"

"It's from the sanctuary in our tent of worship," he said.

I asked if I could go near it, and he said I could. I did, and I saw a tent that, both inside and out, exactly answered the description of the Tabernacle built in the desert for the Israelites, whose design was shown to Moses on Mount Sinai (Exodus 25:40; 26:30). "What is inside the sanctuary," I asked, "that makes so much light?"

He answered, "It's a document inscribed, 'The Covenant between Jehovah and the Heavens.'" He said no more.

Then we were ready to go, so I asked, "When you lived in the natural world, did any of you live with more than one wife?"

"I don't know of anyone," he answered, "because we can't think about more than one wife. Those who have thought about it told us that instantly the heavenly blessings of their souls retreated from the innermost to the outermost parts of their bodies—all the way to their toe nails, and with them the honorableness of manhood. When this was discovered, they were exiled from our territory."

After the man said this he ran to his tent and came back with a pomegranate with lots of golden seeds in it. He gave it to me as a present, and I brought it away as a souvenir to show that we had been with the people who lived in the Golden Age. And then, after a parting word of peace we went away and returned home.

76   The second story: The next day the same angel came to me and said, "Do you want me to guide and accompany you to the people who lived in the Silver Age or era, to hear from them about the marriages of their time?" And he said that they cannot be approached, either, except by the Lord's authority.

It was a spiritual experience, as before, and my guide accompanied me. First we came to a hill where east and south meet, and while we were on its slope he showed me a great expanse of land spread out, and we saw a mountain rising in the distance. Between it and the hill where we stood was a valley, and beyond the valley a plain and a slope gently rising from it. We went down the hill to cross the valley, and here and there to the sides we saw wood and stone carved in the form of people and different animals, birds, and fish.

I asked the angel, "What are they? Are they idols?"

He said, "Absolutely not. They are forms to represent different moral virtues and spiritual truths. The people of that age knew about correspondences, and because every man, animal, bird, and fish corresponds to some quality, each sculpture represents an aspect of some virtue or truth, and a group of several represents the general extended form of the virtue or truth. They are what were called hieroglyphics in Egypt."

We pushed on through the valley, and when we reached the plain, we saw horses and chariots! The horses were equipped and harnessed in various ways, and the chariots had different forms—some carved like eagles, others like whales, others like stags with horns, others like unicorns—and finally we saw some wagons, and stables around to the sides. But when we came closer the horses and chariots disappeared, and instead of them we saw people walking along, two by two, talking and discussing things.

The angel told me, "What looked like horses, chariots, and stables from a distance are images of the rational wisdom of the people from that era. Because of their correspondence, a horse stands for understanding truth, a chariot stands for truth's principles, and stables stand for teachings. You know that everything in this world looks like what it corresponds to."

But we passed by them and went up a long slope and finally saw a city, which we entered. Walking through it we observed its houses from the avenues and squares. They were all palaces made of marble. There were alabaster steps in front of them and columns of jasper beside the steps. We also saw temples of precious stone the color of sapphire and lapis lazuli.

The angel said to me, "Their houses are stone because stones stand for worldly truths, and precious stones stand for spiritual truths. Everyone who lived in the Silver Age acquired his intelligence from spiritual truths and in this way from worldly truths. Silver stands for the same thing."

In our wanderings through the city we saw couples here and there, pair by pair. They were husbands and wives, so we were on the lookout for an invitation somewhere. As we went along in this frame of mind, two of them did call us back into their house. We went up and entered, and the angel, speaking for me, explained to them the reason we came into this heaven. "It's to learn about marriages among ancient people. You are an ancient people."

"We were among the people in Asia," they answered, "and the concern of our era was the study of truths—which gave us intelligence. This concern was the endeavor of our mind and soul. But the concern of our bodily senses was representations of truths in forms. Knowledge of correspondences joined the sensory aspects of our bodies with the perceptive aspects of our minds and gave us intelligence."

Hearing this the angel asked them to tell us something about the marriages in their culture.

The husband said, "There is a correspondence between a spiritual marriage, of truth with good, and a worldly marriage, of a man with one wife. And we studied correspondences, so we saw that religion with its true and good things could only be possible among people who live in real married love with one wife. For the marriage of good and truth is the church among men, so all of us who are here say that a husband is truth and a wife is his good and that good cannot love a truth other than its own nor a truth love any good but its own in return. If it does, the inner marriage that makes the church perishes, and it becomes just an outward marriage. Idolatry corresponds to this, but the church does not. So we call marriage with one wife a sacrament.

And, if marriage with more than one occurred in our culture, we'd call it a sacrilege."

After he said this he led us to an outer room, where there were many works of art on the walls and small sculptures that seemed to be cast in silver. I asked what they were.

They said, "They are pictures and sculptures representing the many qualities, attributes, and delights having to do with the love in marriage. These represent unity of souls, these the joining of minds, these the concord in your hearts, and those the joys that spring from it."

While watching we saw something like a rainbow on the wall, composed of three colors—crimson, blue, and white. And we saw how the crimson shaded off into the blue and tinted the white with dark blue. This color flowed back through the blue into the crimson and made it shine out in a flaming brightness.

The husband said to me, "You do understand this?"

I answered, "Explain it to me."

He said, "From its correspondence the crimson stands for a wife's married love, the white a husband's intelligence. The blue is the beginning of married love, in a husband's insight from his wife, and then the dark blue that tinted the white is married love in the husband. This color seeping back from the blue into the crimson and making it shine out in a flaming brightness stands for the husband's married love flowing back to the wife. Things like this are displayed on the walls while we fasten our eyes on the rainbows pictured here, thinking over the love in marriage, its mutual, ongoing, simultaneous union."

To this I said, "These things are more than secret today, because they're sights that represent unknown things about the married love of one man with one wife."

"They are," he replied. "But they aren't unknown to us here, so they aren't secret."

When he said this a chariot appeared in the distance drawn by white ponies. When the angel saw it he said, "That chariot is a signal to us to go."

Then, as we went down the steps, our host gave us a cluster of white grapes with the vine leaves attached. And the leaves

turned to silver! We brought it away as a souvenir that we had
talked with people of the Silver Age.

77   The third story: The next day the angel guide and companion came up and said, "Get ready, and let's go to the people
living in the western heaven. They come from the people who
lived in the third era, or Copper Age. Their homes spread from
the south throughout the west up to, but not into, the north."

I got ready and went with him, and we entered their heaven
at the south side. There was a magnificent grove of palms and
laurels there. We went through it, and then, right at the western
boundary, we saw giants twice the size of ordinary men. They
asked us, "Who let you in through the grove?"

The angel said, "The God of Heaven."

They answered, "We are guards for the ancient western
heaven. But go through."

We went through, and from a vantage point we saw a mountain as high as the clouds. Between us, at our vantage point, and
the mountain, were town after town with gardens, groves, and
fields in between them. We went through the towns to the mountain and climbed it. Its peak was not a peak but a plain with a big,
wide city on it! And all its houses were made of wood from
resinous trees, and their roofs were made of planks.

I asked, "Why are the houses here made of wood?"

"Because wood stands for good on a material level," answered the angel, "and the people of the third age enjoyed that
kind of good. Copper stands for material good, too, so men of old
called the age when these people lived 'Copper.'

"There are also holy temples here, made of olive wood, and
in their center is a sanctuary where the Word that was given to
the inhabitants of Asia before the Israelite Word, lies in a case. Its
historical books are called The Wars of Jehovah and its prophetic
ones Proverbs. Moses mentions them both in Numbers (21:14–15,
27–30). Today this Word is lost in regions of Asia and is preserved
at present in Great Tartary."

Then the angel led me to a building, and we looked in and
saw its sanctuary in the middle, all in very brilliant light.

"This light is from that ancient Asian Word," the angel said, "for all divine truth shines brightly in the heavens."

Coming out of the building, we heard that it had been announced in the city that two strangers were there and should be questioned to find out where they came from and what they wanted here. A court attendant ran up and ordered us to the judges.

To the question of where we were from and what we wanted here we answered, "We came through the palm forest and also where the giants are who guard your heaven, and then to the place where the towns are. So you can tell that we didn't get here by ourselves, but by the God of Heaven. And what we want is to be taught about your marriages—whether they are monogamous or polygamous."

"What are polygamous marriages?" they responded. "Isn't that fornication?"

Then the judges who were gathered there appointed an informed person to teach us about this matter in his own house. In his house he joined his wife, and here is what they said:

"The earliest or most ancient people had a real love for marriage, so more than anyone else they enjoyed the strength and potency of that love in the world and still do, in their very happy situation in their heaven in the east. And we have preserved their concepts about marriages, among ourselves. We are their descendants, and, like all parents, they gave to us as children rules of life—including this one about marriages: 'Children, if you want to love the Lord and your neighbor, and if you want to be wise and be happy forever, we advise you to live monogamously. If you abandon this principle every heavenly love will escape you and so will inner wisdom, and you will die out.'

"As children we obeyed this precept of our parents and we see the truth of it—that the more you love one partner, the more you grow heavenly and internal, and the more you do not love one partner, the more worldly and superficial you become. A person like this loves nothing but himself and the notions in his mind. He is silly and foolish. This is why all of us in this heaven are monogamous, and because we are, all the boundaries of our heaven are protected against polygamists, adulterers, and fornicators. If polygamists get in, we send them into the northern darkness, if adulterers do, we send them into the western fires, and if fornicators get in, we send them into the false lights of the south."

I heard this and asked, "What do you mean by 'northern darkness,' 'western fires,' and 'false lights of the south'?"

He answered, "Northern darkness is mental dullness and ignorance about the truth. The western fires are loves for evil. And the false lights of the south are falsifications of the truth— spiritual fornications."

After this he said, "Follow me to our treasure house."

We followed him, and he showed us things written by the earliest people on wooden and stone tablets, and then on polished tablets of wood. The second age wrote their writings on parchments, and he brought a parchment with rules of the earliest people copied onto it from the stone tablets. Among the rules was the one about marriages.

After we saw these things and others worthy of note from that ancient time the angel said, "Now it's time for us to be going."

Then our host went out into the garden, picked several twigs from a tree, tied them in a bundle, and gave them to us. He said, "These twigs are from a special tree native to our heaven. Its juice smells of balsam."

We took the little bundle away with us and went back down by a path near the east, which was not guarded. The twigs turned to shining brass! And their tips to gold! It was a sign that we had been among the people of the Third Age, called Copper or Brass.

78   The fourth story: Two days later the angel talked with me again. He said, "Let's finish up the cycle of ages. The last age is left, named for iron. The people of that age stretch into the distance, or the interior, in the northwest. They are all from among the ancient inhabitants of Asia who had the Ancient Word, and their worship comes from that, so it was before Our Lord came to earth. We know this from ancient writings, which named those times in that way. The statue Nebuchadnezzar saw can be taken as a reference to those ages. Its head was gold, its chest and arms silver, its belly and thighs brass, its calves iron, and its feet iron and clay together" (Dan. 2:32–33).

The angel told me these things on the way, which was short-ened and covered more quickly by changes in our state of mind brought on by the characteristics of the settlements we passed through. For space and therefore distances in the spiritual world are appearances according to your states of mind.

When we looked up, we were in a forest of beeches, chest-nuts, and oaks! And looking around, we saw bears to our left and leopards to our right—which astonished me. So the angel said, "These are neither bears nor leopards, but people who guard these northerners. They scent with their noses the atmosphere sur-rounding the life of a passerby, and they attack all the ones who are spiritual, because the people here are worldly. The ones who just read the Word and don't absorb any teachings from it look like bears from a distance, and the ones who use it to confirm untruths look like leopards." But when they saw us they turned away, and we passed on.

After the forest came thickets and then grassy plains divided into fields by box hedges. After these the ground sloped away toward a valley where there was city after city. We bypassed some of them and entered a big one.

Its streets were irregular. So were the houses. They were half-timber and plastered brick. In the squares were temples made of hewn limestone, with a basement below ground and the build-ing above. We went down into one of them by three steps, and all around the walls we saw idols of different shapes, and a crowd of people on their knees adoring them. From a group in the middle protruded the head of that city's tutelary god.

As we left, the angel told me that among the men of old who lived in the Silver Age mentioned above, those idols were images representing spiritual truths and moral virtues, and that when knowledge of correspondences lapsed from memory and died out the images first became objects of worship and later were adored as gods. This is how idolatry arose.

Outside the temple we looked over the people and their clothes. They had faces like steel—bluish gray—and they were dressed like clowns, with skirts around their waists hung from a tight shirt on their chests. And on their heads were sailors' cocked hats.

But the angel said, "Enough of this. Let's find out about the marriages of the people of this age."

We went into the house of an important person with a brim-less, high-crowned hat on his head. He gave us a friendly wel-come and said, "Come in and let's chat."

We walked into the entry hall and sat down there, and I asked him about the marriages of his city and country.

"We don't live with one wife," he said, "but some have two and three, and some more, because we like variety, obedience, and the deference of majesty. We get these attentions from our wives when there are several. With only one there wouldn't be the pleasure of variety but the tedium of sameness, not the flattery of obedience but the annoyance of equality, not the enjoyment of ruling and the honor of it but the disturbance of squabbles over superiority. And what is a woman? Isn't she born subject to the will of a man and to serve, not dominate? So here every husband is like the royal majesty in his own home. This is our love, so it is also the happiness of our life."

But I asked, "Then where is the love in marriage, which makes two souls one, and unites your minds, and makes people happy? You can't divide that love. If divided it becomes a heat that burns out and goes away."

His answer to this was, "I don't see what you mean. What makes a man happy but competition among wives for the honor of being a husband's favorite?"

When he said this the man went to the women's apartment and opened two doors, and something lustful escaped that smelled like filth. It was from polygamous love, which partakes of wedlock and fornication at the same time. I got up and shut the doors.

Then I said, "How can you people in this land survive when you have nothing of real married love, and when you worship idols?"

"As to the love of wedlock," he answered, "we are so vehe-mently jealous for our wives that we let no one farther into our houses than the entry hall. And since there is jealousy, there is love, too. As to the idols, we don't worship them, but we can't think about the God of the Universe except in images present before our eyes, because we can't lift our thoughts above our body's senses or our thoughts about God above things that we can see."

Then, once more, I asked, "Don't your idols have different shapes? How can they present a vision of one God?"

His answer to this was, "It's a mystery to us. Each shape has some hidden thing related to worship of God."

"You are limited to the bodily senses," I said, "without a love of God, or of a partner, which draws on the spiritual plane at all. And it is these spiritual loves that shape a person and make a heavenly person out of a sense-oriented one."

When I said that, something like lightning flashed through the door, and I asked, "What's that?"

"A light like that," he said, "is a sign to us that an ancient person from the east will come. He'll teach us about God—that He is One, the only omnipotent one, who is the first and the last. He warns us not to worship idols, too, but just to regard them as images that represent virtues that radiate from the one God, and together give worship of Him a form.

"This ancient person is our angel, whom we revere and listen to. He comes and raises us up when we lapse into a vague worship of God due to fantasies about the images."

After we heard these things we left the house and the town, and on the way we drew some conclusions from the things we saw in heaven—conclusions about the cycle of married love and how it progressed. The cycle worked around from east to south, from there to west, and from there to north. As to its progress, it diminished in the cycle. In other words, it was heavenly in the east, spiritual in the south, worldly in the west, and sense-oriented in the north. And it also declined to the same degree that the worship of God did.

It led us to this conclusion—that in the first age the love in marriage was like gold, in the second like silver, in the third like brass, and in the fourth like iron, and that it finally ceased to exist.

Then my angel guide and companion said, "Still I take hope that the God of heaven, who is the Lord, will revive that love—because it can be revived."

79   The fifth story: The angel from before who was my guide and companion to the ancient people who lived in the four ages—gold, silver, copper, and iron—came again and said to me, "You'd like to see the age after those ancient ones—what it was, and still is, like. Follow me and you'll see. They are the ones that Daniel prophesied

about, saying that a kingdom would arise after those four ages, when iron would be mixed with clay, that human seed would mix the iron and clay together, but that they would not cohere with one another, as iron does not mix with clay" (Dan. 2:41–43).

And he said, "The 'human seed' that will mix the iron with the clay, although they won't cohere, can be taken to mean the Truth of the Word changed to falsehood."

When he said this I followed him, and on the way he reported these things to me. "They live on the border between the south and the west but a long way past the people who lived in the four earlier ages, and also deeper down."

We went ahead through the south to a region bordering the west and went through a terrible forest. It had swamps where crocodiles raised their heads and gaped at us with their toothy jaws wide open. And between swamps there were terrible dogs, some with three heads like Cerberus, some with two. They all watched us pass with horrible hunger and savage eyes. We entered the western stretches of this region and saw dragons and leopards such as the Book of Revelation describes (12:3; 13:2).

"All those wild animals you saw," the angel told me, "are not wild animals. They are symbolic, and therefore representational, images of desires that the inhabitants have. We're going to visit them. Those horrible dogs represent the desires themselves, the crocodiles their trickery and shrewdness, the dragons and leopards their lies and their twisted attitudes toward anything related to worship.

"Actually the inhabitants they represent do not live just beyond the forest but beyond a large desert that is in between to keep them away and quite separate from the inhabitants of the earlier ages. And they certainly are an alien race and different from them! They do have a head above their chest, a chest above their waist, and waists above their feet, just like the first people, but in their heads is nothing of gold, nor anything of silver in their chests, nor in their waists anything of brass, and indeed nothing in their feet of pure iron. In their heads is iron mixed with clay, in their chests both of these mixed with brass, in their waists both also mixed with silver. In their feet it is mixed with gold.

"By being turned upside-down that way they are changed

from people into human statues with nothing that holds together inwardly, because what was highest has become lowest, so what was a head has become a heel and vice versa. To us from heaven they look like acrobats with their bodies upside-down, walking on their elbows. Or like animals that lie on their backs with their feet up and look at the sky with their heads in the ground."

We passed through the forest and entered the desert, which was no less terrible. It was all heaps of stone and between them gulches that water snakes and vipers crawled out of. And fiery serpents flew out of them.

This whole desert sloped steadily down. We descended the long decline and finally came to the valley peopled by the inhabitants of this region and its epoch.

Here and there were huts that we could see became closer together after a while and joined to form a town. We went into it. The houses were made of tree limbs scorched and mudded together! The roofs were black slate. The streets were irregular. They started out narrow, but they widened out as they went on, becoming quite broad where they ended at public spaces, so there were as many public spaces as streets.

When we entered the city it got dark because we couldn't see the sky. So we looked upward and had light and could see.

Then on the way we asked people we bumped into, "Can you see? Because the sky above you isn't visible!"

They said, "What's that? We see clearly. We're walking in broad daylight!"

When the angel heard this he told me, "Darkness is light to them, and light to them is darkness, the same as to night birds, for they look down and not up."

We went into the huts here and there, and in each hut we saw a man with his woman. We asked if everyone here lives at home with just one wife.

They answered this with a hiss. "Just one wife! Why not say with just one prostitute? What is a wife but a prostitute? By our laws you can only fornicate with one woman. Still, to us it's not dishonest or indecent with several—but not at home. Among ourselves we take pride in it. This way we enjoy freedom and its pleasure more than polygamy. Why can't we have many wives, when all over the world around us they could, and can today?

What is life with one woman but captivity and imprisonment? But here we break open the walls of this jail, escape from servitude, and free ourselves. Who blames a captive who escapes when he can?"

To this we answered, "You talk as if you have no religion, my friend. Who doesn't know that adulteries are profane and infernal, if he has a drop of sense, and that marriages are holy and heavenly? Aren't adulteries for devils in hell and marriages for angels in heaven? Haven't you read the seventh commandment in the Decalogue? And, in Paul [1 Cor. 6:9–10], that there's no way adulterers can come into heaven?"

Our host had a belly laugh at this and looked at me as if I were a simpleton—almost as if I were crazy.

But just then a messenger from the headman of the town ran up and said, "Bring the two strangers into the forum! And if they won't come, drag them there! We saw them skulking in the shadows. They came in secret. They are spies!"

The angel told me that we looked shady to them because we were in light from heaven, which is shade to them. The darkness of hell is light to them. "This is because they don't consider anything a sin, not even adultery, so they see falsehood as the plain truth. In hell falsity shines to the satans, and truth dims their eyes like the darkness of night."

We told the messenger, "We won't be pushed around, let alone be dragged to the forum. But we will go with you on our own volition." And we went.

A great mob was there! Some trial lawyers emerged from it and said in our ear, "Take care not to say anything against religion, our form of government, or proper behavior."

We answered, "We only speak in favor of these things—and according to them." And we asked, "What are your beliefs about marriage?"

The crowd murmured at that and said, "What are our marriages to you? Marriages are marriages."

We spoke up again, "What are your beliefs about fornication?"

The crowd murmured at this, too, saying, "What is our fornication to you? Prostitution is prostitution. Someone guiltless can throw the first stone."

A third time we asked, "Does your religion teach that

marriages are holy and heavenly and that adulteries are profane and infernal?"

At these words many in the crowd gave a horselaugh, jeered, and joked, saying, "Find out about things to do with religion from our priests, not us! We accept what they say without a question, because nothing to do with religion makes any sense intellectually. Haven't you heard that intellect is senseless when it comes to mysteries—which is all that religion is made of? And what do actions have to do with religion? Just mumbling from a devout heart about expiation, satisfaction, and imputation beatifies your soul, eh? Not the things you do."

But then some of the so-called wise men of the town came up and said, "Get out of here. The crowd is smoldering. They'll soon riot! We'll discuss this business alone. There's a walk back of the court. We'll withdraw to there. You come with us."

We followed them. Then they asked us where we were from and what we wanted here.

"To find out about marriages," we said, "whether the ones you have are sacred or not—as they were with the ancient people who lived in the Golden, Silver, and Copper Ages."

Their response was, "Sacred! They're physical acts in the night, aren't they?"

We answered, "Aren't they spiritual acts, too? And what your body does in response to your spirit is spiritual, isn't it? And your spirit does everything it does thanks to a marriage of good and truth. Isn't this a spiritual marriage, which enters the marriage on a natural plane, which is a husband and a wife?"

To this the so-called wise men answered, "You've got this thing too finely honed and high-flown. You soar above rational things to spiritual ones. Who can begin up there, come down here, and decide anything that way?" They added with a sneer, "Maybe you have eagle wings and can fly into the highest reach of heaven and see into everything that way. We can't."

So we begged them, "From whatever altitude or reach the winged ideas of your minds do fly in, do you know, or can you know, that there is such a thing as love in marriage between one man and one wife with all the blessings, pleasures, joys, gladness, and passions of heaven gathered in it? And do you know that the Lord supplies this love according to the way you receive good and truth from Him—in other words, according to the state of the church?"

They turned aside when they heard this and said, "These men are crazy. They go into outer space with their judgment and dream up nothings. They're pulling our legs." Then they turned back to us and said, "We'll give a straight answer to your divinations and dreams." And they said, "What does married love have in common with religion and with inspiration from God? That love goes according to the state of someone's potency, doesn't it? It's the same for people outside the church as with those in it, isn't it? And the same for non-Christians as for Christians. Even the same for the impious as for the pious. Doesn't a person have the vigor of this love according to either heredity or his good health or his temperate life or the heat of the climate? And also, medicines can invigorate and stimulate it. Isn't it the same for animals—especially birds, who love pair by pair? Isn't that love physical? What do physical things have in common with the spiritual condition of a church? The final effect of that love with a wife doesn't differ a shred from the final effect of love with a prostitute, does it? Isn't it the same desire and the same pleasure? So it's wrong to derive the origin of married love from religious principles."

When we heard this we said to them, "You're reasoning from a fit of lust and not from love for marriage. You don't know what married love is at all, because in you it cools right off. What you say confirms for us that you are of the age called, and formed of, iron and clay—which don't hold together—according to the prophecy in Daniel (2:43). So you're making the love in marriage and the love in fornication one thing. Do these two hold together better than iron and clay? People call you wise, and think you are wise, but there's nothing you're less of than wise."

When they heard this they shouted, burning with rage, and called the mob together to throw us out. But then, with a power the Lord gave us we stretched out our hands and fiery serpents, hydras, vipers, and dragons, too, came from the desert and swarmed in and filled the town! The terrified inhabitants fled from this.

"Newcomers from Earth arrive in this place daily," the angel said to me, "and in turn older ones are removed and thrown into chasms west of here that look like lakes of fire and brimstone from a distance. There they are all adulterers, both spiritually and naturally."

80   The sixth story: When he said this I looked toward the western border and sure enough it looked like lakes of fire and brimstone, and I asked the angel, "Why do the hells there look like that?"

He said, "They look like lakes because of distortions of the truth, because water in spiritual terms is truth. It seems like fire around them and in them due to love of evil, and like brimstone due to love of untruth. These three—the swamp, the fire, and the brimstone—are just outward appearances, since they are the correspondences of evil loves that the people have. Every one confined there is an inmate forever, and they work for their food, clothing, and bed. And when they do something evil they get a severe and miserable punishment."

I asked the angel something else. "Why did you say that the people there are spiritual and natural adulterers? Why not evildoers and ungodly people?"

"Because," he answered, "everyone who thinks adulteries are nothing, that is, who believes in them and does them from conviction, which means from an assumption that they are not sins, is at heart an evildoer and ungodly. For a human, married love and religion walk together in step. Every footstep and every stride made in religion and into religion is also a footstep and stride for the married love, and toward the married love, that is special and appropriate to a Christian person."

To the question, "What married love is that?" he said, "It is a desire to live with just one wife, and a Christian person has this desire according to his religion."

Afterwards it pained my spirit that the marriages that were so very holy in the ancient ages had been so recklessly turned into adulteries.

The angel said, "It's the same with religion today, for the

Lord said that in the consummation of the age will be 'the abomination of desolation predicted by Daniel,' and 'there will be great affliction like nothing that has been from the beginning of the world' (Matt. 24:15, 21).

"'Abomination of desolation' means all truth turning to untruth and being taken away. 'Affliction' refers to the condition of the church infested with evils and false concepts. And the 'consummation of the age' that it says these things about means the last period of a church, or its end.

"The end is now! Because no truth is left unfalsified. And turning truth into lies is spiritual fornication, which interacts with worldly fornication, because they are related."

81   As we talked and grieved about these things, the light suddenly shone brighter, narrowing my eyes, so I looked up and saw the whole sky above us seem to glow, and the word *glorification* resounded from east to west.

The angel said to me, "That glorification is a celebration of the Lord for His Advent. Angels of heaven from the east and west are doing it."

From the southern and northern heaven we heard nothing but a gentle murmur.

The angel understood all this, so first he said to me that glorifications and celebrations of the Lord come from the Word, because then they come from the Lord, since the Lord is the Word—that is, the Divine Truth itself in the Word. And he said, "Now they are particularly glorifying and celebrating the Lord through these words that Daniel the prophet said:

> You saw the iron mixed with clay. They will mingle themselves through human seed but will not hold together. But in those days the God of the heavens will make a kingdom arise that will not perish through the ages. That kingdom will break and consume everything, though it will stand for ages itself. (Dan. 2:43–44)

After this I heard something like singing, and deeper in the east I saw a flash of light brighter than the first, and I asked the angel what that one glorified.

He said, "The Lord, in these words from Daniel:

I saw in a night vision, and in the clouds of heaven it was as if the Son of Man was coming! And dominion and the Kingdom is given to Him, and all people and races worship Him—His dominion is the dominion of ages, which will not go away, and His kingdom will not perish. (Dan. 7:13, 14)

"They are also celebrating the Lord by these words in the Book of Revelation:

Glory and strength to Jesus Christ. See him come with clouds. He himself is Alpha and Omega, Beginning and End, First and Last, Who is and Who will be, all-powerful. I, John, heard this from the Son of Man from among the seven candlestands. (Rev. 1:5–13; 22:13; Matt. 24:30–31)

Again I looked into the eastern sky. It was light to the right side, and the brightness reached the southern area, and I heard a sweet sound. I asked the angel, "What are they celebrating about the Lord there?"

He said it was these words in Revelation:

I saw a new sky and a new earth, and I saw the holy city New Jerusalem coming down from God out of heaven, prepared as a wife for her husband. And an angel spoke with me and said, "Come. I will show you the bride, the Lamb's wife." And he carried me away spiritually over a large, high mountain and showed me the city Holy Jerusalem. (Rev. 21:1–2, 9–10)

Also these words:

I, Jesus, am the bright and morning star. And the spirit and the bride say come. He said, Yes, I come quickly. Amen. Also come, Lord Jesus. (Rev. 22:16–17, 20)

After these things, and more, we heard a general glorification from east to west in the sky, and also from south to north, and I asked the angel, "Now what?"

He said, "It's these passages from the Prophets:

Let all flesh know that I, Jehovah, am your Savior and your Redeemer. (Isa. 49:26)

Jehovah, King of Israel, and your Redeemer, Jehovah Zebaoth, says this: I am First and Last, and there is no God other than I. (Isa. 44:6)

In that day they will say, 'Look! This is our God Whom we have hoped for to free us. This is Jehovah whom we hoped for.' (Isa. 25:9)

A voice crying in the desert, 'Prepare a way for Jehovah! Look! The Lord Jehovah is coming in strength. He feeds his flock like a shepherd.' (Isa. 40:3, 5, 10, 11)

A boy is born to us. A son is given to us whose name is Wonderful, Counselor, God, Hero, Eternal Father, Prince of Peace. (Isa. 9:6)

Look! The days are coming, and I will raise up David, the proper branch, who will reign King, and this is His name: Jehovah our Justice. (Jer. 23:5–6; 33:15–16)

Jehovah Zebaoth is His name, and your Redeemer, the Holy One of Israel. They will call Him God of the Whole Earth. (Isa. 54:5)

In that day Jehovah will be there as King over the whole world. In that day there will be one Jehovah, and His name one. (Zech. 14:9)

My heart leapt for hearing and realizing these things! And I went home full of joy! And there I came out of my spiritual state back into my bodily state—in which I wrote down these things that I saw and heard.

Now I'll add this to them—that after His advent the Lord will revive the love in marriage as it was among the Ancient people, because that love comes only from the Lord and is for those who become spiritual through the Word, due to Him.

82   It was after these things that a man from a northern region rushed up, furious, looked menacingly in my face, accosted me in a scorching tone of voice, and said, "Is it you that wants to seduce the world, starting a new church that you take for the 'New Jerusalem' to descend from God out of heaven? And teaching that the Lord will give those who embrace that church's teachings a real love for marriage whose joy and happiness you praise to the skies? It's an invention, isn't it! And you bring this in as a snare, and a lure to attract people to your news, don't you! But give me a summary of what these teachings of the New Church are, and I'll see if they hold together or not."

I answered, "Here are the teachings of the church known as the New Jerusalem:

"First: There is one God, who has the Divine Trinity in him, and He is the Lord Jesus Christ.

"Second: The faith that saves is to believe in Him.

"Third: Avoid evils because they are the devil's and come from the devil.

"Fourth: Do good things because they are God's and come from God.

"Fifth: These good things should be done on a person's own initiative as if they come from him, but he should believe that they come to him and through him from the Lord."

His anger subsided for a few moments when he heard these things. But after some deliberation he again gave me a fierce look, saying, "So these five precepts are the New Church's teachings on faith and charity."

I answered, "They are."

Then he asked harshly, "How can you demonstrate the first, that there is one God, with the Divine Trinity in Him, and that He is the Lord Jesus Christ?"

I said, "This way. God is one and indivisible, isn't He? There is a Trinity, isn't there? If God is one and indivisible, He is one Person, isn't He? If one Person, isn't the Trinity in Him? That He is the Lord Jesus Christ comes from these things: He was conceived by God the Father (Luke 1:34–35), so as to His soul, He is God. And then, as He said Himself: The Father and He are one (John 10:30). He is in the Father and the Father in Him (John 14:10, 11). Whoever sees Him and knows Him sees and knows the Father (John 14:7, 9). No one sees and knows the Father except the One who is in the Father's bosom (John 1:18). All things of the Father are His (John 3:35; 16:15). He is the Way, the Truth, and Life, and no one comes to the Father except through Him (John 14:6). So He is from Him because He is in Him.

"And according to Paul, the whole fullness of the Divinity resides in Him bodily (Col. 2:9).

"And moreover, He has power over all flesh (John 17:2). And He has all power in heaven and in earth (Matt. 28:18).

"It follows logically from this that He is God of heaven and earth."

After that he asked how I demonstrate the second teaching, that faith that saves is to believe in Him.

I said, "I demonstrate it through the Lord's own words: 'This is the will of the Father, that everyone who believes in the Son have eternal life' (John 6:40). 'God loved the world so much that He gave His only Son so everyone who believes in Him will not perish but have eternal life' (John 3:15, 16). 'Whoever believes in the Son has eternal life, but whoever does not believe in the Son will not see life, but the wrath of God remains on him' (John 3:36)."

Then he said, "Demonstrate the third teaching, too, and the ones that follow."

I answered, "What is the use of demonstrating that you should avoid evils because they are the devil's and from the devil, and that you should do good things because they are God's and from God, and that the person should do them on his own volition as if they came from him but should believe that they come to him and through him from the Lord?

"The whole Sacred Scripture from beginning to end confirms that these three teachings are true. What else does it say there, in short, but to avoid evil things and do good things and believe in the Lord God? And moreover, without these three things there isn't any religion. Religion has to do with life, doesn't it? And what life is there except to avoid evil things and do good ones? And how can a person do these things and believe them except as if they came from himself? So if you take these things away from a church, you take away the Sacred Scripture, and religion, too, and a church with these removed is not a church."

When the man heard these things he stepped back and pondered. But he still went away with resentment.

Chapter 5

The Source of Love in a Marriage: It Comes from a Marriage of Good and Truth

83   There are inward and outward sources of love in marriage, and the inner ones are many. So are the outward ones. But the innermost source, or source of all sources, is single. What follows now will demonstrate that this source is a marriage of good and truth.

The reason why no one has as yet found the source of this love in good and truth is that it has escaped notice that there is any union between good and truth. It has escaped notice because good does not come out in the light to be recognized like truth, so knowledge of it has hidden itself away and evaded efforts to track it down. And since good, for this reason, is one of those unnoticed things, no one could suspect a marriage between it and truth.

In fact, to the sight of a rational mind in our world, good seems so distant from truth that there is no connection. You can see that this is true from conversations when good and truth are mentioned. When someone says, "This is good," he does not think about truth at all, and when he says, "This is true," he does not think about good at all. So many people believe, these days, that truth is something totally separate, and so is good. Many also believe that people are intelligent and wise, and therefore human, according to the truths that they think, write, speak, and believe, and not at the same time according to good.

Now to explain that, nevertheless, there is neither good without truth nor truth without good, so there is an eternal marriage between them, and also that this marriage is the source of the love in a marriage—in the following order:

(1) Good and truth are universal elements of creation, so they are in all created things, but they are in the created subjects according to the form of each.

(2) There is no such thing as good alone nor truth alone, but they are always united.

(3) There is a truth in good and from this a good in truth—or a truth that comes from a good and a good that comes from that truth—and they both have, from creation, an inherent inclination to join themselves into one.

(4) In subjects of the animal kingdom the truth of good (the truth that comes from good) is male, and from that good of truth (or good coming from truth) is female.

(5) Sexual love comes from the marriage of good and truth flowing in from the Lord, and so does married love.

(6) Sexual love belongs to the outer or worldly part of people, so it is in common with all the animals.

(7) But love in marriage belongs to the inner or spiritual part of people, so it is strictly for people.

(8) With humans love in marriage is in sexual love like a gem in its matrix.

(9) With people, sexual love is not the source of married love but a place for it to start. It is, so to speak, a worldly outside where a spiritual inside can be implanted.

(10) When the love in marriage has been implanted, sexual love turns around and becomes chaste sexual love.

(11) Man and woman were created to be precisely the image of a marriage between good and truth.

(12) That image is what they are in their deepest being, and as the inner reaches of their minds open up, it comes into the parts that spring from their deepest being.

Now for the explanation of these things.

84   (1) *Good and truth are universal elements of creation, so they are in all created things, but they are in created subjects according to the form of each.* Good and truth are universal elements of creation because the two of them are in the Lord God, the Creator. In fact,

they are He, because He is the Divine Good itself and Divine
Truth itself. But this falls into place more clearly for our intellectual
grasp, and therefore as a concept to think about, if we say "love"
instead of "good" and "wisdom" instead of "truth"—this way:
Divine Love and Divine Wisdom are in the Lord God, the Creator,
and they are He, which is to say, He is love itself and wisdom
itself. Love and wisdom are the same as good and truth. This is
because good is love and truth is wisdom, for love takes form
from good and wisdom from truths.

Since the one pair and the other pair are the same, sometimes
it will be the one expression from here on, and sometimes the
other. But either way it means the same thing. This explanation
comes here at the outset so that when good and truth and love
and wisdom are mentioned later they will not be taken to mean
different things.

85   So since the Lord God, the Creator, is love itself and wisdom
itself, and He created the universe out of Himself—an undertaking
coming from Himself—there cannot help being some good and
truth from Him in each and every created thing. For what is done
by and comes out of anyone bears his imprint. Reason can also
see that this is so from the regular succession of each and every
thing in the created universe. One thing is for the sake of another,
and so one depends on another like a chain made up of links.

Indeed, all things are for the sake of the human race, so an
angelic heaven can come from it. Through the human race creation returns to the Creator it came from. This joins the created
universe with its Creator, and through the conjunction there is
eternal continuation.

This is behind the statement that good and truth are the
universal elements of creation. It is clear to any sensible thinker
that this is true. In every created thing he sees what traces back to
good and what traces back to truth.

86   Good and truth are in created things according to each thing's
form because each creature accepts influence according to its own
form. The continuation of everything is nothing but the perpetual
influence of Divine Good and Divine Truth in the forms that good
and truth create. In fact, being there—continuing to exist—is a
perpetual coming to be, or creation.

Various things can illustrate that an object accepts influence according to its form. Take the influence of heat and light from the sun in all kinds of plants. Each of them accepts heat and light according to its makeup—every tree according to its makeup, every shrub according to its, every plant and every grass according to its makeup. The influence is the same for all, but the reception—according to form—causes each species to remain its species. This same thing can be illustrated by the influence on all kinds of animals according to each one's form. Any peasant can tell when he hears different musical instruments—pipes, flutes, cornets, trumpets, and organs—that they make sounds, according to their own forms, from the same breath, or influence, of air.

87   (2) *There is no such thing as good alone nor truth alone, but they are always united.* When someone wants to shape a feeling into a concept about good, he can only do it by supplying something that embodies good and makes it palpable. Without this, good is a nameless something. What embodies it and expresses it has to do with truth. Just say "Good," and not at the same time this or that thing that is good, or define it abstractly—without some thing it attaches to—and you will see that it is not anything. But with a thing to attach to, it is something. And if you whet your reason you see that good without something else is nothing you can express, so it is unrelated to anything, it gives no feelings, is in no condition—in a word, has no qualities. "Truth" is the same if you hear the word unattached to anything. The thing it attaches to has to do with good, as a sharp intellect can tell.

But the varieties of good are innumerable, and each climbs to its highest and descends to its lowest as on the steps of a ladder. The name changes, too, according to its progress and what it is like, so it is hard for any but the wise to see how good and truth relate to objects and are joined together in them. However, anyone can see that there is no such thing as good without truth nor truth without good, once he knows that each and every thing in the universe relates to good and truth (as explained in nos. 84–85 above).

Various things illustrate, and also confirm, that there is no good alone nor truth alone. For example there is no essence without form nor form without essence. Also, good is essence or being, and it is through truth that essence or being takes form.

Besides, in people there is will and intellect. Good has to do with will and truth with intellect. And will alone does nothing except through intellect, nor intellect alone except from a motive.

Besides, there are two sources of life in the human body—heart and lungs. The heart can produce no sensing and moving life unless the lungs breathe, nor can the lungs without the heart. The heart is related to good and the breathing of the lungs is related to truth. This is also a correspondence. It is the same with each and every thing in the mind and each and every thing in the human body. But this is not the place to bring out further demonstration. However, you can find further confirmations of these things in *Angelic Wisdom about Divine Providence*, nos. 3–26, where it explains them in this order: (1) The universe and every created detail of it came out of Divine Love through Divine Wisdom, or, similarly, out of Divine Good through Divine Truth. (2) Divine Good and Divine Truth come from the Lord as one unit. (3) This unit, in some form, is in everything created. (4) Good is good only to the extent that it is united with truth, and truth is truth only to the extent that it is united with good. (5) The Lord does not let anything be divided, so a person will either be occupied with good and truth together or with evil and untruth together. Besides other confirmations.

88   (3) *There is a truth in good and from this a good in truth—or a truth that comes from a good and a good that comes from that truth—and they both have, from creation, an inherent inclination to join themselves into one.* It is necessary to furnish some specific idea about these things because a grasp of the essential source of the love in marriage depends on it. For, as explained below, the truth in good, or the truth that comes from good, is masculine, and the good in truth, or the good that comes from that truth, is feminine. But this is easier to understand if you say "love" for "good" and "wisdom" for "truth." (No. 84 above shows that they are one and the same.)

Wisdom cannot emerge in a person except from a love of becoming wise. Take this love away, and a person absolutely cannot be wise. The wisdom that comes from this love is what "good's truth or the truth that comes from good" means. But when a person acquires wisdom for himself on the strength of this love, and loves having it in himself, or loves himself on account of it, then a love that is a love of wisdom takes shape. This is what "the good in truth, or the truth that comes from a good" means.

So a man has two loves. The one that comes first is love of becoming wise, and the other, which comes later, is his love for the wisdom. But if this love stays with the man it is a bad love that we call conceit or love of one's own intellect. Later discussions will show that right from creation it was provided that this love would be taken from men to keep it from ruining them and transferred into women so it could become married love, which reintegrates people.

More about these two loves and the transfer of the second one into women appears above (nos. 32–33) and in Chapter 1 (no. 21).

So if you take "love" to mean "good" and "wisdom" "truth," then it stands from the things said now, that there is the truth in good, or truth that comes from good, and from this good in truth, or good that comes from truth.

89   From creation these two have an inborn inclination to join themselves into one because the one is formed from the other—wisdom from love of becoming wise, or truth from good, and love of wisdom from that wisdom, or the good of truth from that truth. This pattern shows that they have a mutual inclination to reunite themselves and join themselves into one.

But this happens for men who have genuine wisdom and for women who have a love for that wisdom in their husbands—which is to say, who have the real love for marriage.

But later articles will tell what wisdom a man must have and a wife must love.

90   (4) *In subjects of the animal kingdom the truth of good (the truth that comes from good) is male, and from it, the good of truth (or good coming from truth) is female.* Nos. 84–86 above have shown that a perpetual union of love and wisdom, or a marriage of good and truth, flows in from the Lord, Creator and Sustainer of the universe, and that the created subjects receive it, each according to its form. Now, a male gets the truth of wisdom from this marriage or union, and the Lord joins the good of love to it according to how

he receives it. And this reception happens in his intellect—which is why a male is born to become intellectual. Reason in its own light can see this from various qualities of a male—mainly his motivation, the way he applies himself, his manner, and his figure.

A male's *motivation* is wanting to know, understand, and become wise—to know in childhood, to understand in adolescence and young manhood, and to become wise from young manhood to old age. This shows that his nature or disposition inclines toward forming an intellect, so it means he is born to become intellectual. But this cannot happen except out of love, so the Lord adds love to him, too, according to his reception—that is, according to his wanting to become wise.

A male *applies* himself to things that are intellectual, or where intellect predominates. Most of them are in the market and the public interest.

His *manner* always comes out of a predominance of intellect. That is why the activities of his life, which are to be taken as "his manner," are rational, and if not, he wants them to seem so. You can also see a masculine rationality in every manly quality he has.

His *figure* is different and quite distinct from a feminine figure. (There is also something about this in no. 33 above.)

In addition to all this, he has fertility. This is from no source other than intellect, for it is from the truth that comes out of good in him. Later discussions will show that this is the source of fertility.

91   By the same token, a woman is born to be willing in response to a man's intellect or, in other words, to be the love of a man's wisdom because she is formed by his wisdom. (More about this appears above, nos. 88–89.) This, too, can be demonstrated from her motivation, the way she applies herself, her manner, and her figure.

A woman's *motivation* is an inclination to love knowledge, learning, and wisdom—not in herself but in a man—and thus to love him. For you cannot love a man just for a figure that *seems* human, but for the endowment that *makes* him human.

A woman *applies* herself to things done by hand called sewing, embroidery, and so forth, for clothing, beautifying herself, and increasing her attractiveness. She also applies herself to the various jobs known as domestic that are attached to men's jobs, called, again, jobs of the market. Women get this from an inclination to join together, be wives, and in this way be one with their husbands.

In her *manner* and *figure* it shows clearly without being explained.

92   (5) *Sexual love comes from the marriage of good and truth flowing in from the Lord, and so does married love.* Nos. 84–87 above show that good and truth are everywhere in creation and thus in all created objects, that they are there according to each object's form, and that good and truth are not two things but go out from the Lord as one. This means that a ubiquitous sphere of marriage goes out from the Lord and pervades the universe from beginning to end, which is to say from the angels all the way to the worms. Such a sphere of the marriage of good and truth goes out from the Lord because it is also a sphere of reproduction—that is, of making offspring and producing fruit—and this is identical with Divine Providence's preservation of the universe by one generation producing another.

Now, since this universal sphere that belongs to the marriage of good and truth enters subjects according to each one's makeup (no. 86), it means that a man receives it according to his makeup, or in understanding things, because he is a form of understanding. And a woman receives it according to hers, or in volition, because she is a form of volition coming from a man's understanding of things. And that sphere is also a sphere of reproducing, so therefore sexual love comes from it.

93   The love in marriage also comes from this because, for people and also for angels, that sphere pours into the matrix of wisdom. For a person can grow in wisdom to the end of his life in the world and afterwards in heaven forever. And his makeup becomes more perfect in the measure that he grows in wisdom. This makeup receives, not sexual love, but love for one person of the other sex, for with her he can unite clear to the core, where heaven is, with its joys—and this union is the union in married love.

94   (6) *Sexual love belongs to the outer or worldly part of people, so it is in common with all the animals.* Every human is born physical. He

becomes worldly-minded on a deeper and deeper level, and as he loves to understand things he becomes rational, and later, if he loves wisdom, he becomes spiritual. (What the wisdom is through which he becomes spiritual is explained later, no. 130.)

Now, just as the person goes step by step from knowledge to understanding and from this to wisdom, his mind, too, changes its form, for it opens more and more and joins itself more closely to heaven, and through heaven with the Lord. This makes him love the truth more and be more interested in good ways to live. In this way, if he stands still on the first threshold in his progress toward wisdom his mind keeps its worldly form. This form receives the influence of that universal sphere that is a marriage of good and truth no differently than the way the lower subjects of the animal kingdom do, called beasts and birds. Because they are merely natural, that makes this man just like them. He loves sex the same way they do.

This is how I mean that sexual love belongs to the outer or worldly part of people, so it is in common with all the animals.

95   (7) *But love in marriage belongs to the inner or spiritual part of people, so it is strictly for people.* Married love has to do with the inner or spiritual person, because the more a person becomes intelligent and wise, the more he develops an inner, spiritual dimension—and the more perfect the configuration of his mind becomes. This form of mind is receptive of married love. It notices and feels the spiritual joy in it, which is made inwardly happy. And from this comes joy on the natural plane, which takes its spirit, life, and being from the inner joy.

96   Married love is only for people because only a human can become spiritual. You see, he can raise his intellect above his worldly loves, look down on them from that height, and assess them—what they are like and how to revise them, set them right, and remove them. No animal can do this, for his loves are totally tied to his inborn knowledge, which therefore cannot be raised to the point of understanding, much less to the point of wisdom. So the love implanted in his knowledge leads an animal the way a dog leads a blind man through the streets. These are the reasons why married love is only for humans. One could say it is native

and appropriate to humans, because people have an inborn faculty that it unites with—the faculty of becoming wise.

97   (8) *With humans love in marriage is in sexual love like a gem in its matrix.* But this is just a comparison, and the next article will explain it. It will also show that sexual love has to do with the outer or natural side of people, and married love has to do with the inward or spiritual side, as already indicated (no. 95 above).

98   (9) *With people, sexual love is not the source of married love but a place for it to start.* It is, so to speak, a worldly outside where a spiritual inside can be planted. The subject here is the real love in marriage and not the common love that is also called conjugal and for some is nothing but a limited sexual love. The real love in marriage, however, is found only among those who crave wisdom and therefore make steady progress toward it. The Lord can tell who they will be and provides married love for them. For them this love does indeed begin with sexual love, or better, *through* sexual love, but it does not originate there. Instead, it originates precisely when wisdom steps onto the scene for a man, for wisdom and this love are inseparable companions.

The reason that married love starts through sexual love is that before you find a partner you love the other sex, with a loving eye for them all, and treat them in a friendly way. Now, a young man is in a process of selection. At the same time, deep in his heart, the natural inclination to join with one woman is gently arousing him outwardly. Besides, marriage arrangements drag out for various reasons until halfway through manhood, and in the meantime the beginning of this love is a sort of lust that for some escapes into a love for active sex. Even they get free rein no more than is good for their health. But these statements are about the masculine sex, because it is an enticement that arouses them physically, but not about the feminine sex.

This shows that sexual love is not the source of real married love but is before it in point of time, though not in point of purpose. For what is first in purpose is first in the mind and its intention, because it is the most important thing. But the only access to this thing is gradually through means to an end. The means are not the most important thing. They just move you on toward the most important thing.

99   (10) *When the love in marriage has been implanted, sexual love turns around and becomes a chaste sexual love.* I say that then sexual love turns around because when love of marriage comes to its source, in the inner parts of the mind, it sees sexual love as being not before itself, but behind—not above itself but below—and in this way something it left behind in passing, so to speak.

It is the same as when someone scrambles from job to job up to some towering rank and from there looks back or down at the jobs he came up through. Or when someone travels to the court of some king. After arriving he turns a look back at the things he saw on the way.

The two stories in nos. 44 and 55 show that then sexual love remains and becomes chaste and even sweeter than before for those who have true married love. This is shown through a description of it by people in the spiritual world.

100   (11) *Man and woman were created to be precisely the image of a marriage between good and truth.* This is because a man is created to *be* a grasp of truth—that is, the image of truth—and a woman is created to *be* a desire for good—which is to say the image of good. And both are gifted, from deep inside, with an inclination to join together into one (see no. 88 above), so the two make one image that is like the image of the marriage between good and truth. I say it is "like" this because it is not that identical thing but similar to it. The good that joins itself with truth in a man, you see, comes directly from the Lord, and a wife's good that joins itself with truth in a man comes from the Lord indirectly through the wife, so that there are two kinds of good, one inner and the other outward, that join themselves with the truth in a husband. And these give a husband a steady grasp of truth and the wisdom that comes from it through the real love in marriage. But more about this is coming later.

101   (12) *That image is what they are in their deepest being, and as the inner reaches of their minds open up, it comes into the parts that spring*

from their deepest being. Every person consists of three things—soul, mind, and body—related to one another in order. The soul is the most inward part of him, the middle part of him is the mind, and the most outward part of him is the body. All that pours into a person from the Lord pours into the innermost part of him, which is his soul, descends from there into the middle part, his mind, and through this into his most outward part, his body. This is how the marriage of good and truth pours into a person from the Lord—directly into his soul, and from there through to the next things, and through these to the most outward. And this is how good and truth make married love together. The concept of this downflowing makes it clear that two partners are the image of this marriage in their most inner selves, and from this in the things that follow down from there.

102   The reason why partners become that image as the inner parts of their minds open up is that the mind is continually opening up from infancy to ripe old age. For people are born as bodies, and as their minds open to the next level above their body they become rational. This rationality becomes purified and, so to speak, emptied of fallacies that flood in from the bodily senses and cravings that flood in from the enticements of flesh, and as this happens one's rationality opens. This takes place only by the agency of wisdom. And when the most inward reaches of the rational mind open up, then a person becomes the image of wisdom, and this is a vessel for the genuine love in marriage.

The wisdom that makes this image and receives this love is both rational and moral wisdom. Rational wisdom looks to the true and good things that show up deep within a person—not as his own but as the Lord's influence. Moral wisdom avoids evil and false things like the plague—especially lascivious ones, which contaminate the person's love of marriage.

103   I'll add to these remarks two stories. Here is the first:

Once, in the morning, before sunrise, I looked toward the east in the spiritual world, and I saw four horsemen seem to fly up out of a cloud gleaming with the flame of the sunrise. On the heads of the horsemen you could see plumed helmets, something like wings on their arms, and lightweight orange tunics on their bodies. Dressed this way as for a race, they rose up and laid the reins on the manes of the horses, which ran as if with winged feet. I followed their course, or rather, flight, with my eyes to satisfy my mind where they were going, and saw three horsemen scatter to three quarters—south, west, and north—while the fourth stayed briefly in the east.

Surprised by these things I looked up into the sky and asked, "Where are those horsemen going?"

The answer was, "To the sages in the countries of Europe, who have intellectual polish and keen insight when it comes to investigating things, and are highly praised among their people for their talents, to have them come and explain the secret source of married love and its virtue, or potency."

These words came from the sky. "Wait a bit, and you will see twenty-seven chariots, three with Spaniards in them, three with Frenchmen or Gauls, three with Italians, three with Germans, three with Hollanders or Netherlanders, three with English, three with Swedes, three with Danes, and three with Poles."

Then after two hours the chariots appeared, drawn by light bay ponies with eye-catching harnesses. They drove swiftly to a large building I could see on the boundary between the east and the south. Everyone in the chariots got out near the building and went inside in good spirits.

Then I was told, "You go, too. Go inside and you'll hear."

I went and entered, and looking over the building inside, I saw that it was square, with its sides facing the four points of the compass. In the sides were three high windows of crystalline glass with frames of olive wood. On either side of the frames partitions came from the walls, forming cubicles, vaulted above, with tables in them. The walls of the cubicles were cedar. The roof was noble white cedar, the floor poplar planks. At the east wall, where windows were not to be seen, a table overlaid with gold was placed. Arranged on it was a tiara studded with precious stones, to go as a token or prize to whoever should solve the problem soon to be proposed.

When I glanced over the walled cubicles (they were like alcoves at the windows) I saw five men in each, from each European country, ready and waiting for the subject they were to consider.

And then suddenly an angel stood in the middle of the palace and said, "The subject of your judgment will be the source of love in marriage and of its energy or potency. Discuss this and decide, write your decision on paper and put it in the silver urn that you see placed beside the gold table. And put the initial of your country on it in this way—France or Gaul, *F;* Holland or the Netherlands, *N;* Italy, *I;* England, *E;* Poland, *P;* Germany, *G;* Hispania, *H;* Denmark, *D,* and Sweden, *S.*"

After saying these things the angel went away, saying, "I'll be back." And then the five countrymen in each alcove by the windows turned their minds to the announcement, reflected, reached a decision according to their best judgment, wrote it on paper, added the initial of their country, and put it in the silver bowl.

In three hours they were all done. The angel came back, picked the papers out of the urn one by one, and read them before the gathering.

104 From the first paper, which he picked at random, he read this:

"We five countrymen in our alcove have decided that the source of married love is the earliest people, in the Golden Age, and they got it from the creation of Adam and his wife. Marriages are from that source, and the source of married love is in marriages. Concerning married love's energy or potency, we derive this from nothing but the climate, or where the sun is in the sky and therefore the heat of the land. We have not examined this by thinking up empty conjectures but from the clear evidence of experience—as from the nations at the Equator where the heat of the day fairly burns, and from nations near that line and from nations living far from it. And also from the cooperation of the sun's heat with the vital heat of animals on earth and birds of the sky in springtime when they mate. Besides, what is the love in marriage but heat? If supplementary heat from the sun is added to it, it becomes sexual energy or potency." This was signed with the letter *H,* the initial of the country they were from.

105 After this he put his hand in the urn again and pulled out a paper from which he read this:

"We countrymen in our booth agree that the source of married love is the same as the source of marriages, which are ratified by law to restrain people's inborn yearning for adulteries that depress their spirits, pollute the thoughts in their minds, foul their morals, and destroy their bodies with infectious disease. For adulteries are not human but bestial, not rational but brutish and thus not Christian by any means, but barbarous. Marriages originated to condemn such things, and married love originated at the same time.

"The same goes for the vigor or potency of this love. It depends on chastity, which is abstinence from roving fornications. The reason is that vigor or potency for those who love only one partner is reserved for one, so it is compressed and concentrated, and then it becomes noble, like a quintessence refined of the impurities that otherwise would disperse it and scatter it everywhere.

"One of us five, a priest, also suggested predestination as the cause of its vigor or potency, saying, 'Marriages are predestined, aren't they? And so is the reproduction in them, and the means to do it.'" This was signed *N*.

Someone, when he heard this, said with a laugh, "Predestination! Oh, what a lovely excuse for feebleness or impotence!"

106   Soon, for the third time, the angel pulled a paper from the urn and read this from it:

"We countrymen in our booth have turned over the reasons for the origin of married love, and we see that this one prevails— that it is the same as the origin of marriages, because that love did not exist before marriages did, and it emerged because when someone courts or desperately loves a girl, he wants with all his heart and soul to possess her as his own beloved, above all others. And once she promises herself to him he sees her as self sees self. It is clearly evident from everyone's fury toward rivals and from jealousy toward violators that this is the source of married love.

"Next we examined the source of this love's energy or potency, and it came out three to two that a partner's vigor or potency comes from having certain liberties with the other sex."

They said they know from experience that in sexual love the potency is better than the potency in married love. This was signed *I*.

When the people at the tables heard it they clamored, "Get rid of this paper and pull another one out of the urn!"

107   He soon pulled out a fourth. He read this from it:

"We countrymen under our window decided that the source

of married love and of sexual love is the same thing, because the one comes from the other—except that sexual love is unconfined, unfocused, promiscuous, and wanders, but married love is limited, focused, strait and narrow, and constant. And so with the circumspection of good sense humanity set it up and ratified it. For otherwise no empire, kingdom, or republic would exist—in fact no society—but people would roam the fields and woods, hordes and hordes of them, with harlots and kidnapped women, and they would steal from camp to camp, to avoid bloody massacres, mayhem, and rapine. It would wipe out the whole human race. This is our opinion about the origin of married love.

"But we trace the vigor or potency of married love from bodily health that lasts right from birth to old age. For a person who has kept his health safe and sound does not lack strength. His fibers, nerves, muscles, and cremasters do not get tired, slack, and weak, but stay in strong condition. Take care of yourself."

This was signed E.

108   For the fifth time the angel pulled a paper from the urn, and he read this from it:

"We countrymen at our table have looked into the origin of married love and of its vigor or potency with rational minds, and from careful deliberation we have seen and confirmed that the origin of married love is nothing but this. Every man has the stimuli and the excitements of it hidden deep in his mind and body. After eyeing many women he finally turns his attention to one female and sets his mind on her until he has a warm glow inside for her. From this time his heat sets one fire after another until there is a conflagration. In this condition his general yearning for the other sex is banished, and marital love takes its place. A young husband, afire like this, does not know but what the energy or potency of this love will never end, for he never experienced a condition without sexual energy and therefore does not know about such a condition and about love cooling off after its delights.

"So the source of married love is this first ardor before marriage, and from this comes its vigor or potency. But after the nuptial torches, the potency changes. It ebbs and flows. But it still lasts, with steady change, ebbing and flowing, until old age—by prudent moderation and by reining in desires that break out of caverns of the mind that are not yet cleaned out. For lust precedes wisdom.

"This is our verdict about the origin and preservation of marital vigor or potency."

This was signed *P*.

109   The angel drew out the sixth paper and read this from it.

"We countrymen of our fraternity have surveyed the causes of the origin of married love, and we agree on two. One is the proper education of children, and the other is preserving the line of descent. We have chosen these two because they converge and look to one target, which is the public good. This is achieved because children conceived and born in wedlock become part and parcel of the family, and since they receive increased parental love because they are of legitimate descent, they are educated to be heirs of all their parents possess, spiritually as well as materially. Reason sees that the public good is based on the correct education of children and preserving the line of descent.

"There is sexual love and the love in marriage. The one love seems the same as the other but is different. Nor is one love next to the other, but one is inside the other. And what is within is more noble than what is outside. And we see that the love in marriage is inside from creation and is tucked away in sexual love like an almond in its shell. So when married love is taken out of its shell, which is sexual love, it gleams to the angels like the gems beryl and moonstone. This happens because the health of the whole human race—which is what we mean by the public good—is due to married love.

"This is our verdict on the origin of this love.

"And now, the source of its vigor or potency we conclude, for well-considered reasons, to be the closing off and separation of married love from sexual love, which a man does in wisdom and a wife does through loving the man's wisdom. Sexual love, you see, is in common with the animals, but the love in marriage is exclusively human. So a person is a person and not an animal in the measure that married love is partitioned off from sexual love. A man gets vigor or potency from his love, and a beast from its."

This was signed *G*.

110   He pulled out the seventh paper and read this from it:

"We countrymen in our room under the light of our window have enjoyed our thoughts and our verdict from them by contemplating the love in marriage. Who would not be happy about it? For when that love is on your mind it is in your whole body at the same time.

"We decided that the source of that love is its joys. Who knows or has known any trace of that love from anything but the pleasure and satisfaction of it? The joys of married love at their source feel like blessings, good fortune, and luck, and as they trickle down from there, they feel like passions and delights, and they end up in the pleasure of all pleasures. So the origin of sexual love is when the inner workings of our mind, and therefore of our body, open up to let those joys flow in. But married love began when its aura first produced it archetypally through the exchange of vows.

"As to the vigor or potency of this love, it comes from the love's ability to pass from your mind to your body in its flow, for your mind is not in your head, but in your body when it feels or acts—especially when enjoying this love. We think the degree of potency and the constancy with which it returns are from that. We also trace the vigor of potency from lineage. If it is excellent in a father it is excellent when passed on to his offspring. Reason and experience agree that this excellence does get reproduced, inherited, and handed down."

This was signed *F*.

111   In its turn the eighth paper came out, from which he read:

"We countrymen in our group have not found the precise source of the love in marriage because it lies down deep in the sanctuaries of the mind. Not even the most perfect knowledge can touch that love at its source with a single ray of comprehension. We made many conjectures, but after pursuing many fine points uselessly we did not know if we were conjecturing in jest or earnest. So whoever wants to dig the source of that love out of the sanctuaries of his mind and place it before his eyes needs a Delphic oracle.

"We did consider that love downstream from its source—how it is spiritual in the mind and like a sweet spring there, flowing into your chest, where it becomes joyful and we call it bosom love. Seen for what it is, it is complete friendship and complete confidence, and it comes from being completely attracted to each other. And when it goes on through your chest it becomes a cheerful love.

"When a young man turns things like these over in his mind, which happens when he chooses one person from the other sex for himself, the fire of love for marriage kindles in his heart. This fire is the beginning of this love, so it is its source.

"The only source we recognize for vigor or potency is that love itself, for love and potency are inseparable companions, but in such a way that sometimes one goes first and sometimes the other. When love goes first and vigor or potency follows it, both are noble, because then potency is the vigor of married love. But if potency goes first and love follows, then both are debased, because then the love comes from bodily potency.

"Therefore we decide what each love is like by the order of succession in which it goes up or down and progresses from its source to its goal."

This was signed *D*.

112   He brought the last, or ninth paper out and read this from it:

"We countrymen of our group have applied our judgment to both of the matters proposed—the source of love in marriage and the source of its energy or potency. As we discussed the fine points of married love's source, so as to avoid shadowy reasoning we distinguished among spiritual, worldly, and physical love of the other sex. We take spiritual love for the other sex to mean the real love in marriage, because it is spiritual. We take worldly love of it to mean polygamous love, because this is worldly, and we take mere physical love of it to be harlotry, because this is purely physical.

"As we looked into our opinions on the real love in marriage we could see that this love is possible only between one man and one woman, and that from creation it is heavenly, deep inside, and the soul and father of all good loves, instilled in our first Parents and capable of being instilled in Christians. It also has such an ability to join, that by means of it two minds can become one mind and two people one person—which is what 'becoming one flesh' means.

"In the Book of Genesis it is clear that this love was instilled at creation, from these words: 'And the man will leave father and mother and be joined to his wife, and they will be one flesh' (Gen. 2:24). It is clear that it can be instilled in Christians, from these words that Jesus said: 'Have you not read that He who made them at the beginning made them male and female?' And he said, 'For this reason a man shall leave his father and mother and be joined to his wife, and the two shall become one flesh? So then, they are no longer two but one flesh' (Matt 19:4–6). So much for the source of married love.

"The source of vigor or potency in real married love, however, we feel, comes from similarity of minds and from unanimity, for when two minds are joined in marriage their thoughts spiritually kiss each other, and this inspires vigor or potency into the body."

This was signed S.

113   Behind a long, low partition set up in the palace in front of the doors, stood some foreigners from Africa. They called out to the Europeans, "Let one of us express an opinion, too, about the source of love in marriage and about its vigor or potency."

Everyone at the tables signaled with their hands to let them do this.

Then one of the Africans came in and took a stand by the table with the tiara on it. He said, "You Christians trace the source of married love from the love itself. In Africa, though, we trace it from the God of heaven and earth. Isn't married love a pure, holy, and chaste love? Don't angels in heaven have it? Isn't the whole human race and the whole angelic heaven that comes from it the seed of that love? Can such an important thing come from anyone but God Himself, Creator and Sustainer of the universe?

"You Christians trace the vigor or potency of marriage from various worldly and rational causes. We Africans trace it from how the person stands in conjunction with the God of the universe. We call this the status of his religion, but you call it an ecclesiastical status. Now, since love is from this, and this is constant and perpetual, it can't help expressing its vigor, which is the image of it and therefore is just as constant and perpetual.

"The real love in marriage is known only to those few who are near to God, so this love's potency is not known to anyone else. Angels in heaven describe this potency in married love as the delight of perpetual spring."

114   Everyone stood up after these statements. And behind the gold table with the tiara on it a window was made—one we had not noticed before! Through it we heard a voice, "The tiara goes to the African." The angel placed it in the African's hand, not on his head, and he went home with it. The natives of the European countries went out, got in their chariots, and returned to their own people in them.

115   The second story: I woke up in the middle of the night. Towards the east, at some height, I saw an angel holding a paper in his right hand. It seemed to gleam white, in sunshine. In the middle of it was writing in gold letters, and I could see what it said: "The Marriage of Good and Truth." The brilliance that glittered from the writing spread in a broad circle around the paper. This circle—or halo—looked like a spring sunrise coming from the paper.

Then I saw the angel with the paper in his hand descending, and the more he descended, the less bright the paper seemed. And the writing, "The Marriage of Good and Truth," changed from gold to silver, from that to copper, then to an iron color, and finally to the color of iron and copper rust.

In the end I saw the angel enter a dark cloud and go through the cloud to the ground, and there the paper, though still in the angel's hand, was invisible.

This was in the world of spirits, where all people go, at first, after death.

Then the angel spoke to me, saying, "Ask the people who come along if they see me, or anything in my hand."

A crowd came—one group from the east, one from the south, one from the west, and one from the north. I asked the arrivals from the east and south (in the world they used to pursue learning) whether they saw anyone with me there and anything in his hand.

They all said, "Nothing at all."

Then I asked the ones from the west and the north (in the

world they had believed in the words of the wise), and they said, "Nothing."

But the last few of these, who had espoused a simple faith of charity in the world—in other words, had some truth from good—said, when the others had left, that they saw a man with a paper—a well-dressed man and a paper with letters written on it. And when they looked closely they said that they read "The Marriage of Good and Truth."

They spoke to the angel, asking, "What does that mean?"

He said, "Everything in all heaven and everything in the whole world is nothing else but a marriage of good and truth. For each and every thing that lives and breathes, as well as what doesn't live or breathe, was created from a marriage of good and truth and in a marriage of good and truth. There is nothing at all created as just truth or as just good. Neither truth nor good by itself is anything, but whatever qualities a thing has, they are the qualities of the marriage through which it exists and comes to be.

"The very substance of divine good and divine truth is in the Lord the Creator. The essence of His substance is divine good, and the existence of His substance is divine truth. The very union of divine good and truth is also in Him, for in Him good and truth become infinitely one.

"Since the two are one in the Creator Himself, they are just as much one in each and every thing that He creates. Through this, besides, the Creator is joined in a permanent covenant like a marriage with all the things He creates."

Next the angel said that the Sacred Scripture, which came directly from the Lord, is as a whole, and in each part, a marriage of good and truth. And the church, formed by doctrinal truth, and religion, formed through the good of a life according to doctrinal truth, comes, for Christians, only from the Sacred Scripture. Therefore it all fits together that the church as a whole and part-by-part is a marriage of good and truth. (*Apocalypse Revealed*, nos. 373 and 483, shows that this is so.)

What it says above about the marriage of good and truth applies to the marriage of charity and faith as well, since good is charity and truth is faith.

Some of those first arrivals who had not seen the angel and

the writing were still standing around, and when they heard these things they mumbled, "Oh, sure. We understand that."

But then the angel said to them, "Turn away from me a little and say the same thing."

They turned away and roared, "It's not true!"

After this the angel talked about the marriage of good and truth in married partners and said, "If their minds were in that marriage (the husband being truth and the wife its good) both would experience the delights of being blessed with innocence, so they would have the happiness that angels have. In this condition the husband would be as prolific as perpetual springtime, so he would have continual drive and energy to propagate his truth, and the wife would always be receptive to him, thanks to love. Wisdom, which men get from the Lord, finds nothing more enjoyable than propagating its truths, and the love of wisdom that wives have in heaven finds nothing more pleasant than receiving the truths just the way they receive in their womb, and in this way they conceive, carry, and bear them. This is what having children is like among the angels. And if you will believe it, all childbirth in the natural world is from this source, too."

After bidding us "Peace," the angel took off from the ground, sailed through the cloud and rose into the sky. And the higher he rose, the more the paper gleamed as before. And then the halo! The one that seemed like a sunrise before! It came down and scattered the cloud that had overshadowed the earth, and the sun came out!

Chapter 6

The Marriage of the Lord and the Church and Its Correspondence

116   We also deal here with the marriage of the Lord and the church and what it corresponds with, because without a knowledge and a grasp of this you can hardly know that the love in marriage is holy, spiritual, and heavenly in its source, and that it comes from the Lord. To be sure, some people in the church do say that marriages have a relationship with the marriage of the Lord and the church, but the nature of the relationship is unknown. So, in order to place this in some intellectual light where it can be seen, we have to deal point by point with this holy marriage and with the fact that it exists among and within those who belong to the Lord's church. They and only they have real married love, moreover. Now, to shed light on these unknown things, the subject breaks down into the following topics:

(1) The Word calls the Lord a Bridegroom and Husband and the church a bride and wife, and it says that the Lord's union with the church and the reciprocal union of the church with the Lord is a marriage.

(2) Also, it calls the Lord a father and the church a mother.

(3) The offspring of the Lord as father and the church as wife and mother are all spiritual, and in the Word's spiritual sense, this is the meaning of sons and daughters, brothers and sisters, sons-in-law and daughters-in-law, and other names, all family relationships.

(4) The spiritual offspring born from the marriage of the Lord and the church are the truths that an intellectual grasp, perception, and all thought come from, and they are varieties of good that love, charity, and all feelings come from.

(5) From the marriage of good and truth that comes from the Lord and flows down, humans receive truth, and the Lord joins good to it, and in this way the Lord makes a church within people.

(6) A husband does not represent the Lord and a wife the church, because a husband and wife both together make a church.

(7) So a husband is not the counterpart of the Lord nor a wife the counterpart of the church in marriages of angels in heaven and people on earth.

(8) But there is a corresponding relationship with married love, impregnating, reproducing, love of children, and things like that, which are in marriages and come from them.

(9) The Word is the connecting link, because it is from the Lord so it *is* the Lord.

(10) The church is from the Lord and is within those who approach Him and live by His teachings.

(11) Married love is aligned with the condition of the church among people, because it goes according to the state of their wisdom.

(12) The church comes from the Lord, so married love does, too.

Now comes the explanation of these things.

117   (1) *The Word calls the Lord a Bridegroom and Husband and the church a bride and wife, and it says the Lord's union with the church and the reciprocal union of the church with the Lord is a marriage.* The following passages establish the fact that in the Word the Lord is called Bridegroom and Husband and the church bride and wife:

He who has the bride is the Bridegroom. But the friend of the Bridegroom, who stands and hears him, rejoices with great joy at the Bridegroom's voice. (John 3:29)

John the Baptist said this about the Lord.

Jesus said, So long as the Bridegroom is with them the sons of the wedding cannot fast. The days will come when the Bridegroom will be taken away from them. Then they will fast. (Matt. 9:15; Mark 2:19, 20: Luke 5:34–35)

I Saw the holy city, New Jerusalem, prepared as a bride adorned for her Husband. (Rev. 21:2)

Apocalypse Revealed (nos. 880–81) shows that "New Jerusalem" refers to the Lord's new church.

The angel said to John, "Come and I will show you the bride, the wife of the Lamb." And he showed him the holy city, Jerusalem. (Rev. 21:9–10)

The time for the the Lamb's wedding has come, and His wife has made herself ready. Blessed are they who are called to the marriage supper of the Lamb. (Rev. 19:7, 9)

The Lord is meant by the bridegroom whom the five prepared virgins met on his way and with whom they entered the marriage (Matt. 25:1–10). This is clear from v. 13, where it says:

Watch, therefore, for you do not know the day nor the hour when the Son of Man will come.

Also in many passages in the Prophets.

118   (2) *Also, it calls the Lord a father and the church a mother.* These passages establish that it calls the Lord a father:

Unto us a child is born, unto us a son is given, and His name shall be called Wonderful, Counselor, God, the Father of eternity, the Prince of peace. (Isa. 9:6)

You, O Jehovah, are our Father. Redeemer from everlasting is Your name. (Isa. 63:16)

Jesus said, "He who sees Me sees the Father who has sent Me." (John 12:44–45)

If you had known Me you would have known My Father also; and from henceforth you have known Him, and have seen Him. (John 14:7)

Philip said, "Show us the Father." Jesus said to him, "He who has seen Me has seen the Father. So why are you saying 'Show us the Father'?" (John 14:8–9)

Jesus said, "The Father and I are one." (John 10:30)

All things whatsoever the Father has are Mine. (John 16:15; 17:10)

The Father is in Me, and I am in the Father. (John 10:38; 14:10–11, 20)

Apocalypse Revealed shows fully that the Lord and His Father are one, just as a soul and a body are one, that God the Father came down from heaven and added a human dimension to Himself to redeem and save people, and that His human dimension is called His Son sent into the world.

119   These passages show that the Word calls the church a mother:

Jehovah said, Plead with your mother; she is not my wife, and I am not her husband. (Hos. 2:2, 5)

You are your mother's daughter, who loathes her husband. (Ezek. 16:45)

Where is the bill of your mother's divorcement, whom I have divorced? (Isa. 50:1)

Your mother is like a vine, planted by the waters, bearing fruit. (Ezek. 19:10)

These things were said about the Jewish church.

Jesus stretched forth his hand towards His disciples and said, My mother and my brothers are those who hear the Word of God and do it. (Luke 8:21; Matt. 12:48–49; Mark 3:33–35)

"The Lord's disciples" means the church.

There stood by the cross of Jesus, His mother. And Jesus seeing the mother and the disciple standing by whom He loved, said unto His mother, Woman, behold your son; and He said to the disciple, Behold your mother. Therefore from that hour the disciple took her into his own home. (John 19:25–27)

This means that the Lord acknowledged the church, not Mary, as His mother. This is why He calls her "woman" and mother of the disciple. He called her this disciple's (John's) mother because John represented the church in respect of the varieties of good that have to do with charity. These are precisely the church in action. For that reason it says that he took her into his own home. (*Apocalypse Revealed* shows that Peter represented truth and faith, James charity, and John the activities of charity [nos. 5, 6, 790, 798, 879], and that the twelve disciples together represented the church in respect to everything it includes [nos. 233, 790, 903, 915].)

120   (3) *The offspring of the Lord as husband and father and the church as wife and mother are all spiritual, and in the Word's spiritual sense, this is the meaning of sons and daughters, brothers and sisters, sons-in-law and daughters-in-law, and other names, all family relationships.* Reason can see with no explanation that no offspring other than these are born of the Lord through the church, so an explanation is unnecessary. After all, every good and truth comes from the Lord, and the church is what receives it and puts it into action. And everything spiritual having to do with heaven and the church relates to good and truth. This is why sons and daughters means, in the spiritual sense of the Word, truths and varieties of good. Sons are truths conceived in a person's spiritual dimension and born in his earthly dimension, and the same goes for daughters as types of good. This is why people who are *re*born of the Lord are called in the Word sons of God, sons of the kingdom, and born of

Him. And the Lord called his disciples sons. The male child that the woman bore and that was snatched up to God (Rev. 12:5) stands for nothing else than that (see *Apocalypse Revealed*, no. 543).

It is because daughters stand for the church's varieties of good that the Word so often mentions the Daughter of Zion, Jerusalem, Israel, and Judah. This stands for no daughter other than an affection for good, which belongs to the church. (See also *Apocalypse Revealed*, no. 612.)

The Lord also calls people who are of His church brothers and sisters (Matt. 12:49; 25:40; 28:10; Mark 3:35; Luke 8:21).

121   (4) *The spiritual offspring born from the marriage of the Lord and the church are the truths that an intellectual grasp, perception, and all thought come from, and they are varieties of good that love, charity, and all feelings come from.* Truths and types of good are spiritual offspring, born of the Lord through the church, because the Lord is good itself and truth itself, and these are not two things in Him but one, and because nothing can come out of the Lord except what is in Him and what He is.

The last chapter, about the marriage of good and truth, showed that a marriage of good and truth radiates from the Lord and flows into people, and they receive it according to the state of their minds and of their lives—those who belong to the church.

The reason why intelligence, perception, and all thought come to people through truth, while love, charity, and all feelings come through good, is that everything about a human relates to truth and good, and there are two things in a person that make him what he is: his will and his intellect. His will is what receives good, and his intellect is what receives truth. The fact that will belongs to love, charity, and feelings, and intellect to perception and thought, has no need to be illustrated by explanation because common sense itself makes the subject clear once it is stated.

122   (5) *From the marriage of good and truth that comes from the Lord and flows down, humans receive truth, and the Lord joins good to it, and in this way the Lord makes a church within people.* The reason why people accept truth, although good and truth leave the Lord as one thing, is that they accept it as their own and make it like a part of themselves. For they mull over the truth as if it came from

themselves and speak from it the same way. This happens because truth is under the light of their intellect that they see it with, and everyone sees it in himself, or in his mind. People do not know where it comes from because they do not see it pouring in the way they see what is in front of their eyes, so they think it is in themselves.

The Lord lets it seem this way to people so that they can be human and so that they can have a reciprocal relationship with Him. Add that by birth people are an ability to find out, comprehend, and become wise, and this ability receives the truth that knowledge, comprehension, and wisdom come from. A woman is created by means of the truth that goes with masculinity and is molded into love of it more and more after marriage, so it follows that she, too, receives truth—from her husband—in herself and joins it with her good.

123   The Lord joins good to the truths that people accept from Him, because a person cannot grasp good as if on his own resources. In fact, he cannot see it in front of his face, because it is not light but heat, and heat is felt, not seen. So when a person is thinking and sees a truth he rarely reflects about the good that is pouring into it from the love that he is disposed to, and that is giving it life. Neither does a wife reflect about the good she has, but about her husband's favor for her, which keeps pace with his intellect's ascent toward wisdom. Without her husband's knowing it she works good into truth—good that she receives from the Lord.

Now a truth comes out of all this—that a person receives truth from the Lord, and the Lord adds good to this truth to the extent that the person applies truth in his actions, which means, according to how much he wants to think wisely and therefore live wisely.

124   The Lord forms a church in a person in this way because then he is joined with the Lord in good from Him and in truth that seems to come from himself. So the person is in the Lord and the Lord in him, according to His words in John 15:4–5. It is the same if we say "charity" for "good," and "faith" for "truth," because good relates to charity, and truth relates to faith.

125   *(6) A husband does not represent the Lord and a wife the church, because a husband and wife both together make a church.* It is a commonplace in the church that just as the Lord is head of the church

a husband is head of his wife. This implies that the husband represents the Lord and the wife the church. But the Lord is head of the church, and people—male and female—are the church. A husband and wife together are even more so. The church is first implanted for them in the man, and through the man, in the wife, because the man accepts its truth in his mind, and the wife gets it from the man. If it works the other way it is in the wrong order. And this does in fact happen—but this is either among men who do not love wisdom, and so they are not of the church, or among those who hang on the beck and call of their wives, like slaves. (Something about this matter appears in Chapter 1, no. 21.)

126 (7) *So a husband is not the counterpart of the Lord nor a wife the counterpart of the church in marriages of angels in heaven and people on earth.* This follows from the words above.

However, this much should be added. It seems as though truth were of first importance in the church because it is first in point of time. Due to this appearance leaders of the church have prized faith, which has to do with truth, above charity, which has to do with good. By the same token the learned have put thought, which is intellectual, before feeling, which is emotional. Because of this, knowledge of what the good in charity is, and of what the response of our will is, lies in the grave, so to speak, and there are even people throwing in dirt so good and feelings will not return from the dead.

But people who have not closed the passage from heaven to their minds by confirming that faith alone makes a church and that thought is all that makes a human being—these people can see, if their eyes are open, that the good in charity really is the most important thing about religion.

Now, the good in charity is from the Lord, and the truth in faith is in a person as if it came from himself, and these two make the connection between the Lord and man, and man and the Lord—the kind of link the Lord meant by the statement that He is in them and they in Him (John 15:4–5). So it is clear that this connection is religion.

127 (8) *But there is a corresponding relationship with married love, impregnating, reproducing, love of children, and things like that, which*

are in marriages and come from them. These things are so thoroughly unknown, though, that they can enter your mind with some light only if you first have some grasp of *correspondence.* Without that clear in your mind it would be impossible to understand the things in this article, however much they were explained. But what correspondence is, and that things in nature do correspond to spiritual things, is amply shown in *Apocalypse Revealed* and also in *Arcana Caelestia,* and especially in *The Doctrine for the New Jerusalem Concerning the Sacred Scriptures.* And particularly in a story about it that comes later.

Just for the intellect that is not yet acquainted with all that and is in the dark, these few remarks:

The love in a marriage corresponds to a response to genuine truth, its chastity, purity, and holiness. Impregnation corresponds to the power of the truth. Reproducing corresponds to the increase of truth, and love for infants corresponds to protecting the truth and good.

Now, the truth shows up in people as if it were their own, and the Lord adds good to it, so clearly these correspondences are between man's worldly or outward plane and his spiritual or inward plane.

But the stories that follow shed more light on this.

128   (9) *The Word is the connecting link, because it is from the Lord, so it is the Lord.* The Word is the Lord's means of connection with people and people's with the Lord, because in essence it is Divine Truth united with Divine Good and Divine Good united with Divine Truth. *(Apocalypse Revealed* shows that these are united in each and every part of the Word in its heavenly and spiritual sense—nos. 373, 483, 689, 881.) This means that the Word is a perfect marriage of good and truth. It is from the Lord, and also what is from Him also is He, so consequently when a person reads the Word and gets true ideas out of it, the Lord adds good.

You see, a person does not see how the good affects him, because he reads it with his intellect, and intellect only absorbs what has to do with intellect, namely truths. From the pleasure that pours in when your intellect is enlightened, your intellect can tell that the Lord is adding good.

But this happens only for those who read it to become wise.

And people who want to find out genuine truths from the Word and by means of them form a church within themselves do have this purpose—to become wise. On the other hand, those who read it only for the glory of learning, and those who read thinking that just reading or hearing it will breathe faith into them and lead to salvation—they receive no good from the Lord. This is because the one group of people just wants to save themselves by the mere sound of it, which has nothing of the truth in it, and the other group want to be famous for their learning, so nothing of spiritual good is involved, but only a worldly pleasure that comes from the world's praise.

The Word is called a Covenant—Old and New—because it is a connecting link, and a covenant is a connecting link.

129   (10) *The church is from the Lord and is within those who approach Him and live by His teachings.* Today people do not deny that the church is the Lord's and that since it is the Lord's it is from the Lord.

The reason why the church is among those who approach Him is that His church in the Christian world is from the Word, and the Word is from Him—from Him in such a way that it is He. It has Divine Truth united with Divine Good in it, and this, too, is the Lord. This is exactly the meaning of the Word that "was with God and was God," from which is the life and light of men, and which "was made flesh" (John 1:1–14).

Moreover, it is with those who approach Him because it is with those who believe in Him—that He is God, Savior, Redeemer, Jehovah Justice, the Door where you enter the Sheepfold (i.e., the church), the Way, the Truth, and Life; that no one comes to the Father except through Him; that He and the Father are one; and the other things that He teaches. I tell you, no one can believe these things unless it is of His doing.

The church can be with only those who approach Him because He is God of heaven and earth, as He also teaches. Whom else would you approach, and who else *could* be approached? The church can be only with those who live according to His instructions because for others the connection is not there, for He says:

Whoever keeps My commandments and does them, he is the one who loves Me, and I will love him and make My home with him. But surely whoever does not love Me does not keep My commandments. (John 14:21–24)

Love is joining together, and joining with the Lord is a church.

130   (11) *Married love is aligned with the condition of the church among people, because it goes according to the state of their wisdom.* It has often been said before, and it will often be said again, that for people the love in marriage is according to the state of their wisdom. So now to throw some light on what wisdom is and on the fact that it comes to the same thing as religion.

People have knowledge, intelligence, and wisdom. Knowledge has to do with being acquainted with something, intelligence has to do with understanding it, and wisdom has to do with living it. Wisdom viewed as a whole is acquaintance, understanding, and life all at once. Knowing about things comes first. It builds understanding, and these two build wisdom—which happens when you live intelligently according to the truths that you know about. So wisdom has to do with both understanding and life, together. And it becomes wisdom when it partakes of understanding and therefore is part of life, and it finally is wisdom when it is made part of life and therefore part of understanding.

The earliest people on this earth did not know of any wisdom but the wisdom that was part of life. This was the wisdom of the ones who used to be called Wise Men. But the ancient people who came after those earliest people took the wisdom of reasoning for wisdom, and they were called Philosophers. Today, though, many people call it wisdom just to know things, for the schooled, the learned, and the trained are called wise. So wisdom has slid from its peak to its valley.

Now, something should also be said about what wisdom is at its source, on its way, and based on that, in full flower. Things that have to do with religion, called spiritual things, reside deep within a human being. The ones called civil that have to do with public matters have a lower place, and the ones having to do with knowledge, experience, and skill, called mundane, form the foundation for the others.

The reason why things having to do with religion, called spiritual, reside deep within a person is that they tie in with heaven, and through heaven with the Lord—for nothing but this enters a person through heaven from the Lord.

Things called civil that have to do with public matters take their place below spiritual matters because they tie in with the world, since they are worldly matters—statutes, laws, and codes that fetter people to make them into a stable, unified society and country.

The things that have to do with knowledge, experience, and skill, called mundane, supply the foundation because they tie right in with the body's five senses, and these are the lowest things. The inward things of your mind and the deepest things in your soul rest on them, so to speak.

Now, what has to do with religion and is called spiritual resides deep inside, and what resides deepest within becomes the head. What follows, below this, called civil matters, provides a body, and the lowest part, which is called worldly, supplies the feet. So this establishes the fact that when the three come one after the other by their rank, a person is a complete human being. For then everything flows down, just the way what is in your head influences your body, and through your body, your feet. So spiritual matters enter civil ones, and through civil ones, they enter worldly ones.

Now, what is spiritual is in the light of heaven, so this light enlightens what follows in order, and the heat of heaven, which is love, gives it life, and when this happens, a person has wisdom.

Granted that wisdom has to do with life and therefore with understanding, the question is, what *is* wisdom in life? Pulled together in a summary, it is this: To avoid bad things because they harm your soul, they harm the public, and they harm your body, and to do good things because they are a benefit to your soul, the public, and your body.

This is the wisdom that we refer to as the wisdom that married love attaches itself to, for it attaches itself through the fact that this wisdom avoids the evil of adulteries as a plague on your soul, the public, and your body. And since this wisdom wells up from spiritual matters having to do with religion, this means that married love goes according to the condition of the church, because it goes according to the condition of the wisdom in a person.

This is also what we meant by what has been said so many times already—that to the extent that a person is spiritual, he is under the influence of real married love, for a person becomes spiritual through what is spiritual in religion.

(More appears below about the wisdom that love in marriage attaches itself to. See nos. 163–65.)

131   (12) *The church comes from the Lord, so married love does, too.* This follows from what has already been said, so I refrain from reinforcing it with more words. Besides, all the angels in heaven will testify that real love in marriage comes from the Lord, and also that this love is in keeping with the condition of their wisdom, and the condition of their wisdom keeps pace with the condition of their religion. (The stories after this chapter, seen and heard in the spiritual world, make it clear that the angels do testify to this.)

132   I add two stories. Here is the first:
Once I was talking with two angels. One was from an eastern heaven, the other from a southern one. When they noticed that I was thinking about things not yet known about the wisdom of married love they said, "Do you know anything about the Wisdom Games in our world?"
I said, "Not yet."
"There are lots of them," they said, "and those who love truths out of a spiritual interest in them, or because truths are truths and they lead to wisdom—these people come together at a set time to discuss and settle subjects that require a deeper under-standing." Then they took me by the hand, saying, "Follow us, and you'll see and hear. The notice came today."
They led me across a plain to a hill. At the foot of the hill was an avenue of palms reaching clear to its top! We entered it and went up. At the top or summit of the hill we saw a woods. Its trees formed a sort of theater on a rise in the ground, and inside it was a level place paved with stones of different colors. Chairs were placed in a square around this, where the lovers of wisdom sat. In the center of the theater was a table with a paper on it that was sealed with a seal.
The people who were seated on chairs invited us to some

chairs that were still vacant, and I said, "The two angels brought me here to watch and listen, but not to sit in."

Then the two angels went to the table in the center of the floor, broke the seal of the paper, and read before the ones sitting down some unknown things about wisdom that were written on the paper, for them to discuss and turn over this time.

The things had been written and put on the table by angels of the third heaven. There were three "mysteries."

First: What is the image of God, and what is the likeness of God that man was created in?

Second: Why are people not born with any skill that love requires, when the birds and animals, both noble and lowly, are born with the skills that all their loves require?

Third: What do the Tree of Life and the Tree of Knowing Good and Evil stand for, and what does eating from them refer to?

Written below these things was, "Reduce these three things to one statement, write it on a new sheet of paper, and put it on this table. We shall see. If the statement weighs out just and true on the scales, each of you will get wisdom's award."

When they had read these words the two angels went away and were swept up into their heavens.

Now the people sitting in chairs began to discuss and turn over the mysteries before them. They spoke in turn, first the ones seated on the north, then those on the west, afterwards those on the south, and finally those on the east. They took up the first subject of discussion, which was, "What is the image of God, and what is the likeness of God that man was created in?"

Then to start out, these words from the Book of Genesis were read before everyone: "And God said, Let us make man in our own image, after our likeness. And God created man in His own image, in the image of God created he him" (Gen. 1:26–27). "In the day that God created man, in the likeness of God made He him" (5:1).

Those who sat on the north spoke first, saying, "The image of God and the likeness of God are the two lives that God breathed into man—the life of his will and the life of his intellect, for it is written, 'Jehovah God breathed into the nostrils of Adam the breath of lives; and man became a living soul' (Gen 2:7). 'Into' his 'nostrils' means He breathed into his comprehension the concept that he could want good and understand truth, so the breath of lives was in him. And the life was breathed in by God, so the image and likeness of God stands for the integrity that that wisdom and love, and that righteousness and good judgment, give him."

Those seated on the west agreed with this, but they added, "This condition of integrity that God breathed in he continually breathes into every person since Adam. But it is in a person as if in a vessel, and a person is an image and likeness of God according to what kind of vessel he is."

Then the third in turn, those seated at the south, said, "The image of God and the likeness of God are two distinct things, albeit united in man from creation. And we can see from a kind of inner light that a person can lose the image of God, but not the likeness of God. We see this as if through latticework from the fact that Adam kept the likeness of God after he let the image of God go, for after the curse it says, 'Behold the man is as one of us, knowing good and evil' (Gen. 3:22). And later it calls him the likeness of God and not the image of God (Gen. 5:1). But we yield to our colleagues who are sitting on the east—so they have better light—to say precisely what the image of God is and precisely what the likeness of God is."

Then, after it became quiet, the ones sitting on the east rose out of their chairs, looked upwards to the Lord, and after sitting back down on their chairs, said, "The image of God is a vessel for God. And God is Love itself and Wisdom itself, so the image of God is the vessel that receives love and wisdom from God, in man. But the likeness of God is the perfect likeness and full appearance that love and wisdom are in a person and therefore totally his own. In fact, a human being has no other feeling than that he loves by himself and has wisdom by himself—or wants good and knows the truth on his own—when indeed not a particle of it is from himself, but from God. Only God loves by Himself and is wise by Himself, because God is Love itself and Wisdom itself.

"The likeness, or appearance, that love and wisdom, or good and truth, are in a person just as if they were his is what makes a human being human and able to be joined with God and in that way live forever. It springs from that, that a human is human due to the fact that he can want good and know the truth just as if he did it himself, and still know and believe that it comes from God. For God puts His image in a person according to the way the person knows and believes this. It is different if one believes that it is from himself, and not from God."

After they said this a fervor came over them springing from their love of truth, and they said, "How can a person receive anything of love and wisdom and keep it and reproduce it unless he feels that it is his? And how can there be conjunction with God through love and wisdom unless a person has something responsive to conjunction? For without this mutuality no conjunction is possible. And what responds to conjunction is that the person loves God and is aware of the things that are from God as though they were from himself and yet believes that they are from God. Also, how can man live forever except in conjunction with Eternal God? So how can a human being be human without the likeness of God in him?

Everyone approved when they heard these things, and they said, "Let's make this concluding statement from these things:

"A person is a vessel for God, and a vessel for God is the image of God. And God is love itself and wisdom itself, so a person is a vessel for those. And the vessel is the image of God so far as it receives.

"And a person is the likeness of God due to the fact that he feels within himself that the things that are from God are in him just as if his own. And yet this likeness makes him an image of God exactly to the extent that he acknowledges love and wisdom, or good and truth, not to be something of his own in him—therefore not from himself—but only something in God, and therefore from God."

133   After this they took up the second object of discussion, "Why are people not born with any skill that love requires, when the birds and beasts, both noble and base, are born with the skills that all their loves require?"

First they affirmed the truth of the proposition in various ways, for example, that as for man, he is born without knowledge—not even the knowledge of the love in marriage. And they asked, and learned from expert witnesses that an infant cannot even get himself to his mother's nipple from inborn knowledge, but the mother or nurse must move him there. And all he knows is how to suck, and he learned this by constantly sucking *in utero*. And later he does not know how to walk nor make a sound in any human language—not even express the feelings of his love, as animals can. Furthermore, he does not know what food is good for him, as animals do, but he grabs what he comes on, whether it is clean or not, and puts it in his mouth.

The experts said that without instruction a human does not even know how to distinguish one sex from the other, and absolutely nothing about how to love the other sex. And not even young boys and girls know these things without instruction, although trained in various fields. In a word, man is born just a body, like the worms, and he stays a body unless others teach him to know, understand, and be wise.

After this, they demonstrated that the animals—noble as well as lowly—animals on earth, those that fly in the sky, reptiles, fish, bugs called insects—are born with all the knowledge of their life's love. They know everything nutritious for them, all the places where they can live, everything about sexual love and propagation, and all about rearing their young. They demonstrated these things by remarkable memories they recalled of things they saw, heard, and read in the natural world—as they called our world where they had lived—where there are real and not representative animals.

When the truth of the proposition was established in this way they turned their minds to tracking down and finding the ends and means to unwrap and figure out this mystery. Everyone said that these things must result from Divine Wisdom so that humans can be human and animals animals, and in this way the imperfection of a human's birth becomes his perfection and the perfection of an animal's birth is its imperfection.

134   Then the Northerners began to present their thoughts and said, "Man is born free of knowledge so he can receive all knowledge. If he were born knowing things he could not receive other skills besides the ones he was born with, and moreover, he could not adopt them as his own."

They illustrated this by a comparison. "A newborn person is like ground with no seeds planted in it, but ground that can take all seeds, grow them, and bring them to fruit. But an animal is like ground already planted, full of grass and plants, which does not accept seeds other than the ones in it. Or if it did it would choke them. This is why a person grows for many years, during which he can be cultivated like soil and, so to speak, bring forth all kinds of grain, flowers, and trees. But an animal matures in a few years, during which he can be cultivated only in what he was born to."

Then the Westerners spoke and said, "A person is not born knowing things, as an animal is, but he is born as an ability and an inclination—an ability to know and an inclination to love. He is born an ability not just to know, but also to understand and be wise. And also when he is born he is the most perfect inclination not just to love things related to himself and the world but also to love those that relate to God and heaven.

"So when a person is born to his parents he is an organism living only in external senses with nothing inward at first, so that he can become more and more human—first worldly, then rational, and at last spiritual. This he would not become if he were born with the skills and loves that beasts are born with. Inborn skills and dispositions give that process a limit, but an inborn ability and inclination limit nothing. So a person can perfect his knowledge, understanding, and wisdom forever."

The Southerners took it up and made their pronouncement, saying, "A person cannot acquire knowledge out of himself but gets it from others because no knowledge is inborn in him. And because he cannot get any knowledge out of himself, he cannot get any love there, since where there is no knowledge there is no love. Knowledge and love are inseparable companions and cannot be separated any more than will and intellect can, or feeling and thought—indeed, no more than being and form. So as a person gathers knowledge from others, love attaches itself to the knowledge as its friend. The all-embracing love that attaches itself is love of knowing, understanding, and being wise. Only people, and not animals, have this love, and it pours in from God.

"We agree with our companions from the west, that a person is not born with any love, and therefore not with any knowledge, but he is only born with an inclination to love, which gives him the ability to receive knowledge—not from himself, but from others.

That is to say, through others—through others because they do not receive any knowledge from themselves, either, but from God.

"We also agree with our companions on the North that a newborn human is like soil with no seeds planted in it, but where all kinds, both noble and lowly, can be planted.

"We'll add these ideas. The animals are born with worldly loves, so they have the skills that correspond to these loves. And they do not get any knowledge, grasp, understanding, or wisdom from the skills, but through them they are led by their loves almost as the blind are led through the streets by dogs. Intellectually they are in fact blind. Or better yet, they are like sleep-walkers, who do what they do from blind skill, with their minds asleep."

Last the Easterners spoke. They said, "We agree with the things our brothers said—that a person knows nothing by himself, but by and through others, so that he may come to know and acknowledge that everything he knows, understands, and has wisdom about is from God; and that in no other way can a person be conceived, born, and created by the Lord and become His image and likeness. For he becomes an image of the Lord by knowing and believing that all the good associated with love and charity, and all the truth that goes with wisdom and faith are things he has received, and is receiving, from the Lord, and not a shred from himself. And the feeling that all this is in himself as if it came from himself is what makes him the likeness of the Lord. He feels this because he is not born with skills but acquires them, and what you acquire seems to come from yourself. Also, the Lord grants this feeling to man so he will be human and not animal, since it is through the things you want, think about, love, know, understand, and have wisdom about as if on your own that you get skills and raise them into your understanding, and by using them, raise them to wisdom. In this way the Lord joins a person to Himself and the person joins himself to the Lord. This could not happen if the Lord had not provided that man should be born in total ignorance."

When all this was said everyone wanted to draw a conclusion from the discussion, and it came out like this: "Man is born with no knowledge so he can gain all knowledge and move on to understanding it, and through this to wisdom. And he is born with no love so that he can achieve all love by using his skills intelligently, and so that he can achieve love for the Lord through loving his neighbor. This joins him to the Lord, which makes him become human and live forever."

135   After this they picked up the paper and read the third subject of investigation, which was, "What do the Tree of Life and the Tree of Knowing Good and Evil stand for, and what does eating from them mean?"

Everyone asked the ones from the east to unfold this mystery, because it calls for deeper understanding, and the ones from the east have a blazing light. In other words, they have the wisdom of love. The garden of Eden, where the two trees were placed, stood for this wisdom.

They said, "We'll do the speaking, but no one gets anything from himself, but from the Lord, so we'll be speaking from Him, and yet by ourselves as if it came from us."

Then they said, "A tree stands for man, and its fruit stands for the good that has to do with life. So the Tree of Life stands for a person who 'lives from' God, or God living in a person. And love and wisdom, as well as charity and faith (that means good and truth), make the life of God in people, so these things are what the Tree of Life stands for. For this reason it stands for man's eternal life. The Tree of Life in Revelation 2:7 and 22:2, 14, which you could eat from, stands for the same thing.

"The Tree of Knowing Good and Evil stands for people believing that they have life in themselves and not from God—in other words, believing that love and wisdom, and charity and faith, that is, good and truth, are something of your own in you and not God's. People believe this because they think, will, speak, and act as if by themselves, in all likeness and appearance. And in this belief a person persuades himself that God put Himself into him—infused His Divinity into him—so this is why the Serpent said, 'God knows that the day you eat the fruit of that tree your eyes will be opened, and you will be like God, knowing good and evil' (Gen 3:5).

"Eating from those trees means receiving something and making it your own. Eating from the Tree of Life means receiving eternal life, and eating from the Tree of Knowing Good and Evil means accepting condemnation. This is why both Adam and his wife were cursed along with the serpent. The serpent means the devil in respect to self-love and pride in your own intelligence. That tree belongs to self-love, and people who are proud because of that love are that kind of tree.

"So the people who believe that Adam knew and did good by himself and that this was his perfection are making a terrible mistake. In fact, it was because he believed this that Adam was cursed, for this is the meaning of eating from the Tree of Knowing Good and Evil. For this he fell from his state of perfection, which he had because he believed that he knew and did good due to God and not at all by himself—which indeed is what eating from the Tree of Life means.

"Only the Lord, when He was in the world, knew by Himself and did good by Himself, because Divinity Itself was in Him from birth and was His. And so it was also from His own power that He became Redeemer and Savior."

From these and the other ideas they drew this conclusion:

"The Tree of Life and the Tree of Knowing Good and Evil, and eating from them, means that man's life is God in him and that in this way he has heaven and eternal life. And it means that the death of a human being is the persuasion and belief that man's life is not God but himself, which brings him hell and eternal death, which is condemnation."

136   After this they looked at the paper the angels left on the table, and they saw a postscript: "Wrap these three statements into one."

They compared them and saw that the three went together in a series, and this is the series—or the summary of it:

"Man was created to receive love and wisdom from God, yet in all ways seemingly by himself, for the sake of reception and conjunction. And on account of this man is born without any love or any skill, and also without any power to love and be wise by himself. So if he attributes to God all the good that goes with love and all the truth that goes with wisdom, it makes the man alive, and if he attributes it to himself, it makes him dead."

They wrote this on a fresh sheet of paper and put it on the table. Suddenly, in a bright light, angels were there! They carried the paper off into heaven. After it was read there the people sitting in the chairs heard voices, "Good ... Good ... Good ..." And instantly someone appeared from there, as if flying. He had two wings on his feet and two on his temples, and in his hand he had prizes. They were robes, caps, and laurel wreaths. He landed and gave opaline robes to those who sat on the north, and scarlet robes to those on the west. He gave the ones on the south caps with the edges decorated with bands of gold and pearl, and with the left side turned up and decorated with diamonds cut like flowers. But to the ones on the east he gave laurel wreaths with rubies and sapphires in them.

Everyone left the Wisdom Games decorated with these prizes and went home. And when they made a display for their wives, their wives came out to meet them, with gorgeous decorations from heaven themselves! They admired these.

137   The second story: As I was thinking about the love in marriage I saw two naked babies appear out of the distance with baskets in their hands and doves flying around them. And up closer they still seemed naked, becomingly decorated with garlands. Little garlands of flowers decorated their heads, and bands of lilies and blue roses draped crosswise from one shoulder to their waists ornamented their chests. And round and round both of them was a sort of chain they shared, woven of little leaves with olives worked in.

When they came still closer they seemed neither to be babies nor naked, but two people in the flower of youth dressed in robes and shirts of shining silk with very beautiful flowers woven in. When they were near me the warmth of spring from heaven breathed on me with a pleasant fragrance like the first blossoms in gardens and fields, through them.

They were two married partners from heaven. Then they spoke to me. The things I had just seen were on my mind, so they asked, "What did you see?"

I told them that at first they looked like naked babies to me, then like babies decorated with garlands, and finally like adults wearing clothes embroidered with flowers. And I said that just then the spring and its pleasantness breathed on me.

They laughed cheerfully at that and said that to themselves

they did not look like babies as they went along, nor were they naked, nor did they have garlands, but that all the while they looked the same as now. But they said that their married love is represented that way from a distance—its innocent state in their looking like naked babies, its delights by the garlands, and the same thing now by the flowers woven into their robes and shirts.

And they said, "You said that as we approached the warmth of spring with its pleasant scent of a garden breathed on you, so we'll tell you why." They said, "We have been married for centuries now, and we're always in the flower of youth, as you see us. Our first state was like the state of a young man and woman when they join themselves in marriage. We thought then that that state must be the very blessing of our life. But from others in our heaven we heard, and noticed it ourselves later, that it was a state of heat not moderated by light and that gradually it is moderated as a husband's wisdom gets more perfect and his wife loves it in him. This happens as a result of the things they do, and according to them—things they help each other do in society. Then come the delights according to how the heat and light—which is to say the wisdom and love of wisdom—are moderated.

"When we approached, a warmth like spring breathed on you because married love and the warmth of spring go together in our heaven. For warmth is love for us, and the light that warmth unites with is wisdom. The things we do are like an atmosphere that enfolds both of them. What are heat and light without being in something? And in the same way, what are love and wisdom without being put to use? There's no marriage in them, because something for them to be in just isn't there.

"In heaven, where there is the warmth of spring there is a real love of marriage. The reason for this is that there is spring only where heat and light are together in equal amounts, or where there is as much light as heat and vice versa. And, take it from us, love delights in wisdom, and, the other way around, wisdom delights in love, just the way heat delights in light, and, the other way around, light delights in heat."

He said more. "For us in heaven there is always light and never the shadows of evening, much less night, because our sun does not rise and set like your sun but always stays halfway between the zenith and the horizon, which we call 'forty-five degrees in the sky.' This is why the heat and light coming from our sun make perpetual spring, and a perpetual spring breeze always breathes on those who have love and wisdom together in equal amounts. And our Lord breathes nothing but activity through the eternal union of heat and light. This is where germination comes from in your world, too, and the mating of your birds and animals in the spring. You see, the warmth of spring releases things inside them, all the way to the most inward, called their souls. It does something to them and puts its marriage in them and makes their breeding instinct satisfy itself, due to a constant drive to produce the fruits of activity—which is propagation of their species.

"But for people the influence of spring warmth from the Lord is constant, so they can enjoy marriage in all seasons, even winter. For men are born vessels for light—that is, wisdom from the Lord—and women are born vessels for heat—that is, love for the man's wisdom from the Lord.

"So now that's why the warmth of spring with its pleasant smell like new blossoms in gardens and fields seemed to breathe on you as we approached."

After saying these things the man offered me his right hand and led me to houses where there were married partners who were in the same flower of youth as he and his wife. He said, "These wives that look like young women now were elderly women in the world, and their husbands that look like young men now were decrepit old men there. The Lord returned them to this blooming youth because they loved each other, and following their religion they avoided adulteries as terrible sins."

He said, "Only those who reject the horrible joys of adultery know the blessed joys of married love. And no one can reject them unless he has wisdom from the Lord. No one gets wisdom from the Lord unless he does useful things from a love of doing them."

Then I also saw the furnishings of their homes. Everything had a heavenly form and flashed with gold that seemed to be aflame from the rubies studding it.

Chapter 7

About "Chaste" and "Unchaste"

138   Now then, I am still at the outset in regard to working through the details of married love, and married love in detail can only be recognized indistinctly and as if in the dark unless its opposite appears to a certain extent, too. Its opposite is anything unchaste, which does appear, somewhat hazily, when you describe "chaste" and "unchaste" together, because chastity is just the separation of what is unchaste from what is chaste.

However, Part 2, at the end of this book, deals with unchasteness, which is totally opposite to chastity, where its variations are described fully under the heading, "The Foolish Pleasures of Illicit Love."

But the illustration of what chastity and unchasteness are, and for whom, follows this order:

(1) "Chaste" and "unchaste" apply only to marriages and to things that have to do with marriages.

(2) "Chaste" applies only to monogamous marriages, or marriage of one man with one wife.

(3) Marriage can be chaste only if Christian.

(4) True married love is chastity itself.

(5) All the pleasures of real married love are chaste—even the most physical ones.

(6) For those whom the Lord makes spiritual, married love grows more and more pure and becomes chaste.

(7) The chastity of a marriage emerges through totally renouncing fornication for religious reasons.

(8) "Chastity" does not apply to babies, little boys and girls, or

teenaged boys and girls before they have felt sexual love.

(9) "Chastity" does not apply to born eunuchs nor to those who are made eunuchs.

(10) "Chastity" does not apply to those who do not think adultery is a religious evil, and still less to those who do not think adultery hurts society.

(11) "Chastity" does not apply to those who abstain from adulteries just for various superficial reasons.

(12) "Chastity" does not apply to those who think marriages are unchaste.

(13) "Chastity" does not apply to those who have renounced marriage and have vowed perpetual celibacy, unless they still have a love for a life of real marriage.

(14) Marriage is a better condition than celibacy.

Now comes an explanation of these things.

139   (1) *"Chaste" and "unchaste" apply only to marriages and things that have to do with marriages.* This is because real married love is chastity itself (this comes later), and its opposite, called love of fornication, is unchasteness itself. So married love is chaste just to the extent that it is freed from the other love, for to that extent its destructive opposite is removed. This shows what the purity of married love, called chastity, is.

There is such a thing as married love that is not chaste and yet is not unchaste, as between partners who for various outward reasons abstain from lascivious actions enough not to think about them. Yet if in their spirits the love is not purified, it is still not chaste. Its outward form is chaste, but in it there is no essential chasteness.

140   "Chaste" and "not chaste" apply to things having to do with marriage because marriage is etched on either sex from deep within all the way to the surface. This leads a person's thoughts and feelings and, behind the scenes, his bodily acts and motions.

The truth of this is easier to see in the unchaste. The unchasteness that besets their minds comes out in the sound of their speech and in the fact that they turn everything in conversation—even chaste things—to something lewd. (The sound of speech comes from your voluntary feelings, and your speech comes from the thought in your intellect.) This is a sign that their will and everything to do with it, and their intellect and everything to do with it, or their whole mind and therefore their whole body, inside and out, seethes with unchasteness.

I have heard from angels that their ears pick up the unchasteness in consummate hypocrites no matter how chastely they talk, and angels can also tell from the aura that these people exude. This, too, is a sign that they have unchastity in their innermost minds and therefore deep inside their bodies, and that it is veiled over outwardly as if by a shell painted with various colored patterns.

From the Children of Israel's statutes it is clear that an aura of lewdness exudes from the unchaste, because every single thing that a person who was defiled in certain ways touched, even with his hand, was unclean.

These ideas lead to the conclusion that the same goes for chaste people. That is to say, that for them each and every thing from inmost to outmost is chaste, and that the chastity of married love does this. This is where the saying comes from in the world: "To the pure all things are pure, and to the impure all things are impure."

141   (2) *"Chaste" applies only to monogamous marriages, or marriage of one man with one wife.* Chaste applies only to these marriages because married love for them is not seated in the worldly plane of the person but reaches into the spiritual, and it gradually opens a way for itself to spiritual marriage itself—the marriage of good and truth—which is its source. It joins itself with that. Married love comes in as wisdom increases, and this happens as the Lord implants religion, as already demonstrated in many places. This cannot happen to polygamists, since they split married love, and when it is divided this love is not unlike sexual love, which is worldly in its own right. But something applicable to this subject appears in the discussion of polygamy later.

142   (3) *Marriage can be chaste only if Christian.* This is because the real love of marriage a person has keeps pace with the state of religion in him, and he gets this from the Lord (as earlier discussions have shown—nos. 130–31, and elsewhere). It is also because

religion's genuine truths are in the Word, and the Lord is present in them there. This means that there can be chaste marriage only in the Christian world. If it is not there, at least it can be there.

Christian marriage means marriage of one man and one wife. In the proper place it will come out that this marriage can be implanted in Christians and pass to children by heredity from parents who have the real love of marriage, and that it can yield an innate ability and inclination to understand religious and heavenly things.

The chapter on polygamy will show that if Christians have more wives than one, they commit adultery not only on the worldly level but the spiritual level as well.

143   (4) *True married love is chastity itself.* The reasons are: (a) It is from the Lord and corresponds to the marriage of the Lord and the church. (b) It descends from the marriage of good and truth. (c) It is just as spiritual as the church is among people. (d) It is the basic love and the chief of all heavenly and spiritual loves. (e) It is the proper nursery of the human race and, from this, of the angelic heaven. (f) For this reason the angels of heaven have it, too, and from it spiritual offspring are born to them, which are love and wisdom. (g) So this practice takes a place ahead of all the other activities in creation.

What comes from this is the fact that real married love, because of its origin, and when its essence is seen for what it is, is pure and holy enough to be called purity and holiness and therefore chastity itself.

But article 6, which follows (no. 146), shows that it is not totally pure among people nor among angels, even at that.

144   (5) *All the pleasures of real married love are chaste—even the most physical ones.* This follows from the things explained above—that real married love is chastity itself and delights are its life, that the delights of this love ascend and enter heaven, and on the way they pass through the joys of heavenly love that the angels have in heaven, and besides, that these delights join together with the joys of the angels' married love. This was mentioned above.

Besides this, I have heard it from angels that they themselves find those pleasures better and fuller when they come from chaste marriages on earth. Some unchaste people were hanging around nearby. Someone asked, "Even the physical pleasures?" They nodded and said quietly, "Why not? These pleasures are the fulfillment of the others, aren't they?"

(Where these pleasures associated with love come from, and what they are like appears in no. 69 above and in the stories—especially the ones to follow.)

145   (6) *For those whom the Lord makes spiritual, married love grows more and more pure and becomes chaste.* Here are the reasons:

(a) First love, meaning the love before the wedding and just after the wedding, brings with it something of sexual love—something afire for the body itself that is not yet tempered by love of the spirit.

(b) A person changes from worldly to spiritual gradually. You see, he becomes spiritual as his rationality, which is midway between heaven and earth, begins to take its life from what pours out of heaven. This happens as he turns toward wisdom and takes pleasure in it (see no. 130 above). And so far as he does this, his mind rises into a higher atmosphere that contains the light and warmth of heaven, or in other words the love and wisdom that angels enjoy. For the light of heaven acts in unison with wisdom and the warmth of heaven with love. And as wisdom and its love grow between partners, their married love becomes that much purer. This happens gradually, so it follows that their love becomes more and more chaste. You might compare this spiritual purifying to the purifying of natural spirits that chemists do, which they call purging, fractional distillation, purifying, repeated distillation, refining, decantation, and sublimation. And you could compare purified wisdom with alcohol, which is fully distilled spirits.

(c) Now, spiritual wisdom in its own right warms more and more to love of wisdom, which makes it grow forever. This happens as it becomes more perfect, so to speak, through purging, purifying, distillation, refining, decantation, and sublimation. This happens by polishing the intellect and drawing it away from the misconceptions that the senses create and getting your will away from bodily lusts. So obviously married love, whose parent is wisdom, gradually becomes more and more pure, or chaste, in the same way.

(The story in no. 137 shows that the first state of love between partners is a state of heat untempered with light, but that it is gradually tempered as the husband matures in wisdom and the wife loves the wisdom in him.)

146   But note that totally chaste and pure married love is not found among men or angels. There is always something less than chaste and pure attached and connected to it—though this is a different type of thing than something *un*chaste. Indeed, it is chaste above and not chaste below. The Lord puts a hinged door between, so to speak, which is opened by decision, and takes care that it does not stand ajar so that what is chaste and what is not chaste do not cross over to each other and mix together.

Indeed, on the worldly plane people are born contaminated and full of evils. Their spiritual side is not, because it is born of the Lord, for it is *re*born. Rebirth is a gradual separation from the evil inclinations that people are born with.

(No. 71, above, shows that no love of men or angels is totally pure, nor can be, but the Lord considers mainly your goal, purpose, or voluntary intent, so in the measure that a person has these and is loyal to them he is introduced into purity and makes progress toward it.)

147   (7) *The chastity of a marriage emerges through totally renouncing fornication, for religious reasons.* The reason is that chastity is the removal of unchasteness. A general rule is that in the measure that one removes the bad there is room for the good to replace it. And furthermore, in the measure that you hate evil, you love good, and vice versa. So in the measure that you renounce fornication, the chastity of marriage steps in.

Anyone can see from common sense that love of marriage is purified and set right as you renounce fornication. You see it as soon as it is said and heard, before it is demonstrated. But not everyone has common sense, so it is important to illustrate this by giving proof.

The proof is that married love cools as soon as it is divided, and cooling spoils it. The heat of unchaste love extinguishes it. The two opposite kinds of heat cannot occur together, because the one banishes the other and robs it of strength.

By this token, when the heat of married love removes and rejects the heat that belongs to love of fornication, the married love begins to become pleasantly warm, and, aware of its delights, it starts to bud and blossom like apple trees and roses in the spring. The trees and roses do this because of the springtime blend of light and warmth from the sun of the natural world, but love does it because of the springtime blend of light and warmth from the spiritual sun.

148   Innate in every person from creation, and therefore from birth, is an inner marriage drive and an outer one. The inner one is spiritual, and the outer one is worldly. First the outward one governs the person's condition, and as he becomes spiritual the inner one does. So if he sticks with the outward or worldly drive, the inner or spiritual one is veiled over to the point where he knows nothing about it—in fact, to the point where he calls it a silly notion. But on the other hand, if the person becomes spiritual he begins to notice the inner drive somewhat. Then he notices something of what it is like and gradually feels its pleasantness, joys, and delights. And as this happens, the veil mentioned above, between outward and inward, starts to become thinner, then melts, so to speak, and finally dissolves and disappears.

But when this process is done, the external drive remains, but the inner one keeps cleaning it and purifying it of its dregs. This goes on until the outside is like a face for the inside, and it gets its joy from the inner blessedness, and also its life and the delights of its potency.

This is what the renouncing of fornication is like, which enables the chastity of marriage to emerge.

You may think that the outward marriage drive remaining after the inner one has separated from it, or it from the inner one, is just the same as when they are not separated. But I have heard from angels that the outward and inward drives are completely different. An outward drive that comes from within—call it an outside from within—has no part in anything lascivious, because the inward element cannot enjoy lewd pleasures but only chaste ones, and it brings chaste pleasures to its outside where it can feel them.

An outside separated from the inside is quite different. The angels said this is lascivious, throughout and in every part. An outward marriage drive that comes from an inner one they compared to a choice fruit whose pleasant taste and smell seep into its skin and form it to correspond with what is inside. They also compared an outward marriage drive that comes from an inner one to a pantry whose provisions never diminish, but what is taken out is constantly being replaced.

But an outward one separated from the inward one they compared to wheat in a winnower. If you scatter the wheat all around, only the chaff is left, and a gust of wind blows it away. This happens to the love in marriage unless you renounce fornication.

149   The chastity of a marriage does not come from renouncing fornication unless it is done for religious reasons. This is because a person does not become spiritual without religion. He remains worldly. And if a worldly person renounces fornications, his spiritual level still does not renounce them. So it seems to him that he is chaste by renouncing them, but unchasteness still lies hidden within, just like infected tissue in a superficially healed wound.

(No. 130, above, shows that married love keeps pace with the religious condition of a person. Article 11, below, has more on this subject.)

150   (8) *"Chastity" does not apply to babies, little boys and girls, or teenaged boys and girls before they have felt sexual love.* This is because "chaste" and "unchaste" apply only to marriages and to things associated with marriage (see no. 139, above). Chastity is not applicable to those who know nothing about marriages, for it is like nothing to them, and there is no feeling from it or thought about it. But after that void, something does emerge when you feel the beginnings of marriage, which is love for the other sex.

It is because people do not know what chastity is that they commonly call teenaged boys and girls chaste before they feel sexual love.

151a   (9) *"Chastity" does not apply to born eunuchs nor to those who are made eunuchs.* "Born eunuchs" primarily means those who from birth lack love's bodily member. The beginning and middle lack a basis to build on, so they cannot emerge. And if they do emerge there is no point distinguishing between chaste and unchaste, for to them there is no difference between the two. But there are many differences.

It is almost the same with made eunuchs as with born eunuchs. But made eunuchs—they are both men and women—can only observe the love of marriage like a fantasy, and its delights like fables. If they have any inclination in them it is neuter—which is neither chaste nor unchaste. Since it is neuter, you cannot call it chaste or unchaste.

152a   (10) *"Chastity" does not apply to those who do not think adultery is a religious evil, and still less to those who do not think adultery hurts society.* You cannot apply the word "chastity" to these people because they do not know what chastity is, nor that it exists, for chastity has to do with marriage, as the first article in this discussion showed. People who do not think that adultery is a religious evil also make marriages unchaste, when on the contrary it is the religion of married partners that makes marriages chaste. So nothing is chaste to them, and so it is useless to mention chastity in their presence.

These are confirmed adulterers. Still, those who do not think adultery hurts society understand even less than the rest what chastity is—or that it exists—for they are adulterers on purpose. If they say that marriages are less unchaste than adulteries, they say it with their mouths but not their hearts, because marriages are chilling to them. When they speak from this chill about chaste warmth, they cannot have an idea of the chaste warmth in married love.

Part 2, about the folly of adulterers, will show what these people are like and what kind of ideas they have in their minds, and therefore what they are saying to themselves.

153a   (11) *"Chastity" does not apply to those who abstain from adulteries just for various superficial reasons.* Many people believe that mere bodily abstinence from adulteries is chastity, when in fact it is not chastity unless it is in your spirit, too, at the same time. A person's spirit, which in this case means the response of his mind to feelings and thoughts, is what makes something chaste or unchaste, because chastity or unchastity in his body comes from his spirit. For his body is exactly the same as what his mind or spirit is like. So this means that people who abstain from adulteries bodily and not in spirit, or who abstain from them in spirit for bodily reasons, are not chaste.

There are many reasons that make a person abstain from bodily adulteries, and refrain in spirit for bodily reasons, but really, whoever does not quit bodily adulteries for spiritual reasons is unchaste. For the Lord says that if anyone looks at someone else's woman with a desire for her he has already committed adultery with her in his heart (Matt. 5:28).

It is impossible to list all the reasons for abstaining from adulteries in body only, for they vary with the condition of a marriage and also according to bodily condition. That is to say, some people abstain from them for fear of civil law and its penalties, others for fear of losing their reputation and therefore its honors, others for fear of the diseases from them, others for fear of disagreements at home with their wives and the disquiet that results in their life, others for fear of vengeance from a husband or relative, and still others for fear of being beaten up by the servants. And then, some people abstain out of poverty, or avarice, or because of weakness due to disease, because they are worn out, or because of age or impotence. Some of them, because they cannot or dare not commit bodily adulteries, condemn spiritual adulteries too. Thus they speak morally against them and in favor of marriages. But if they do not disavow adulteries in spirit, and in spirit because of religion, they are still adulterers, for they still commit adultery, in mind if not in body. When they are spirits after death, they speak openly in favor of adulteries.

This all shows that even the ungodly can avoid adultery as harmful, but only a Christian can avoid it as a sin. So now the truth of the proposition stands—that "chastity" has nothing to do with those who abstain from adulteries for various superficial reasons.

154a   (12) *"Chastity" does not apply to those who think marriages are unchaste.* These people do not know what chastity is nor that it exists—like those mentioned above (no. 152a) and like those who think only celibacy is chaste, discussed in the next article.

155a   (13) *"Chastity" does not apply to those who have renounced marriage and have vowed perpetual celibacy, unless they still have a love for a life of real marriage.* "Chastity" does not apply to these people, because the love in marriage is thrown away once they make a vow of perpetual celibacy, and chastity only applies to that love. Also, love of the other sex is still there from creation and therefore from birth. When this tendency is restrained and subdued it can only turn into a heat that seethes inside some people. Then it surges from their body into their mind, infests it, and in some cases contaminates it. And it can happen that a mind contaminated by this also contaminates religious matters and degrades them from their inner place where they have holiness, down into superficialities, where they become nothing but words and postures.

For this reason the Lord provides that this celibacy only occurs among people who have an external worship, because they do not approach the Lord or read the Word. The imposition of celibacy together with the vow of chastity does not endanger their eternal life as it would for those who worship inwardly. In addition, many people living in that condition did not do it of their own free will. Some did it before they had enough rationality to be free, and some because of worldly influences.

Among those who adopt celibacy to get their minds away from the world and to make room for divine worship, the ones who had a love for the life of real marriage before their vows, or develop it afterwards, and it remains in them, are chaste to that extent, for a love of married life is what chastity does have to do with.

And for this reason all monastics are finally released from their vows after death, and set free, and are given a choice between married and unmarried life, according to the inner vows and desires of their love. Then if they enter married life, there are weddings in heaven for the ones who also loved the spiritual side of worship. But those who choose unmarried life are placed with people like themselves, who live at the edges of heaven.

I have asked angels whether heaven accepts women who

have pursued piety and have given themselves up to divine worship, and have withdrawn themselves from worldly illusions and the lure of the flesh, and on that account have vowed perpetual virginity—and whether they become first among the blessed, according to their faith.

The angels said that they are accepted, but when they notice the aura of married love there they become depressed and uncomfortable, and then—some of their own free will, some through asking permission, and some by command—they go away or are sent away. And when they are outside that heaven, paths open for them leading to companions who had enjoyed the same condition of life in the world. Then they change from worried to happy and rejoice among themselves.

156a   (14) *Marriage is a better condition than celibacy.* This is established by what was already said about marriage and celibacy. A married condition is preferable because it comes from creation, because its source is the marriage of good and truth, because it has a correspondence with the marriage of the Lord and the church, because the church and married love are constant companions, because its purpose is the primary purpose of all creation—the orderly propagation of the human race and also the heaven of angels, for this comes from the human race.

In addition, marriage is human fulfillment, because a person becomes fully human through it, as the next chapter will show. No celibate people are fully human.

But if you offer the proposition that the celibate state is better than the married state and open the proposition to examination, to be affirmed and established by presenting proofs of it, what comes out of it is that marriages are not holy, and chaste marriages do not exist, and even that chastity in the feminine sex is nothing other than their abstaining from marriage and vowing perpetual virginity, and on top of this, that people who vow perpetual celibacy are meant by the eunuchs who made themselves eunuchs for the kingdom of God (Matt. 19:12). Besides many other things that are not true because they come from an untrue proposition. (The eunuchs who made themselves eunuchs for the kingdom of God is a reference to spiritual eunuchs—those who are married and abstain from the evils of fornication. Clearly this does not mean the Italian castrati.)

151b   I add to these things two stories. The first:

While I was going home from the Wisdom Games (described in no. 132 above) I saw on the way an angel dressed in blue. He came up beside me and said, "I see that you are coming from the Wisdom Games and that the things you heard there make you happy. I can tell that you are not entirely in this world, because you are in the natural world at the same time, so you don't know about our Olympic Seminars where the wise men of old gather and find out from newcomers out of your world what changes and developments wisdom has been going through—and still is. If you like, I'll lead you to a place where many of the old philosophers and their children—in other words, their students—live."

He led me toward the boundary between the north and the east, and then, from a rise, I looked in that direction. I saw a city! To one side of it were two hills. The one nearer the city was lower than the other.

"That city is called Athens," he told me. "The lower hill is Parnassus and the higher one is Helicon. They call them this because in and around the city the old philosophers of Greece live—like Pythagoras, Socrates, Aristippus, Xenophon—with their students and novices."

I asked about Plato and Aristotle.

He said, "They and their followers live in another place, because they used to teach rational concepts that have to do with knowledge, while the philosophers who live here taught moral concepts that apply to life." He said that students from this city of Athens are often sent to educated Christians to report what they think these days about God, the creation of the universe, the immortality of the soul, the human condition compared to that of animals, and other things having to do with inner wisdom. "Today a crier has announced an assembly," he said, "an indication that the scouts have come across new arrivals from Earth, from whom they have heard things worth looking into."

We saw many people going out of the city and its environs, some with laurels on their heads, some holding palms in their hands, some with books under their arms, and some with pens in their hair by their left temples.

We joined in with them and went up together. What did we see on the Palatine Hill but an octagon called the Palladium. We went in. What did we see inside but eight hexagonal alcoves, with a library in each and also a table where the laureates sat together. And in the Palladium itself we saw seats carved out of stone, where the others sat down.

Then a door opened on the left, and two newcomers from Earth were brought in through it. After the greetings, one of the laureates asked them, "What is the news from Earth?"

They said, "It's new that some people resembling animals, or animals resembling people, have been found in the woods, and from their faces and bodies they were known to have been born humans, lost or left in the woods at the age of two or three." They said they could not speak any thoughts nor learn to pronounce words in any language. They didn't know what food was good for them, either, as animals do, but put whatever they found in the woods into their mouths, clean and unclean alike. And other things like that. "Some of our scholars have conjectured from these things, and some have inferred, many things about the human condition compared to the animal state."

When they heard these things some of the ancient philosophers asked what they did conjecture and infer.

The two newcomers answered, "Many things. But they boil down to these: (a) By nature and birth, man is more stupid and therefore more lowly than all animals, and this is all he amounts to if he is not taught. (b) He can be taught, because he has learned to articulate sounds and to speak with them. By this means he began to express thoughts, step by step, more and more, to the point where he can pronounce laws for society—though animals are equipped with many of the laws from birth. (c) Animals have rationality the same as people. (d) So if animals could talk they would reason about everything as skillfully as people do. An indication of this is that they think from reason and good sense the same as people do. (e) That intellect is just a modification of the sun's light, working with heat, by means of the ether, so it is just an activity of your inner nature, and it can rise to the point where it seems like wisdom. (f) So it is useless to believe that people live after death any more than animals do—except perhaps for a few days after death, in the life breathing out of their body like a ghostly cloud before it dissipates into nature, not much different than the way a twig in ashes looks like what it used to be. (g) So religion, which teaches that there is life after death, is invented to keep the simple shackled inwardly by its laws, as they are shackled outwardly by civil laws."

To these things they added that only the clever scholars worked it out this way, and not the intelligent ones. The philosophers asked what the intelligent ones thought. They said they had not heard, and that this was their own opinion.

152b   When they heard these things everyone sitting at the tables said, "Oh, what times these are on earth! Alas, what changes wisdom has undergone! How changed it is into foolish cleverness! The sun has set and is under the earth diametrically opposite its meridian! Who can't tell from the account of those people lost and found in the woods that man is like that if he is not taught? He is what he's taught to be, isn't he? Isn't he born more ignorant than the animals? Doesn't he learn to walk and talk? If he didn't learn to walk would he stand on his feet? And if he didn't learn to talk could he even mumble any thoughts?

"Doesn't everyone turn out as he is taught—foolish from false concepts and wise from truths? And when foolish from false concepts, he has the complete fantasy that he is wiser than anyone who is wise due to truths, doesn't he? Aren't there foolish and insane people who are no more human than those people they found in the woods? Isn't that what people are like when they have lost their memory?

"From all these things we conclude that an untaught person is neither a person nor an animal, but he is a vessel that can receive what does make you human, and so he is not born human but becomes human. And a person is born in such a form as to receive life from God, so that he can be something that God can put everything good into, and can bless him forever through a union with Himself.

"We can tell from what you say that wisdom today is so dead or foolish that people know nothing at all about the human condition as compared to the animal state. This is why they do not know about the human condition after death. And as for those who can know this but do not want to, and therefore deny it, as many of your Christians do—we might compare them to the people found in the woods. Not that they are stupid for lack of instruction. They have made themselves stupid through false observations, which are shadows of the truth."

153b   But then someone standing in the middle of the Palladium, holding a palm in his hand, said, "Please unfold this mystery. How can someone created in the form of God be changed into the form of a devil? I know that angels in heaven are forms of God and that angels of hell are forms of the devil, and the two forms are opposite to one another—one a form of folly, the other a form of wisdom. So tell how someone, created in the form of God, can go from day into such night that he can deny God and eternal life."

The teachers responded to this one by one—first the Pythagoreans, then the Socratists, and afterwards the others.

But among them was a Platonist. He spoke last, and his opinion was the best. Here it is.

"People in the Saturnian or Golden Age knew and acknowledged that they were forms to receive life from God and that therefore wisdom had been inscribed on their souls and hearts. So they saw truth in the light of truth, and through truth they could be aware of good from the joy of loving it. But the human race in the following ages withdrew from acknowledgement that all the truth of wisdom, and therefore the good of love, that people have, continuously flows down from God. As they did, they stopped being a place for God to inhabit. And then conversation with God and association with angels stopped, too. For the inner part of their minds changed its direction of being raised by God upwards to God, and it turned out toward the world more and more, and thus God turned them to Himself through the world. In the end they were turned around in the opposite direction—downwards to their own selves.

"A person who is inwardly upside-down and therefore turned away cannot see God, so people separated themselves from God and became forms of hell or the devil.

"It follows from this that in the first ages they acknowledged in their heart and soul that all the good of love and all the truth of wisdom from it in them were from God, and also that these were God's in them. So they realized that they were only vessels of life from God and were therefore called images of God, sons of God, and born of God. But in the following ages they acknowledged it, not in heart and soul, but with a sort of induced faith, then with a memorized faith, and finally just with their mouths. And to acknowledge something like that with your mouth only is not to acknowledge it, but in fact to deny it in your heart.

"You can see from these things what wisdom is like today on earth among Christians, when they can get inspiration from God by written revelation, yet they do not know the difference between man and animals. So there are many who think that if people live after death the animals will survive, too, or that animals do not live after death so man will not survive, either.

"Our spiritual light, which enlightens the sight of the mind, has become darkness to them, hasn't it? And the light of nature that they have, which only enlightens physical sight, has become dazzling."

154b   After all this, everyone turned to the two newcomers and thanked them for coming and speaking to them. And they asked them to report to their brothers these things they had heard.

The newcomers answered that they would encourage their friends to see the truth that in the measure that they attribute every good of charity and truth of faith to the Lord, not to themselves, they are humans and become angels of heaven.

155b   The second story: Early one morning a very beautiful song I heard somewhere up above me woke me up. And then in that first stage of waking up, which is more inward, peaceful, and sweet than the rest of the day, I was able to stay for some time in a spiritual condition, as if outside my body, and give keen attention to the feeling being sung. The singing of heaven is nothing but a mental feeling coming from the mouth as melody, for it is the sound, apart from the words, of someone voicing a feeling of love. This gives the words their life.

In the state I mentioned, I could tell it was a feeling that had

to do with the delights of married love, made into a song by some
wives in heaven. I noticed this because of the sound of the song,
in which those delights varied in marvelous ways.

After this I rose up and looked around—in the spiritual world.
A golden rain seemed to appear in the east, below the sun there!
It was the early morning dew coming down so copiously. When
the sun's rays hit it, it looked like a kind of golden rain before my
eyes. This made me even more wide awake. I went out (in the
spiritual world), happened to meet an angel on the way, and
asked him if he saw the golden rain coming down from the sun.
He answered that he saw it whenever he was thinking about
married love.

Then he looked that way and said, "The rain is falling above
a dwelling where three husbands are, with their wives. They live
in the middle of the Eastern Paradise. We see that rain falling
from the sun over the dwelling because wisdom about married
love and its delights dwells with them—wisdom about married
love with the husbands and wisdom about its delights with the
wives. But I notice that you are thinking about the delights of
married love, so I'll take you to that house and introduce you."

He led me, through places that seemed like paradise, to
houses built of olive wood with two cedar columns outside the
door, and he introduced me to the husbands and asked them to
let me join them and speak with their wives. They nodded and
called their wives.

The wives cast a penetrating look into my eyes.

I asked why.

They said, "We can tell exactly how you feel about love for
the other sex and how your feeling affects you, and this tells us
how you think on the subject. We see that you're thinking about
it intensely but yet chastely." And they said, "What do you want
us to tell you about it?"

I answered, "Please say something about the delights of love
in marriage."

The husbands nodded, saying, "Please do explain something
about the delights. Their ears are chaste."

And the wives asked, "Who told you to ask us about the
delights of that love? Why not ask our husbands?"

"This angel who is with me." I answered. "He said in my ear

that wives are the vessels of married love and can sense it because they are loves by birth, and all delights have to do with love."

They answered this with a smile on their lips. "Be careful. Don't say such a thing, unless you say it ambiguously, because it's a nugget of wisdom hidden deep in the hearts of our sex. We don't reveal it to any husband except one who has a real love for marriage. There are many reasons, which we keep well hidden."

Then the husbands said, "Our wives know all about our mental state. Nothing is hidden from them. They see, sense, and feel whatever comes out of our will. On the other hand, we know nothing about what goes on inside them. Wives have this gift because they are very tender loves. They also amount to forms of ardent zeal to preserve the friendship and confidence of marriage, which keeps life happy for both. They see to this for their husbands and for themselves, thanks to a wisdom that is inherent in their love. It is so discreet that they don't want to say they love, so they can't say it. Only that they are loved."

"Why is it that they don't want to and therefore can't?" I asked.

The wives said that if the least thing like that slipped from their mouths, a chill would come over their husbands and separate them from bed, chamber, and sight.

"But this happens to husbands who do not hold marriages sacred, so they do not love their wives from a spiritual love. It works differently for those who do love in this way. In their minds the love is spiritual, and the earthly love in their bodies comes from that.

"In this house we get the natural love from the spiritual, so we trust our husbands with our secrets about the delights of married love."

Then I politely asked them to explain some of those secrets to me, too.

They glanced at a window on the south side, and there a white dove appeared! Its wings shimmered as if with silver, and its head was capped as if with a gold crown. It stood on a branch bearing an olive. When it began to spread its wings the wives said, "We'll tell you something. While the dove is there it's a sign to us that we may."

Then they said, "Every man has five senses—sight, hearing, smell, taste, and touch. But we have a sixth sense that is a sense of all the delights of married love in our husbands. And this sense is in our hands when we touch our husbands' chests, arms, hands, or cheeks—especially their chests—and when they touch us. All the happiness and pleasures of the thoughts in their minds and all the happiness and joys in their souls, and the cheer and mirth in their hearts, come across to us from them and take form, and we can perceive them, sense them, touch them, and tell them apart as clearly and distinctly as ears can tell the notes of a tune and a tongue can tell the flavors of fine foods.

"In a word, you might say the spiritual joys of our husbands wear a natural embodiment for us. So our husbands call us the sense organs of chaste married love, and therefore of its delights.

"And yet this sense of our sex comes out, is supported, continues, and gets better in the degree that our husbands love us due to wisdom and discernment and we, on our part, love them for those same things in them.

"In heaven, this sense that our sex has is called wisdom at play with its love and love with its wisdom."

These things made me want to know more—like the different kinds of delights.

They said, "They are infinite. But we don't want to tell you more, so we can't. The dove in our window with the olive branch under his feet has flown away."

I waited for it to come back, but it was no use.

Meantime, I asked the husbands, "Don't you have the same sense of married love?"

"We have a general sense," they said, "but not the specific one. We get a general happiness, a general joy, and a general pleasantness from the specific happiness, joy, and pleasantness our wives have. And this general feeling that we get from them is like a calm peacefulness."

When this was said, a swan appeared outside the window! It was standing on the branch of a fig tree. It spread its wings and flew off.

When the husbands saw this they said, "This is a sign to us to be quiet about married love. Come back another time, and maybe more things will come out." And they withdrew.

We went away.

Chapter 8

The Union of Souls and Minds by Marriage, Which is the Meaning of the Lord's Words That They Are No Longer Two, But One Flesh

The Book of Genesis, and the Lord's words as well, make it clear that from creation a man and a woman have a built-in inclination and also an ability to join together just like one, and that man and woman still have that inclination and ability in them.

We read in the Book of Creation, called Genesis, that

Jehovah God built the rib that He took from the man into a woman. And He led her to the man, and the man said, "This at last is bone of my bones and flesh of my flesh. The name to call her is woman ['ishshah] because she was taken out of man ['ish]. So a man shall leave his father and his mother and cling to his wife, and they will be one flesh." (2:22–24)

The Lord also says the same thing in Matthew:

Haven't you read that He who made male and female from the beginning said, "On account of this a man will leave father and mother and cling to his wife, and the two will be one in flesh"? So they are no longer two but one flesh. (19:4–5)

This shows clearly that woman was created from man and that each has the inclination and the ability to unite into one again. It is also clear that this means unite into one person, from the Book of Genesis, where it calls the two of them together a person. For it says, "In that day God created a person. He created them male and female. And he gave them the name 'human'" (5:1, 2). It says there that He called their name Adam, but *Adam* and *human* are the same word in Hebrew. The two of them together are also called a person in Genesis 1:27 and 3:22–24.

"One flesh" also means "one person," which is clear from the places where the Word says "all flesh," meaning mankind, as in Gen. 6:12, 13, 17, 19; Isa. 40:5, 6; 49:26; 66:16, 23–24; Jer. 25:31; 32:27; 45:5; Ezek. 20:48; 21:4–5; and other places.

Arcana Caelestia, which explains the spiritual sense of the two books, Genesis and Exodus, points out the meaning of the man's rib that was made into a woman, the flesh that was closed up in place of it—and thus what "bone of my bones and flesh of my flesh" means—and what the "father and mother" whom the man would leave after marriage means, and what clinging to his wife means. The book points out that "rib" does not mean rib, nor "flesh" flesh, nor "bone" bone, nor "cling" cling. The words designate the things that the objects correspond to spiritually, and therefore stand for.

It is clear that this refers to spiritual things that make one person out of two, because married love joins them together, and that is a spiritual love.

I have often said already that a man's love of wisdom is carried over to his wife, and it will be established more fully in the articles that follow this. At this point it would not do to depart from the stated subject and digress—the subject being the joining together of two married partners into one flesh by the union of their souls and minds.

Here is the way the explanation will be organized:

(1) Each sex has inherent from creation an ability and an inclination so that they can, and want to, join together just as if into one person.

(2) The love in marriage joins two souls, and therefore two minds, into one.

(3) The will of a wife joins itself with a man's intellect, and the man's intellect with the wife's will, on that account.

(4) The inclination to unite is constant and perpetual for a wife but inconstant and variable for a man.

(5) The wife excites conjunction in the man according to her love, and the man receives it according to his wisdom.

(6) This conjunction takes place steadily from the first days of marriage, and among those who have a real married love, it becomes deeper and deeper forever.

(7) A wife's union with her husband's rational wisdom happens from within, but with his moral wisdom it happens from the outside.

(8) For the sake of this union as a goal a wife has perception about her husband's feelings and also great cleverness in molding them.

(9) Wives keep this perception to themselves and hide it from their husbands for reasons that are necessary to stabilize married love, friendship, and confidence—and therefore the happiness of living together and the felicity of their life.

(10) This perception is a wife's wisdom. A man cannot have it, nor can a wife have a man's rational wisdom.

(11) A wife is always thinking from love about a man's inclination toward her, with joining herself to him on her mind. A man is different.

(12) A wife joins herself to a man by involving herself in what he wants.

(13) A wife joins in with her husband by the aura of life that her love gives off.

(14) A wife is joined together with her husband by absorbing the vigor of his manhood, but this happens according to the spiritual love they both have.

(15) In this way a wife accepts an image of her husband in herself, so she sees, perceives, and feels his feelings.

(16) There are activities appropriate to a man and activities appropriate to a wife, and a wife cannot take up the functions that belong to a man, nor a man the functions that belong to a wife, and do them right.

(17) These activities, when done to help each other, also join the two together into one and make a unified home as well.

(18) Depending on the things mentioned above that join them

together, married partners become more and more one
person.

(19) Those who enjoy the real love in marriage can tell that
they are one integrated person and therefore one flesh.

(20) The real love in marriage, viewed in itself, is a union of
souls, minds joined together, a drive to join together in
their breasts leading to a drive to join bodily.

(21) The attributes of this love are innocence, peace, tranquillity,
deep friendship, full confidence, and a desire in heart and
soul to do everything good for each other. And from all
these things come blessedness, happiness, joy, passion, and
from the eternal enjoyment of these, heavenly bliss.

(22) These things are not to be had in any way except in a
marriage of one man with one wife.

Now comes the explanation of all these topics.

157   (1) *Each sex has inherent from creation an ability and an inclination
so that they can, and want to, join together just as if into one person.* It is
already clear from the Book of Genesis that woman was taken
from man (see above). This means that each sex has the ability
and inclination to join together into one, because whatever is taken
from something takes along and keeps the identity it got from
there and makes it its own. This identity is homogeneous with the
other, so it wants to reunite, and when it does reunite it is just like
being in itself when in the other, and vice versa.

The idea that one sex is capable of joining with the other, or
that they can unite, is no problem. Neither is the idea that they
have an inclination to join themselves together. Firsthand experience teaches both things.

158   (2) *The love in marriage joins two souls, and therefore two minds,
into one.* Every person is made up of soul, mind, and body. His
soul is his most inward part, his mind is midway, and his body is
most outward. Because the soul is the most inward part, its source
is heavenly. Because the mind is in the middle, its source is spiritual. Because the body is most outward, its source is material. The
parts with heavenly and spiritual sources are not in a place, but
have something that seems like place. This is also known in the

world, because people say that extent and place do not apply to spiritual things. Since spaces are appearances, distances and presence are appearances, too. In small treatises on the spiritual world I have often stated and demonstrated that the appearances of distances and presence there go according to resemblances, nearness, and relationships of love.

These things have been said to make it known that people's souls and minds are not in a place like their bodies, because, again, their source is heavenly and spiritual. And because they do not occupy space they can be joined together as if into one even when their bodies are not.

This happens especially between married partners who love each other mutually and deeply. But since woman came from man and the joining together is a kind of reunion, you can see from reason that it is not joining together into one but getting together, nearer and closer according to love—to touch, in the case of those who have the real love of marriage. This coming together can be called spiritual living together, which happens for partners who love each other tenderly, whatever their physical distance. There are many practical examples in the natural world, too, to confirm these things.

All this makes it clear that married love joins two souls and minds together into one.

159   (3) *The will of a wife joins itself with a man's intellect, and the man's intellect with the wife's will, on that account.* This is because a man is born to become intellect and a woman to become will that loves the man's intellect. This means that the union in marriage is a union of the wife's will with the man's intellect, and in return a union of the man's intellect with the wife's will. Anyone can see that this union of intellect and will is a very close one, and that it amounts to an association where the one capability can enter into the other and get delight out of the union, and in it.

160   (4) *The inclination to unite is constant and perpetual for a wife but inconstant and variable for a man.* The reason is that love cannot do anything but love, and unite itself in order to be loved in return. This is its whole essence and life. Women are born loves, while the

men they unite themselves with to be loved in return are receivers.

Also, love is always at it. It is like heat, flame, and fire, which go out if their activity is shut off. This is why wives' inclination to unite themselves with men is constant and perpetual.

A man, however, does not have that same inclination toward a wife, because a man is not love but only a receiver of love. His state of receptiveness comes and goes according to worries that get in the way, according to the variations of warmth and lack of it in his mind, for different reasons, and according to the ebb and flow of his body's vigor, which does not come back regularly and at specific times. As a consequence, for men that inclination to join together is inconstant and variable.

161   (5) *The wife excites conjunction in the man according to her love, and the man receives it according to his wisdom.* Men today do not notice that love and therefore conjunction are excited in men by women. In fact, they all deny it. The reason is that wives maintain that only the men love and they themselves receive, or that the men are the love and they themselves are obedience. And it brings joy to their hearts when the men believe this.

There are various reasons why wives insist on this, and all the reasons have to do with the prudence and circumspection of wives. Something about this will be said later, particularly in the chapter about causes of coldness, separation, and divorce among married partners.

The excitement or instigation of love in men comes from wives because men have nothing about them of married love or even love for the other sex, but it resides only in wives and women. I saw living proof of this in the spiritual world. There was once a discussion of these things there, and the men, persuaded by their wives, maintained that they are the ones who love, and not their wives, and that their wives receive love from them. To settle the debate about this mystery, all women, including their wives, were removed from the men, and when they were, the very atmosphere of sexual love went away. With this gone, the men went into a very strange state of mind that they had never felt before. It made many of them complain.

Then, while they were still in that state women were brought to them, and wives to the husbands, and they spoke to the men tenderly. But the men had become cold to their charms. They turned away and said among themselves, "What is this? What is a woman?" And when some of the women said that these were their wives, they answered, "What is a wife? We don't understand you."

But when the wives became hurt, and some cried over this thoroughly frigid indifference on the men's part, the atmosphere of feminine sex and marriage, which was kept away from the men up to that point, came back. Then the men instantly returned to their previous state of mind—those who loved marriage into their previous state, and those who loved sex into theirs.

This convinced the men that nothing of married love nor even of sexual love resides with them, but only with wives and women. But afterwards the wives, in their prudence, still induced the men to believe that love resides with men and that a certain spark of it can come across from them to the women themselves.

This experience is brought in here to make it known that wives are loves and men the receivers.

Men are receptive according to the wisdom they have—particularly this wisdom from religion: that only your wife is to be loved. This is obvious from the fact that when you love only your wife, the love is concentrated. It stays strong, is steady, and lasts, because it is on a high plane. Otherwise it would be like throwing wheat from the barn to the dogs, creating poverty at home.

162   (6) *This conjunction takes place steadily from the first days of marriage, and among those who have a real married love, it becomes deeper and deeper forever.* The first warmth of marriage does not unite, for it comes out of sexual love, which is bodily and in that way spiritual. Anything in your spirit that comes from your body does not last long. But bodily love that comes from your spirit does last. Spiritual love, and bodily love that comes from spiritual, enters the married partners' souls and minds together with friendship and trust. When these two join with the first love of marriage it becomes married love, which opens up their hearts and breathes the sweetness of love into them—more and more deeply as the two join themselves to the first love. It enters them, and they enter it.

163   (7) *A wife's union with her husband's rational wisdom happens from within, but with his moral wisdom it happens from the outside.* Men's wisdom is of two kinds, rational and moral. Their rational wisdom has to do with intellect, while their moral wisdom has to do with intellect and life together. You can infer this and see it by just examining and exploring it. But to make known what "men's rational wisdom" and "men's moral wisdom" means, here are a few specifics.

Things having to do with their rational wisdom go by various names. In general they are called knowledge, intelligence, and wisdom, but in particular, rationality, judgment, character, learning, and keen perception.

Knowledges, however, are many, because they come with the specialties of each person's work, for there is the special knowledge of clergymen, administrators, of their various officials, of judges, of doctors and pharmacists, of soldiers and sailors, of tradesmen and workers, of farmers, and so on. Also belonging to rational wisdom are all the kinds of knowledge that young people learn in schools and that afterwards bring them to competence. They, too, have various names, like philosophy, physics, geometry, mechanics, chemistry, astronomy, jurisprudence, politics, ethics, history, and others. Through these, as through doors, you enter the rationality that rational wisdom comes from.

164   On the other hand, having to do with men's moral wisdom are all the moral virtues that have respect to life and go into it, and also the spiritual virtues that spring from love to the Lord and love for your neighbor and that converge in these loves.

The virtues that have to do with men's moral wisdom also have various names and are called temperance, sobriety, honesty, kindliness, friendliness, modesty, sincerity, courtesy, civility, and also earnestness, industry, alertness, lavish giving, eagerness, liberality, generosity, energy, courage, prudence, and many more.

Spiritual virtues that men have are love of religion, charity, truth, faith, conscience, innocence, and many others.

In general all these different virtues relate to love and zeal for religion, for the public good, for the country, for the populace, for parents, for wife, and for children. Justice and judgment dominate in all of these virtues. Justice is involved in moral wisdom, and judgment in rational wisdom.

165   A wife's connection with her husband's rational wisdom is an inward one. This is because rational wisdom belongs only to men's intellect, and it climbs into a light that women are not in. This is the reason why women do not speak in the terms of rational wisdom but hold their peace and just pay attention in the company of men when things like that are being discussed. Still, it is obvious that wives inwardly participate in these things, because they do pay attention and inwardly recognize and agree with things they hear and have heard from their husbands.

Wives' connection with their husbands' moral wisdom, however, is an outward one. This is because women share most of the virtues of moral wisdom, and the virtues come from the will of a man's intellect, with which a wife's will unites and makes a marriage. I said that the wife's connection with these virtues is from the outside, because a wife knows more about them in a man than the man knows about them in himself.

166   (8) *For the sake of this union as a goal a wife has perception about her husband's feelings and also great cleverness in molding them.* Wives know about their husbands' feelings and cleverly mold them. This, too, is among the secrets about married love that are hidden away inside of wives. They know about the feelings from the three senses of sight, hearing, and touch, and they mold them without their husbands' knowing a thing about it.

Now, these things are among the secrets of wives, so it would not do for me to expose them in detail. But it is appropriate for the wives to do it, so four stories, in which wives reveal these things, follow chapters 7, 9, and 12. Two stories are about the three wives living in the house with the appearance of golden rain falling above it, and two are about the seven wives sitting in the rose garden. If you read these stories you will see the secret uncovered.

167   (9) *Wives keep this perception to themselves and hide it from their husbands for reasons that are necessary to stabilize married love, friendship, and confidence—and therefore the happiness of living together and the felicity of their life.* I said it was necessary for wives to hide and conceal from husbands their perceptions of the husbands' feelings because if they let it out it would alienate the husbands from bed, bedroom, and home. The reason is that most men have a deep

marital coldness for many reasons, which appear in the chapter about the causes of coldness, separation, and divorce among married partners. If wives disclosed the feelings and inclinations of their husbands, this coldness would break from its den and chill the inner parts of their minds first, then their hearts, and from there the most outward parts that have to do with love, which are devoted to reproduction. With these things chilled, married love would be banished so far that no hope of friendship, confidence, the blessings of living together, and its happiness of life would survive. Yet wives are continually nourished by hope of these.

Disclosing that they know their husbands' feelings and amorous inclinations brings with it a declaration and publicizing of their own love, and it is well known that the more wives say about that, the more husbands become cold, and want to get away.

These things show the truth of the statement that there are necessary reasons why wives keep their perception to themselves and hide it from their husbands.

168   (10) *This perception is a wife's wisdom. A man cannot have it, nor can a wife have a man's rational wisdom.* This is due to the difference between masculine and feminine. It is masculine to perceive from intellect and feminine to perceive from love. Besides, intellect perceives things above the body and out of the material world, for that is where rational and spiritual sight goes. But love does not go past what it feels. When it does it draws on the connection with a man's intellect established at creation. For intellect is light, and love is warmth, and things having to do with light are seen, while things having to do with warmth are felt.

All this shows that because of the general difference between masculine and feminine, a man cannot have the wisdom of a wife, nor a wife the wisdom of a man. A woman does not have a man's moral wisdom inasmuch as it draws on his rational wisdom.

169   (11) *A wife is always thinking from love about a man's inclination toward her, with joining herself to him in mind.* This fits in with what was explained above (see no. 160)—that the inclination to unite with a man is steady and lasting for a wife but unsteady and alternating for a man. Consequently, a wife is continually thinking

about her husband's inclination to her, with a view to joining herself with him. To be sure, a wife's thought about her husband is interrupted by her household problems, yet it stays in the feelings of her love, and for women these are not separate from thoughts as they are for men.

But I pass these things on as told to me. See the two stories about the seven wives sitting in the rose garden, which follow one of the chapters (nos. 293–94).

170   (12) *A wife joins herself to a husband by involving herself in what he wants.* These are well known household matters, so I omit an explanation of them.

171   (13) *A wife joins in with her husband by the aura of life that her love gives off.* Out of every person comes, in fact pours, a spiritual atmosphere of the feelings that belong to the person's love. It surrounds the person and puts itself into the natural sphere of the person's body, and these join together.

It is common knowledge that a natural sphere continually flows out from a body—not just from people, but from animals, too. In fact, from trees, fruits, flowers, and also metals. It is the same in the spiritual world, but the spheres flowing out from things there are spiritual ones. And the ones that come from spirits and angels are more deeply spiritual, because they are feelings of love, so they are inner feelings and thoughts. This is the source of every sympathy and antipathy, and also of every union and separation, with the resulting presence and absence, in the spiritual world. For similarity or like-mindedness causes conjunction and presence, while difference and discord cause separation and absence, because those atmospheres make distances there.

Some people also know what those spiritual atmospheres do in the natural world. Married people's inclinations toward each other are from no other source. These spheres unite people who are similar and feel alike but separate those who disagree and have discord. Compatible spheres are happy and pleasant, but discordant spheres are unhappy and unpleasant.

I have heard from angels, who have a clear awareness of these spheres, that there is nothing inside nor on the outside of a person that is not renewing itself—by breaking down and rebuilding—and the continual waves of sphere are from this. They said that this aura wraps around a person in back and in front, but thinner at his back and thicker at his chest, and that the part at his chest associates itself with his breathing. And this is why two partners whose souls are at odds and whose feelings are out of tune lie in bed turned away from each other, back to back. On the other hand, partners whose souls and feelings are in harmony lie turned toward each other.

They also said that because spheres come from every part of a person and extend outward for quite a distance around him, they do not just join and separate two partners outwardly, but inwardly as well. And this is where all the differences and variations of married love come from.

Last they said that the sphere of love coming from a tenderly loving wife in heaven seems like a sweeter fragrance, more remarkably pleasant than the sphere you notice in the world from a newlywed in the first days after the wedding.

These things make the stated truth plain, that a wife is joined to a man through the aura of her life that comes from her love.

172   (14) *A wife is joined together with her husband by absorbing the vigor of his manhood, but this happens according to the spiritual love they both have.* I also have it from the mouths of angels that this is true. They have said that what husbands expend reproductively wives receive all throughout themselves and attach themselves to its life, and in this way wives lead a life that is like-minded with their husbands'—and more and more like-minded. This is what makes an active union of souls and a conjunction of minds.

They said the reason is this—that a husband's soul is in his fertility, and so is his inner mind, which connects with the soul. They added that this was provided from creation so that a wife can take to herself a man's wisdom, which makes his soul, and in this way they become, as the Lord said, one flesh. And it was also provided so that a human male might not leave his wife after conception because of some fantasy.

But they added that wives take on their husbands' lives and

make them their own in relation to married love, because love, which is a spiritual union, joins. And they said that this, too, was provided for many reasons.

173   (15) *In this way a wife accepts an image of her husband in herself, so she sees, perceives, and feels his feelings.* It is evident from reasons given above that wives accept within themselves things that have to do with their husbands' wisdom and are part of their souls and minds, and this is how they change themselves from virgins to wives.

Here are the reasons why this logically follows: (a) Woman was created from man. (b) This implants an inclination to unite, and to reunite, so to speak, with a man. (c) From this union with her counterpart, and on account of it, a woman is the love of a man by birth and becomes more and more his love through marriage, because then love steadily concentrates on joining the man to herself. (d) Attentions to the life's wishes of her one husband join her with him. (e) The couple are joined by their surrounding atmospheres, which unite them wholly and in each part, according to what kind of married love the wives have and also according to what kind of wisdom their husbands have to receive the love. (f) They are also joined by the wives' taking to themselves the husbands' vitality. (g) This makes it clear that something is always being transferred from husband to wife and is etched on her as her own.

As a consequence of all this, a husband's image is formed in a wife. From this image the wife perceives, sees, and feels in herself the things that are in her husband, so it is as if she felt herself in him. She perceives through communicating, sees by watching closely, and feels by touch. The three wives in their home and the seven in the rose garden (in the stories, nos. 155b, 208, 293–94) made it clear to me that a wife feels her husband receiving her love as their hands touch cheeks, arms, hands, and chests.

174   (16) *There are activities appropriate to a man and activities appropriate to a wife, and a wife cannot take up the functions that belong to a man, nor a man the functions that belong to a wife, and do them right.* It is not necessary to illustrate that there are activities appropriate to

a man and activities appropriate to a wife, by listing them, because they are many and varied. Everyone knows how to classify them in order by genera and species if he turns his mind to an inspection of them.

The main activities by which wives unite themselves with husbands are in the rearing of babies of either sex and of girls up to the age when they can marry.

175   A wife cannot take on the activities proper to a man, nor on the other hand a man the activities proper to a wife, because they differ like wisdom and the love of it, or like thought and an affection for it, or like intellect and an inclination toward it. The activities that belong to men particularly have to do with intellect, thought, and wisdom, while the functions that belong to women particularly have to do with will, feeling, and love. A wife performs her duties with these as a starting point, and a man starts from those other abilities. So their activities are different by nature. Still they are interlinked.

Many people think that women can do men's jobs if only they are started in them at an early age, like boys. They can be introduced to the practice of the jobs but not the judgment that the correctness of the work depends on inwardly. On this account, women who have been introduced to men's functions are obliged to consult men in matters of judgment, and then if the decision is up to them they choose from the men's advice what favors their own love.

Some people also say that women are as able as men to raise the sight of their intellect into the areas of light that men participate in and see into things on that same level—an opinion induced on them through writings of certain learned authoresses. But these writings, examined in the spiritual world, with the authoresses present, turn out not to involve judgment and discernment but ingenuity and eloquence. And the products of these two skills seem as if they are lofty and erudite from elegance and polish in the composition of sentences—but only to people who call all cleverness wisdom.

Men cannot undertake the activities that belong to women and do them right, either, because they do not have women's dispositions, which are totally different from men's dispositions. It is because the masculine sex's inclinations and perceptions are so different, from creation and therefore by nature, that this was among the statutes given to the Children of Israel: that a man's clothing must not be on a woman nor a woman's clothing on a man, because this is an abomination. (Deut. 22:5) The reason was that everyone in the spiritual world dresses according to his disposition, and the two different dispositions of woman and man can only be united between two people, and never in one person.

176   (17) *These activities, when done to help each other, also join the two together into one and make a unified home as well.* In some respects a husband's activities join together with a wife's and a wife's attach to her husband's, and these connections and attachments are a mutual help and happen according to mutual help. These are things the world knows. But the main thing that allies the souls and lives of two partners, makes them share, and brings them together, is their mutual concern for educating children. On this ground the husband's activities and the wife's activities are different, and at the same time they fit together. They differ because a wife's particular job is taking care of the breast-feeding and rearing of babies of either sex and also the instruction of girls up to the age of consent and the company of men. But a husband's particular job is seeing to the instruction of boys, after childhood up to puberty, and after that until they are in charge of themselves. Yet these activities mesh through consulting and supporting one another and helping each other in many other ways.

    It is well known that these activities—as united as they are different, or as much in common as they are individual—bring the partners' souls together into one, and that the love called parental love is what makes it happen. It is also well known that these activities, keeping their difference and their cooperation in view, make a united home.

177   (18) *Depending on the things mentioned above that join them together, married partners become more and more one person.* These ideas fit in with the ones under article 6 (see above), explaining

that conjunction takes place steadily from the first days of marriage, and that for those who have real married love conjunction becomes deeper and deeper forever. They make one person as their married love increases. And in heaven the heavenly and spiritual life of the angels makes this love genuine, so two partners there are called two when they are called husband and wife, but one when they are called angels.

178   (19) *Those who enjoy the real love in marriage can tell that they are one integrated person and therefore one flesh.* The truth of this is not going to be verified by any earthly mouth, but by the mouths of angels, because the real love in marriage is not to be found among people on earth today. Besides, people on earth are densely enshrouded in a body that deadens and swallows up the sensation that two partners are a united person and just like one flesh. And furthermore, those in the world who love their partners only outwardly and not inwardly do not want to hear this. They think lasciviously about this union, on account of the flesh.

It is different with angels in heaven, because they have a spiritual and heavenly love in marriage and are not enveloped in such a dense body as people on earth. I have heard people who have lived for centuries with their partners in heaven verify that they feel themselves united that way, husband with wife and wife with husband, and they can tell they are mutually in each other, and vice versa, and just like one flesh, although separate.

They said the cause of this phenomenon, so rare on earth, is that they can sense in their flesh the union of their souls and minds, because your soul not only does things deep within your head, but also deep within your body. The same goes for the mind, which is in between soul and body. It seems to be in your head, yet it is also active in your whole body. They said, "This is why actions that the soul and mind intend spring instantly from the body. And this is why souls and minds, after leaving their bodies in the former world, are complete humans. Now, soul and mind are closely connected with the flesh of the body, so that they participate in and cause the body's actions. Consequently, the union of soul and mind with a partner is felt physically, too, as in one flesh."

When the angels said all that, I heard from some spirits who were standing there that it was angelic wisdom and too lofty. But the spirits were worldly-minded and not spiritual-minded.

179   (20) *The real love in marriage, viewed in itself, is a union of souls, minds joined together, a drive to join together in their breasts leading to a drive to join bodily.* No. 158, above, shows that married love is a union of souls and an interconnection of minds. It is a drive in their breasts to join because the breast is a meeting place, like a royal court, and the body is like a populous city around it. It is like a meeting place because everything from your soul and mind that ends up in your body runs into your breast first. It is like a royal court because the government of everything in your body is there. For your heart and lungs are there. Your heart, through your blood, and your lungs, through respiration, reign throughout. That your body is like a populous city surrounding it, is obvious.

Therefore, when married partners' souls and minds are united and it is a real love of marriage that unites them, the result is that the loving union pours into their breasts and through their breasts into their bodies and causes an effort to join together. And all the more, because married love projects this drive to its outer parts, wanting to complete its happy pleasures. And since the breast is at the crossroads, it is easy to see why married love finds the seat of its delightful sensation there.

180   (21) *The attributes of this love are innocence, peace, tranquillity, deep friendship, full confidence, and a desire in heart and soul to do everything good for each other. And from all these things come blessedness, happiness, joy, passion, and from the eternal enjoyment of these, heavenly bliss.* The reason these things are in married love and therefore come from it is that its source is the marriage of good and truth, and this marriage is from the Lord. The nature of love is that it wants to communicate with another whom it loves from the heart. Indeed, it wants to give the person joy and obtain its own joy from doing that. The Lord's divine love for people is infinitely more so. He made people a vessel for both the love and the wisdom that radiate from Him. And since He made people vessels, he made man to receive wisdom and woman to receive love for the man's wisdom.

For that reason He infused the love of marriage into people

from deep inside them. In this love He could bring together every blessing, happiness, joy, and satisfaction that comes only from Divine Love through His Divine Wisdom together with life. Consequently, these things come together in people who have the real love of marriage, since they are the only receptive ones.

Innocence, peace, tranquillity, deep friendship, full confidence, and a desire in heart and soul to do everything good for each other are mentioned because innocence and peace have to do with your soul, tranquillity has to do with your mind, deep friendship has to do with your breast, full confidence has to do with your heart, and a desire in heart and soul to do everything good for each other involves your body in all of these attributes.

181   (22) *These things are not to be had in any way except in a marriage of one man with one wife.* This is the conclusion from everything that has been said so far. And it will also be the conclusion from everything that will be said from here on. Therefore, a demonstration of this proposition by specific comments is not called for.

182   I add two stories to this. Here is the first:

Some weeks later [see no. 151b] I heard a voice from the sky saying "Come on! There is another meeting on Parnassus! We'll show you the way!"

I went, and when I came close I saw someone on Helicon, announcing and advertising the meeting with a trumpet. And as before, I saw people going up from the city of Athens and its outskirts, with three newcomers from Earth among them. The three were Christians—one a priest, another a politician, and the third a philosopher. On the way, these three entertained the others with much talk, mainly about ancient philosophers, whom they named.

"Will we see them?" they asked.

The others said, "You will, and be introduced if you want to, because they are friendly."

They asked about Demosthenes, Diogenes, and Epicurus.

"Demosthenes is not here, but with Plato," they were told. "Diogenes lives with his students at the foot of Helicon, because he considers worldly matters to be nothing and sets his mind on heavenly things only. Epicurus lives at the border in the west and does not come in to us, because we distinguish between good inclinations and bad, and we say good inclinations are the same thing as wisdom and bad ones are against wisdom."

When they had climbed the hill Parnassus, some attendants brought water from a fountain there in crystal tumblers and said, "This is water from the fountain that the ancient people fabled was broken open by the hoof of Pegasus and was later dedicated to the nine virgins. But to them the winged horse Pegasus meant the comprehension of truth, which wisdom comes from. The hoofs on his feet stood for experiences that lead to worldly comprehension, and the nine virgins stood for all kinds of things one is acquainted with and knows.

"Today these are called myths, but they were correspondences, which was the way the earliest people spoke."

The people accompanying the three newcomers told them, "Don't be surprised. The attendants are taught to talk about this, and for us, drinking water from the fountain stands for being taught about truths, and about varieties of good through truths, and in this way being wise."

After this they went into the Palladium and with them the three newcomers from earth—the priest, the politician, and the philosopher.

Then the laureates who sat at the tables asked, "What's the news from Earth?"

They answered, "This is new. Someone is claiming that he talks with angels and has sight that opens into the spiritual world just the way it opens onto the natural world, and he brings a lot of news from there. Some of the things are that a person lives on as a person after death, just the way he lived before in the world, that he sees, hears, and speaks just as before in the world, that he is clothed and well groomed just as before in the world, that he gets hungry and thirsty, eats and drinks as before in the world, that he enjoys the pleasure of marriage as before in the world, that he sleeps and wakes as before in the world, that there is land there and lakes, mountains and hills, plains and valleys, springs and rivers, gardens and parks. Also that there are palaces and homes and cities and towns, just as in the natural world. And that there are writings and books, and jobs and businesses. And also precious stones, gold, and silver. In a word, he says that each and every thing that exists on earth is there, and the things in heaven are infinitely more perfect. The only difference is that everything in the spiritual world comes from a spiritual source, and therefore is spiritual, because it comes from the sun there, which is pure love.

"And he says that everything in the natural world is from a natural source and therefore is natural and material, because it is from the sun there, which is pure fire. In a word, a person is fully human after death. In fact, more fully human than before in the world. For before, in the world, he was in a material body but in this world he is in a spiritual body."

When all this was said, the ancient sages asked, "What do they think about these things on earth?"

The three said, "We know that they are true because we are here and we have looked into them all and put them to the proof. So we'll tell what people on earth say and think about these things."

Then the priest spoke. "People of our order called them visions when they first heard it, then fictions. Afterwards they said the man was seeing ghosts. Finally they were at a loss and said, 'Believe it if you want to. We have always taught that a person will not have a body after death until the day of the Last Judgment.'"

They asked him, "Aren't there any intelligent people among them, who can show them and convince them of the truth—that a person lives on as a person after death?"

The priest said, "There are some who show them, but they don't convince them. The ones who do point it out say, 'It is against sane reason to believe that a person does not live on as a person until the Last Judgment Day and is a soul without a body in the meantime. What is a soul, and where is it meanwhile? Is it a breath? Or some kind of wind flitting in the air? Or a being hidden in the middle of the earth? Where is its limbo? Have the souls of Adam and Eve, and everyone since them, been flying around in the universe for six thousand years now, or sixty centuries? Or are they kept closed up in the middle of the earth, waiting for the Last Judgment? What could be more anxious and pitiful than such a wait? You might compare their luck to the luck of people bound with chains and hobbled in prison, mightn't you? If this is the fate of a person after death, wouldn't it be better to be born a donkey than a man? Isn't it against reason to believe that a soul can have its body put back on? Isn't the body eaten up by worms, rats, and fish? Can a skeleton of bones burnt by the sun or collapsed into dust be put into this body again? How can these ghastly and putrid things be brought together and united with souls?'

"But when they hear arguments like that they don't answer them with any rational thought. They stick fast to their faith, saying, 'We hold reason under obedience to faith.'

"About gathering everyone from graves on the day of the Last Judgment they say, 'This is a matter of Omnipotence.' And when they speak of Omnipotence and faith, reason is banished. And I can tell you that then sound reason is like nothing, and to some it is like an apparition. In fact, they can say to sound reason, 'You're insane!'"

When the wise Greeks heard all this, they said, "Paradoxes as contradictory as those demolish themselves, don't they! Yet sound reason can't demolish them in the world these days! What can be more paradoxical to believe than what they say about the Last Judgment—that then the universe will perish, and that the stars will fall out of heaven onto the earth, which is smaller than the stars! And that then the bodies of people, whether corpses or mummies of people eaten away, or turned to dust, will be united with their souls! When we were in the world we believed in the immortality of people's souls from reasoning by the evidence that reason afforded us. We also assigned the blessed a place that we called the Elysian Fields. We thought that the blessed were human images or likenesses, but rarefied because they were spiritual."

After saying these things, they turned to the second newcomer, who had been a politician in the world. He admitted that he had not believed in life after death, and he had thought that the news he heard about it was fiction and was made up. "Thinking about it I said, 'How can souls be bodies? Doesn't all of the man lie dead in the grave? Aren't his eyes there? How can he see? Aren't his ears there? How can he hear? Where does he get a mouth to speak with? If something of a person lived after death, could it be anything but some kind of ghost? How can a ghost eat and drink, and how can it enjoy the delight of marriage? Where does it get clothes, a home, a bed, and so forth? And ghosts, which are images in the air, seem to exist and yet they do not.' In the world I thought things like that about the life of people after death. And now that I see all and have touched everything with my own hands I'm persuaded by these very senses that I am a human just as in the world, to the point that I can't tell but what I'm living the way I lived—with the difference that I have sounder reason. Sometimes I'm ashamed of what I used to think."

The philosopher told similar things about himself, but with the difference that he classed the news he had heard about life after death with the opinions and hypotheses that he had gathered from the ancients and the moderns.

The wise men were astonished when they heard these things. The ones of the Socratic school said that from this news from earth they could tell that the inner minds of people had been gradually closed up, and that now in the world faith in falsity shines like truth, and clever nonsense like wisdom.

And they said, "Since our times the light of wisdom has worked its way down from deep in the brain to the mouth, under the nose, where wisdom seems to be the glitter of language to you, so that mouthed words seem like wisdom."

One of the students there, when he heard this, said, "How stupid the minds of people on earth are today. If only the disciples of Heraclitus and Democritus were here, who laugh at everything and weep at everything. We'd hear great laughing and great weeping."

After the meeting ended they gave the three newcomers from earth souvenirs of their district—small copper plates with some hieroglyphics engraved on them—which they went away with.

183   The second story: In the east I saw a grove of palms and laurels placed in spiral curves. I went to it, entered, and walked a few times around on the curved paths, and at the end of the paths I saw a garden, forming the center of the grove. A little bridge separated it, with a gate at the grove end and a gate at the garden end. I approached, and a keeper opened the gates.

"What is the name of the garden?" I asked him.

He said, "Adramandoni," which means married love's delight.

I went in, and there were olive trees, with trailing vines hanging from tree to tree, and flowering shrubs under and among them. In the middle of the garden was a grassy circle, where husbands and wives and young men and women were sitting two by two, and in the middle of the circle, where the ground rose, was a little spring leaping high from the force of its stream.

When I came closer I saw two angels in purple and scarlet talking with the people sitting on the grass. They were talking about the source of married love and its delights. And since the conversation was about that love there was eager attention and complete reception, which put an excitement like the fire of love in the angels' speech.

From the conversation I gathered this, in summary. They started with the difficulty of investigating and finding out the sources of married love, since its source is the Divinity of heaven, for it is Divine Love, Divine Wisdom, and Divine Activity. The three things go out from the Lord as one thing, so they pour into the souls of people as one thing, and through their souls into their minds and into their inner feelings and thoughts there. Through these they go on to people's bodily desires, and from these, through their chests, into the genital region. All the things that came from the original source are together there, and, together with the things that follow, they make married love.

After saying these things, the angels said, "Let's have fellow-ship in our talk, through questions and answers, because something learned only from hearing may sink in, but it doesn't stay unless the listener thinks about it on his own, too, and asks questions."

Then some in the married group said to the angels, "We have heard that the source of married love is the Divinity in heaven, because it comes flowing into people's souls from the Lord. And because it is from the Lord it is love, wisdom, and activity, the three essentials that together make one Divine Essence. And nothing that is not Divine Essence can radiate from Him and flow into a person's inmost part, called his soul. And in working down into the person's body these three are turned into their analogue or their correspondence.

"So now we want to ask, first, what is meant by the third essential that goes out from Divinity—called activity?"

The angels answered, "Love and wisdom without activity are only abstract notions in thought, and, moreover, they drift away like the wind after staying a while in your mind. But in activity the two join together and become one thing, called a reality. Love cannot hold still and do nothing, because love is precisely the action of life. Nor can wisdom exist and be sustained except due to love, and with love when it is doing. And doing is activity. So we define 'activity' as doing good on account of love, through wisdom. Activity is good itself.

"These three, Love, Wisdom, and Activity, flow into people's minds, so that shows where we get the expression that all good is from God. For everything done from love by wisdom is called good, and activity also takes place. What is love without wisdom but some kind of foolishness? And what is love with wisdom without activity but a wind in the mind? Love and wisdom with activity, though, do not just make the person, they also *are* the person. In fact (this may surprise you) they perpetuate the person! For a man's soul is in a perfect human form in his semen, enveloped in substance made of the purest things in nature, which form a body in the mother's womb. This activity is the supreme activity, and the final one, of Divine Love through Divine Wisdom."

Finally the angels said, "The point must be this—that every fertilization, all propagation, and all prolification originate in the stream of love, wisdom, and activity from the Lord. They are from the direct flow from the Lord into people's souls, from the indirect flow into the souls of animals, and from a still less direct flow into what is deep within plants. In all cases this happens on the lowest plane, coming from the highest.

"It is clear that every fertilization, propagation, and prolification is a continuation of creation. For creation can only come from Divine Love, through Divine Wisdom, in Divine Activity. Therefore, everything in the universe is generated and formed from activity, in activity, and for activity."

Afterwards the people sitting on their grassy couch asked the angels where the innumerable and indescribable delights of married love come from.

"They come from the activities of love and wisdom," the angels answered. "You can see this from the fact that a person enjoys the stream and potency of married love to the extent that he loves to have the wisdom of some real activity, and he has the delights to the extent that he has this stream and potency.

"Useful activity does this because when love acts in wisdom, love and wisdom enjoy each other and play almost like children, and they happily join together growing up. It's as if they become engaged, have a wedding, are married, and have children. And this goes on steadily, with variations, forever. This goes on between love and wisdom inwardly during an activity. The joys of this at their sources are unnoticed, but they become more and more evident as they gradually work down from there and enter your body. They go step by step from the soul into the deeper parts of a person's mind and from there to its outer parts and from there into the depths of his heart and from there into his genital region.

"But a person doesn't notice a trace of these heavenly wedding games in his soul, though they do steal into his inner mind in the guise of peace and innocence, and into the outer parts of his mind in the guise of blessedness, happiness, and joy, into the depths of his heart as the joys of inner friendship, and into his genital region—thanks to the steady flow all the way from his soul with its own sensation of married love—as the delight of all delights.

"These wedding games of love and wisdom in action in your soul continue as they go on toward your chest cavity and stay there, and there they stand out perceptibly in an infinite variety of delights. And on account of the chest's marvelous communication with the genital region, the delights there become the delights of married love, which rise above all the delights that there are in heaven and earth. They rise above them because the activity of married love is much higher than all other activities, since it is where the continuation of the human race comes from, and from the human race the angelic heaven."

The angels added to these ideas, "Those who do not enjoy the love—which comes from the Lord—of being wise for the sake of usefulness, know nothing about the innumerable variety of delights that are involved in real married love. For the way to the soul is closed for people who do not love to get wisdom from genuine truths but love to get unsound minds from untruths, and who, because of their unsound minds, do bad acts on account of some love. This makes the heavenly wedding games of love and wisdom in their souls cease, after being more and more interrupted, and along with them the love in marriage, its flow, its potency, and its delights also cease."

To these things the listeners said, "We can see that the love in marriage is according to love, from the Lord, of being wise for the sake of usefulness."

The angels responded, "Just so."

Then garlands of flowers appeared on the heads of some, and they asked why.

"Because they have understood more deeply," the angels said.

Then they all left the garden, and the ones with garlands were in the middle of the group.

Chapter 9

Marriage Changes the Conditions of Men's and Women's Lives

184   The learned and the wise know what "conditions of life" and "changes in them" means, but unlearned and plain people do not, so something should be said about this first.

The condition of a person's life means what his life is like. Every person has two faculties that make up his life, called intellect and will. Therefore, the condition of a person's life is what his life is like in terms of intellect and will. This makes it clear that "changes in the conditions of your life" means changes in what it is like in terms of things having to do with intellect and things having to do with will.

This chapter undertakes to show that every person is continually changed in respect to these two things, but in different ways before marriage and after it. This will be done in this order:

(1) The condition of a person's life is always changing, from infancy to the end of life, and after that to eternity.

(2) The same goes for his inner form—the form of his spirit.

(3) These changes are not the same for men and for women, since by creation men are the image of knowledge, intellect, and wisdom, and women are the image of loving those same things in men.

(4) Men's minds are raised into a higher light and women's are raised into a higher warmth, and a woman feels the pleasure of her warmth in the light of a man.

(5) The conditions of men's and women's lives are different before marriage and after marriage.

(6) After marriage the conditions of the partners' lives are changed and go on according to the ways their minds are joined together through married love.

(7) Also, marriages impose different configurations on the souls and minds of the partners.

(8) A woman really is formed into the wife of a man according to the description in Genesis.

(9) The wife works this transformation in unknown ways, and this is what Genesis means by the woman being created while the man was sleeping.

(10) The wife performs this transformation by joining her disposition with the man's inner disposition.

(11) The purpose is for both of their dispositions to become one, and thus for both of them to be one person.

(12) The wife performs this transformation by making the husband's affections her own.

(13) The wife performs this transformation by accepting the output of the husband's soul with the delight arising from the fact that she wants to be the love of her husband's wisdom.

(14) In this way a virgin is made into a wife and a young man into a husband.

(15) In a marriage of one man with one wife, sharing real married love, the wife becomes more and more a wife and the husband more and more a husband.

(16) And in this way their forms are continually perfected and made more excellent from within.

(17) Children born of two people in real married love receive from their parents a marriage of good and truth. From this they acquire an inclination and an ability—in the case of a son, to perceive things that have to do with wisdom, and in the case of a daughter, to love things that wisdom teaches.

(18) This happens because a child's soul comes out of its father, and its clothing comes from its mother.

Now comes the explanation of these topics.

185   (1) *The condition of a person's life is always changing, from infancy to the end of life, and after that to eternity.* The ordinary states of human life are called babyhood, childhood, adolescence, youth,

and old age. We know that every person whose life goes on in the world gradually passes from one stage to the next, and in this way from the first to the last. The transitions into these states are only noticeable through the spaces of time in between. But reason sees that they go on from moment to moment, thus continually. For it is the same with a person as with a tree, which, from the time its seed is planted in the ground, springs up and grows through every little moment of time—even the smallest. These ongoing moments are also changes in condition, for a following one adds to the one before it something that completes its condition.

The changes that happen within a person are more perfectly continuous than the ones that happen on the outside of him. The reason is that the interiors of a person, which means the things that have to do with his mind or spirit, are on a higher level, raised above his outer life, and among things on the higher level, thousands of things happen in the same moment that it takes for one thing to happen outwardly.

The changes that happen inwardly are changes in the state of your free will as to feelings, and changes in your intellectual state, which are thoughts. The heading refers particularly to the continuous changes of conditions in these two areas. The changes of condition in these two "lives" or faculties are constant in a person from infancy to the end of his life, and afterwards to eternity, because there is no end of knowing, less of understanding, and still less of wisdom. For their extent has infinity and eternity in it from the Infinite and the Eternal whom they come from. This is where the ancient people got the philosophical idea that everything can be divided to infinity—to which should be added that similarly everything can be multiplied to infinity. Angels assert that the Lord perfects them in wisdom to eternity, which is to infinity as well, because eternity is infinity of time.

186   (2) *The same goes for a person's inner form—the form of his spirit.* This is continually changing like the condition of the person's life, because there is nothing without a form, and a condition induces a form. So it is the same thing whether you say the state of a person's life is changed, or his form is changed.

All the feelings and thoughts of a person are in forms and

therefore come from forms, because forms are their embodiments. If feelings and thoughts were not embodied in things that have forms, they could be in skulls emptied of brains, which would be like sight without eyes, hearing without ears, and taste without a tongue. We know that these organs are the embodiments of these senses and are forms.

The condition, and therefore the form, of a person's life is always changing, because a truth that the wise have taught and still teach is that no two things are the same, or absolutely identical—much less many things—just as no two people's faces are alike, much less many people's faces. The same goes for successive events. A following state of life is not the same as the one before it. It springs from this that change in the state of a person's life is perpetual, so change of form is also perpetual—especially the form of his inner dimensions.

But, since these remarks do not teach anything about marriages but just prepare the way for ideas about them, and since they are only intellectual philosophical explorations, which are hard for some people to grasp, they are passed over with these few words.

187   (3) *These changes are not the same for men and for women, since by creation men are the image of knowledge, intellect, and wisdom, and women are the image of loving those same things in men.* It was explained above (see no. 90) that men were created an image of intellect and that women were created an image of loving the intellect of men. It follows that the changes of condition that go on in men and women from infancy to maturity are for making the images complete—intellectual for men and voluntary for women. This makes it evident that the changes are different for men than for women. But in both, the outer form, that of the body, is completed according to the completeness of the inner form, of the mind. For mind acts in body, and not the other way around.

This is why children in heaven grow up to be tall, good-looking people according to the growth of their intelligence—differently than infants on the earth do, who are clothed in a material body, like the animals. But they are alike in that first they grow in inclination toward the kind of things that allure their bodily senses, afterwards, step by step, to the kind that attract their taste for deep truth, and rung by rung to the kind that teach their will to respond.

And at an age midway between immaturity and maturity, an interest in marriage steps in—a virgin's interest in a youth and a youth's interest in a virgin. Virgins in heaven, the same as on earth, hide their inclinations toward marriage with an inborn skill, so that the young men there do not know but what they themselves are turning the virgins toward love. It seems so to them because of masculine arousal. But they receive this, too, from love filtering into them from the fair sex—an inflowing that is specifically discussed in another place.

These things establish the truth of the proposition that men have different changes of condition than women do, since men are by creation images of knowing, understanding, and wisdom, and women images of a love for those things in the men.

188   (4) *Men's minds are raised into a higher light and women's are raised into a higher warmth, and a woman feels the pleasure of her warmth in the light of a man.* The "light" that men are raised into means intelligence and wisdom, because spiritual light, which comes from the sun of the spiritual world, which essentially is love, acts together with intelligence and wisdom. And the warmth that women are raised into means the love of marriage, because spiritual warmth, which comes from that world's sun, is essentially love. And for women it is the love that joins them together with intelligence and wisdom in men—which is called the love of marriage in its entirety and becomes that love through fulfillment.

I spoke of elevation into higher light and warmth because it is elevation into the light and warmth that the angels of the higher heavens are in. And it actually is just like rising up from a cloud into the air, and from the lower level of air to a higher one, and from there into space. So for men, being raised into a higher light is being raised into higher intelligence, and from this into wisdom. And there is such a thing as being raised higher and higher into wisdom. But for women, being raised into a higher warmth is being raised into more chaste and pure married love, always approaching the "marriage" lying hidden deep within them from creation.

Seen for what they are, these risings up are openings of the mind. For the human mind has different levels just as the world has levels of the atmosphere. The lowest is water, the higher is air, higher still is space, and above that is a highest one. The human mind is raised into regions like that as it is opened—in men through wisdom and in women through the real love in marriage.

189 We say that in man's light a woman feels the delight of her warmth, but this means she feels the delights of her love in a man's wisdom, because wisdom is the container, and where love encounters something analogous to itself, that is where it has its joys and delights. But this does not mean that warmth is delighted with its light outside of any forms, but in forms. And spiritual warmth has more delight with spiritual light, because these forms are alive with wisdom and love and therefore receptive.

This can be illustrated to some extent by warmth and light playing, so to speak, in plants. Outside them is just a plain combination of heat and light, but in them it is a kind of play between heat and light, because there they are in forms or containers. For they go through them in marvelous winding paths, and deep inside there they aspire to produce fruit, and their pleasures breathe out onto the air all around, besides. They fill the air with fragrance. And the game of spiritual warmth with spiritual light is still more lively in human forms, where the warmth is the love in marriage and the light is wisdom.

190 (5) *The conditions of men's and women's lives are different before marriage and after marriage.* Before marriage there are two stages for each sex, one before the inclination to marriage and another after it. The changes of these states, and therefore mental developments, steadily progress according to their continual growth. But there is not room to describe these changes here, for they are various and they differ in different people.

Before marriage, inclinations toward marriage are only things imagined in the mind, and they become more and more noticeable in the body. But the conditions of the inclinations after marriage are conditions of joining together and of having children. It is obvious that these circumstances are different from the earlier ones the way accomplishments differ from intentions.

191   (6) *After marriage the conditions of the partners' lives are changed and go on according to the ways their minds are joined together through married love.* After marriage the changes of condition and the way they follow one another, for both man and wife, are according to the married love they have. The changes either join or separate their minds. This is because married love ebbs and flows, but it can also turn off for married partners. It ebbs and flows for those who love each other more inwardly. It is interrupted in them at times, yet inwardly it remains permanent in its warmth. But this love turns off in those partners who only love each other outwardly. For them it is not interrupted from time to time for the same reasons, but by alternate chill and warmth. The reason for this difference is that in these people the body is in the lead, and its enthusiasm spills out and takes over the lower parts of the mind. But in those who love each other inwardly the mind is in the lead and takes over the body.

It seems as if love rises from the body into the soul, because as soon as the body is enticed the enticement goes through your eyes like doors into your mind. This is how it goes through sight as an entrance into your mind and right into your love. But even so it does descend out of your mind and acts in lower things according to their arrangement. So a lascivious mind acts lasciviously, and a chaste mind chastely. The chaste mind arranges the body, and the unchaste mind is arranged by the body.

192   (7) *Also, marriages impose different configurations on the souls and minds of the partners.* In the natural world it goes unnoticed that marriages bring different configurations to souls and minds because souls and minds there are wrapped up in a material body, and the mind rarely shines through this. And also, people of this era, more than in ancient times, learn from infancy to put expressions on their faces that deeply hide their mental feelings. This is the reason why it goes unnoticed what the conditions of the mind before marriage and after marriage are like.

But it is palpably clear from souls and minds in the spiritual world that the forms of souls and minds are different after marriage than they were before it. For then they are spirits and angels, who are nothing other than minds and souls in a human form, stripped of the slough that was made of elements in the water and earth and of vapors from water and earth diffused in the air. Once these are cast off, the forms of minds as they used to be inside their bodies are easy to see, and then it is easy to see that those who live in marriage are one way and those who do not are another.

In general, the married have an inner charm in their faces, for the man receives from his wife the beautiful flush of her love, and the wife receives from her husband the sparkling luster of his wisdom, for two married partners there are united in soul. And more than this, a human completeness appears in both of them.

This is in heaven, because there are no marriages anywhere else. Below heaven, though, there are only civil marriages, which are made and broken.

193   (8) *A woman really is formed into a wife according to the description in Genesis.* In Genesis it says that the woman was created out of the man's rib and that when she was brought to him the man said, "This is bone from my bones and flesh from my flesh, and she shall be called *'ishshah,* woman, because she was taken from *'ish,* man (2:23–24). In the Word the ribs of the chest stand for nothing other than truth on a worldly plane. The ribs that the bear carried in his teeth (Dan. 7:5) stand for this, because bears stand for those who read the Word in its worldly sense, and they see the truth there without understanding it. The chest of a man stands for something essential and particular that is different from what the chest of a woman stands for. This thing is wisdom (see no. 187 above). For truth supports wisdom just as a rib supports the chest. These things have this meaning because all human things are in the chest as in their center.

These observations establish that woman was created from man by the transfer of his own wisdom, which comes from worldly truth. The love for this wisdom was transferred from the man to the woman so it could become married love. And it shows that this was done so there would not be self-love in the man, but love for his wife. She, on account of a natural inborn quality in her, can do nothing but change the self-love in a man into his love for her. And I have heard that this is done by the wife's own love, without the man or wife being conscious of it. This is why no one who has the pride of his own intelligence from self-love can ever love a partner, with a real married love.

Once this unknown fact about woman's being created from man is understood, one can see that similarly a woman is, so to speak, created or formed from a man in marriage, and that this is done by the wife, or rather through the wife by the Lord, who pours into women the inclinations to do this. For the wife receives into herself the image of the man through taking his affections to herself (see no. 183 above) and through joining the man's inner will with hers. More about this follows. She also does this by taking the output of his soul into herself. More about this follows, too.

These things make it clear that a woman is formed into a wife according to the inner meaning of the description in Genesis— by the things she receives from her husband and from his breast, and transfers to herself.

194   (9) *The wife works this transformation in unknown ways, and this is what it means by the woman being created while the man was sleeping.* It says in Genesis that Jehovah God made a heavy sleep fall on Adam, so he fell asleep, and then He took one of his ribs and built it into a woman (2:21–22). The heavy sleep and the man's falling asleep stand for his complete unawareness that a wife is formed and in this sense created from him. This is clear from the presentation in the last chapter and also in this one about the inborn prudence and watchfulness of a wife not to let anything be known about her love, nor about taking the motives of the man's life to herself and in this way transferring his wisdom into herself.

The explanation above (nos. 166ff.) shows that a wife brings this about with her husband unaware and as if sleeping—in other words, by hidden means. In that place it also shows that the skill to bring this about is inherent in women from creation and therefore from their birth, for reasons that are necessary to preserve the love, friendship, and confidence of married love, and thus the happiness of living together and productive life. So for this to be done right the man is told to leave his father and mother and cling to his wife (Gen. 2:24; Matt. 19:4–5). In a spiritual sense, the father and mother whom the man leaves mean his own will and his own intellect. A person's own will is to love himself, and his own intellect is to love his wisdom. And to cling means to give himself over to loving his wife.

(No. 193, above, and other places, show that these two things of his own are fatal ills to the man if they stay in him and that love of them both turns into the love in marriage as the man clings to his wife—i.e., receives her love.)

(There are other passages in the Word that can sufficiently confirm that sleeping means being ignorant and unaware, that father and mother stand for the two things of a person's own— one associated with will and the other with intellect—and that to cling means to give yourself over to loving someone. But this is not the place for the passages.)

195   (10) *The wife performs this transformation by joining her disposition with the man's inner disposition.* A man has rational wisdom and moral wisdom, and a wife unites herself with the things that have to do with moral wisdom in a man (see nos. 163–65 above). Things having to do with rational wisdom form the man's intellect, and those belonging to moral wisdom form his will. A wife unites herself with the ones that make up the man's will. It is the same thing to say that a wife unites herself and to say that she unites her will with the man's will, because a wife is born will and so she does what she does from will.

We say she unites herself with the man's inner will because a man's will resides in his intellect, and a man's intellectual side is the innermost part of a woman (according to what was related about the formation of woman from man in no. 32 above, and other places after that). Men also have an outward will, but this often draws on pretense and dissembling. A wife notices these things and she joins herself with this outer will only in pretense or playfully.

196   (11) *The purpose is for both of their dispositions to become one, and thus for both of them to be one person.* This is because whoever joins himself to someone's will also joins the person's intellect to himself. For, seen as what it is, intellect is nothing but the servant and

attendant of free will. The feeling of love shows clearly that this is true. With a nod it sets the intellect thinking. Every feeling of love is a property of your will, for what someone wants he also loves.

It follows from these things that whoever joins a person's will to himself joins the whole person to himself. This is why it is inherent in a wife's love to unite her husband's will to her will, for in this way a wife becomes her husband's and her husband becomes hers. So both are one person.

197   (12) *The wife performs this transformation by making the husband's affections her own.* This is the same thing as the last two articles above, because affections belong to will. For affections, which are nothing but derivatives of love, form your will, make it up, and compose it. But in men they are in intellect, and in women they are in will.

198   (13) *The wife performs this transformation by accepting the output of the husband's soul with the delight arising from the fact that she wants to be the love of her husband's wisdom.* This coincides with the explanations above (nos. 172–73), so further explanation is passed over.

The pleasures of marriage for women have no other source than that women want to be one with their husbands just as good is one with truth in spiritual marriage. It was specifically demonstrated in a chapter of its own that married love comes down from this marriage. From that you can picture how a wife joins a man to herself the way good joins truth to itself, and how in return a man joins himself to his wife according to the reception of her love in himself just as truth in turn joins itself to good according to the reception of good in itself. And in this way a wife's love takes form by a man's wisdom just as good takes form by truth. For it is indeed the form of good.

It also becomes clear from these things that the pleasures of marriage for a wife are principally from the fact that she wants to be one with a husband—consequently, that she wants to be the love of her husband's wisdom. For then she feels the delights of her warmth in the man's light (as explained in article 4, no. 188).

199   (14) *In this way a virgin is made into a wife and a young man into a husband.* This springs as a consequence from previous things in

this chapter and in the chapter before it about married partners joining into one flesh. A virgin becomes, or is made, a wife because in a wife are things taken out of her husband, and in this way adopted, that were not in her before as a virgin. A young man becomes, or is made into, a husband because in a husband are things taken from his wife that make him more able to receive love and wisdom—things that were not in him before as a young man. But these things are for those who enjoy the real love in marriage. (In the last chapter, no. 178, it showed that the real love in marriage is between those who feel they are an integrated person and just like one flesh.) From these things it is clear that the virginal state changes into a wifely state for women, and the state of young manhood changes into the state of a husband for men.

An experience in the spiritual world convinced me that this is so. Some men said that being together with a woman before marriage was the same as being together with a wife after marriage.

When the wives heard this they were very indignant and said, "There's simply no comparison! It's as different as fantasy and reality!"

To this the men came back, "You're females the same as before, aren't you?"

The wives raised their voice at this and answered, "We aren't 'females,' but wives! You're infatuated and not in real love, so you're talking foolishly."

Then the men said, "If you're not females, you're still women."

They answered, "When we were first married we were women, but now we're *wives*."

200   (15) *In a marriage of one man with one wife, sharing real married love, the wife becomes more and more a wife and the husband more and more a husband.* Real married love joins two more and more into one person (see nos. 178–79 above). And a wife becomes a wife by conjunction with her husband and according to it. The same goes for a husband's conjunction with his wife. And the real love of marriage goes on to eternity. So consequently a wife becomes more and more a wife and a husband more and more a husband. The reason for this is precisely that in a marriage with real married love, both become more and more inwardly human. For that love

opens the deeper parts of their minds, and a person becomes more and more human as these are opened. To become more human, for a wife, is to become more a wife, and for a husband it is to become more a husband.

I have heard from angels that a wife becomes more and more a wife at the rate that her husband becomes more and more a husband but not vice versa. For a chaste wife loves her husband—this is rarely if ever missing—but love from a husband in return does fail. It is missing if his wisdom is not being raised up. Wisdom is the only thing that receives a wife's love. (See nos. 130, 163–65 about this wisdom). But the angels said these things about marriages on earth.

201   (16) *And in this way their forms are continually perfected and made more excellent from within.* The most perfect and highest human form is in two forms that make one form by joining together, which happens when two make one flesh in accordance with creation. Then the man's mind is raised into higher light and the wife's mind into higher warmth, and then they bud, flower, and bear fruit like trees in springtime (see nos. 188–89 above). The next article will show that the perfecting of this form bears noble fruit—spiritual in heaven, natural on earth.

202   (17) *Children born of two people in real married love receive from their parents a marriage of good and truth. From this they acquire an inclination and an ability—in the case of a son, to perceive things that have to do with wisdom, and in the case of a daughter, to love things that wisdom teaches.* It is well known, broadly from reports and specifically from experiments, that children take from their parents tendencies toward the kind of love and life their parents have. But they do not take or inherit the affections themselves and the lifestyles that come from them, only inclinations and capabilities for them. The wise men in the spiritual world (in the two stories about them brought in earlier) demonstrated this.

You can see clearly from the Jewish race, which today is just like their fathers in Egypt, in the desert, in the Land of Canaan, and in the Lord's time, that descendants if not split up also bear a resemblance to their parents in their affections, thought patterns, languages, and lifestyles. And these close resemblances are not just in their minds but also in their faces. Who cannot tell a Jew by his looks?

Other races are the same. It can be concluded from these things, not falsely, that inclinations toward qualities resembling their parents' qualities are inborn.

But the very same thoughts and actions do not persist, due to Divine Providence, so distorted inclinations can be put right. And due to Providence an ability to do this is also implanted, which enables parents and teachers to effectively improve children's behavior and for them to change their own later when they have their own judgment.

203   We say that children get from their parents a marriage of good and truth because every soul is endowed with this from creation. It is the thing that flows into a person from the Lord and makes his human life. This marriage carries through by stages from the soul all the way to the most outward parts of the body. But on the way the person himself changes it in these stages and his body in many ways—sometimes into its opposite, which is called a marriage, or legal relationship, of the bad and the false. When this happens the mind is shut off from below and is sometimes twisted into a sort of backward spiral. But for some it is not closed off but stays half open above—and wide open for some.

From both of these kinds of marriage children get inclinations from their parents—different ones for sons than for daughters.

The reason why this inclination comes from marriage is that the love in marriage is the basic love of all, as demonstrated above (no. 65).

204   There is a reason why children born of people who are in real married love get inclinations and abilities—if a son, to perceive things having to do with wisdom and if a daughter, to love the things that wisdom teaches. The marriage of good and truth has been implanted in every soul from creation, and also in everything that derives from the soul. For we already showed that this marriage fills the universe from top to bottom and from people all the way down to worms. And we already pointed out that an ability is put into each person by creation for the lower parts of the mind to open until they join the highest parts of it, which are in the light

and warmth of heaven. This shows clearly that those who are born from such a marriage, more than others, inherit a readiness and ability to join good to truth and truth to good, or to be wise. Consequently, they also have the ability to absorb things having to do with the church and heaven. In many places above, it was already shown that married love exists in unity with these things.

From these things the purpose for which the Lord the Creator provided marriages of true married love and still provides them is obvious.

205   I have heard from angels that the people who lived in the earliest ages live today in heaven, house by house, family by family, and nation by nation the same as they lived on earth. And hardly anyone from a household is missing. The reason is that they had real married love. Therefore their children inherited inclinations toward the marriage of good and truth, and their parents easily introduced them more and more deeply into this marriage by education. And afterwards, when they developed judgment, the Lord introduced them to it as if on their own.

206   (18) *This happens because a child's soul comes from its father and the soul's clothing from its mother.* No one who is wise questions that the soul is from the father. You can also see this obviously from the souls and also from the faces, which are the images of souls, in the descendants that come from the fathers of families in a direct line. For the father comes back as if in effigy, if not in the children, then in the grandchildren and great-grandchildren. This happens because a soul makes up the most inward part of a person, and this can skip the next offspring but still come out and show itself in later descendants.

The fact that the soul is from the father and its clothing from the mother can be illustrated by analogues in the vegetable kingdom, where the earth or soil is the common mother. She takes seeds into herself as into a womb and clothes them. In fact, she figuratively conceives, carries, gives birth, and rears them, as a mother does her offspring from a father.

207   I'll add to these remarks two stories. This is the first:

At a later time I looked toward the city of Athens, mentioned in earlier stories, and I heard an unusual clamor coming from it. There was an element of laughter in it and in the laughter an element of indignation, and in the indignation an element of grief. Yet that did not make the noises dissonant, but consonant, because one sound was not at the same time as another. They came one after another. In the spiritual world you distinctly notice varieties and mixtures of feelings in sound.

I asked from a distance, "What's the matter?"

They said, "A messenger came from the place where arrivals from the Christian world first show up, saying that he heard from three of them there that in the world they came from, they and others believed that the blessings and happiness after death would be total rest from labors, and that the blessings would be rest from management, duties, and jobs, because these are labors.

"Our messenger has now brought the three here, and they stand waiting outside the gate, so a clamor went up. And on consideration they decided not to bring them into the Palladium on Parnassus as before, but into the great auditorium there, so they can break the news they have from the Christian world. Some people were appointed to introduce them properly."

I was in spirit, and distances for spirits are according to their feelings. I felt like seeing and hearing them, so I found myself present there, and I saw them introduced and heard them speaking.

The elders or wiser ones were seated at the sides of the auditorium, and the rest were in the middle. A raised platform was in front of them. To this the younger men brought the three newcomers, with the messenger, with due ceremony, through the center of the auditorium. And once it quieted down one of the elders there greeted them and asked, "What is new from Earth?"

They said, "Much is new, but please name a subject."

The elder said, "What is new from Earth about our world and heaven?"

They answered, "When we new spirits came into this world we heard that here and in heaven there's management, administration, duties, business, studies in all disciplines, and wonderful craftsmen. And yet we thought that after passing over, or being carried across, from the natural world into this spiritual one we would come into eternal rest from work. And what are duties but work?"

To this the elder said, "By 'eternal rest from work' did you understand eternal leisure, where you would continually sit and lie down, gathering delights in your breast and drinking in pleasures with your mouth?"

To this the three newcomers laughed politely and said that they had supposed something like that.

The answer to that was, "What do pleasures and delights and the happiness from them have to do with inactivity? Idleness collapses your mind—it doesn't open your mind up. In other words, it makes a person dead, not alive. Picture someone sitting in complete idleness, hands hanging down, eyes downcast or staring, and picture him surrounded with pleasures at the time. Wouldn't his head and body both get drowsy, and wouldn't the lively smile on his face droop? And with every fiber relaxed, wouldn't he nod and sway until he fell on the ground? What loosens and tones up all the parts of your body like a focused mind? And where does mental focus come from unless it comes from management and jobs, when they are done from delight?

"So I'll tell you the news from heaven. There's management, administration, higher and lower courts there, and there are also trades and employment."

When the three newcomers heard that there are higher and lower courts in heaven, they said, "Why is that? Isn't everyone in heaven inspired and led by God? Don't they know what's just and right from that? What do the courts do?"

The elder man answered, "In this world we are taught and learn about what is good and true and also what is just and fair, the same as in the natural world. We don't learn this directly from God, but indirectly through others. And every angel, like every person, thinks truth and does good as if by himself. It is mixed and impure according to the angel's condition.

"And also some angels are plain and some are wise, and the wise ones have to judge, when the plain ones, in their simplicity and ignorance, are undecided about what is just, or wander away from it.

"But since you have just come into this world, if you feel like it, follow me into our city, and we'll show you everything."

They left the auditorium, and some of the elders also went with them.

First they went to the great Library, which was divided into smaller libraries according to fields of knowledge. When they saw so many books, the three newcomers were astonished and said, "Are there books in this world, too? Where do you get parchment and paper? Where do you get pens and ink?"

The elders answered this. "We notice that in the former world you thought that this world was empty because it is spiritual. You thought so because you cherished a notion of spirit without matter, and without matter it seemed like nothing to you, thus like a vacuum, when instead everything is complete here. Everything here is *substantial* and not material. Material things come from substantial things. We who are here are spiritual people, because we are substantial, not material. This is why all the things in the natural world are here in their perfection—even books and literature and many other things."

When the three newcomers heard the things called "substantial," they thought it must be so, both because they saw the written books and because they heard the statement that substance is the source of matter.

To further assure them about these things they were taken to where the scribes lived who were making copies of books by the city's wise men. They inspected the writing and were surprised that it was so neat and refined.

After this they were led to museums, schools, and colleges, and to where those people's literary contests were. Some were called games of the Heliconians, others games of the Parnassians, others games of the Athenians, and others games of the Virgins of the Spring. They said that these last were called this because virgins stand for affections having to do with knowing things, and a person has intelligence according to his affection for knowing things. The games called this were spiritual exercises and trials of skill.

Later they were led around in the city to rulers, administrators, and their officers, and by them to wonderful structures that were made in a spiritual way by tradesmen.

After they saw these things the elder spoke with them again about the eternal rest from work that the blessed and happy enter after death, and he said, "Eternal rest is not idleness, because from idleness the mind, and from the mind the whole body, gets weariness, numbness, lethargy, and sleepiness, and these are death, not life, and still less are they the eternal life that angels of heaven live. So eternal rest is rest that dispels those things and makes the person live, and this must be something that lifts your mind. So it is some study and work that excites, enlivens, and pleases your mind. This happens in pursuit of some usefulness that you work for, on, and at. For this reason the entire heaven as the Lord sees it is one continuous activity, and every angel is an angel according to participation. The joy of usefulness carries him the way a following current does a ship, and it puts him in eternal peace and the rest that peace brings. This is what eternal rest from work means.

"The fact that an angel is alive according to how eagerly he applies his mind because he is occupied shows clearly in the fact that everyone has married love with its strength, potency, and joy, according to how he applies himself to his real calling."

Then the three newcomers were convinced that eternal rest is not idleness but the joy of some work that is useful. Some young women came with needlepoint and sewing, their handwork, and gave it to the newcomers. And the young women sang a song with an angelic tune as the new spirits went away. The song expressed the feeling of doing useful things, and its pleasures.

208   The second story: As I was musing about the unknown things having to do with married love that are kept hidden by wives, the golden rain mentioned before appeared again. And I remembered that it fell over a residence in the east, where three married loves lived—in other words three married couples who loved each other tenderly. When I saw that, I hurried there as if invited by the sweetness of my reflections about that love.

As I came nearer the rain changed from golden to purple, then to scarlet, and when I was close, it looked like opaline dew. I knocked, and the door was opened, and I said to the attendant, "Tell the husbands that the one who was here before with an angel is back again and asks if they will let him come in to talk."

The attendant returned and gave me the husbands' consent, and I went in.

The three husbands with their wives were together in the courtyard, and they returned my greeting kindly. I asked the wives if the white dove in the window came back again.

"Just today!" they said, "And it spread its wings, too, so we guessed you would be here asking us to reveal one more secret about the love in marriage."

I asked, "Why do you say 'one' when I came here to learn many?"

They answered, "They're secrets. And some are so far beyond your wisdom that your intellect can't grasp them. You pride yourself over us for your wisdom, but we don't pride ourselves over you for ours. And yet ours goes far beyond yours, because it enters your inclinations and feelings. It sees them, notices them, and feels them. You know absolutely nothing about the inclinations and feelings of your love, and yet they are what your intellect thinks from and follows—so it is due to them and according to them that you are wise.

"And yet wives know them so well in their husbands that they see them in their faces and hear them from the sounds of the speech in their mouths. Yes, indeed. They feel them on their chests, arms, and cheeks. But from a zeal of love for your happiness, and ours at the same time, we pretend that we don't know them. And yet we manage them so skillfully that whatever our husbands like, find pleasing, and want, we comply with, permitting and submitting. We bend them only when they'll bend but we never force them."

"Where do you get this wisdom?" I asked.

They answered, "It's built into us from creation and therefore from birth. Our husbands think it's like instinct, but we say it comes from Divine Providence so that men's wives can provide them happiness. Our husbands have told us that the Lord wants a male human being to act in freedom, following reason. This freedom of theirs, which has to do with inclinations and affections, the Lord Himself modifies from within, and through wives from the outside. And in this way He forms a man and his wife into an angel of heaven. Moreover, if love is forced it changes its essence and does not become this kind of love. But we'll talk more plainly about these things. Our motivation in prudently regulating our husbands' inclinations and affections is this strong so that they'll see themselves as acting freely according to their reason. Here's why. We have delight from their love, and we love nothing more than for them to get delight from our delights. If these delights cheapen for them, they get dull for us."

After they said these things, one of the wives went into a room indoors, came back, and said, "My dove is still fluttering its wings, which is a sign for us to disclose more."

They said, "We've noticed various changes in men's inclinations and feelings, such as that husbands get cold toward their wives when they think wayward thoughts against the Lord and the church, that they get cold when they are proud of their own intelligence, that they get cold when they look at other women lustfully, that they get cold when their wives direct them in love, and other things, and that they get cold in various ways. We notice this in the way their eyes, ears, and bodies react under our scrutiny.

"From these few examples you can see that we know better than the men whether they are all right or not. If they cool off toward their wives they aren't all right, but if they warm up to their wives they're all right. So wives are always thinking up ways to have their husbands warm up to them and not cool off, and they think about this with a perspicacity that men can't see through."

When I had heard these things it sounded as if the dove was mourning, and the wives said, "This is a signal to us that we crave to divulge deeper secrets, which we aren't allowed to do. You might tell men what you've heard."

"I intend to," I answered. "What harm can it do?"

After talking about this among themselves the wives said, "Tell them the secrets if you like. The power of wives to persuade is no secret to us. They'll tell their husbands, 'That man's playing games. They're stories. He's cracking typical male jokes about how things seem. Don't believe him, believe us. We know that you're the lovers and we just obey.'

"So tell about it if you want to. But husbands still won't rely on your mouth, but on the mouths of their wives, which they kiss."

Chapter 10

General Observations About Marriages

209   There are so many things to say about marriages that they would swell this little book into a huge volume if they were told in detail. One could go into detail, you see, about similarity and difference among married partners, about the worldly love in marriage rising into a spiritual love in marriage and about how the two are united, about how the one waxes and the other wanes, about each one's varieties and differences, about the intelligence of wives, about a general atmosphere of marriage coming from heaven and its opposite from hell and how these inflow and are accepted, and many other things. If these things were presented one by one it would expand this book into a big enough document to wear a reader out. For this reason, and to avoid being pointlessly wordy, these things are all brought together into general observations about marriages.

Like the earlier chapters, though, these are broken down into the following articles.

(1) Married love's particular sense is the sense of touch.

(2) The ability to be wise grows in people who have real married love, but for those who do not have married love it shrinks.

(3) For people who have real married love the happiness of living together grows, but for those who do not, it shrinks.

(4) For people who have real married love the unity of their minds grows, and with it friendship, but in those who do not, these shrink.

(5) People who have real married love constantly want to be one person, but those who do not have married love want to be two.

(6) People who have married love focus on the permanence of marriage, but the reverse holds true for those who do not.

(7) Married love resides in chaste wives, but their love still depends on their husbands.

(8) Wives love the bonds of matrimony, provided that the men love them.

(9) In its own right, women's intelligence is modest, tasteful, peaceable, yielding, pliant, and tender, but men's intelligence in its own right is heavy, rough, hard, bold, and liberty loving.

(10) Wives do not experience arousal the way men do, but they have a state of being ready to accept.

(11) Men have sexual potency in proportion to their love of putting forth truths of their wisdom and doing useful things in keeping with their love.

(12) Making love is at the husband's discretion.

(13) There is an aura of marriage that radiates from the Lord, through heaven, into each and every thing in the universe, all the way to the lowest of them.

(14) The female sex receives this aura and passes it on to the male sex, and not the other way around.

(15) Where there is real love in marriage the wife accepts this aura, and the husband accepts it only through his wife.

(16) Where there is love that is not the love of marriage, the wife does accept the aura of marriage, but the husband does not accept it through her.

(17) Real married love can be present in one spouse when it is not present in the other.

(18) There are various similarities and various differences between married partners, inner as well as outer.

(19) The various similarities can unite with each other but not with the differences.

(20) For people who yearn for real married love the Lord provides someone similar, and if someone similar is not available on earth, He provides someone in heaven.

(21) The more a person lacks or rejects married love, the more that person is like an animal.

Now to explain these ideas.

210   (1) *Married love's particular sense is the sense of touch.* Every love has its sense. Love of seeing from a love of understanding has the sense of sight, and its pleasures are symmetry and beauty. Love of hearing due to a love of paying attention and obeying has the sense of hearing, and its pleasures are harmony. Love of recognizing things wafting around in the air, from a love of noticing things, has the sense of smell, and its pleasures are fragrances. Love of nourishing yourself due to love for absorbing good and true things has the sense of taste, and its pleasures are fine foods. Love of knowing objects due to love for exploring and self-protection has the sense of touch, and its pleasures are things that feel good.

The reason why love of joining yourself with a companion out of love for uniting good and truth has the sense of touch is that this sense participates in all the senses, and so it draws tribute from them. It is a well-known fact that this love carries all the senses mentioned above along with it and attaches to itself their pleasures.

We can see that the sense of touch belongs to married love and is intrinsic in it, due to its extraordinary and exquisite intensity whenever it comes into play. But I will leave it to lovers to explain this further.

211   (2) *The ability to be wise grows in people who have real married love, but for those who do not have real married love it shrinks.* The reason the ability to be wise increases for people who have real married love is that married partners have this love on account of, and in keeping with, wisdom, as many demonstrations in earlier passages have shown. Then, too, the sense that belongs to this love is touch, which is common to all the senses and also full of delights, so it opens the inner reaches of the mind as it opens the inner reaches of the senses and with them the organs of the whole body. This means that people involved in this love love nothing more than being perceptive, since people are perceptive to the extent that the more inward reaches of their minds are open. This opening, in fact, lets intellectual thoughts rise into a higher light and voluntary responses rise into a higher warmth. The higher light is wisdom, and the higher warmth is a love for wisdom. The spiritual joys that people with real married love have, united with earthly joys, make for a pleasantness that in turn brings an ability to be wise.

This is why angels have married love in keeping with their wisdom, and it is why this love, with its joy, increases in keeping with the growth of their wisdom. It is also why the spiritual off-spring that are born from their marriages are qualities of wisdom, from the father, and qualities of love, from the mother. Angels love these offspring with a spiritual parental love. This love joins itself to their married love and keeps raising it higher, and it unites the partners.

212   The opposite happens to people who do not have married love because they do not have love of being wise. They enter marriages only for the sake of sex—a purpose that has an inherent love of being foolish. Actually every purpose, in its own right, is a love, and at its spiritual source lasciviousness is folly. Folly means mental derangement due to untruths, and the worst folly is folly due to making truths false to the point where they are thought to be wisdom. In the spiritual world there is clear evidence or proof that people who do this are against married love. They flee into caverns there and shut the doors at the first whiff of married love, and if the doors are opened they rave like the insane people in our world.

213   (3) *For people who have real married love the happiness of living together grows, but for those who do not, it shrinks.* The reason the happiness of living together grows among those who have real married love is that they love each other with every sense. The wife does not see anyone more lovable than the man, and the man likewise. In fact, no one is more lovable to hear, smell, or touch. This is the source of their happiness in living together in house, bedroom, and bed. You husbands can confirm that this is

so from the first joys of marriage, which are at their fullest, because then one loves his wife alone, of all women. We know that people who do not have any married love are the opposite.

214   (4) *For people who have real married love the unity of their minds grows, and with it friendship, but for those who do not, these shrink.* The chapter dealing with marriage joining souls and minds together (this is what the Lord's words mean—that they are no longer two but one flesh) showed that unity of minds grows for those who have real married love (see nos. 156b–181).

The reason the unity grows, however, as friendship unites itself to love, is that friendship is like the face of the love and is also like its clothing, for it not only adds itself to the love like clothing but also unites itself with the love like a face.

The love before friendship is like love for the other sex, which fades after the vows, but love united with friendship lasts after the vows and also becomes more steadfast. It also enters your heart more deeply. Friendship leads it in and makes it real married love, and then that love makes its friendship a married friendship, too. This is very different from the friendship of any other love, for it is complete.

It is well known that the opposite happens in the case of people who do not have real married love. For them the first friendship, which comes during their engagement and then in the first days after their wedding, falls away more and more from the inward levels of their minds and gradually withdraws toward their skin. In people who contemplate separation it goes away altogether, but in those who do not contemplate separation love remains in their extremities but cools inside them.

215   (5) *People who have real married love constantly want to be one person, but those who do not have married love want to be two.* Essentially, married love is nothing but two people wanting to be one. That is, they want two lives to become one life. This wish is their love's constant effort—the wellspring of all its actions.

Investigations by philosophers confirm that effort is precisely the essence of motion, and an intention is a living effort in a person. This is clear, too, to people who think about it with skilled reason. So it follows that people who have real married love always make an effort—in other words want—to be one person.

People who do not have married love are just the opposite, as they well know. They do not grasp what the Lord's words mean—that they are no longer two, but one flesh (Matt. 19:6)—because, due to the separation of their souls and minds, they always think that they are two people.

216   (6) *People who have real married love focus on the permanence of marriage, but the reverse holds true for those who do not.* People who have real married love focus on permanence because eternity is in that love. Its permanence comes from the fact that the love in the wife and the wisdom in the husband grow forever, and during the growth or progress the partners enter deeper and deeper into the blessings of heaven, which have their wisdom and its love stored away in them. So if the notion of permanence were erased or slipped their minds for some reason, it would be as if they were thrown out of heaven.

The following experience gave me a clear view of what the condition of married partners in heaven is like when the idea of permanence slips their minds and in place of it a notion of impermanence slips in.

Once two married partners from heaven were with me by permission, and then some smooth-talking scamp took away their idea of the permanence of marriage. When it was gone they began to wail, saying that they could not live any more and that they felt a distress they never felt before. Their angel friends in heaven noticed this, and the scamp was removed and thrown out. Then the idea of permanence instantly came back to them, which cheered them with heartfelt happiness, and they hugged each other tenderly.

Besides this, I heard two married partners who sometimes cultivated the notion of permanence, sometimes the notion of impermanence. The reason was that inside they were not alike. When they had the idea of permanence they were happy with each other, but when they had the notion that it was temporary, they said, "It isn't a marriage any more."

The wife said, "I'm not a wife any longer but a mistress."

The man said, "I'm not a husband any more but an adulterer."

So when they found out about this inner difference the man left the woman and the woman left the man. Still, they both had the idea of the permanence of marriage, so later they were put together with partners like themselves.

These things clearly show that people who have real married love look for permanence, and that if this slips from the inmost core of their thought they are separated as far as married love goes, although not, at the same time, as far as friendship goes, for this resides on the surface. Married love resides within.

It is the same in marriages on earth. When partners love each other tenderly they think about the permanence of the covenant and do not think at all about death ending it. If they do, they grieve. Still, they are revived by hope at the thought of its continuing after death.

216a   (7) *Married love resides in chaste wives, but their love still depends on their husbands.* The reason is that wives are born loves, so it is built into them to want to be one with their husbands, and they continually nurture their love due to thinking from this wish of theirs. As a result, to back off from the effort to unite themselves with their husbands would be to back off from themselves.

Husbands are different. Since they are not born loves but receivers of the love that comes from wives, the wives' entrance with their love depends on the husbands' accepting it, while to the extent that they do not accept the wives' entrance, the wives with their love stand outside and wait. This happens only in the case of chaste wives, though. It is different with unchaste wives.

These observations establish that the love in marriage resides with wives but that their love depends on their husbands.

217   (8) *Wives love the bonds of matrimony, provided that the men love them.* This follows from the things said in the last article. In addition, due to something inherent, wives want to be wives and to be called wives. They find this title becoming and honorable, so they love the bonds of marriage. Chaste wives do not want to be wives just in name but in actuality—which takes place through closer and closer ties with their husbands—so they love the bonds of

marriage as the foundations of its covenant. This is true the more their husbands love them in return, or the more the men love the bonds, which is the same thing.

218   (9) *In its own right, women's intelligence is modest, tasteful, peaceable, yielding, pliant, and tender, but men's intelligence in its own right is heavy, rough, hard, bold, and liberty loving.* We can readily see that men and women are like that, from their bodies, faces, voices, speech, bearing, and behavior. The body shows that men have hard skin and flesh, but women soft. The face shows that men are sterner, more resolute, rougher, more tawny, and bearded, therefore less beautiful. But women are softer, more yielding, more tender, fairer, and therefore beautiful. The voice shows that men have a low one but women a high one. Speech shows that in men speech is bold and spirited, but in women modest and peaceable. Bearing shows that men's is stronger and firmer but women's is not so strong and less vigorous. Behavior shows that men's is more extreme but women's is more tasteful.

I have seen clearly how much the disposition of men differs from that of women right from birth, from watching boys and girls in groups. I have often seen them through a window in a large city, overlooking a street where twenty or more of them gathered every day. The boys there, following their inborn nature, played together making a commotion, shouting, wrestling, punching and throwing stones at one another. But the girls sat quietly by the doors of the houses, some playing with babies, some dressing dolls, some sewing little pieces of linen, some kissing each other. What surprised me was that they kept looking with pleased expressions at the boys who were behaving that way.

I could see clearly from these things that a man is born intellect and a woman love, and I could see what intellect is like in its early stages and what love is like in its. And in this way I could see what a man's intellect would be like if it developed without joining together with feminine love, and later married love.

219   (10) *Wives do not experience arousal the way men do, but they have a state of being ready to accept.* Clearly, men produce semen, which results in arousal, and women do not have arousal because they do not produce semen. But I report from what I have heard

that women have a state of being ready to accept and therefore to conceive. I am not supposed to describe what this state in women is like, and besides, only they know it. But they have not disclosed whether their love finds pleasure in that state or is unhappy, as some say. Only this is generally known—that it is not permissible for a husband to tell his wife that he is able and not willing, for this markedly hurts the receptive state, which becomes ready in response, when the husband is able.

220   (11) *Men have sexual potency in proportion to their love of putting forth truths of their wisdom and doing useful things in keeping with their love.* This is one of the mysteries known to ancient people and lost today. The ancient people knew that each and every thing that goes on in the body comes from a spiritual source—for example, that actions flow from intent, which is intrinsically spiritual. Speech flows from thought, which is also spiritual, and physical sight, too, from spiritual sight, which is intelligence. Physical hearing is from spiritual hearing, which is intellectual concentration together with the will's acceptance. The physical sense of smell, too, is from the spiritual one, which is perception. And so on.

The ancient people could see that men's production of semen is similarly from a spiritual source. They concluded from many proofs, both of reason and experience, that it comes from truths, which make up intellect. They also said that from the spiritual marriage that is a marriage of good and truth that flows into each and every thing in the universe, males receive only the truth and whatever is related to truth and that this is formed into seed on its way through the body. This is why seeds, taken spiritually, are truths.

As to how seed is formed, they said that since the male soul is intellectual, it is truth, for the intellect is nothing else. So as the soul moves down, so does truth. They said this happens because a soul, which is deep within a person and every animal and is essentially spiritual, follows a descending course from an inherent drive to reproduce itself and an intent to reproduce itself. They said when this is going on, the soul, undiminished, takes form, clothes itself, and makes semen. They also said that this can happen thousands and thousands of times because a soul is spiritual substance, which does not have size but completeness, and the process is not selection of one part of the soul, but emergence of the whole thing, nothing of it being lost. This is why a soul is complete in the tiniest vessels, which are seeds, just as it is in its largest vessel, which is a body.

Since the soul's truth is the source of the seeds, it follows that men's potency depends on their love of bringing forth the truths of their wisdom. Since useful actions are the good things that truths produce, potency also depends on men's love of doing useful things. Some people in this world know that active people, not idle ones, have sexual ability.

I have also asked how a man's soul can generate a female soul. The answer I received was that it is due to intellectual good, because in essence this is truth. For the intellect can grasp that this is good—or that it is true that it is good. Will is different. It does not think good and truth but loves and does them. (No. 120 above shows that for this reason sons in the Word stand for things that are true and daughters for things that are good. *Apocalypse Revealed*, no. 565, shows that seed in the Word stands for truth.)

221   (12) *Making love is at the husband's discretion.* This is because men have the sexual ability mentioned above, and it varies for them according to their state of mind and the condition of their bodies. Intellect is not steady in its thoughts in the way that will is in its feelings. Intellect is sometimes carried up, sometimes down. Sometimes it is in a peaceful and clear state, sometimes in a turbulent and dark one, sometimes involved in pleasant subjects, sometimes in unpleasant ones. Since an active mind is also in a body, the body experiences similar states. This is why a husband draws back from marital love sometimes and sometimes goes after it, and it is why his potency goes away in one state and comes back in the other. These are the reasons why the husband decides when to make love. This is why wives, from the inherent wisdom that they have, never press anything like that.

222   (13) *There is an aura of marriage that radiates from the Lord, through heaven, into each and every thing in the universe, all the way to the lowest parts of it.* It was pointed out above, in its own chapter, that love and

wisdom, or goodness and truth—which are the same thing—radiate from the Lord. These two married qualities continually radiate from the Lord because they are He Himself. Everything comes from Him, and the things that come from Him fill the universe, because otherwise nothing that exists could continue to exist.

There are many spheres that go out from Him, like the sphere of preserving the created universe, the sphere of protecting goodness and truth from evil and untruth, the sphere of reformation and regeneration, the sphere of innocence and peace, the sphere of mercy and grace, and others. Embracing them all is the sphere of marriage, because this is also the sphere of having offspring, and in this way it is the primary sphere of preserving the created universe through generation after generation.

This sphere of marriage fills the universe and reaches throughout it from its beginnings to its ends, as we can see from what was already pointed out—that there are marriages in the heavens, the most perfect in the third or highest heaven, and that besides being among humans this sphere is in all the members of the animal kingdom in the world, even to the worms. Not only that, it is in all the members of the vegetable kingdom, from olive trees and palms all the way to the small grasses.

This sphere is more universal than the sphere of warmth and light that comes from the sun in our world. Reason can be convinced of this by the fact that the sphere of marriage also operates in the absence of the sun's heat, as in winter, and in the absence of its light, as at night, especially among humans. It operates this way because it is from the sun of the angels' heaven, which always gives equal portions of warmth and light—that is, a union of goodness and truth. It is always an atmosphere of spring, you see. The changes in good and truth, or in the heat and light of this sphere of marriage, are not variations in the sphere, like the variations from changes of the sun's heat and light on earth, but instead the changes originate in the recipients of the goodness and truth.

223   (14) *The female sex receives this sphere and passes it on to the male sex.* I have seen it shown by experience (see no. 161 above about this) that the masculine sex has no married love, but that it is only in the feminine sex and comes across to the masculine sex from

there. The following explanation agrees with this. The masculine form is an intellectual form, and the feminine is a form of intent, and an intellectual form cannot become warm with the warmth of marriage by itself but needs the warmth of a union with someone whom it is implanted in by creation. For this reason masculine nature cannot receive the love in marriage except through a volitional feminine nature joined to itself, since this feminine nature is also a form of love.

This same thing could be more fully confirmed from the marriage of goodness and truth, and, for a worldly-minded person, from the marriage of the heart and lungs, since the heart corresponds to love and the lungs to intellect. But since not very many people know about these things, confirming it through them would darken the matter rather than throwing light on it.

It is due to this transfer of the marriage sphere from the feminine sex to the masculine that the mind is aroused just by the thought of the other sex. It follows that the propagating pattern, and thus the arousal pattern, comes from the same source, for if warmth does not join light in the world, nothing flourishes or is stimulated to bear fruit there.

224   (15) *Where there is real love in marriage the wife accepts this aura, and the husband accepts it only through his wife.* It is unknown today that among those who have real married love the husband receives this sphere only through his wife, and yet it is no secret in its own right, because a bridegroom and newlywed can know it. Everything that comes from a bride or a new wife nurtures a love of marriage, does it not? But at that time what comes from others of her sex does not. It is like this with people who are living together in real married love. Besides, since both men and women are surrounded by the sphere of their life—thickly in front and thinly in back—we can see why husbands who love their wives well face their wives and look at them fondly during the day. On the other hand, men who do not love their wives turn away from them and look at them with narrowed eyes during the day.

You can tell real married love by the husband's accepting the sphere of marriage only through his wife, and this distinguishes it from counterfeit, false, or frigid married love.

225   (16) *Where there is love that is not the love of marriage, the wife does accept the aura of marriage, but the husband does not accept it through her.* This sphere of marriage flowing into the universe is Divine in its source, and on its way through heaven among the angels it is heavenly and spiritual. It is worldly among people, animal among animals and birds, merely bodily among worms, and it is without life in plants. Beyond this, it varies in specific creatures according to their makeup.

    Now, since the feminine sex accepts the sphere directly and the masculine sex indirectly, and since they accept it according to their makeup, the sphere, which is holy in its source, can be turned into something unholy in those who receive it. In fact, it can even be turned around into its opposite. This opposite sphere is called meretricious in women of this kind and adulterous in men of this kind, and since these women and men are in hell, that is where the sphere comes from. But this sphere, too, varies widely, so there are many different kinds of it, and a man attracts and chooses the kind that agrees with him, conforms with his natural bent, and suits him.

    We may conclude from this that a man who does not love his wife gets that sphere from some source other than his wife. It can still happen that his wife also inspires the sphere without his knowing it, when he is aroused.

226   (17) *Real married love can be present in one spouse when it is not present in the other.* This is because one might be heartily devoted to chaste marriage, while the other does not know what "chaste" means. One can love things having to do with the church while the other loves only things that have to do with the world. One can be mentally in heaven, the other in hell. The love of marriage can therefore be in one and not the other. Their minds clash inwardly, because they are going in opposite directions. And even if it does not show, still the one who does not have a love of marriage looks on his partner by covenant as a loathsome hag. And so on.

227   (18) *There are various similarities and various differences between married partners, inner as well as outer.* It is well known that there are similarities and differences between married partners, and

that the outward ones show; but the inward ones show to the partners only after a time of living together and to others only by telltale signs. There is no point in listing the recognizable similarities and differences, though, because mentioning and describing their diversity could fill many pages. Some of the similarities can be deduced and inferred from the differences, discussed in the next chapter, that make married love cool off.

Similarities and differences in general have their source in inborn inclinations, varied by education, associates, and mindsets that have been absorbed.

228   (19) *The various similarities can unite with each other but not with the differences.* There are many varieties of similarity, and they can be more or less distant ones. Even remote similarities, though, can in time be united by various means—mainly through accommodations to wishes, shared duties, courtesy, refraining from unchaste things, a common love of babies and care of children, but most of all through conforming in religious matters. Things having to do with religion do join inwardly remote similarities, while other things unite only outwardly distant ones.

Differences, however, cannot be joined together, because they have a mutual aversion.

229   (20) *For people who yearn for real married love the Lord provides someone similar, and if someone similar is not available on earth, He provides someone in heaven.* The reason is that the Lord provides all the marriages based on real married love (nos. 130–31 above show that they are from Him). I have heard angels describe how marriages are provided in heaven, as follows.

The Lord's Divine Providence over marriages and in marriages is most detailed and most universal because all the joys of heaven well up from the joys of married love like sweet waters out of a flowing spring. This is why it is provided that the pairs for married love are born. Under the Lord's watchful eye the two are continually being educated for their marriage, both the boy and the girl unaware of it. Then, when the time comes (she is a marriageable young woman, and he is a young man ready to marry), they meet somewhere as if by fate and see each other. Right away, as if by some instinct they know that they are partners, and as if from some inner voice the young man thinks to himself, "She's mine," and the young woman thinks to herself, "He's mine." After this has sunk into both their minds for a few days they decide to speak to each other, and they become engaged.

The angels said "as if by fate," "instinct," and "inner voice"— even though that means by Divine Providence—because it seems that way while they are unaware. It is actually the Lord who opens their inner similarities for them to see.

230   (21) *The more a person lacks or rejects married love, the more that person is like an animal.* The reason is that people are spiritual in the measure that they have married love, and in the measure that they are spiritual they are human. We are in fact born for a life after death, and we achieve it because a spiritual soul is in us and we can be raised up to spiritual life through our intellectual ability. Then if our will is raised at the same time, thanks to an ability that it, too, has, we live a heavenly life after death.

The reverse happens if our love is opposite to the love in marriage, because in the measure that we are preoccupied with this opposite love we are worldly, and merely worldly people are like animals in their desires, their objectives, and their pleasures. They do have one difference from animals, though. They have the ability to raise their intellect into the light of wisdom and also the ability to raise their will into the warmth of heavenly love. These abilities are not taken away from anyone.

So even though merely worldly people are like animals in their desires, objectives, and pleasures, they still live after death— but in a state in keeping with the life they lived before.

We may conclude, therefore, that people approach the state of an animal in proportion to their rejection of married love. It might look as though these things can be contradicted because there are people who lack or reject the love of marriage, who are still people. But the ones I have in mind are those who make nothing of married love because they love adultery, so that they lack and reject married love.

231   Three stories are added to these remarks. The first is this.

Once I heard outcries that were gurgling up from below as if through water—one to the left, "Oh, how just!" another to the right, "Oh, how learned!" and another behind me, "Oh, how wise!" It occurred to me to wonder if there are also just, learned, and wise people in hell, so I wanted to see if people like that are there, and a voice from the sky told me, "You shall see and you shall hear."

I went out of the house, in spirit, and saw an opening in front of me. I went to it and looked down, and there I saw steps. I went down them. When I was down below I saw flatlands planted full of trees mixed with thorns and nettles.

I asked if this was hell.

They told me, "It's a lower land that is just above hell."

Then I went ahead, following the outcries one at a time, to the first, "Oh, how just!" where I saw a group of people who in the world had been judges influenced by friendship and bribes, then to the second outcry, "Oh, how learned!" where I saw a group of people who in the world had been reasoners, and the third outcry, "Oh, how wise!" where I saw a group of people who in the world had been provers.

I turned back from these to the first group, who were judges influenced by friendship and bribes, and who were pronounced "just." I saw on one side something like an amphitheater built of bricks and roofed with black tiles. I was told that they called it the Judgment Seat. There were three entrances into it on the north side and three on the west side but none on the south and east. This indicated that their decisions had nothing to do with justice but were arbitrary.

In the middle of the amphitheater was a hearth that the hearth attendants were throwing sulfur and pitch torches into. The flickering light from them threw on the plastered walls images of evening and night birds. The hearth and the flashes of light from it in shapes of those images represented their decisions. They could tint the matter of any issue with deceptive coloration and impose on it any form they chose.

After half an hour I saw old and young men in robes and cloaks come in. They took off their caps and sat down on chairs at tables, to sit in judgment. Then I heard and saw how skillfully and ingeniously they bent justice and turned it upside down into an appearance of justice, in consideration of friendship. They did it to the point where they could not see that injustice was any different than justice and they saw justice as injustice. Their belief in things like this showed on their faces and could be heard in their speech.

Then I was given enlightenment from heaven, by which I could tell whether each case was just or unjust, and I saw how purposefully they covered injustice over and gave it the appearance of justice. They selected the favorable laws, and they brought the other people over to their side through skillful reasoning.

After deliberation the sentences were delivered to the clients, who were their friends and patrons, and these went a long way shouting, "Oh, how just! Oh, how just!" to pay back the favor.

After this I spoke about them with angels of heaven and told them something of what I saw and heard. The angels told me that judges like that seem to others to be gifted with incisive intellectual brilliance, when in fact they see nothing at all of what is just and fair. "If you take away friendship for someone, they sit in judgment as mute as statues and just say, 'I assent. I agree with this or that.' The reason is that all their judgments are prejudices, and prejudice dogs the case from beginning to end. So they see nothing but what favors their friend. Everything against him they set aside, and if they do take it up again they wrap it up in reasonings, as the spider wraps her prey in strands, and eat it up. This is why they see nothing of justice unless they follow the web of their prejudice. They've been investigated to see if they can see justice and were found not to. The inhabitants of your world will be surprised that this is so, but tell them this is a truth that angels of heaven found out.

"In heaven we view them as monsters, not people, because they have no vision of justice—monsters with heads made of what has to do with friendships, chests of what has to do with injustice, feet of what has to do with giving proofs, and soles of what has to do with the justice that they push aside and walk on if it doesn't favor a friend. But you're about to see what they look like from heaven, for their end is near."

Then the earth suddenly opened up! Tables tumbled on tables, and the judges were all swallowed up along with the whole amphitheater and thrown into caverns and imprisoned.

Then someone said to me, "Do you want to see them there?"

And I did see them—with faces like polished steel, with bodies from the neck to the waist as if carved from stone and dressed in panther skins, and with feet like snakes. And I saw the law books that they had placed on the tables turned into playing cards. And now in place of judging they were given the job of making red lead into a dye to daub the faces of prostitutes with and turn them into beauties.

After I saw these things I wanted to go to the other two groups—the one where the mere reasoners were and the other, where the mere provers were. And then someone told me, "Take a little rest. You'll be given angels from a community right above them, as companions. Through them you'll get light from the Lord, and you'll see remarkable things."

232   The second story: After a while I again heard from the lower land the voices I had heard before, "Oh, how learned!" and "Oh, how wise!" and I looked around to see if the angels would come then, and there they were! They were from the heaven just above those who were shouting "Oh how learned!"

I spoke with them about the shouting, and they said, "These are the learned who only reason 'Is it?' or 'Is it not?' and rarely think 'It is.' Therefore they are like winds that blow and go away, or like the bark on hollow trees, or like shells on almonds without any kernel, or like rinds on fruits without pulp. You see, their minds are without inner judgment and are connected only with their bodily senses, so if the senses themselves don't judge, they can reach no conclusion. In a word, they're just sense-oriented, and we call them reasoners. We call them reasoners because they never conclude anything but pick up whatever they hear and discuss whether it is, always contradicting. They love nothing more than to attack actual truths and mangle them in this way by putting them in question. These are the ones who consider themselves more learned than everyone else in the world."

When I heard these things I asked the angels to lead me down to them. They took me to a cave with steps that led to the lower land, and we went down and followed the shouts, "Oh, how learned!" What did we see but several hundred people standing in one place and stamping on the ground with their feet.

Surprised at this at first, I asked, "Why do they stand like that, beating the ground with the soles of their feet?" I said, "They could hollow out the ground with their feet!"

The angels smiled at this and said, "They seem to stand still like this because they never think that something is so, but only whether it is so and argue about it. And since the thought gets no further, they seem to tread and wear away one single patch of ground and go nowhere."

Then I went closer to the crowd, and, surprisingly, they looked to me like people with not unpleasant faces, dressed in fine clothes. But the angels said, "They look like that in their own light, but if light from heaven flows in, their faces change, and so do their clothes." This happened, and then they seemed to be burnt dark in their faces and dressed in black sacks. But with this light taken away they appeared as before.

I soon spoke with some of them and said, "I heard a crowd around you shouting, "Oh how learned," so please let me talk with you a little to discuss some matters of highest learning."

They answered, "Say what you please, and we'll satisfy you."

"What would the religion through which a person is saved be like?" I asked.

"We'll divide this question into several questions," they said, "and until we argue them out, we can't give the answer. The first question will be whether religion is anything. The second, whether there is salvation or not. The third, whether one religion does more than another. The fourth, whether heaven and hell exist. The fifth, whether there is eternal life after death. And many more questions."

I asked about the first—whether religion is anything. They began to discuss this with a lot of arguments about whether there is religion and whether the thing *called* religion is anything. I asked them to refer it to the group, and they did. The general response was that the subject required so much inquiry that it could not be finished within the evening.

I asked, "Could you finish it in a year?"

Someone said, "It couldn't be done in a hundred years."

"Meantime," I said, "you're without religion."

He answered, "It must first be shown whether there is religion, mustn't it? And whether the thing called religion is anything.

If it is, it must also be for the wise. If it is not, it must be only for the masses. We know that religion is called a bond. 'But,' you ask, 'a bond for whom?' If only for the masses, it is in itself nothing. If for the wise as well, it exists."

When I heard these things I said, "There's nothing you have less of than learning, because all you can think is whether something exists, and turn it every which way. Who can become learned unless he knows something for certain and goes ahead in that knowledge as a man goes forward step by step and in this way steadily approaches wisdom? Otherwise you don't even touch the facts with your fingernail but put them more and more out of sight. Debating only about whether something exists is like debating about a cap you never put on or a shoe you never wear, isn't it? What can spring from that except that you don't know whether anything exists, whether there is such a thing as salvation or eternal life after death, whether one religion does more good than another, whether heaven and hell exist? You can't think anything about these things as long as you stay stuck in the first step and trample the sand there, without going forwards, putting one foot in front of the other. Be careful that your minds don't harden into statues of salt while you stand like this outside the door of decision. You could be the companions of Lot's wife!"

After saying these words, I went away, and in their resentment they threw stones after me. By then they looked to me like statues of stone, with nothing of human reason in them.

I asked the angels about their fate, and they said, "Their fate is that they are lowered into an abyss and into a wasteland there and are forced to carry burdens, and then they babble and talk nonsense because they can't produce anything from reason. From a distance there they look like donkeys carrying loads."

233   The third story: After this, one of the angels said, "Follow me to the place where they're shouting 'Oh, how wise!'" And he said, "You'll see monstrosities of people. You'll see faces and bodies of people, and yet they aren't people."

"Are they animals, then?" I said.

"They aren't animals," he answered, "but animal people, for they're people who absolutely cannot see whether the truth is true or not, and yet they can make anything true that they want to. We call people like that 'provers'."

We followed the shouting and came to the place. We saw a group of men, and around the group a crowd, and in the crowd some of noble descent. When these heard the provers confirm everything they were saying and heard themselves favored with such open agreement, they turned around and said, "Oh, how wise!"

But the angel said to me, "Let's not go up to them. Let's call one out of the group." We called one, and we went aside with him and talked about various things. He "proved" each thing until it absolutely seemed like the truth.

We asked him if he could also prove just the opposite.

He said, "Just as well as the other things." Then he said, frankly and from his heart, "What is truth? Is there anything true in the nature of things other than what a person makes true? Tell me whatever you like, and I'll make it into the truth."

I said, "Make it true that faith is the sum total of religion."

He did this so cleverly and skillfully that the learned ones standing around were amazed and applauded. Afterwards I asked him to make it true that charity is the sum total of religion, and he did, and then that charity has no place in religion. He dressed up both arguments and adorned them with such imagery that the bystanders looked at each other and said, "Isn't he wise!"

But I said, "Don't you know that living right is charity and believing right is faith? One who lives well believes well, doesn't he? And so faith is a matter of charity and charity of faith, isn't it? Don't you see that this is true?"

He answered, "Let me make it true and I'll see," and he made it true and said, "Now I see." But he promptly made the opposite into the truth, and then he said, "I also see that this is true."

We smiled at this and said, "Aren't they opposites? How can you see two opposite things as true?"

Indignant at this, he answered, "You're wrong. Both are true, because nothing is true but what a person makes true."

Standing nearby was someone who in the world had been an ambassador of the highest rank. He was amazed and said, "I know that there is something like this in the world, but you're still out of your mind. Try making it true that light is darkness and darkness is light."

"I can do this easily," he answered. "What are light and darkness but conditions of the eye? Isn't light changed to darkness when the eye comes out of the sun, and when it stares at the sun? Who doesn't know that then the condition of the eye changes, and that makes the light seem like shadow? But on the other hand, when the eye's original condition returns, the shade seems like light. Doesn't an owl see the dark of night as the light of day and the light of day as the dark of night, and even the sun itself as an opaque, black ball? If some person had eyes like an owl, which would he call light and which darkness? So what is light but a condition of the eye? And if it's a condition of the eye, isn't light darkness and darkness light? So the one thing is true, and the other thing is true."

Afterwards the ambassador asked him to make it true that a raven is white and not black.

He answered, "I can do that easily, too," and said, "Take a needle or a razor and slit the feathers or quills of a raven. Aren't they white inside? Then take off the feathers and quills and look at the raven's skin. Isn't it white? What's the black that surrounds it but a shade, from which the color of the raven is not to be judged? As to black being just a shade, talk to experts in the science of optics, and they'll say so. Or grind black stone or glass to a fine powder, and you'll see that the powder is white."

The ambassador's response was, "Doesn't the raven look black to you?"

The prover answered him, "You're human. Do you want to think anything because of appearances? You can certainly say from the appearance that a raven is black, but you can't think it. As, for example, you can say, going by the appearance, that the sun rises, moves forward, and sets, but being a man you cannot think this, because the sun stands still, and the earth moves. It's the same with the raven. Appearance is appearance. Say what you like, the raven is completely white. Besides, it grows white as it ages. I've seen this."

Next we asked him to say from his heart whether he was joking or whether he believed that nothing is true except what a person makes true, and he answered, "I swear that I believe it."

Then the ambassador asked him if he could make it true that he was out of his mind.

He said, "I can, but I don't want to. Who isn't out of his mind?"

After this the prover of everything was sent to angels who examined what he was like, and after the examination they said that he did not have even one grain of intellect, "because everything above his rational level is closed off, and only what is below his rational level is open. Above the rational level is the light of heaven, but below the rational level is worldly light, and this light is the kind that can confirm whatever you please. If heavenly light doesn't flow into worldly light, a person doesn't see whether something true is true and consequently that something false is false. Seeing these two things is due to heavenly light in worldly light, and heavenly light is from the God of heaven, who is the Lord. So the universal prover is neither man nor animal, but he is an animal man."

I asked the angel about the fate of such people and whether they can be the same as living people, since human life comes from heavenly light, and that is where human intellect is from.

The angel said, "When people like that are alone they can't think anything and talk about it, but they stand silent like machines, just as if in a deep sleep. They wake up, though, as soon as they hear anything that catches their attention. The ones who get like this," he added, "are evil to the core. The light of heaven can't radiate into them from above, but only something spiritual, through the world, which gives them their ability to prove things."

After this I heard a voice from the angels who examined him, saying to me, "Draw a general conclusion from what you heard."

I drew this one. "Being able to prove anything you want is not a matter of intelligence. Being able to see that something true is true and something false is false, and to confirm this, is a sign of intelligence."

After this I looked at the group where the provers were standing, with a group around them shouting, "Oh how wise!" and I saw a dark cloud envelop them. Screech owls and bats were flying in the cloud, and I was told, "The screech owls and bats flying in the dark cloud are corresponding images and are therefore their thoughts objectified. It's because in this world the proving of untruths to the point that they seem like truths is represented in the form of night birds whose eyes are lit by a false light inside, by which they see objects in the dark as though it were light. A spiritual false light like this is characteristic of people who prove untruths until they look just like truths, and afterwards say and believe that they are true. They habitually look at everything from below and nothing from above.

Chapter 11

The Causes of Coldness, Separations, and Divorces in Marriages

234   The causes of separations and divorces relate closely to the causes of coldness in marriages, so these are all dealt with together here. Feelings of coldness arise gradually after marriage, and are the cause of separation, as are matters that come to light after marriage and induce the coldness. But divorces result from adulteries, because adulteries are totally opposite to marriage, and opposites bring coldness into one partner or both. This is why the causes of coldness, separations, and divorces are discussed together in one chapter.

But the close connection of the causes is easier to see when you look at the whole series. Here is their sequence:

(1) There is spiritual heat, and there is spiritual cold. Spiritual heat is love, and spiritual cold is love removed.

(2) In marriages, spiritual coldness is souls not together and minds not connected. This makes for indifference, discord, contempt, loathing, and aversion. In the end, these things lead many to separate from bed, bedroom, and home.

(3) The causes of coldness taken one by one are many—some inner and some outer. Some are "contingent" causes.

(4) The inner causes of coldness depend on religion.

(5) One inner cause is the rejection of religion by both partners.

(6) Another cause is that one partner has religion and the other does not.

(7) A third is that they have two different religions.

(8) A fourth is saturation with religious falsity.

(9) These are causes of inner coldness, but, in many people, not causes of outward coldness as well.

(10) There are also many outward causes of coldness, and one of them is a difference in dispositions and manners.

(11) Another is thinking that the love in marriage is the same as the love in fornication, except that the one is legally permissible, and the other is not permissible.

(12) A third is contention for dominance between the partners.

(13) A fourth is failure to settle on any goal or career, which promotes roving lust.

(14) A fifth is an external difference in class and condition.

(15) There are also several causes of separation.

(16) One is an unhealthy mind.

(17) Another is an unhealthy body.

(18) A third is impotence before marriage.

(19) Adultery is cause for divorce.

(20) There are also many "contingent" causes of coldness, and one is sex being commonplace because it is always allowed.

(21) Another is that living with a married partner under contract and the law seems coerced and not free.

(22) A third is the wife being over assertive and lecturing about love.

(23) A fourth is the man's thinking day and night that his wife is willing, while the wife, on her part, thinks that the man is not.

(24) The body grows just as cold as the mind, and as the mental coldness increases it shuts the body off outwardly.

Now for the explanation.

235   (1) *There is spiritual heat, and there is spiritual cold. Spiritual heat is love, and spiritual cold is love removed.* The one source of spiritual heat is the sun of the spiritual world—for there is a sun there. It radiates from the Lord, who is within it. Being from the Lord, that sun is an expression of pure love. To the angels it looks fiery, just as the sun of our world does to people. It looks fiery because love is spiritual fire. That sun puts out both heat and light, but since it

is pure love, the essence of its heat is love, and the essence of its light is wisdom. This shows where spiritual heat comes from, and that it is love.

Now to explain in a few words where spiritual cold is from. It is from the sun of the natural world and from its heat and light. The sun of the natural world was created to receive spiritual heat and light into its own heat and light and carry these things, through the atmospheres, to every last thing on earth. The purpose was for heat and light to produce results from the intentions that are the Lord's in His sun. Also, heat and light were for clothing spiritual things in the right clothes—materials to make the Lord's intentions work in nature. This happens when spiritual heat joins earthly heat, from within it. But the opposite happens when earthly heat is separated from spiritual heat, as it is with those who love natural things and reject spiritual things. For them spiritual heat becomes cold.

The reason why these two loves become opposites like this, though created to work together, is that in such a case the master heat becomes the servant heat, and vice versa. To prevent this, spiritual heat, which is master by birth, withdraws. Spiritual heat then grows cold for those people, because it becomes the opposite. This shows what spiritual cold is—spiritual heat removed.

In what I am saying, heat means love, because living creatures feel spiritual heat as love. I have heard in the spiritual world that worldly-minded spirits grow intensely cold when they are beside an angel who is in a state of love, and so do spirits of hell when influenced by heat from heaven. Yet, among themselves, with the heat from heaven shut off from them, they burn with great heat.

236   (2) *In marriages, spiritual coldness is souls not together and minds not connected. This makes for indifference, discord, contempt, loathing, and aversion. In the end, these things lead many to separate from bed, bedroom, and home.* There is no need to comment on the well-known fact that this happens to married partners while their first love is passing away and growing cold. The reason is that coldness toward marriage resides in the human mind above all other coldness. Marriage itself is inscribed on the soul, so that soul may beget soul and the soul of a father may be ingrafted in his offspring. So

this coldness begins in the soul and passes down to the subordinate parts, one after another, infecting them, and so it makes sadness and depression out of the joys and delights of first love.

237   (3) *The causes of coldness taken one by one are many—some inner and some outer. Some are "contingent" causes.* The world knows that there are many reasons for coldness in marriages and that it comes from many outward causes. But it is not common knowledge that the causes are from origins deeply hidden within the person, and from there they go into lower parts until they finally appear outwardly. The causes are first separated broadly into inner and outer and then are examined in detail in order to show that the outward causes themselves are not the causes but that they come from the real causes, which, again, are deep within.

238   (4) *The inner causes of coldness depend on religion.* A person's love for marriage originates in his most inner reaches—in other words, in his soul. Just the fact that the child's soul comes from the father's might convince everyone. You can tell, because father and child have similar dispositions and affections, and also features shared with the father that remain even in remote descendants. And souls are created with an inborn ability to propagate. Also, using the vegetable kingdom for an analogy, when a plant germinates it already has, latently, deep within it the propagation of seed and everything that comes from the seed, whether tree, shrub, or bush. This force to propagate or give form, in seeds of the vegetable kingdom and souls of the other kingdom, is from no source but an environment of marriage—or in other words an environment of good and truth—that constantly radiates from the Lord the Creator and Preserver of the universe, and permeates everything (see nos. 222–25 above). In it is the effort of these two—good and truth—to join themselves into one entity. This effort to marry resides in our souls and is the origin of our love in marriage.

The chapter on the marriage of good and truth (nos. 83–102; and elsewhere) has shown very fully that the same marriage that makes this universal environment of good and truth also makes the church among people, so the evidence is there for your reason to see clearly that the source of the church and the source of love in marriage are in the same place and in one continual embrace. But more on this subject appears (no. 130 above) where we showed that a person's love in marriage is aligned with the state of the church in him, so this love comes from religion, which determines what the church in him is like.

Moreover, people are created with the potential to become more and more inwardly human, so they can be led or lifted closer and closer to the marriage of good and truth. This means they can approach the real love in marriage and even find out how happy it is. Religion is the only way to be led or lifted this way, clearly, when you consider the statement just above—that the origin of the church and the origin of love in marriage are in the same place and in mutual embrace there, so they have to be linked together.

239   The point is that where there is no religion there is no married love, and where this love is missing there is coldness. A marriage is cold when it lacks married love (see no. 235 above), so marital coldness also comes when the church or religion is missing. You can tell this is true by the general ignorance, these days, about real married love. Who knows, these days, that religion is the source of married love? Who will acknowledge it? Who is not surprised? This is due to one thing—that although there is religion, there are no truths of religion, and what is religion without truths? (*Apocalypse Revealed* shows fully that there are no truths. Also see the events recorded there, no. 566.)

240   (5) *One inner cause of coldness is the rejection of religion by both partners.* There is no good love in those who toss holy church matters to the back of their minds instead of having them before their faces, or put them behind their backs instead of in their hearts. If they demonstrate any good love bodily, it still is not in their spirits. With people like this the good things outside veil evils like a glittering gold garment covering a putrid corpse. The veiled-over evils inside, generally speaking, are hatreds that cause inner struggles against everything spiritual—for everything that they reject about the church is intrinsically spiritual. The true love in marriage is the most basic of all spiritual loves (see no. 65), so

their inner hatred is clearly against it and their own inner love is for the opposite—which is the love of adultery. So they, more than others, deride the truth that for everyone the love in marriage is aligned with the state of the church in him. In fact, they might even laugh out loud at the mere mention of a real love in marriage. But so be it.

But they must be excused in spite of that, because it is just as hard for them to see the difference between embraces in marriage and embraces in fornication as it is for a camel to squeeze through the eye of a needle. People like this have more extreme coldness toward the love in marriage than others do. If they do cling to their partners it is only for some of the external reasons mentioned above (no. 153a), which restrain and bind them. Their inner dimensions which have to do with the soul and therefore the mind, close off more and more, and are blocked off in the body, so that love for the other sex also degenerates, or becomes insanely lascivious within their bodies and therefore on the lowest plane of thought. If they want, they can read the story in no. 79, which applies to them.

241 (6) *A second cause of coldness is that one has religion and the other does not.* This is because the soul of one is open to receive married love, and the soul of the other is closed to it, so their souls have no alternative but discord. The soul of the one without religion is closed, the other's open. This means that their two souls cannot live with each other, and when married love is banished from the souls, coldness follows—but only for the partner who has no religion. This coldness is dissipated only by accepting a religion compatible with the other partner's religion—providing that this is a true religion. Otherwise a coldness descends on the soul of the partner without religion, working down into his body and all the way out to his skin.

As a final effect of this coldness, the unreligious partner cannot bear to look the other straight in the eye, or speak sharing the same breath except in a reluctant tone of voice, or touch the other person with his hand—hardly with his back—not to mention the insanities from that coldness that creep into his private thoughts.

This is why marriages of that kind are self-dissolving. Besides, an un-pious person has a low opinion of his partner, as everyone knows, and no one without religion is pious.

242   (7) *A third cause of inner coldness is that the partners have two different religions.* Here is why. In this kind of partnership good cannot be linked to the truth that corresponds to it. As we have said, the good of a husband's truth is a wife, and the truth of a wife's good is a husband. So two souls with different religions cannot make one soul. The fountain of that love is closed, which makes them enter a married state on a lower level—a marriage of good with a truth other than its own or of truth with a good other than its own. There is no agreement of love between these. So the coldness begins with the partner who has accepted falsities from his religion, and it builds up as he goes a different direction from the other.

    Once I was going through the streets of a big city, looking for a place to stay. I went into a house where married partners of different religions lived. I did not know this yet, but the angels spoke up and said, "We can't stay with you in this house, because the partners there have religions that don't agree with each other." They could tell this from the lack of togetherness within the people's souls.

243   (8) *A fourth cause of inner coldness is religious falsity.* The reason is that untruth in spiritual matters either takes away religion or defiles it. It takes religion away from people who have genuine truths that are falsified. It defiles the religion of people who do labor under false notions but do not have any genuine truths to be falsified. These people may have some good qualities that the Lord can join those false notions to, in practice, because their false ideas are like so many discordant tones that skillful combinations worked in artfully can make into harmony that is pleasant. Some married love is possible for these people, but it is not possible for people who have falsified in themselves the genuine truths of the church. They are the ones responsible for the prevailing ignorance about the real love in marriage, or the negative attitude about its

being possible. The insanity, settled in many people's minds, that adulteries are not evils of religion, also comes from them.

244   (9) *For many people, the causes of inner coldness mentioned above are not causes of outward coldness as well.* So far, we have been pointing out causes of inward coldness and explaining them. If these produced similar coldness outwardly, it would cause as many separations as there are instances of inner coldness—which are as many as the marriages mentioned above—between people with religious falsities, different religions, and no religion. But it is a well-known fact that many people live together as if they did have love and friendship for each other. The next chapter, on the reasons for apparent love, friendship, and favor between married partners, tells where people with inward coldness find this love and friendship.

    There are many forces that join worldly minds together, but without joining souls, and some are mentioned above (no. 183). But within lies a hidden coldness, so you sometimes observe it and sense it. The feelings of people like this go off in different directions, but when they put their thoughts into words and actions they agree with each other in order to seem friendly and favorable to one another. Therefore they know nothing about the pleasantness and delight of real married love, let alone its happiness and bliss, which for them are little more than myths.

    The story in nos. 103–14, above, is about people like this. On the source of married love, they make things up like the nine companies of the wise, brought together from different kingdoms.

245   A rebuttal to the above demonstration can be made on the grounds that the father's soul *does* reproduce even if it is not in union with the mother's soul—even if a coldness residing there separates them, in fact. The reason why souls or offspring are conceived in spite of this, however, is that the man's intellect is not closed off enough to keep it from rising into the light where his soul is. But the love of his will is not raised into the warmth that corresponds to the light there. Only a life that makes him spiritual instead of worldly can do this. This is why a soul is still conceived. But as it is descending, becoming seed, elements of the

man's worldly love cover it over. This is where hereditary evil springs from.

I add to this something unknown from heaven. Between two disunited souls, especially partners, the union takes place in love on an intermediate level. Otherwise there would be no conception among people.

In addition to what I have said about marital coldness and how its seat is in the highest region of the mind, see the last story in this chapter (no. 270).

246   *(10) There are also many outward causes of coldness, and one of them is a difference in dispositions and manners.* Similarities and differences are internal and external. Inward differences come exclusively from religion, which is rooted in the soul. It comes down from parents to children through their souls as a primary inclination. The soul of every person takes its life from the marriage of good and truth, and the church is from this marriage. Because the church varies and is different in different parts of the world, the souls of all people are varied and different, too. So this is the source of the inner similarities and differences, and the marital combinations we are dealing with follow suit.

But outward similarities and differences do not have to do with soul, but the worldly mind. "Worldly mind" means the outward feelings and the inclinations they produce. These are gradually introduced after birth, mainly by education and being with others, and by the habits this develops. When someone says, "I have a mind to do this or that," it shows his feelings and his leaning toward that thing. Also, this outward mind is usually shaped by the persuasions a person accepts about this or that kind of life. This is where we get inclinations to marry even unequals or refuse to marry our equals. Still, after the partners live together for a while these marriages vary according to the similarities and differences that come from heredity and also education, and differences lead to coldness.

The same goes for differences in manners—for example, in the marriage of a coarse man or woman with a refined woman or man, or a neat man or woman with a sloppy partner, of a quarrelsome man or woman with a peaceable partner—in a word, of a rude man or woman with a well-bred partner. Marriages between different types like these are a bit like the mating of different animal species that do not run together because of their differences—sheep and goats, stags and mules, hens and geese, sparrows and noble birds, even dogs and cats. In the human race, not faces but habits reveal these differences.

So this is the source of coldness.

247   (11) *A second external cause of coldness is thinking that the love in marriage is the same as the love in fornication, except that the one is legally permissible, and the other is not permissible.* Reason can clearly see that coldness comes from this way of thinking when it considers that the love in fornication is the exact opposite of the love in marriage. Therefore, when someone thinks that the love in marriage is the same as the love in fornication, the two loves become alike in his mind, and the person views a wife as a harlot and a marriage as unclean. The man becomes an adulterer in spirit if not in body. What inevitably happens is that this situation produces a flood of contempt, loathing, and aversion—and thus an icy coldness—between the man and his woman, for nothing stores more marital coldness in it than the love of fornication does. This love changes into coldness, so it can virtually be called that very thing—marital coldness.

248   (12) *A third outward cause of coldness is contention for dominance between the partners.* This is because one main object of married love is a union of wills and the freedom this brings. Vying for the upper hand or control throws this right out of the marriage. It divides the intentions, splitting them into sides, and changes freedom of agreement into slavery. While this rivalry lasts, the spirit of the one broods on violence against the other. If you could open their minds and see in with spiritual sight, they would look like fighters with daggers, and you would notice them alternately hate and favor each other—hate in the heat of struggle and favor when hoping for control and full of lust. After one of them wins, the aggressions leave the outward mind and withdraw to the inner mind to hide there restlessly. This leaves the subdued, servant partner, and also the victor or master, cold.

The victor becomes cold because the love of marriage is gone, and its absence is what cold is (no. 235). The heat of victory replaces married love. This heat is totally out of agreement with the warmth of marriage, and yet it may provide concord on the surface through the medium of lust. After an unspoken agreement between the partners it seems as if married love had produced friendship, but the difference between the friendship of marriage and servile friendship in a marriage is like the difference between light and shade, living fire and the illusion of fire. It is like the difference between someone who is fleshed out and someone who is skin and bone.

249 (13) *A fourth outward cause of coldness is failure to settle on any goal or career, which promotes a roving lust.* People are created for useful activity because it is a container for good and truth. Creation and the love in marriage both come from the marriage of good and truth (see the chapter on the origin of married love, nos. 83–102).

"Goal or career" means any work at something useful. Therefore, while a person is at work on some study or business— something useful—it keeps his mind within bounds like a circle, within which his mind gradually is pulled together into a truly human form. His mind can look out, as if from a house, at the different lures out there and use sane reason inside to keep them out. Therefore it also keeps out the bestial follies of lusting for fornication. This is why marital warmth lasts better and longer with men like this than with others.

It is just the opposite with those who give themselves up to laziness and idleness. Their minds are without restraint and dimensions, and a person like that lets all sorts of useless and silly things that are physical and worldly flood his whole mind, and he drifts into loving them. Clearly, that banishes the love of marriage, too, because laziness and idleness make the mind stupid and the body slack. The whole person becomes insensitive to every vital love—especially married love, which life's zest and cheer spring from as from a fountain. Marital coldness, however, is different in these people than in the others. It is indeed a lack of married love, but by default.

250 (14) *A fifth outward cause of coldness is an external difference in class and condition.* There are many inequalities of class and

condition that, as the people live together, erode the married love that started before the wedding. But they can all be categorized as inequalities of age, class, and wealth. No need to prove that unequal ages bring coldness into marriages—like the marriage of a boy with an old woman, or an adolescent girl with a worn-out old man. The same goes for class inequalities, as in the marriage of a prince and a servant, or a highborn lady and a servant. It is clearly the same with wealth, unless the partners have similar dispositions and manners to bring them together and one partner attends to the other's inclinations and natural desires. But in all these cases, if one complies because the other is of a better class or richer, it only joins them by servitude, which is a cold way to be joined. Their marriage is not of the spirit and heart, but only of the mouth and in name. The lower-class one boasts of it, and the higher-class one blushes with shame.

In the heavens, however, there is no inequality of age, rank, or wealth. As to age, all the people there are in the bloom of youth and stay that way forever. As to class, they all regard others according to what useful functions they perform. The more outstanding look on the less eminent people as brothers. They do not think that rank matters more than important duties, but the other way around. And when virgins are given in marriage, they do not know their family tree, because no one there knows who his father was on earth. The Lord is the Father of them all.

It is the same with wealth, there. Wealth there is talents for wisdom, and they have all the wealth they need, in proportion to these.

(No. 229, above, is about how marriages are entered into in heaven.)

251   (15) *There are also several causes of separation.* There is separation from bed and separation from the house. Separation from bed has many causes, and so does separation from the house. Here we are dealing with legitimate causes. The reasons for separation coincide with the reasons for having a mistress, and they have their own chapter in Part 2 of this book, so the reader is referred to that chapter (Chapter 20) to see the reasons in their due order. The legitimate causes of separation are below.

252   (16) *One legitimate cause of separation is an unhealthy mind,*
because the love of marriage is a union of minds. Therefore, if the
mind of one turns away from the mind of the other, the union
dissolves, and love vanishes with it. A list of unhealthy conditions
that separate partners will show what these conditions are. For
the most part they are as follows: mania, frenzy, insanity, actual
foolishness and idiocy, loss of memory, severe hysteria, extreme
simplicity with no perception of what is good and true, great
stubbornness against yielding to what is just and fair, the greatest
pleasure in gabbling and talking of nothing but insignificant and
trivial things, unchecked desire to tell secrets about the home,
also to quarrel, strike blows, take revenge, do evil, steal, lie, deceive,
blaspheme; neglect of children, lack of self-control, self-indulgence,
excessive wastefulness, drunkenness, uncleanness, lack of shame,
practice of magic and witchcraft, impiety, and many others.

When we say legitimate causes of separation here, we mean
legitimate as far as the other partner is concerned, not legally
justified. Separation from the house, in fact, is seldom decreed by
a judge.

253   (17) *Another legitimate cause of separation is an unhealthy body.*
This does not apply to temporary diseases that strike one or the
other partner during marriage, and then go away. It means incur-
able diseases that do not go away. Pathology teaches what they
are. There are many of them, such as diseases that infect the whole
body to a degree that may lead to fatal results by contagion—like
harmful and infectious fevers, leprosy, venereal diseases, gangrene,
cancer, and similar illnesses. Also diseases that weigh the whole
body down so much that they prevent companionship and give
off harmful discharges and noxious vapors either from the surface
of the body or from within it, especially from the stomach and
lungs. On the surface of the body: malignant pox, warts, pimples,
consuming scurvy, infectious itch, especially if the diseases make
the face repulsive. From the stomach: foul, rank, smelly, and crude
belches. From the lungs: smelly, putrid breath exhaled from tumors, ulcers, abscesses, from contaminated blood, or from contaminated fluid in it.

There are also other diseases of various names, in addition, like lipothymy, which is total languidness of the body and lack of vital forces; paralysis, which is a loosening and relaxation of the membranes and ligaments that serve for motion; certain chronic diseases arising from loss of the sinews' elasticity and the ability of the nerves to stretch from an excessive density, viscosity, and acidity of the fluids; epilepsy; permanent illness from stroke; certain wasting diseases that consume the body; obstruction of the bowels; chronic intestinal disease; hernia; and other diseases like these.

254   (18) *A third legitimate cause of separation is impotence before marriage.* This is a cause of separation because marriage's purpose is offspring, which is impossible for the impotent. Knowing this beforehand, they purposely deny their wives this hope that suckles and strengthens their marital love.

255   (19) *Adultery is cause for divorce.* The many reasons for this are rationally clear and yet are hidden today. In the light of reason, marriages are holy and adulteries profane, so marriages and adulteries are exactly opposite to each other. When opposites act on each other, the one destroys the very last spark of life in the other. This happens to the love in marriage when a married man commits adultery intentionally and therefore with a set purpose. Those who know something about heaven and hell can see these reasons in a clearer, rational light. They know that marriages are in heaven and from heaven and that adulteries are in hell and from hell. They know that marriage and adultery cannot join together any more than heaven and hell can. They know that if the two are joined together in a man, heaven instantly departs and hell enters. So this is why adultery is the cause of divorce.

This is why the Lord says, "Whoever puts away his wife except for whoredom and marries another commits adultery" (Matt. 19:9). He says that the man commits adultery if he puts away his wife except for whoredom and takes another, because to "put away" for this reason is a complete separation of minds. This is called divorce. But acts of "putting away" for other reasons are the separations already discussed. If a person takes another wife after separations like these, it is adultery—but after divorce, it is not.

256   (20) *There are also many "contingent" causes of coldness, and one*
is sex being commonplace because it is always allowed. This is a contingent cause of coldness because it happens to people who think
about marriage and a wife lasciviously but not to those who think
of marriage in a holy way and have confidence in a wife. Pleasures
become commonplace and tiresome when overdone, as you can
see from games and theater, concerts, dances, banquets, and similar enjoyments that in themselves are pleasant because they are
refreshing. It is the same with living together and intercourse
between married partners—especially those who have not taken
the unchaste love of the other sex out of their love for each other,
and when they lose their sexual ability they think foolishly that
sex is commonplace because it is continually allowed. It goes
without saying that this is a cause of coldness for such a man. As
a cause it is contingent, because it is in addition to coldness—the
basic cause—and becomes one more reason. Wives have an inborn
prudence, and they can put their husbands off in various ways to
prevent the coldness caused in this way.

However, it is totally different with those who have a chaste
opinion of their wives. For sexual love to be continually allowed
and commonplace is precisely the delight of an angel's soul, and
it is the container of their married love. For they enjoy the pleasure
of that love continually and the ultimate activity of it whenever
the husband's mind is present and free of care—at the pleasure of
his judgment.

257   (21) *Another contingent cause of cold is that living with a married*
partner under contract and the law seems coerced and not free. This
happens only to people whose marital love is cold at the core. It
adds to the inner cold and becomes an accessory or contingent
cause. With people like this, extramarital love smolders inside
because they consent to it and favor it, for the coldness of the one
love is the other love's warmth. This heat may not be felt, but it is
still present, right in the midst of the cold, and if this heat were
not there within the cold, sexual interest would not return. This
smoldering heat is what causes a feeling of coercion, aggravated
to the extent that one partner sees the agreement by contract or

the justice of the law as bonds not to be broken. It is different if both partners loose the bonds.

For those who have detested extramarital love, and who think that the love in marriage is not only heavenly but is heaven, the situation is opposite—and still more for those who perceive that this is so. The covenant with its agreements and the law with its obligations are written on their hearts and are more deeply inscribed all the time. For them the bond of their love is not fixed by the contracted covenant or the legal enactment, but both of these are implanted from creation in the very love that they have. This is where the covenant and the law in the world come from, and not the other way around. So everything about their love feels free.

The only freedom possible is the freedom of love. And I have heard from angels that the freedom of true married love is the ultimate freedom, because that is the love of loves.

258   (22) *A third contingent cause of coldness is the wife being overassertive and lecturing about love.* Among the angels in heaven, wives make no refusal and resistance as some wives on earth do, and angel wives in heaven talk about love instead of keeping quiet as some wives on earth do. I am not allowed to give the causes of these differences because it would not be proper for me to do it. But see the four stories that follow these chapters, where angel wives, who freely disclose the differences to their husbands, tell about them. They are the three wives in a house with a golden shower that I saw over it [nos. 155b, 208], and the seven sitting in a rose garden [nos. 293–94]. These stories are supplied to disclose everything about the love in marriage, which is the subject under consideration both in general and in particular.

259   (23) *A fourth contingent cause of coldness is the man's thinking day and night that his wife is willing, while the wife, on her part, thinks that the man is not.* I pass on without comment on the fact that the one thing makes husbands cold and the other makes wives stop loving. Husbands who study the secrets of married love know that if a man thinks his wife desires or wants him whenever he sees her by day or lies beside her at night, it chills him to his

fingers and toes. And on the other hand, if a wife thinks her husband is able and not willing, she loses her love. This is added to make the book complete and cover the whole subject of the delights of wisdom about love in marriage.

260 (24) *The body grows just as cold as the mind, and as the mental coldness increases it shuts the body off outwardly.* These days people think that a person's mind is in his head and not at all in his body—yet both soul and mind are in both head and body. The soul and the mind are the person. They constitute his spirit, which lives after death, and my books have shown fully that this has a perfect human form. This is why someone can speak something with his physical mouth, and at the same time represent it by a gesture, the instant he thinks of it. And as soon as he wills anything, he can instantly do it and make it happen by the parts of his body. This would not be so if the soul and mind were not together in the body and did not constitute the spiritual person. This shows that when married love is in the mind, its effigy is in the body. And love is warmth, so it opens the outward parts of the body, from within. Conversely, the absence of love, which is coldness, works from inside to close the outward parts of the body.

All this shows why angels have potency forever, and why people do not have it when they are in a state of coldness.

261 I add to this three stories. First:

In the upper northeast quarter, in the spiritual world, are places of instruction—for boys, for youths, for men, and for old men. People who die in infancy and are being brought up in heaven are sent to these places. So are those who have just arrived from the world and want to learn about heaven and hell. This region is in the east so that the Lord's influence can inform every-one—for the Lord is the east, because He is in the sun there, which is pure love from Him. The essence of the sun's warmth is therefore love, and the essence of its light is wisdom. The Lord inspires the people with this love and wisdom from that sun according to what they accept, and they receive according to their love of becoming wise. After a period of instruction, those who have become intelligent are sent out and are called the Lord's disciples. First they go west, and those who do not stay there go to the south, and some go through the south to the east. This introduces them to the communities where they will live.

Once I was thinking about heaven and hell, and I began to want a basic knowledge of what they are both like, because a person with a basic knowledge can grasp the details later. They fit in like parts of the whole. With this desire I looked north toward the place in the east where the instruction goes on, and a path opened, so I followed it that way and went into one of the schools where young men were. I went to the head teachers there and asked if they knew the general facts about heaven and hell.

They said they knew a little bit about them, "But if we look eastward toward the Lord, we'll be enlightened and know."

They did this and said, "There are three basic facts about hell, but they are just the opposite of the facts about heaven. The basic facts of hell are three loves—the love of ruling due to self-love, the love of having what belongs to others due to love of the world, and the love of fornication.

"The basic facts of heaven are the three loves opposite to these—the love of ruling due to a love of being useful, the love of having worldly goods due to a love of putting them to good use, and real married love."

When they said that, I left, saying, "Peace," and went back home. When I got home, a voice from heaven told me, "Examine these three basic facts inside and out, and then we shall see them in your hand." It said "in your hand" because whatever a person surveys with his faculty of understanding appears to the angels written on his hands.

262   After this I examined the first basic love of hell—the love of ruling due to self-love; and then the corresponding love of heaven—the love of ruling due to a love of being useful. I was not allowed to consider the two loves separately, because they are opposites, and the mind does not grasp the one without the other, so you have to contrast them against each other to perceive each one. A nice, beautiful face shines out when compared with an ugly, deformed face.

While examining the love of ruling due to self-love, I could tell that this love is extremely hellish, so those in the deepest hell have it, and the love of ruling due to a love of being useful is extremely heavenly, so those in the highest heaven have it. The love of ruling due to a self-love is the ultimately hellish love because it comes from the person's own self, which is born evil itself, and evil itself is exactly opposite to the Lord. Therefore, the further people go in that evil, the more they deny God and the things of the church that are holy, worshiping themselves and nature. If people with that love will please explore it in themselves, they will see. Also, it is the kind of love that rushes on, rung by rung, all the way to the top if it goes unbridled and does not meet an impassable barrier. And it is not restrained there, but laments and grieves if there is no higher step.

Among politicians this love mounts up until they want to be kings and emperors, and they would like to control everything in the world and be called kings of kings and emperors of emperors. But among clergymen the same love mounts so high that they even want to be gods and if possible rule everything in heaven and be called gods of gods. What comes next will show that neither the clergymen nor the politicians admit in their hearts that there is any God.

Those, on the other hand, who want to rule due to a love of doing useful things do not want to rule on their own account, but for the Lord—for the love of usefulness is from the Lord and is the Lord Himself. They think dignities are just ways to be useful, which they think is far more important than the dignities. The others think status is far more important than doing useful things.

263   While I was thinking about these things, an angel from the Lord said, "You are going to see how hellish this love is and be convinced, right now!"

Suddenly, to my left, the earth opened, and I saw a devil coming up out of hell. He had a square cap, pressed down on his forehead clear to his eyes. His face was full of pimples as if he had a burning fever, his eyes were ferocious, and his chest swelled up like a top. He belched smoke out of his mouth like a furnace. His sides were all on fire. In place of feet were bony ankles without flesh, and his body gave off a stinking, unclean heat.

I was terrified at the sight of him, and shouted, "Don't come near! Tell me where you're from."

"I am from the lower regions," he answered hoarsely. "I belong to a group of two hundred, and of all societies we are the greatest. All of us are emperors over emperors, kings of kings, dukes among dukes, and princes among princes. No one there is a mere emperor, king, duke, or prince. We sit upon thrones over thrones and send orders from there to the whole world and beyond."

I said, "Don't you see you're insane, with this fantasy of being the greatest?"

"How can you talk that way?" he answered. "We can see we're just what I said, and our comrades admit it."

I didn't want to tell him "You're insane" again, when I heard this, because he really was insane with his fantasy. And I found out that this devil was only a manager in someone else's household when he lived in the world, and he acquired such an inflated ego that he despised the whole human race compared to himself and indulged in the fantasy that he was worthier than a king or even an emperor. It led him to deny God and consider all the holy things of the church of no account to him but only to the stupid masses.

"About you and your two hundred," I finally said—"how long will you glory among yourselves there?"

"To eternity," he said. "Except that the ones who torment others for denying that they are the greatest sink down. We can glorify ourselves, but we're not allowed to harm others."

Then I said, "Do you know what happens to the ones who sink down?"

"They sink into a kind of prison where they are called viler than the vile, or most vile," he said, "and they work."

Then I told this devil, "Be careful. Don't sink down yourself."

264 After this the earth opened again, but to my right, and I saw another devil rising up. On his head was what looked like a tiara wrapped in the coils of something like a serpent, whose head rose up from the top of it. His face was leprous from his forehead to his chin, and so were both hands. His waist was naked and black as soot, and something like a hearth fire dimly glowed through. His ankles were like two vipers. The other devil saw him, and fell on his knees and adored him.

"What are you doing that for?" I asked.

"He is the God of heaven and earth," he answered, "and is omnipotent."

I asked the other one, "What do you say to that?"

He said, "What should I say? I have all power over heaven and hell. The fate of all souls is in my hand."

I asked again, "How can someone who is emperor of emperors submit himself like this, and how can you receive his adoration?"

"He is my servant anyway," he said. "What is an emperor before God? In my right hand is the thunderbolt of excommunication."

So I said, "How can you be so insane? In the world you were a minor clergyman, and you labored under the fantasy that you also had the keys, with their power to bind and loose. So you raised your spirit to the height of insanity where you think now that you're God Himself."

This made him angry. He swore he was God and that "the Lord has no power in heaven, because He has transferred it all to us. We need only command, and heaven and hell reverently obey. If we send anyone to hell, the devils immediately receive him. So do the angels if we send anyone to heaven."

I asked further, "How many are in your group?"

"Three hundred. And all of us are gods," he said, "but I am the god of gods."

Then the earth opened under their feet, and each sank down into his hell. I could see that there were workhouses under their hells, and the ones that harm others sink down into them. Everyone in hell can have his own fantasy and glory in it, but he is not allowed to harm anyone else.

They are the way they are down there, because they are in a spiritual state, and after the spirit separates from the body one gains full freedom to act according to his feelings and the thoughts that come from them.

Afterwards I had a look into their hells. The hell where the devils were "emperors of emperors and kings of kings" was full of filthiness. They looked like various wild beasts with ferocious eyes. Similarly in the other hell where they are gods and gods of gods. In this hell dreadful birds of night called *ochim* and *ijim* appeared flying around them. This is how the images of their fantasies looked to me.

These experiences showed me what political self-love and ecclesiastical self-love are like. One is the wish to be emperors, and the other is the wish to be gods. People do wish for this and try to attain it, so far as these loves go unchecked.

265   Then a hell opened where I saw two people, one sitting on a bench with his feet in a basket of snakes. They seemed to creep up over his chest to his neck. The other sat on a blazing donkey, and at the animal's sides red snakes crawled along, following the rider with their necks and heads lifted up. I learned that these were popes who had taken dominions away from emperors, had defamed them and had treated them badly at Rome, where they came to supplicate and adore them. The baskets of snakes and the blazing donkey with serpents at its sides depicted their love of ruling due to self-love. But I found out that things like this appear only to those who look at them from a distance. There were several clerics there, and I asked them if these were those same popes. They said they knew they were. They had been acquainted with them.

266   After I had seen these sad and dreadful things, I looked around and saw two angels standing not far from me and chatting. One had a woolen toga of bright, glowing purple, with a tunic of shining linen under it. The other had similar clothing of scarlet, and a tiara set with a number of rubies on the right side of it.

I approached them, said, "Peace," and asked respectfully, "What are you doing down here?"

"The Lord sent us here from heaven by command, to speak with you about the good life people have who want to rule because they love to do useful things," they answered. "We're worshipers of the Lord. I'm the prince of a community. This is the high priest there."

The prince said he was a servant of his community because he served it by being of use to it. The other said he was the minister of the church there, because in their services he administered the holy services for the use of their souls. Both said they have perpetual joy. Eternal happiness is in them from the Lord.

And they said that everything in that community is bright with gold and precious stones and magnificent with palaces and gardens. "This is because our love of ruling isn't from self-love, but from loving to be useful. Loving to be useful is from the Lord, so all useful activities in the heavens are bright and shining. Everyone in our community has this love, so the light there, coming from the fiery glow of the sun, gives the atmosphere a golden appearance. The fiery glow of the sun corresponds to that love."

At these words I saw an aura like that light around them and noticed an aroma from it. I told them so and asked them to add something more to what they had said about the love of being useful.

They went on to say, "We certainly did seek the status that we have, but only to perform useful functions more fully and spread them more widely. Also, we are surrounded with honor and accept it—but for the good of the society and not on our own account. For our brothers and associates among the common people there hardly know that the honors due to our status are not in us and that the usefulness of what we do is not from ourselves. But we don't feel that way. We feel that the honors of our status are outside us and in fact are like clothing that covers us. But we think the useful things we do are from the love for them that is in us from the Lord, and the blessedness of this love comes from communication with others through useful occupations.

"And we know by experience that so far as we are useful for the love of it, the love increases, and as it does, so does the wisdom that brings the communication about. But the blessedness dies away to the extent that we keep our functions to ourselves and do not communicate them. Then the things we do become like food hidden away in your stomach, which does not spread out to nourish your body and its parts, but goes undigested and causes nausea.

"In a word, all heaven is nothing but a vessel for useful activities, from beginning to end. And what are useful activities but love of your neighbor put into action? And what holds the heavens together except this love?"

I listened to this and asked, "How can anyone know whether he does useful things out of self-love or for the love of the useful things? Every man—good or evil—does useful things, and does them from some love. Suppose that there were a community all of devils in the world and another community only of angels. I think the devils in their community, from the fire of self-love and the glow of their own glory, would do as many useful things as the angels in theirs. So who can know where the useful acts originate, and what love they come from?"

The two angels answered, "Devils do useful things for the sake of themselves and for the sake of fame—to be promoted to honors or became rich. Angels do not do useful things for these reasons, but for the sake of being useful and for the love of it. A person cannot tell the difference, but the Lord can. Everyone who believes in the Lord and avoids evils because they are sins does useful acts from the Lord. But everyone who does not believe in the Lord and does not avoid evils for the reason that they are sins does useful things from himself and for the sake of himself. This is the difference between the useful things that devils do and the ones that angels do."

After the two angels said this, they went away, and in the distance it looked as if a chariot of fire carried them up into their heaven, like Elijah.

267   The second story: After quite a while I went into a certain grove and was walking around, thinking about people who have a lust that gives them a fantasy of having everything in the world, and at a distance I saw two angels talking together and looking at me from time to time. So I went toward them, and as I approached they said, "We have a feeling you're thinking about what we were saying, or else we're talking about what you're thinking about. Affections can do this by communicating back and forth."

So I asked them what they were talking about. They said they were talking about fantasy, lust, intelligence, and just now about people who like to envision and imagine owning everything in the world. Then I asked them to tell what they thought about those three things—lust, fantasy, and intelligence.

They started talking and said, "Everyone is born greedy for things, inwardly, but has outward intelligence from education. And no one is inwardly intelligent, still less wise—in his spirit— except from the Lord. For everyone is kept from lusting for evil to the extent that he pays attention to the Lord and also keeps united with Him. Without this, a person is nothing but lust. Yet outwardly, as to his body, he has intelligence due to education. For people lust for honors and riches, or status and wealth, but you do not get these unless you seem moral and spiritual and therefore intelligent and wise, so people learn to appear like that from infancy. This is why a person turns his spirit upside-down and recovers it from selfishness as soon as he gets among people or in company, and speaks and acts according to an idea of proper behavior and integrity, which he has learned from infancy and keeps in his bodily memory. He is very careful not to let any of the insane selfishness in his spirit show. So everyone who is not inwardly led by the Lord is a dissembler, a deceiver, a hypocrite, and therefore a person in appearance, yet not human. You could say that his shell or body is wise, and his kernel or spirit is insane, and that his outside is human and his inside bestial. People like this turn the backs of their heads upward and the fronts downward, so they walk as if they are depressed, with their heads hanging down and their faces turned to the earth. When they shed their bodies, become spirits, and are set free, they turn into the insanity of their own greedy wants. For people who are preoccupied with self-love have a burning desire to rule the universe and even to extend the limits of it to increase their dominion. They are never satisfied.

"The ones who are preoccupied with worldly love want to have everything in the world. It gives them grief and envy if others put away any of its treasures. Therefore, to keep them from becoming pure greed instead of people, while in the spiritual world they are allowed to think under the influence of fear—fear of losing their reputation and with it their dignity and wealth, and fear of the law and its penalty. They are also allowed to apply their minds to some study or occupation that keeps them on the surface and thus in a state of intelligence, no matter how delirious and insane they are under the surface."

Then I asked whether everyone who is preoccupied with lust also lives in its fantasies.

They said, "Those who think secretly and indulge too much in their own imagination by talking to themselves do live in the fantasy of their lust. They almost separate their spirit from its connection with their body, and what they envision overwhelms their ability to understand, and they delight in a pretense that they own everything. A person finds himself in his delirious fantasy after death if he has made his spirit something separate from his body, and if he would not withdraw from the delight of this madness by using religion to think about evils and false ideas, and if he thought still less about unbridled self-love and how it destroys love of the Lord, and how unbridled love of the world destroys love for the neighbor."

268   Next, the two angels wanted to see the people who get from their worldly love a hallucinating greed or fantasy of owning all riches. I wanted to, also. We could tell that we were inspired to want this so that we would know about them, so we looked at each other and said, "Let's go."

The people lived under the earth below our feet, but above hell, and we noticed an opening and stairs there. We went down, and someone told us to approach the people from the east to keep from entering the dark cloud of their fantasy, which would cloud our understanding and our vision at the same time.

And what did we see but a house, made of reeds so it was full of chinks. It stood in a thick cloud, which wafted continually, like smoke, through the chinks in three of the sides. We went in and saw fifty people here and fifty there, sitting on benches, but turned away from the east and south so that they looked toward the west and north. In front of each was a table with fat purses on it, and lots of gold coins around the purses.

We asked, "Are these the riches of everyone in the world?"

"Not of everyone in the world," they said, "but of everyone in the kingdom." They hissed when they spoke and had round faces with a reddish glow like a snail shell. The pupils of their eyes seemed to glitter in clear green, which was from the light of fantasy.

Standing among them we asked, "Do you believe that you possess all the riches of the kingdom?"

They said, "We do possess them."

"Who does?" we asked.

They said, "Each of us."

"What do you mean, 'each'?" we asked. "There are many of you."

"Each of us knows that his are all mine," they said. "No one is allowed to even think, let alone say, 'Mine are not yours,' but we can think and say, 'Yours are mine.'"

The coins on the table appeared to be of pure gold, even to us. But when we let in the light from the east, the "coins" were little grains of gold that they magnified by common united fantasy. They said that everyone who entered there had to bring some gold with him, which they divide into small bits and then into little grains, which they enlarge into bigger coins by the unanimous power of fantasy.

Then we said, "Weren't you born men of reason? Where do you get this hallucinating foolishness?"

"We know that it is a flight of fancy, but it is deeply pleasing to our minds, so we come in here and are as delighted as if we did own everything," they said. "But we only stay a few hours. After that we go out, and our sanity returns every time. And still," they said, "time and again the pleasant hallucination comes over us, and we come in and go out by turns, so we are alternately wise and foolish. We also know that a hard lot awaits those who take other people's goods."

"What *is* their lot?" we asked.

"They are swallowed up and thrown naked into some infernal prison where they have to work first for clothing and food, and then for a few small coins, which they collect and put their heart's delight into," they said. "But if they do evil to their companions, they have to give up part of their little coins as a fine."

269   After this we went up from those lower regions into the south, where we were before, and there the angels told many memorable things about the greed, not hallucinatory or imagined, that is inborn in every person.

"While they are in the grip of this greed, they seem like fools, yet to themselves they seem extremely wise. They vibrate between this foolishness and the rationality that they have outwardly, so they see, admit, and confess their insanity. But when they are rational they long for their folly, and they plunge back into it as if from a restricting, unpleasant element into a free and delightful one. So deep down inside, what they like is greed, and not intelligence.

"From creation, every person is made up of three basic loves—love of one's neighbor, which is also love of doing useful things, love of the world, which is also love of having wealth, and self-love, which is also love of ruling others. Love of one's neighbor or of being useful is a spiritual love, but love of the world or of having wealth is a material love, and love of self or of ruling others is a physical love. A person is human when love of his neighbor or being useful makes his head, worldly love makes his body, and self-love his feet. But if love of the world is his head, he is only a person like a humpback, and when self-love is his head, he is a person standing on his hands, not his feet, with his head down and his buttocks up. When love of his neighbor is his head and the other two loves in the right order are his body and feet, the person has the face of an angel and a beautiful rainbow around his head, when seen from heaven. If worldly love is his head, he is seen from heaven with a pale face like a dead person and a yellow circle around his head. But if self-love is his head, he seems, from heaven, to have a dusky face, with a white circle around his head."

So I asked, "What do the circles around his head represent?"

"They represent the person's intelligence," the angels said. "A white circle around the head with the dusky face represents that his intelligence is in superficial things or things around him, but in inner matters, he is foolish. A person like that is sane in body but insane in spirit. And no one has sanity in spirit except from the Lord. This happens when he is born anew, or when the Lord creates him again."

After these words the earth opened to my left, and I saw a devil coming up through the opening with a bright white circle around his head.

"Who are you?" I asked.

"I am Lucifer, Son of the Dawn," he said. "And because I made myself like the Most High I was cast down." He thought he was Lucifer, but he was not.

I said, "If you were cast down, how can you rise again out of hell?"

"There I'm a devil, but here I'm an angel of light," he said. "Don't you see the bright halo around my head? And if you wish, you'll also see that I'm super-moral among the moral, super-rational among the rational—even super-spiritual among the spiritual. I also know how to preach, and have preached."

"Preached what?" I asked.

"Against frauds, adulterers, and all hellish loves," he said. "In fact, I used to call Lucifer—myself—a devil, and I hurled an oath against him—me—and they praised me to the sky. This is why I am called the Son of the Dawn. And it even puzzles me, but in the pulpit I thought I was speaking uprightly and piously. But I know why. I was all on the surface, and the surface was at that time separated from what I was inwardly. But even though I found this out, I couldn't change myself, because I was too proud to look to God."

"How could you talk like that," I said, "when you yourself are a fraud, an adulterer, and a devil?"

He answered, "I'm one person on the outside or in my body, but another inside, or as a spirit. In my body I'm an angel, but in my spirit a devil. In a body I follow my ability to understand, but as a spirit I follow my will. My ability to understand carries me upward, but my will carries me downward. When I go by what I understand, there is a white halo around my head. When my ability to understand gives in completely to my will and becomes my will's ability to understand—which is what happens to us in the end—the halo grows dark and dies out, and then we can no longer rise into this light."

Then he talked about his double condition—external and internal—more rationally than anyone else. But he suddenly saw the angels with me. His face and voice flared out. He turned black. Even the halo around his head turned black, and he sank down into hell through the opening he came out of.

This is what the people on the scene made of it—that what a person is like depends on what his love is like, not what his ability to understand is like, because love easily carries intellect over to its side and makes it a servant.

"Where do devils get such rationality?" I asked the angels.

"It comes from the conceit of self-love," they said. "For self-love is surrounded with conceit that can raise their intellect right into the light of heaven. For every man's intellect can be elevated according to the knowledge in it, but only a life that follows the truths of the church and reason can lift up someone's will. This is why even atheists whose self-love makes them conceited about their reputations and therefore proud of their own intelligence, enjoy a more sublime rationality than many others do. But only when they are engaged in intellectual thought, not when they are living by the feelings of their will. Now, the will with its feelings possesses the inner person, but intellectual thought possesses the outer person."

The angel also told why a person is made up of the three loves already mentioned—love of being useful, worldly love, and self-love. It is so that his thought can come from God as if it came from himself. The angel said that a person's highest qualities turn upward toward God, his intermediate ones turn outward toward the world, and his lowest downward toward himself. Because the lowest ones turn downward, the person thinks just as if thought came from himself, though it comes from God.

270   The third story: One morning I had been sleeping, and my thoughts ran to the things we don't know about the love in marriage, and eventually I came to this one: Where does the true love in marriage reside, in the human mind, and so where does marital coldness reside?

I knew that there are three levels of the human mind, one above another, and that worldly love dwells in the lowest, spiritual love in the next, and heavenly love in the highest, and I knew that on each level there is a marriage of good and truth. Now, good goes with love, and truth goes with wisdom, so there is a marriage of love and wisdom on each level. And this marriage is the same as the marriage of one's will and his faculty of understanding, because your will is what receives love, and your faculty of understanding is what receives wisdom.

In the depth of this thought, what did I see but two swans flying towards the north, and soon two birds of paradise flying towards the south, and also two turtledoves flying in the east. I was following them with my eye when I saw the two swans wheel from the north toward the east and the two birds of paradise turn from the south. They joined the two turtledoves in the east and flew together to a tall palace there, surrounded by olive trees, palms, and beeches. It was a palace with three tiers of windows, one above the other. I watched them and saw the swans fly into the palace through opened windows in the lowest tier, the birds of paradise through windows opened in the middle tier, and the turtledoves through ones in the highest tier.

As I was watching this, an angel stood beside me and said, "Do you understand the things you have seen?"

I said, "Partly."

He said, "This palace represents the way the dwelling places of married love are arranged in the human mind. The highest part of it, where the turtledoves entered, represents the highest level of the mind, where married love resides in the love of good and its wisdom. The middle part, where the birds of paradise entered, represents the middle level, where married love resides in love of truth with its intelligence. And the lowest part, where the swans entered, represents the lowest level of the mind, where married love resides in the love of what is just and right with its knowledge.

"The three pairs of birds also stand for the same things—the pair of turtledoves stands for married love in the highest level, the pair of birds of paradise married love in the middle level, and the pair of swans married love in the lowest level. The three kinds of trees around the palace—the olives, the palms, and the beeches— stand for the same things.

"In heaven we call the highest level of the mind heavenly, the middle level spiritual, and the lowest natural, and we think of them as the stories of a house, one above another, with steps going up from one to another like a staircase. Each level, you might say, has two rooms—one for love, the other for wisdom— and in front a bedchamber, so to speak, where love with its wisdom, or good with its truth, which is to say the will with its intellect, lie with each other in bed. That palace depicts all the secrets of married love in a metaphor."

When I heard this I had a burning desire to see the palace. I asked, "Since it is a representative palace, do they let anyone go in and look around?"

"Only people in the third heaven," the angel answered,

"because to them everything that represents love and wisdom becomes real. They were the ones that told me what I've told you. They said something else, too—that true married love resides in the highest region surrounded by mutual love, in the marriage chamber or room of the will and, also surrounded by what wisdom perceives, in the marriage chamber or room of the intellect, and they lie together in bed in the bedroom at the front in the east."

"I asked, "Why are there the two rooms?""

He said, "The husband is in the marriage chamber of the intellect, and the wife is in the one of the will."

I asked, "Since the married love resides there, where does marital coldness reside?"

"That also is in the highest level," he said, "but only in the room of the intellect. The room of the will there is closed. Whenever it wants, intellect and its truths can go up into the highest level, into its room, by a spiral stairway. But if the will and the good of its love does not go up with it to the adjacent room, this room is shut, and coldness gets into the other room—marital coldness. When this coldness toward a wife is there, the faculty of intellect looks down from this highest level to the lowest, and if fear does not hold it back, it goes down there to get warmed by illicit fire."

Then he would have told me still more about the love in marriage, according to the symbols of it in that palace, but he said, "Enough for now. First see if these things are over most people's heads. If they are, why say more? But if not, there is much more to be told."

Chapter 12

The Reasons for a Pretense of Love, Friendship, and Thoughtfulness in Marriages

271   We have considered the reasons for coldness and separations, so the next topic in order is the reasons for a pretense of love, friendship, and thoughtfulness in marriages. Everyone knows that married couples live together and have children these days even though coldness separates their minds. This would not happen unless there were an appearance of love that at times is like the warmth of genuine love, and imitates it. The following pages will show that such appearances are necessary and useful and that homes, and therefore communities, could not hold together without them.

Besides, a conscientious person might be shaken by the idea that if he and his mate disagree in their minds and become that alienated inwardly it is their own fault and something against them, and they could grieve in their hearts on account of it. Yet there really is nothing they can do about inner differences, and all they have to do is to quiet the troubles that arise from their consciences by keeping up an appearance of love and approval. This may even bring back a friendship with the love of marriage within it—for one partner if not for the other.

But this chapter takes up a lot of different subjects, so it comes in articles, like the previous ones. These are the articles:

(1) In the natural world nearly every couple can get together

as to outward feelings, but not as to inner ones—if they are conspicuously incompatible.

(2) In the spiritual world people join together according to inward affections, and not according to outward ones, unless the outward and inward affections are in harmony.

(3) In the world, the affections that lead to matrimony are ordinarily the ones on the surface.

(4) But without deeper feelings that join the minds together, the marriage ties loosen in the home.

(5) All the same, worldly marriages should last to the end of either partner's life.

(6) In the case of marriages where the inward feelings do not unite the couple, there are outward ones that simulate inner ones and keep the couple together.

(7) These outward feelings create an appearance of love or of friendship and thoughtfulness between the married partners.

(8) These appearances are pretenses of marriage that are commendable because they are useful and necessary.

(9) These pretenses of marriage have the wisdom of justice and judgment when a spiritual person is joined together with a worldly person.

(10) They have the wisdom of expedience, for various reasons, in the case of worldly people.

(11) They allow improvement and make it easier to get along.

(12) They keep order in the home and allow the partners to help each other.

(13) They provide for the care of infants and cooperation in the care of children.

(14) They keep peace in the home.

(15) They help preserve reputation outside the home.

(16) They are for the sake of various favors expected from the married partner or the in-laws and for fear of losing these.

(17) They help the partners excuse faults that might damage one's reputation.

(18) They help bring people back together.

(19) If the wife is still thoughtful to the man when he loses his

potency, a friendship resembling the friendship of marriage may spring up as they grow old.

(20) There are many different types of pretended love and
friendship between married partners if one is dominated
and must obey the other.

(21) There are hellish marriages in the world between married
partners who inwardly are the bitterest enemies and outwardly are like the closest friends.

The explanation of these topics follows.

272   (1) *In the natural world nearly every couple can get together as to
outward feelings, but not as to inner ones—if they are conspicuously
incompatible.* The reason is that in the world, a person has a material
body full of selfish motives like the dregs that sink to the bottom
as wine clarifies. The bodies of people in the world are made up
of such things. This is why the inner feelings of the mind do not
appear, and with many people hardly a trace of them shows
through. Either the body absorbs them and enfolds them in its
dregs, or, by pretenses learned from infancy, hides them deeply
from the sight of others. So one person adopts the feelings he sees
in another and attracts the other's feelings to himself, and in this
way they join themselves together. They join together because
every affection gives pleasure, and the pleasures bind their more
worldly minds together.

It would be different if you could see inner feelings in a face
or in gestures, like the outward one, or hear them in a tone of
voice, or if the nostrils could pick up the scent of their pleasure, as
in the spiritual world. Then if the inner feelings were different
enough to be out of tune, they would separate the people's minds
from each other, and the couple would keep their distance according to how much they noticed their feelings clash.

These thoughts show that nearly everyone in the natural
world can be united as to outward feelings, but not as to inner
ones if these disagree conspicuously.

273   (2) *In the spiritual world they join together according to inward
affections, and not according to outward ones, unless the outward and*

inward affections are in harmony. This is because the material body—which, I repeat, could receive all affections and express them in form—has been dropped off by then. Stripped of that body, the person is reduced to his inner feelings, which his body used to conceal, so people not only feel these similarities and differences, or sympathies and antipathies, but they show them in their faces, speech, and gestures. Therefore, like joins like, there, and people who are not alike separate. This is why the Lord arranges the entire heaven according to all the varieties of feelings that come from the love of good and truth, and hell just the other way around—according to all the varieties of feelings that come from love of evil and falsity.

Angels and spirits have inner and outer feelings, just like people in the world, and outward feelings cannot hide inner ones there, so the inner ones show through and make themselves known. Therefore their outward and inward feelings unite and reflect each other, and then the outward feelings mirror the inner ones, on the people's faces, in the tones of their speech, and also in their body language. Angels and spirits do have both mind and body, and this is why they have inward and outward feelings. Feelings and thoughts have to do with the mind, while sensations and their pleasures have to do with the body.

It often happens that friends meet after death, remember their friendship in the former world, and then believe they will be together in a life of friendship as before. But when an association that is only on the basis of outward affections becomes apparent in heaven, the people separate according to their inward affections, and from that encounter some are sent north, some west, and each to a distance where they never see or know each other again. For wherever they settle, their faces change so as to express their inner affections. This shows that in the spiritual world everyone joins together according to inward affections, and not according to outward ones unless the outward and inward affections are in harmony.

274   (3) *In the world, the affections that lead to matrimony are ordinarily the ones on the surface.* This is because inner feelings are rarely

considered, and if they are, their pattern is not always clear in the woman, for she has a natural gift of withdrawing them into the inner recesses of her mind.

Many superficial inclinations lead men into marriage. The primary one these days is to improve family matters with wealth in order to be rich and have plenty. Another is seeking status, either to have influence or to become more successful. Then there are various seductions and yearnings, too, which leave no room for looking into the harmony of inner dispositions. These few observations show that ordinarily marriages are made with superficial motives, in the world.

275   (4) *But without deeper feelings that join the minds together, the marriage ties loosen in the home.* We say in the home because it is a personal matter. It happens because the fires kindled in courtship and blazing on the wedding day gradually cool down afterwards and finally turn cold on account of differences in the people's inner dispositions. Then, as we know, the superficial motives that led and lured them into marriage diverge and no longer keep the couple together.

The previous chapter demonstrated that all the different causes of coldness—internal, external, and contingent—well up from differences in inner dispositions. So it is clearly the truth: unless inward feelings within the surface ones join the minds together, the marriage ties in the home come untied.

276   (5) *All the same, worldly marriages should last to the end of either partner's life.* We bring this up to make a necessity, a requirement, and a truth more clear for the mind—that if a real love of marriage is not there, it must be feigned, so there will seem to be a marriage. It would be different if entering marriage were not a pact to the end of life but one that could be dissolved at will, as with the Israelite Nation. They took it upon themselves to cast off wives for any reason, as these statements in Matthew show: The Pharisees came to Jesus, saying, "Is it lawful for a man to put away his wife for any cause at all?" And when Jesus answered, "It is not lawful to put away a wife and marry another except for whoredom," they replied, "Yet Moses commanded to give her a bill of divorcement and put her away." And the disciples said, "If the case of a

man with a wife is like this, it is not expedient to marry" (19:3–10). So marriage is a covenant for life. Therefore, appearances of love and friendship between married partners are a necessity.

It comes from Divine law that a contracted marriage is to last till the end of life in the world, so it is also rational law and therefore civil law. Divine law provides that a man may not "put away" his wife and marry another except for fornication, as above, and rational law is based on spiritual law, for Divine law and rational law are one law. From rational law and Divine law—or rather, from Divine law *through* rational law—you can see the great many irregularities, and the social shambles that would come from broken marriages or husbands getting rid of wives at will, before death.

The account (in nos. 103–15) about people gathered from nine kingdoms discussing the origin of married love shows these irregularities and their social consequences fully, so there is no need to add more reasons. These reasons do not obstruct separations, though, when permitted for their own reasons (see nos. 252–54), nor keeping a mistress (see Part 2).

277   (6) *In the case of marriages where the inward feelings do not unite the couple, there are outward ones that simulate inner ones and keep the couple together.* Inner feelings means inclinations toward each other that come from heaven and that both people share in their minds. The outward feelings are the ones in their minds that come from the world. They are just as much mental inclinations or feelings, of course, but they are on a lower plane of the mind, while the others are on a higher. You might suppose that they are alike and agree, because they both are in the mind. But they are not alike, though they might seem alike. For some people they are ways to conform, for others, thoughtful pretenses.

The two people have some common interests, implanted with the first marriage vows. Their minds may disagree, but the common interests remain in their shared possessions, and for many, shared occupations, and the various needs of the household. This leads them to share thoughts and certain secrets. The bed they share and their love for infants bring them together, and so do other things that are also written in the marriage commitment and therefore on their minds. This is where the outward affections that resemble inner ones come from, especially. However, the affections that do no more than imitate are partly from this source and partly from another. But more about both will come later.

278   (7) *These outward feelings create an appearance of love or of friend-ship and thoughtfulness between the married partners.* The appearance of love, friendship, and approval between married partners comes from the marriage covenant, which is binding to the end of life, with the shared responsibilities it assigns to the partners. From these common responsibilities are born the superficial affections already mentioned, which resemble inner ones. There are also useful and necessary reasons that in part produce these affections that join the partners outwardly, so that outward love comes to resemble inner love, and outward friendship comes to resemble inner friendship.

279   (8) *These appearances are pretenses of marriage that are commend-able because they are useful and necessary.* We call them pretenses be-cause they exist between people whose minds are not in agreement and who have an inner coldness for that reason. If the people live a proper and decent life together on the surface, you might still say the fellowship of their life together is pretense—but it is a pretense of marriage. This is useful and therefore commendable, so it is entirely different from hypocritical pretenses. These pre-tenses provide all the good benefits spelled out below in articles 11–20. They are commendable because they are necessary, and they are necessary because doing without them would banish all the good things, when yet the couple have a duty to live together, imposed by their contract and the law.

280   (9) *These pretenses of marriage have the wisdom of justice and judgment when a spiritual person is joined together with a worldly person.* This is because the spiritual person does what he does out of justice and judgment, so to him the pretenses are not alien to his inner feelings but are coupled with them. He acts in earnest and looks to improvement as a goal. If it fails to come, he concen-trates on compromise for the sake of order in the home, mutual assistance, the care of children, and peace and quiet. Justice leads

him to do this, and he brings it about with his judgment. This is how a spiritual person lives with a worldly person, because a spiritual person acts spiritually even with worldly people.

281   (10) *These pretenses of marriage have the wisdom of expedience, for various reasons, in the case of worldly people.* A spiritual person loves what is spiritual, so he acquires wisdom from the Lord. A worldly person loves only what is worldly, so he has only his own wisdom. Between two partners, one spiritual and the other worldly, living together in marriage, the love in marriage is warmth for the spiritual one and coldness for the worldly one. Clearly warmth and coldness cannot exist together, and the heat cannot warm the cold person up until the coldness goes away. Nor can the cold seep into the one with warmth until the warmth goes away. This is why inner love is not possible between a spiritual partner and a worldly one. But the spiritual one can have something like inner love, as the article above points out.

But between two worldly partners inner love is not possible, because both are cold. Any warmth they have comes from lewdness. But even they can live together at home with their separate minds and put on a face of love and friendship between themselves in spite of their different minds. Their outward feelings, which mostly have to do with wealth, possessions, honor, and status, can seem ardent. This ardor makes them afraid to lose these things, so the pretenses are necessary for them—principally the necessary ones mentioned in articles 15–17 below. Some of their motives might have something in common with the motives of the spiritual person (see no. 280), but only if the worldly person's prudence has a touch of intelligence.

282   (11) *These pretenses allow improvement and make it easier to get along.* The reason why the pretenses of marriage that seem like love and friendship between married partners of different minds improve the situation is that a spiritual person joined to a worldly one by marriage covenant just wants to make his or her mutual life better. This is done by sensitive and refined conversation and by doing things the other person likes, and if it falls on deaf ears

and set ways, the person makes allowances to keep order in household matters, and for the sake of working together, and for the babies and children—this kind of thing. For what a spiritual person says and does is flavored by justice and judgment (as above, no. 280).

But when neither partner is spiritual but both are worldly, it can work the same way, though for other purposes—whether to improve matters and make it easier to get along, or because one wants to make the other act his way, or to dominate the other, or to have the other serve his purposes, or for peace in the house, or for their reputation, or to gain benefits from the partner or the in-laws, and other reasons.

But some people do these things from the prudence of their good sense, some from native civility, some for fear of doing without comforts they have always enjoyed. And for many other reasons they more or less pretend thoughtfulness as if it came from a love of marriage.

Outside the home there are also things people do for each other as if from married love (while neglecting them at home) for the purpose of their reputation, or if not that, just for show.

283   (12) *Pretenses do keep order in the home and allow the partners to help each other.* Every household with children, their tutors, and other servants, is a society like society at large, which indeed emerges from this like a whole from its parts. And the welfare of this small society depends on order just as the welfare of the large one does. So, just as it is up to the leaders to discern and foresee how to have order and keep it, in a complex society, it is up to married partners to do it in their private one. But you cannot have this order if the husband and wife are of different minds, because it draws their discussions and help for each other in different directions, divided like their minds. This tears the arrangement of the small society apart. Therefore, to keep order and watch out for themselves and their household at the same time (or their house-hold and themselves), so that it does not go to ruin and rush into disaster, the two in charge have to agree and work together. If they cannot do this by being of one mind, at least they should do it

by putting on a show of marital friendship. This is fitting and proper. It makes things go well. It brings households into agreement for practical necessities, as everyone knows.

284   (13) *Pretenses provide for the care of infants and cooperation in the care of children.* It is a well-known fact that for the sake of infants and children married partners make what looks like a marriage by acts of love and friendship like the ones in a true marriage. They both love the children, and it makes each partner appear kind and thoughtful toward the other. A mother's and father's love of their infants and children joins them together, like the heart and lungs in your chest. The mother's love for them is like the heart, and the father's is like the lungs. The reason for the comparison is that the heart corresponds to love and the lungs to intellect. A mother's love is spontaneous and a father's is calculated. With spiritual people a marriage bond comes through this love, due to judgment and compassion—due to compassion because the mother carried the children in her womb, bore them in pain, and then, with untiring care, nurses, feeds, cleans, clothes them, and brings them up.

285   (14) *Pretenses keep peace in the home.* Most of the outward pretenses of marriage or friendship to keep peace and quiet at home are the man's because men have a natural inclination to do what they do by intellect—which involves thinking. Intellect becomes involved in many things that upset, distract, and disturb the mind, so if the home were unpeaceful their vital spirit would slacken and their inner life half die. This would destroy their health, both physical and mental. Men's minds become obsessed with fear of these perils and many others unless there is shelter at home with their wives to quiet the intellectual turmoil. Also, peace and quiet puts their minds at rest to gratefully accept the thoughtful things their wives do—wives who do everything possible to sweep away the mental clouds that they are keenly aware of in their husbands. And besides, peace and quiet add charm to the presence of wives. So a show of real married love, for the peace and quiet of the home, clearly is useful and necessary.

In addition, wives do not pretend the way men do, and even if they seem to, it comes from real love, because they are born to love the intellect in a man. So in their hearts, if not vocally, they gratefully accept the thoughtful things that their husbands do for them.

286   (15) *Pretenses help preserve reputation outside the home.* Men's success depends for the most part on their reputation for being law-abiding, sincere, and upright, and furthermore, their reputations depend on their wives, who know their husbands' private lives. So if the disunion of their minds broke out in open unfriendliness, quarrels, and hateful threats, and if the wife and her friends and servants told everybody, it could easily turn to reproach that would give the man a bad name. All the men can do to avoid this is to pretend they care for their wives, or else be separated from their homes.

287   (16) *Pretenses are for the sake of various favors expected from the married partner or the in-laws and for fear of losing these.* This happens particularly in marriages of mixed class and condition (see no. 250, above), for example, when a man marries a wealthy wife and she hides her money away or invests her wealth—or worse, if she boldly insists that her husband owes it to her to support the household from his own property and income. Everyone knows that this necessitates imitations of married love. It is also common knowledge that the same thing happens when a man marries a woman whose parents, relatives, and friends are in high office, lucrative business, or commercial work and can set him up in better conditions. The man makes a pretense of marital love. In both cases, the pretenses are clearly for the fear of losing the advantages.

288   (17) *Pretenses help the partners excuse faults that might damage one's reputation.* Married partners fear a bad reputation for various faults, some serious and some not. There are flaws of the mind and of the body that are less serious than the ones listed in the previous chapter (nos. 252, 253) as the causes of separation. Here we mean flaws that the other married partner bears in silence to avoid disgrace. Besides these, some people have committed crimes that would be punishable by law if everyone knew. Not to mention lack

of the potency that men ordinarily take pride in. There is no need to explain that people pretend love and friendship with a married partner in order to be excused flaws like these and avoid disgrace.

289   (18) *Pretenses help bring people back together.* The world knows that married partners who for various reasons do not think alike alternately disagree, then trust, are alienated and then back together, even quarrel, then come to terms and make up, so that the appearances of friendship reconcile them. Reconciliation can also take place after separation and be neither alternate nor temporary.

290   (19) *If the wife is still thoughtful to the man when he loses his potency, a friendship resembling the friendship of marriage may spring up as they grow old.* One of the main reasons why the minds of married partners drift apart is that the wife's favorable attitude toward the man fades away as his potency wanes and his love decreases, because coldness is reciprocal just as warmth is. Without love, they both lose their friendship and even their consideration for each other, unless they are afraid of the danger to their family life. This is clear from reason and experience. Then, if the man quietly takes the responsibility and the wife stays chastely considerate of him, a friendship can emerge from it that will closely resemble married love, because it exists between married partners. Experience shows that this kind of friendship can come to an aged couple from the peace, security, good nature, and great kindness of their close relationship in living together and companionship.

291   (20) *There are many different types of pretended love and friendship between married partners if one is dominated and must obey the other.* One of the things we know in this world today is that rivalries over rights and authority spring up between married partners, once their newly married state has passed. They vie for their rights, as the conditions of their contract make them equal and give them equal dignity in the performance of their roles. They vie for authority, as men insist on being the leaders in domestic affairs because they are men and think women inferior because they are women.

        These family rivalries of our day come from only one source— failure to appreciate real love in marriage and lack of sensibly perceiving its blessings. Without these, you do not have love in marriage, but a counterfeit of it—lust. From this lust, without genuine love, comes strife over power. Some get this from their pleasure in the love of ruling, some have been introduced to it by designing women before marriage, and others do not know it. Men who have this ambition and get the upper hand after the struggles of rivalry reduce their wives either to the level of rightful possessions or to obedience under their will, or to slavery. It depends on the amount and kind of ambition each particular man has inborn and latent in himself. If wives with this ambition get the upper hand after the give-and-take of rivalry, they reduce their husbands either to equal rights with themselves or to obedience under their will, or to slavery. But after wives win the staff of authority, they still retain a lust that passes for married love, so they lead a companionable life with their husbands—the lust being restrained by law and the fear of justified separation in case they extend their authority past acceptable limits.

It would take many words to describe the kind of love and friendship there is between a dominating wife and a servile husband or a dominating husband and a servile wife. In fact, there would not be enough pages to list the varieties of it under headings and discuss them, for they are varied and different. They vary according to the kinds of ambition that men have, and the kinds wives have, and men's ambitions are different from women's. Men like that have no friendship of love except a foolish one, and wives like that have the friendship of a false love from selfish desire. But the next article tells how wives gain power over men.

292   (21) *There are hellish marriages in the world between married partners who inwardly are the bitterest enemies and outwardly are like the closest friends.* Actually wives like that, in the spiritual world, forbid me to tell the public about these marriages. They are afraid I would divulge their art of gaining power over men, and they are very anxious to keep it hidden. But men in that world urge me to tell why they have a gut hatred for their wives and a fury stirred up against them in their hearts, so to speak, on account of their secret arts, so all I will say is this. Men have said that they

unconsciously contracted a terrible fear of their wives, and it made them totally obedient to their wives' will, more submissive to their nod than the lowest slaves, so they were practically worthless. And wives did this not just to men with no position in the world, but also to men of high standing; in fact, even valiant and renowned generals. And they said that once they had this terror they did not dare speak to their wives except in a friendly way, nor do anything to them except what pleased them, though they nursed a murderous hate for their wives in their hearts. Yet their wives talked and acted courteously with them and listened compliantly to some of their requests.

Now, the men really wondered where such negative inner feelings and such outward sympathy could arise from, so they asked women who knew the secret art what the reasons were. The men said they had it from the women's own lips that deep within themselves women conceal knowledge of how to put men under the yoke of their authority if they want to. Coarse wives do it by alternate scolding and kindness, and others by continual hard and unpleasant looks, and others do it in other ways. Refined wives do it by obstinately pushing their requests without letup, and by doggedly opposing their husbands if the husbands are hard on them, and insisting on their equal rights under the law. They make themselves so stubborn this way that even if they are run out of the house they will come back whenever they please and take the same stand. They know that by nature there is no way men can hold out against pressure from their wives and that once the husbands concede the authority, they are submissive. Then the wives act polite and soft for the husbands under their power.

The real reason why wives dominate through this craft is that a man acts from intellect and a woman from will, and will can be persistent but intellect cannot. I learned that the worst of this kind, who are inwardly baited with ambition to rule, can doggedly hold onto their stubborn ways even in a struggle to the death. I have also heard the women's excuses for taking up the practice of this art. They said they would not have taken it up if they had not foreseen the extreme contempt, future rejection, and their ruin in the end, if their husbands got the upper hand over them, so they had to take up arms. They added a warning to men to let their wives have their rights and not consider them lower than slaves during their periods of coldness. They also said that many of their sex are not in a position to exercise these arts because of their inborn timidity, but I added, "because of inborn modesty."

From all this it is clear now what marriages we mean by infernal marriages in this world between partners who are inwardly the bitterest enemies and outwardly like the most intimate friends.

293   Two stories belong here. The first is this:

I was once looking through a window toward the east and saw seven women sitting in a rose garden by a spring, drinking water. I focused my eyes and looked hard to see what they were doing, and they could tell I was staring at them, so one of them invited me with a nod, and I left the house and hurried over to them. When I arrived there I asked politely where they came from.

"We are wives," they said, "and we are here talking about the joy of married love. And for many reasons we have settled it that the joy of married love is also the joy of wisdom."

This answer made my mind so happy that I could see I was in my spirit and therefore had deeper and clearer perception than ever before. So I said to them, "Let's get each other's opinions about these pleasures." They nodded "yes," and I asked, "How do you wives know that the joy of married love is the same as the joy of wisdom?"

"We know this," they said, "from the fact that the wisdom in our husbands is the counterpart of our delight in married love. You see, for us the joy of this love ebbs and flows and takes its whole character according to the wisdom in our husbands."

When I heard this, I asked, "I know that you respond to the sweet talk of your husbands and to the liveliness of their minds. It thrills your whole breast. But I am surprised that you say their wisdom does it. Tell me—what is wisdom? And what kind of wisdom can do that?"

That made the wives indignant, and they answered, "You don't think we even know what wisdom is and what kind of wisdom does this, but for all that, we think about the wisdom in our husbands all the time, and we learn it every day from their own mouths. For we wives think about how our husbands are from dawn to dusk. Hardly a few minutes are wedged into a day when our intuitive thoughts completely leave them or are somewhere else—though our husbands think very little during the day about how we are. This intuition is how we know what wisdom of theirs takes delight in us. Our husbands call this wisdom spiritual on a rational plane and spiritual on a moral plane. They say that spiritual rational wisdom has to do with intellect and concepts, and spiritual moral wisdom, they say, has to do with your intentions and the way you live. And they join these two wisdoms together into one. They sum it up this way—the pleasures of this wisdom coming from their minds translate into joy in our breast, and from ours into theirs, and so the pleasures return to the wisdom they came from."

And then I asked, "Do you know anything else about how your husbands' wisdom makes you happy?"

"We do," they said. "There is spiritual wisdom. Rational and moral wisdom come from it. Spiritual wisdom is to acknowledge the Lord the Savior as God of heaven and earth and to gather the truths of the church from Him. The truths come through the Word and through preaching that is from the Word. Spiritual rationality comes from this. Spiritual morality is living according to those truths, from Him. Our husbands say these two things—spiritual rationality and morality—are the overall wisdom that brings about the real love in marriage.

"They have told us the reason, too. This wisdom opens out the innermost parts of their minds, and that leaves their bodies open to carry love freely like a stream from its highest beginning to its end. The life of married love depends on the strong, plentiful flow of this 'stream.'

"The rational and moral spiritual wisdom of our husbands has a specific purpose and scope in marriage—to love only a wife and to reject every selfish desire for anyone else—and to the extent that it succeeds, the love reaches a higher level and more perfection. And at the same time, it gives us that much more special and exquisite feelings of delight in response to the joy of our husbands' feelings and the charm of their thoughts."

Then I asked, "Do you know how the communication happens?"

"Every relationship by love needs an action, a reception, and a reaction," they said. "Our love finds a state of delight in starting something, or doing. The wisdom of our husbands is a condition of receiving or reception and also of reacting or reaction, so far as they notice. And we notice their reaction with joy in our breast, in keeping with our state of mind, which is always open and ready to receive anything at all that is connected with, and that comes from, our husbands' virtue—which means connected with, and coming from, our own full state of love, too."

They also said, "Be careful not to think that the joys we have been talking about mean the more outward pleasures of this love. We don't ever speak of them, but of the delight in our hearts, which are always in response to the state of our husbands' wisdom."

After this a dove seemed to appear in the distance flying with a leaf of a tree in its beak. But as it came nearer it proved to be a little boy instead of a dove, with a piece of paper in his hand. Coming up to us he held the paper out to me and said, "Read this in front of the virgins of the spring."

And I read these words, "Tell the Earth dwellers you are with, that genuine married love does exist. It has thousands of delights, and the world still knows hardly any of them. But it will know them when the church betroths herself to the Lord and marries."

And then I asked, "Why did the boy call you virgins of the spring?"

"We are called virgins when we are sitting at this spring," they answered, "because affection for the truths of our husbands' wisdom is what we are, and affection for truth is called a virgin. Also, a spring stands for the truth of wisdom, and the rose garden we are sitting in stands for the delights of wisdom."

Then one of the seven twined a wreath of roses and sprinkled it with spring water and put it on the boy's cap, around his little head, and said, "Here are some joys of intelligence. You see, that cap stands for intelligence, and a wreath from this rose bed is the joys in it."

Decorated that way, the boy set off, and in the distance he again looked like a dove, flying—but with a garland on its head.

294   The second story: I saw the seven wives again some days later, in a rose garden, but not the same one. It was a magnificent rose garden. I had never seen one like it before. It was round, and the roses there formed a kind of rainbow arch. Its outer circle was roses or deep crimson flowers, inside that were others of a golden yellow, inside those were others of a deep blue, and onion green or bright green flowers were innermost of all. In this rainbow rose garden was a pool of transparent water. The seven wives sitting there, called the Virgins of the Spring before, again saw me at the window and invited me to join them.

When I came, they said, "Did you ever see anything more beautiful on earth?"

I said, "Never!"

"The Lord creates a thing like this in a moment," they said, "and it stands for something that is new on earth. Everything that the Lord creates is representative. See if you can guess what the new thing is. We'll guess it's the joy of married love."

When I heard this I said, "The joy of married love! You told me so much about it so eloquently before, from your wisdom! After I left you I told some wives in our vicinity about your conversation. I said, 'I've learned something, and now I know that delight springs up in your hearts from your married love, and you can share it with your husbands according to their wisdom. So the eyes of your spirit are on your husbands all the time, dawn to dusk, and you try to bend and lead their minds toward becoming wise so you can enjoy those delights.'

"I also told them that what you mean by wisdom is moral and rational spiritual wisdom, and in marriage it is the wisdom of loving only a wife and rejecting all selfish desires for anyone else.

"But the wives there only laughed at these things and said, 'What's this? Those words are silly. We don't know what married love is. We don't have any even if our husbands do, so how can we have any delight in it? And as to what you call the most outward pleasures of this love, sometimes we violently refuse them, because we find them disagreeable—hardly different from rape. In fact, you wouldn't find any sign of such love in our faces if you looked for it. So you're teasing, or joking, if you say that we think about our husbands from dawn to dusk like those seven wives, and wait on their pleasure and whims just to get delights like that out of them.'

"I remembered these words of theirs so I could repeat them to you. They fly in the face of everything you told me at the spring. In fact, they're the exact opposite. And I swallowed it all eagerly and believed it!"

"Friend," the wives sitting in the rose garden answered, "you don't know how wise and prudent wives are, because they completely hide it from men, and they hide it for no reason but to be loved. Every man who is not spiritually, but only naturally rational and moral, is cold toward his wife. It lurks concealed in his deepest levels. The wise and prudent wife keeps track of this exquisitely and keenly and hides her love for marriage to just that extent. She draws it into her breast and hides it there so deeply that not the least bit of it shows in her face, voice, or gesture. The reason is that to whatever extent the love appears, the man's marital coldness pours out from the depths of his mind where it resides, and into the outward man. It makes his body completely frigid, so it makes him want to separate from bed and bedroom."

Then I asked, "Where does cold like this come from, that you call marital cold?"

"It comes from their spiritual folly," they said, "and every man who is spiritually foolish is cold to his wife, deep down inside, and warm toward prostitutes. The love in marriage is the opposite of the love in fornication, so that married love cools when love for fornication is warm. And when coldness reigns in a man he can't stand any feeling of love, nor therefore any breath of it, from his wife.

"This is why the wife so wisely and prudently hides it, and to the extent that she does hide it by denying and refusing, a lewd element filters in to revive and restore the man. This is why the wife of a man like that has none of the heartfelt delights that we have, but only pleasures that are the pleasures of folly for the man, because they are the pleasures of loving fornication.

"Every chaste wife loves her husband—even an unchaste husband—but only wisdom can receive her love, so the wife does all she can to turn his folly into wisdom—in other words, to make him lust after no one but herself. She does this in a thousand ways, being very careful not to let him discover any of them, for she knows that you can't force love, but it finds its way in spontaneously. Therefore women get to know their husbands' every state of mind, from sight, hearing, and touch, but husbands, on the other hand, have no way of knowing any state of mind in their wives.

"A chaste wife can give her husband withering looks, speak harshly to him—even be angry and quarrel—and yet cherish a gentle and tender love for him in her heart. But in a moment she can forgive and forget, so these outbursts of anger and these poses are clearly for the benefit of wisdom in the husband, and his receptiveness to love.

"Another reason why wives have such a way of concealing the love inborn in their heart and marrow is to keep marital coldness from breaking out in the man. That would douse the fire of his lustful warmth, too, and make him a dry stick instead of green wood."

After the seven wives had said these things and many other things like them, their husbands came with clusters of grapes in their hands. Some tasted delicious, and some tasted horrible, and the wives said, "Why did you bring the bad wild grapes, too?"

"We could tell in our souls, which are one with yours," the husbands answered, "that you were talking with that man about the real love in marriage and how its joy is the joy of wisdom, and also about love of fornication and how its joy is the pleasure of folly. These pleasures are the bad-tasting wild grapes, but the others are the grapes that taste delicious."

They supported the things their wives had said and added, "The pleasures of folly look like the delights of wisdom on the surface, but not inside—exactly like the good and bad grapes we brought. For the wisdom of unchaste people is like the wisdom of chaste people on the surface but totally different underneath."

After this the little boy came again with a piece of paper in his hand and held it out to me, saying, "Read."

This is what I read. "Something you need to know is that the joy of married love rises to the highest heaven, and both there and on the way there it joins together with the joy of all heavenly loves, and so they enter a happiness that lasts forever. The reason is that the joy of married love is also the joy of wisdom.

"You must also know that the pleasures of a love for fornication sink to the lowest hell, and both there and on the way there they join together with the pleasures of all hellish loves, and so they enter an unhappiness consisting of never having any heartfelt joys. The reason is that the pleasures of loving fornication are also the pleasures of folly."

After this the husbands left with their wives and kept the little boy company all the way to a path that he followed to heaven. They knew what community he was sent from, and it was a community of the new heaven. The new church on earth will be associated with it.

Chapter 13

Commitments and Weddings

295   Commitments and weddings, and the ceremonies that go with them, are dealt with here mainly on an intellectual basis, because the purpose of the things written in this book is for the reader to agree as a result of seeing truths by his rationality. This is how his spirit is convinced. Things that your spirit is convinced of take precedence over things that come through faith in authority without the counsel of reason. These things go no further into your head than your memory, and there they mix with fallacies and false concepts, so they are inferior to rational intellectual convictions.

Anyone can seem to speak rationally from these memorized concepts, but this is backwards, for in that case he is thinking the way a crab walks—with his eyes following his tail. It is different if he thinks intellectually. When he does this his rational insight selects from his memory things appropriate to confirm the truth seen as it is. This is why this chapter brings in many things that are accepted customs, like the man choosing, parents being consulted, pledges being given, a marriage covenant being agreed on before the wedding, its being consecrated by a priest, and the wedding being celebrated. Plus many other things that are brought in so that a person will see rationally that they are attributed to married love as being necessary to promote it and fulfill it.

This study is divided into the following articles, in this order:

(1) The man, not the woman, chooses.

(2) It is proper for the man to court and ask the woman to marry him, and not the other way around.

(3) It is proper for a woman to consult her parents or those who are in place of parents, and then consider it in her own mind, before she consents.

(4) After they announce their consent they should give pledges.

(5) Consent should be strengthened and confirmed by a solemn commitment.

(6) Commitment prepares them both for married love.

(7) Commitment joins the mind of one with the mind of the other to make the marriage spiritual before it becomes physical.

(8) This is how it works for people who think about marriages chastely, but it works differently for those who think about them unchastely.

(9) During the time of engagement, physical union is not allowed.

(10) After a period of engagement, there should be a wedding.

(11) Before the celebration of the wedding a marriage agreement should be settled in the presence of witnesses.

(12) The marriage should be declared sacred by a minister.

(13) The wedding should be celebrated with good fellowship.

(14) After the wedding the spiritual marriage also becomes a bodily marriage and thus complete.

(15) This is the development of married love by proper stages from its first warmth to its first torch.

(16) Rushed into without development by proper stages, married love burns out its core and is squandered.

(17) The mental states of both, following one after another in order, flow into the character of the marriage, but it is different for spiritual people than for worldly people.

(18) This is because there is progressive order and simultaneous order, and the second kind is from the first and in keeping with it.

The explanation of these points follows.

296   (1) *The man, not the woman, chooses.* This is because a man is born to be intellect but a woman is born to be love, and also because men generally have a love for the other sex, but women have a love for one person of the other sex. Also, while it is not

improper for men to talk about a love and proclaim it, this is improper for women. Still, women have the say in choosing one of their suitors.

Respecting the first point—that men have the choice because they are born to intellect—this is because intellect can examine compatible things and those that are not compatible and tell them apart and choose appropriately through judgment. It is different for women. They are born to be love, so they do not see by that light, and therefore for them decisions to marry would only follow the tendencies of their love. Though they may have skill in telling the differences in different men, still appearances win their love.

As to the second reason why men have the choice and not women, men generally have love for the other sex and women have love for one person of the other sex. The one with love for the other sex is free to look around and also to decide. It is different for women. It is innate in them to love one person of the other sex. If you wish to confirm this, ask the man on the street about monogamous and polygamous marriage, and rarely will you hit on one who is not going to answer in favor of polygamous marriage, which is also love for the other sex. But ask women about those marriages and nearly all, except prostitutes, are going to reject polygamous marriages. This leads to the conclusion that women have love for one of the other sex, which is the love in marriage.

As to the third reason—that it is not improper for men to talk about a love and publicize it, and that it is improper for women—it is self-evident. And it follows from this that it is the man's part to declare his love, and if this is so, then the choice is also up to him.

We know that women do have freedom to choose one of their suitors, but this type of choice is narrow and limited, while men's choice is broad and unlimited.

297   (2) *It is proper for the man to court and ask the woman to marry him, and not the other way around.* This comes from his having the choice, and also it is respectable and proper for men to court and ask women to marry, but not for women. If women courted and solicited, not only would they be reproached, but also they would have a cheap reputation after they asked, or after marriage they

would be considered wanton people whom there is no living with, without coldness and loathing. So in this way marriages would be turned into tragic scenarios. Also, wives make it praiseworthy in themselves that they surrendered to the earnest pleas of men, as if conquered. Who cannot foresee that if women courted men they would rarely be accepted? They would either be scornfully rejected or enticed into wantonness and prostitute their modesty as well.

Furthermore, men do not have any love for the other sex innately, as shown above, and without that love, life has no inner charm. So men need to be pleasant to women in order to improve their lives with that love, politely, courteously, and humbly courting and begging them for this sweet addition to their lives. Besides, the beauty of this sex's face, body, and manners, more than the male sex's, is appropriate for devotion.

298   (3) *It is proper for a woman to consult her parents or those who are in place of parents, and then consider it in her own mind, before she consents.* Parents should be consulted because they consider it and take thought from judgment, knowledge, and love. From *judgment* because they are older, and their age strengthens their judgment so it notices things that work together and things that are incompatible. From *knowledge* of the suitor as well as their daughter. They find out things about the suitor, and they know things about their daughter. So with joint vision they decide about both of them at once. From *love* because to take care for their daughter's good and look out for her household is to do the same for their own.

299   It would be quite different if a daughter consented to a suitor, without consulting her parents or those in place of parents, because she cannot, from judgment, knowledge, and love, evaluate this matter that has to do with her future welfare. Not from *judgment*, because her judgment about married life is still in a state of ignorance and not in a state to compare one reason with another and ascertain men's habits from their natural inclinations. Not from *knowledge* or inquiry, because she knows little beyond household matters of her parents and other friends, and she is not good at finding out the kind of things that are private and personal to her suitor. Not from *love*, because in daughters during this first

marriageable state—and in the next—love obeys the desires of the senses and not yet the wishes of a keen mind.

Yet it is right for a daughter to think this thing over by herself before she consents, so as not to be made captive unwillingly to a man she does not love. For that way she does not give consent on her own behalf. And yet consent makes a marriage and initiates her spirit into married love. But unwilling or extorted consent does not initiate her spirit, though it can initiate her body. And in this way it turns purity, which resides in her spirit, into passion—spoiling married love in its first warmth.

300   (4) *After they announce their consent they should give pledges.* Pledges means gifts, which are assurances, testimonies, and first favors. They are delightful after the consent. The pledges are *assurances* because they are tokens of consent. This is why two parties say, "Give me a token," when they agree to something. And we call two people "given in pledge," which means confirmed, when they have vowed marriage and confirmed the vows with gifts. The pledges are *testimonies* because the pledges are like perpetual eyewitnesses of mutual love, and so they are also reminders of it—especially if they are rings, scent bottles and pendants hung where they are seen. A certain image of the bride's and groom's souls is in them. The pledges are *first favors* because married love pledges itself eternal good will, which the gifts are the first fruits of. The pledges are *delightful,* as is well known. It makes your mind happy to look at them, and because love is in them these favors are dearer and more precious than any others. The couple's hearts are in them, so to speak.

Since the pledges support married love, people in ancient times also had the established custom of gifts after consent, and after accepting them the couple were pronounced bride and groom.

But note that it is a matter of choice whether to give the gifts before the formal commitment or after it. If before, gifts are assurances and testimonies to the commitment. If afterward, they are the same thing for the wedding as well.

301   (5) *Consent should be strengthened and confirmed by a solemn commitment.* Here are the reasons for commitments. (a) So that

after them the souls of both will incline toward each other. (b) To limit a general love of the other sex to one masculine or feminine person of the other sex. (c) To make known their mutual inner feelings and let these feelings be joined in the inner happiness of love, by inclination. (d) So that each one's spirit may enter marriage and be brought closer and closer together. (e) So that married love can progress properly from its first warmth clear to the blaze of the wedding. Consequently, (f) so that married love can advance and grow from its spiritual origin by the right steps.

The state of engagement can be compared to the condition of spring before the summer, and this state's inner delights compare to the blossoming of trees before they bear fruit.

There are engagements in the heavens, too, because the beginnings and the progress of married love proceed in order for the sake of their influencing the completed love that begins on the wedding day.

302   (6) *A commitment prepares them both for married love.* The reasons brought out in the last article establish that a formal commitment prepares one mind or spirit to be united with another mind or spirit, or, to say the same thing, one love with another love.

It should also be mentioned that real married love is inscribed in this order: It goes up and it goes down. From its first warmth it goes steadily upwards towards the souls in an effort toward joining together on that level, by more and more inward openings of their minds. And there is no love that more eagerly sets these openings-up in motion, or that more vigorously and nimbly opens the mind's inner dimensions, than the love in marriage does. For the soul of each urges this.

But in the same moment that this love is going up toward the souls it also goes down toward the bodies and clothes itself by the agency of the body. But note that married love in its descent is like what it is in the height that it ascends to. If it exists in the heights, it comes down chaste, but if it does not exist in the heights it comes down unchaste. The reason is that the lower parts of the mind are unchaste, but its higher parts are chaste, for the mind's lower parts cling to the body, but the higher ones separate themselves from the lower parts. But more about these things appears below (no. 305).

These few remarks will establish that a commitment prepares each partner's mind for married love, yet each in a different way, according to what they love.

303   (7) *A commitment joins the mind of one with the mind of the other to make the marriage spiritual before it becomes physical.* This can pass without bringing in further confirmations by reason, as it is a conclusion from what was already said (nos. 301–2).

304   (8) *This is how it works for people who think about marriages chastely, but it works differently for those who think about them unchastely.* Among the chaste—those who think from religion about marriages—marriage of the spirit comes first, and marriage of the body follows. They are also the ones in whom love rises toward their soul and comes down from that height (concerning this see no. 302, above). These people's souls separate themselves from unrestricted love of the other sex and consign themselves to one with whom they look forward to a perpetual and eternal union and its growing blessings as things that foster the hope that is always restoring their minds.

But it is totally different for the unchaste—the ones who do not think about marriages and their holiness from religion. For them there is marriage of the body and none of the spirit. If anything of spiritual marriage does show up during the engaged state—if it rises due to elevated thought about it—it nevertheless falls back down to the selfish desires that are in the will of the flesh. And so, because of the unchaste things there it dives headfirst into the body and pollutes the foundations of its love with that alluring fire. This makes it go out as quickly as it lit in the beginning, and it disappears into midwinter cold. This hastens its loss. With these people the engaged state serves for almost nothing except to fill their lusts full of lasciviousness and contaminate married love.

305   (9) *During the time of engagement, physical union is not allowed,* because this destroys the sequence ascribed to the love in marriage. For there are three regions in human minds. The highest is called heavenly, the middle spiritual, and the lowest worldly. A person is born in this lowest but rises into the higher, called spiritual,

through a life in keeping with the truths of religion, and into the highest through marriage of love and wisdom. All bad lusts and wantonness reside in the lowest region, called worldly, but there are no bad lusts or wantonness in the higher region called spiritual, for the Lord leads a person into this region as he is reborn. In the highest region, though, called heavenly, is the chastity of marriage in married love. A person is raised into this region by a love of usefulness—and by the real love of marriage, because the foremost forms of usefulness come out of marriage.

These observations show in brief that the love in marriage should be raised from the lowest region into the highest from the time it first kindles, in order to be chaste and so it can be sent from chasteness through the middle region and the lowest, into the body. When this happens, this lowest region is purified of its unchastities by the love's coming down from chasteness. In this way the lowest level of the love becomes chaste.

Now, if bodily unions coming before their time topple the regular order of this love, the result is that the person acts from the lowest region, which is unchaste from birth. It is well known that coldness toward marriage and scornful neglect of the married partner begin there and arise from it.

But still the results of premature unions can differ in various ways. Likewise the results of the time of betrothal dragging on too long, or of too much haste. But these results are hard to describe because they are so many and so varied.

306   (10) *After a the period of engagement, there should be a wedding.* There are ceremonies that are only formalities, and there are ceremonies that are formalities and essentials at the same time. Weddings are among the latter. The reasons that follow establish that weddings are among the essential things that should be religiously made public and formally celebrated.

(a) The wedding ends the previous state begun with a commitment—which was mainly a state of spirit—and it begins the later state to be begun by marriage. This is a spiritual and bodily state at the same time, for then your spirit enters your body and directs from there. Therefore, on that day the couple drop the state and name of bride and groom and put on the state and name of spouses and bed companions.

(b) The wedding is an introduction and entrance to a new state, which is such that the young woman becomes a wife and the young man a husband, and both of them one flesh. This happens when love unites them through the most outward plane. Earlier pages showed that marriage does in fact change a young woman into a wife and a young man into a husband, and also that marriage unites two into one human form so that they are no longer two but one flesh.

(c) The wedding is a step toward fully separating love for the other sex from married love. This happens as the consent of one person's love becomes bound to the other person's love through a full opportunity to join together.

(d) It seems as if the wedding only fills the gap between those two states and thus is just a formality that can be omitted. But all the while this essential thing is in it—that the new state already mentioned is to be entered then with a covenant, and consent is to be declared in the presence of witnesses and also consecrated by a priest, besides the other things that make it last.

Since there are essential things in a wedding, and since a marriage becomes legitimate only after it, they celebrate weddings in heaven, too (see no. 21, above, and later nos. 27–41).

307   (11) *Before the celebration of the wedding a marriage agreement should be settled in the presence of witnesses.* Properly, a marriage agreement should be settled before the wedding is celebrated so the statutes and laws of genuine married love are known and kept in mind after the wedding, and also ties that bind minds to lawful marriage. For after certain beginnings of marriage the states before engagement come back, at times, when memory fades and forgetfulness of the agreed-on contract creeps in. In fact, because one unchaste thing leads to another, the contract is blotted out, and if recalled to memory at the time, it becomes despised. But society has taken on itself the protection of this covenant to avoid these transgressions, and it has appointed penalties for those who break the contract.

In a word, a contract made before the wedding makes the sacred promises of real married love public, supports them and binds people without self-restraint to obey them. In addition, the right to have children, and the children's right to inherit their parents' goods, are made lawful.

308
(12) *The marriage should be declared sacred by a minister.* The reason is that marriages are spiritual in their own right, and therefore holy. For they come down from the heavenly marriage of good and truth, and things having to do with marriage correspond to the divine marriage of the Lord and the church. So they are from the Lord Himself and are in keeping with the condition of the church in the ones who enter the contract.

Now, because the clergy on earth administers the things that are ministerial in the Lord—that is, things having to do with His love—and thus things having to do with blessing, it is proper for marriages to be declared sacred by a minister. And because they are the chief witnesses at that time, it is proper for them to hear, accept, confirm, and in this way establish, consent to the covenant.

309
(13) *The wedding should be celebrated with good fellowship.* The reasons are that the love before the wedding—the love of a bride and groom—descends at that time into their hearts, and they feel the joy of marriage as it spreads from there into their entire bodies. This makes them want to celebrate, so they break into celebration, as much as is fitting and proper. To foster these feelings it is important that their souls rejoice together, so that in this way they are introduced to the joys of marriage.

310
(14) *After the wedding the spiritual marriage also becomes a bodily marriage, and thus complete.* All the things a person does in his body flow into it from his spirit. For it is well known that the mouth does not speak by itself, but the mind's thoughts speak through it, and that the hands do not move, nor do the feet walk, by themselves, but the mind's intention acts through them. So the *mind* speaks, through its organ, and the *mind* acts, through its organs, in the body. This makes it clear that whatever your mind is like, that is what the speech of your mouth and the actions of your body are like. From these things it follows as a conclusion that by constant

influence your mind directs your body to do the things it wants, when it wants them. So people's bodies, from an inner point of view, are nothing but the outward forms of their minds, structured to do the soul's bidding.

These things are said first to make clear why minds or spirits should first couple with each other as in marriage, before bodies do—namely, so that marriages will be marriages of spirit when they become bodily marriages. And consequently so that the partners will love each other in spirit and therefore in body.

Now to look at marriage in the light of these concepts. When the love in marriage joins two people's minds and forms them into a marriage, then it also joins and forms their bodies for this same thing. For, as was said, the form of your mind is also the form of your body, inwardly, with the only difference that your body is organized on the outside to bring about what your mind settles on for the inward form of your body.

But a mind regulated by married love is not only inwardly all throughout, everywhere, in your whole body, but it is also inwardly in the organs devoted to generation, situated in their own place below the other bodily parts. When people are united in married love, the contours of their minds come to completion in these organs of generation. Consequently, the feelings and thoughts of their minds are directed there. The things that minds do from other loves differ in that other loves do not extend to there.

The conclusion from these things is that whatever married love is like in two people's minds or spirits, it is like in these organs.

But it is self-evident that after the wedding the marriage of the spirit also becomes a marriage of the flesh and thus complete, and consequently that if a marriage is chaste in spirit and draws on the spirit's holiness, it is chaste when it is fulfilled in your body. And the opposite is true if the marriage is unchaste in spirit.

311   (15) *This is the development of married love by proper stages from its first warmth to its first torch.* We say from its first warmth to its first torch because the warmth of life is love, and the warmth—or love—of marriage keeps growing, and it finally grows as if into a flame or torch. We say to its first torch because this means the first state after the wedding, when the love is ablaze. But earlier chapters have described what it becomes after this flame, in the

marriage itself. This part of the book, however, explains its progress from the first starting post to this first turning post.

Everything goes forward in a regular succession from beginnings to results, and in any chain of events that takes up from there, these results become beginnings. Also, every intermediate thing of a series is the result of what comes before it and the beginning of what follows. And in this way purposes always go through causes into effects. This can be established and illustrated enough for reason to see it by means of things known and seen in the world. But we pass by all that because here we are only dealing with the order by which love goes forward from its point of departure to its goal, except to say that afterwards this love develops, for the most part, as it did from its first warmth to its first torch. For then it unfolds according to what the first heat was like in its own right. If this first heat was chaste, its chasteness becomes stronger as it goes, but if it was not chaste, its unchasteness increases as it goes on, until it is stripped of all the chasteness it had from outside but not from within at the time of engagement.

312   (16) *Rushed into without development by proper stages, married love burns out its core and is squandered.* Certain ones in heaven put it this way. By core they mean the interiors of your mind and body. When married love is rushed into it burns these out, or consumes them, because then that love starts from a flame that devours and corrupts the sanctuaries where married love should settle as in its starting point, and where it should begin from. This happens if a man and woman rush into marriage without the right order, not looking to the Lord, not consulting reason, rejecting formal commitment, and obeying only their flesh. If that love begins from flesh's fire, it becomes superficial and not internal, thus not married love. You might call it a shell and not a kernel, or physical—meager and dry—because drained of its true essence. (More about this appears in no. 305, above).

313   (17) *The mental states of both, following one after another in order, flow into the character of the marriage, but it is different for spiritual people than for worldly people.* It is a rule that should be recognized for its truth in the literate world, that the final condition is of the same quality as the successive steps from which it was formed

and exists, for this discloses what inflowing is and how it works. Inflowing refers to everything that comes before and goes to make up what follows, and through things following in order makes up the final result, like all that comes first in the case of a person, and goes to make up his wisdom. Or like all that precedes for a politician and makes up his good judgment, or everything that precedes for a theologian and makes up his learning. The same goes for everything that comes before from infancy and makes up a man. Also what goes forward in order from the seed and sprout and makes a tree, and then what goes from the flower and makes its fruit. The same goes for all that comes before and goes on for a husband and wife and makes their marriage. This is what inflowing means.

As yet it is not known in the world that all the things that come before in a mind make up sequences and that the sequences link themselves together, one next to another and one after another, and these together make up the end result. But this is brought up here because it is a truth from heaven. For it makes known what influx does, and what the end result is like, where the sequences just mentioned exist together, formed step by step.

These observations show that the mental states of both partners, following one after another in order, influence the condition of the marriage. But after marriage the partners are totally unaware of the sequential things that are in their souls, impressed on them from things that preceded. And yet these are the things that give form to married love and make up the mental states by which they interact. A different state is formed from a different development in spiritual people than in worldly, because spiritual people go ahead in the right order and worldly in the wrong order. For spiritual people look to the Lord, and the Lord provides and conducts the process, but worldly people look to themselves and go at the process backwards. So the condition of their marriage is inwardly full of unchaste things. And however many unchaste things there are, there are that many frigidities, and however many of these there are, there are that many obstructions to innermost life. They clog the current and dry up the spring.

314 (18) *This is because there is progressive order and simultaneous order, and the second kind is from the first and in keeping with it.* This is

brought in as a reason that confirms the last article above. It is well known that there is progressive and simultaneous order. But people do not know that the simultaneous order comes from the progressive order and is in keeping with it. But it is extremely hard to make it understandable how the progressive things carry over into the simultaneous and what kind of order they form there, because as yet the learned do not have any notion that would serve to make it clear.

A preliminary idea of this mystery cannot be introduced in a few words, and to introduce it at length here would take our minds off a clearer view of married love. So the things briefly brought out about these two orders, progressive and simultaneous, and about the one influencing the other, in *The Doctrine for the New Jerusalem Concerning the Sacred Scriptures*, will be enough to shed some light.

It says, "In heaven and on earth there is progressive order and simultaneous order. In progressive order one thing follows another from highest all the way to lowest. But in simultaneous order one thing is next to another from innermost all the way to outermost. Progressive order is like a column with steps from the top to the bottom, but simultaneous order is like a structure holding together from the center to the surface.

"Progressive order becomes simultaneous in the end in this way: the highest elements of progressive order become the inmost things of simultaneous order, and the lowest things of progressive order become the outermost things of simultaneous order. By comparison it is like a column of steps being collapsed to become a structure on one plane. This is how the simultaneous is formed from progressive entities. And this is in each and every thing in the spiritual world and in each and every thing in the natural world." (See nos. 38, 65 in that book, and much more about it in *Angelic Wisdom about Divine Love and Divine Wisdom*, nos. 205–29.)

It is the same with the progressive order leading to marriage and with the simultaneous order in marriage. Namely, the simultaneous is from the progressive and in keeping with it. One who knows that progressive order flows into simultaneous order can understand the reason why angels can see in a person's hand all his mind's thoughts and intentions. And also that wives can tell their husbands' feelings from their husbands' hands on their breasts. This has been mentioned various times in the stories. The reason is that hands are the most outward parts of a person, where the thoughts and conclusions of his mind reach their final point, and become "simultaneous" there. Also for that reason it says in the Word that it is "written on the hands" [Is. 49:16; Rev. 13:16; 20:4].

315   I add to this two stories. This is the first:

One time I saw something happening in the sky not far from me. I saw a cloud separated into little clouds. Some of these were blue and some dark, and it seemed as if they were bumping into each other. flashing across them were striped rays that seemed now sharp like sword points, now blunt like broken swords. The rays now darted out, now retreated, just like boxers. That is, these little clouds of different colors seemed as if they were fighting among themselves. But they were playing. And since this meteorological phenomenon appeared not far from me, I raised my eyes, focused my eyesight, and saw boys, young men, and old men going into a house built of marble, with a foundation of porphyry. The phenomenon was above this house.

Then I spoke to one of the people going in and asked, "What's this?"

"It's a school where young men get a start in various things that have to do with wisdom."

When I heard this I went in with them. I was in spirit. That is, in the same state the people in the spiritual world are in—called spirits and angels. Looking around in the school I saw a raised chair at the front, benches in the middle, seats all around the sides, and a balcony over the entrance. The raised chair was for the young men who took turns answering the problems that were proposed, the benches were for the scholars, the seats at the sides were for those who had answered wisely before, and the balcony was for the older ones who would be arbiters and judges. In the middle of the balcony was a dais where a wise man they called the chief teacher sat. He proposed the problems that the young men would answer from the chair.

When they were assembled the man rose up from the dais

and said, "Please respond to this problem, and solve it if you can. What is the soul, and what is it like?"

Everyone was astounded when they heard these words, and they murmured. Some of the group on the benches called out, "Who among men, from Saturn's time to this time of ours, has been able to see and understand with any rational thought what the soul is, much less what it is like? Isn't this beyond everyone's intellectual range?"

But a response to this came back from the balcony, "This is not beyond understanding but is within reason and in plain sight. Just answer."

And the young men chosen that day to go up to the chair and respond to the problem, stood up. They were five whom the elders had examined and found to be strong thinkers, and then they sat on couches beside the chair. Then, in the order they were seated in, they went up. When each went up to the chair he put on a tunic of silk, opal in color, and over it a robe of soft wool with flowers woven into it, and on his head a skullcap with a garland of roses surrounded by little sapphires on the crown of it.

I watched the first one dressed this way go up. He said, "What the soul is and what it is like has not been revealed to anyone from the day of creation. It is a mystery among the treasures of God alone. But this is disclosed, that a soul resides in a person like a queen. Where her court is, learned seers have conjectured. Some guess that it is in a little gland between the cerebrum and the cerebellum, called the pineal gland. They put the seat of the soul there because the whole person is regulated from these two brains, and that gland regulates them. Because what governs your brains also governs your whole body, from head to heel." And he said, "Therefore this has seemed true, or like the truth, to many in the world. But after a long time it has been rejected as fiction."

After he said this he took off the robe, tunic, and skullcap. The second of those chosen put it on and went to the chair. His proposition about the soul was, "Not in all heaven and in all the earth is it known what the soul is and what it is like. It is known that it exists and that it is in people, but where it is, is a guess. This is certain— that it is in your head, since the intellect thinks there and will intends there, and in the front of the head, in the face, are a person's five senses. Nothing gives life to intellect, will, and senses except the soul that resides in the head. But where in your head its court is I dare not say. But I have agreed with those who give it a seat in the three ventricles of the brain. Sometimes I agree with those who place it in the *corpora striata* there, sometimes with those who place it in the medullary substance of each brain, sometimes with those who place it in the cortical substance, sometimes with those who place it in the *dura mater*. For there has been no lack of votes, so to speak, in confirmation of each of the places.

"There have been votes for the three ventricles in the brain because they are vessels for the animal spirits and all the lymphs of the brain; votes for the *corpora striata* because they make the medulla through which the nerves go out and through which both brains connect with the spine, and from the nerves and brains, fibers go out that weave the whole body together; votes for the medullary substance of each brain because this is the collection and gathering of all the fibers that are the beginnings of the whole person; votes for the cortical substance because the first and the last ends, and thus the beginnings, of all fibers and thus of all senses and motions, are there; votes for the *dura mater* because this is the common covering of each brain and extends from there, by a kind of continuation, over the heart and over the viscera of the body.

"As for me, I do not advocate one theory more than another. Please judge and choose which you prefer."

He got down from the chair when he had said this, and he turned the tunic, robe and skull-cap over to the third, who said these words when he got up into the chair. "What am I, a youngster, doing with such a sublime theme? I call on the learned ones sitting on the sides here, I call on you wise men in the balcony, I even call on the angels of the highest heaven. Can anyone get any idea about the soul from the light of his reason? But like the others I can speculate about its seat in a person. And I guess that it's in the heart and for that reason in the blood. This is my guess because by its blood the heart reigns in body and head. It sends the great vessel called the aorta out into the whole body, and it sends the carotid arteries into the whole head. This accounts for the general agreement that the soul sustains, nourishes, and vivifies the whole organic system—both head and body—by the heart through the blood. The fact that Holy Scripture says 'soul and heart' so many times lends credence to this. For instance, that God is to be loved 'with the whole soul and with the whole heart,' and that God creates in a person 'a new soul and a new heart' (Deut. 6:5; 10:12; 11:13; 26:16; Jer. 32:41; Matt. 22:37; Mark 12:30, 33; Luke 10:27; and other places). And it says plainly that 'the blood is the soul of the flesh'" (Lev. 17:11, 14).

Some raised their voices, saying, "Learned! Learned!" They were clergymen.

Then the fourth put on the third one's clothes, got into the chair and said, "I, too, suspect that no one is keen and sharp-witted enough to be able to discern what the soul is and what it is like. So, in my opinion, when they try to pry into it they dull their edge on nothings. But from childhood I have stuck faithfully with the opinion that ancient people had, that a person's soul is in all of him and in every part of him, thus just as much in his head and every part of it as in his body and every part of it. And I think it's been a hoax contrived by modern people to designate the soul's seat somewhere, and not everywhere. Besides, soul is spiritual substance, which dimensions and location do not apply to, while residence and completeness do. And who doesn't mean 'life' when he says 'soul'? Isn't life throughout and in each part?"

Many in the auditorium applauded when he said this.

Then the fifth stood up and, furnished with the same clothing, he spoke out from the chair. "I'm not going to take up time saying where the soul is—whether in some part or everywhere in the whole. But from my stock and store I disclose my feelings about this: what the soul is and what it is like.

"No one can think of the soul except as like something pure, comparable to ether or air or wind, in which the vital element is from rationality, which man has more than beasts. I have based this opinion on the fact that when a person dies he is said to breathe out or give up his soul or spirit. And so a soul living after death is thought to be such a breath, with thinking life in it, called the soul. What else can the soul be?

"But I heard someone saying from the balcony that the problem of what the soul is and what it is like is not beyond understanding but within reason and in plain sight, so I beg and pray you yourself to unlock this eternal mystery."

The elders in the balcony looked at the master teacher who had proposed the problem. He could tell from their nods that they wanted him to go down and teach. He went down from the dais at once, crossed the auditorium, got into the chair, spread his hand out and said, "Please listen. Who does not believe that soul is the inmost and subtlest essence of a person? And what is essence without form but a figment of the imagination? So a soul is a form. But I'll tell what form. It is the form of everything belonging to love and everything belonging to wisdom. Everything having to do with love is called affections, and everything having to do with wisdom is called perceptions.

"Perceptions due to feelings and thus with feelings make one form in which there are innumerable forms in such order, series, and coherency that they can be called one thing. They can be called one thing because you cannot remove anything from it or add anything to it and keep it what it is. What is a human soul but such a form? Aren't all the things related to love and all the things related to wisdom essentials of that form? And in a person these things are in his soul and, by means of his soul, are in his head and body.

"You are called spirits and angels, and in the world you thought that spirits and angels are like winds or atmospheres, thus like minds and souls. And now you see clearly that in truth you are really and actually people who lived and thought in a material body in the world. And you know that a material body does not live and think, but a spiritual substance in that body does. And this you called a soul. You didn't understand its form, though you have seen it now, and you do see it.

"All of you are the souls about whose immortality you have heard, thought, said, and written so much. And you are forms of the love and wisdom from God, so you can never die. And so soul is the human form that nothing can be taken away from and nothing can be added to, and it is the inmost form of all the forms of your whole body. And the forms that are more outward get both their essence and their form from within, so you, just as you appear to yourselves and to us, are souls.

"In a word, the soul is the person himself, because it is the innermost person. For this reason its form is fully and perfectly a human form. Yet it is not life but is the vessel of life from God nearest to God, and in this way it is a place where God lives."

When he had said these things many applauded, but some said, "We'll think about it."

Then I went home. And I noticed that in place of the earlier aerial phenomenon over the high school a bright white cloud appeared, without stripes or rays sparring among themselves. The cloud came in, penetrating the roof and lighting up the walls. And I heard that they saw things written—this among others: "Jehovah God . . . breathed a soul of lives into the man's nose, and the man was made into a living soul" (Gen. 2:7).

316   The second story: Walking along one time, at rest in my soul and in the peace of a happy mind, I saw a park in the distance, with a covered walk in the middle of it, leading to a small palace. And I saw young women and young men and husbands and wives going in. I approached in spirit, and asked a keeper standing in the entrance if I could go inside, too.

He looked at me, and I said, "Why are you looking at me?"

"I'm looking at you," he answered, "to see if the peaceful happiness in your face includes something of the happiness of married love. Past this walk is a small garden with a house in the middle of it, where two newlyweds are. Their male and female friends are coming today to wish them happiness. I'm not acquainted with the people I let in, but I was told that I'd know them by their faces. If I see the happiness of married love in them I am to let them in, and not others."

All angels can see other people's heartfelt joy in their faces, and the delight of their love. The delight he saw in my face was that I thinking about the love in marriage. This thought shone from my eyes and went from there to the more inward parts of my face. So he said I could go in.

The covered walk I entered through was made of fruit trees connected to each other by their limbs. They made an unbroken wall of trees on either side. Through the walk I went into the little garden, which breathed a pleasant fragrance from its shrubs and flowers. The shrubs and flowers were pair by pair, and I heard that little gardens like that appear around houses where there are, or have been, weddings, and that for that reason they are called wedding gardens.

Then I went into the house, where I saw the two married partners holding hands and talking together because of their genuine married love. And then I could read in their faces the image of married love, and what is alive about it in their conversation.

After I and many others had offered them congratulations and wished them happiness, I went out into the little wedding garden, and on the right side of it I saw a group of young people. Everyone who came out of the house was hurrying to this group. They hurried there because the conversation there was about the love in marriage, and this conversation draws everyone's soul to itself by some hidden force.

Then I listened to a wise man talking about it, and the things I heard were briefly these: The Lord's Divine Providence is over marriages and in marriages very particularly and therefore very generally, in the heavens, because all the happiness of heaven wells up from the joys of married love, like fresh waters from the fresh current of a spring. And because of this, the Lord provides that pairs are born for marriage, and they are continually being educated for marriage, both the boy and the girl, without knowing it. And when the time is fulfilled the young woman, marriageable by then, and the young man, ready to marry by then, meet somewhere as if by fate and see each other. And then instantly, as if by some instinct, they know that they are partners. And, from some inner voice within them, the young man thinks, "She is for me," and the young woman thinks, "He is for me." And after this has been on both of their minds a few days they talk with each other on purpose and make vows. They say "as if by fate" and "as if by instinct" and mean by Divine Providence, because these things seem that way, since the couple do not know about it.

The wise man confirmed that pairs are born for marriage and are brought up for marriage without either one's knowing it, by the marriage-like resemblance visible in their faces. Also by the inmost and eternal union of their souls and minds. Unions, which are like that in heaven, are not possible without foresight and provision by the Lord.

After the wise man said these things and the group applauded, he went on, "Marriage is in people, masculine as well as feminine, in the smallest details. But yet the marriage is one thing in a male and another in a female. Also, in the masculine of marriage is something that can join with the feminine of marriage, also in the smallest details, and vice versa." He confirmed this by the marriage of will and intellect in everyone—"two things that act together in the most specialized aspects of your mind and the most specialized of your body. You can see from this that something of marriage is in every substantial thing—even the smallest. And this comes clear from the composite resources that are put together from simple resources, as that there are two eyes, two ears, two nostrils, two cheeks, two lips, two arms and hands, two sides, and two feet. And inside the person are the brain's two hemispheres, the heart's two ventricles, the lungs' two lobes, two kidneys, two testicles, and where there are not two of things, still they are divided in two. There are two of them because one belongs to will and the other to intellect, which act marvelously together to make a unit. So two eyes make one vision, two ears one hearing, two nostrils one smell, two lips one speech, two hands one work, two feet one walk, two hemispheres of the brain one habitation of the mind, the heart's two chambers one bodily life through blood, the lungs' two lobes one respiration, and so on. And masculine and feminine united through the real love in marriage make one fully human life."

While he was saying these things there appeared on the right a red lightning flash and a white flash on the left. They were both gentle and entered through our eyes into our minds and enlightened them, too. And after the flashes it thundered. It was a gentle murmur floating down from an angelic heaven and growing louder.

When we heard and saw these events the wise man said, "These are a sign and a warning to me to add something to what I said. The right member of these pairs stands for their goodness and the left stands for their truth. This comes out of the marriage of good and truth, which is inscribed on the person in general and on every single part in him. Good has to do with will and truth with intellect, and both together have to do with unity. For this reason the right eye, in heaven, is the good of sight, the left is its truth, and the right ear is the good of hearing and the left its truth, as the right hand, too, is the good of a person's power and the left its truth. The same goes for the other pairs. And since the right and left have those meanings, the Lord said, 'If your right eye offends you, pluck it out . . . and if your right hand offends you, cut it off' (Matt. 5:29–30).

"By this He meant that if good becomes bad it should be rejected. Also, he told the disciples to throw their net on the right side of the boat, and when they did it they caught a huge number of fish (John 21:6–7), by which He meant that they should teach the good of charity, and in this way they would gather people."

After he said these things the two flashes appeared again, more gentle than before. And then we noticed that the left flash took on its white brilliance from the red fire of the right flash. Seeing this he said, "This is a sign from heaven confirming what I said, because in heaven something fiery is good and something bright white is truth. And the fact that the left flash seemed to get its brilliance from the red fire of the right flash is a sign to show that the brilliance of light—or light—is nothing other than the brightness of fire."

When they had heard these things everyone went home afire with the good and truth of joy kindled by the flashes and the talk about them.

Chapter 14

Remarriage

317   The questions might be raised, whether married love, which is love of one man and one woman, can be set aside or transferred or added to after the death of a partner, and also whether remarriage has something in common with polygamy and thus whether it can be called progressive polygamy—besides other questions that have a way of adding problems to problems for people who argue the point.

So I thought it worthwhile to let the following topics about repeated marriages stand trial, so that the masters of investigation, who reason in the dark about these marriages, can see some light.

The topics are:

(1) Remarriage after the death of a partner depends on the married love that preceded.

(2) It also depends on the state of the marriage the partners had lived in.

(3) Nothing stands in the way or is against those who did not have a real married love, if they marry again.

(4) Those who have lived together in real married love do not want to marry again, unless for reasons not connected with married love.

(5) The state of marriage of a young man with a virgin is different from the state of marriage of a young man with a widow.

(6) And the state of marriage of a widower with a virgin is different from that of a widower with a widow.

(7) The variations and diversities of these marriages, as to love and its characteristics, are beyond number.

(8) A widow is in a worse situation than a widower.

An explanation of these topics follows.

318

(1) *Remarriage after the death of a partner depends on the married love that preceded.* Real married love is like a balance, weighing your inclinations to marry again. In the measure that the previous married love approached true married love, the inclination to remarry goes away, and in the measure that the previous love veered off from true married love, an inclination to marry again tends to enter. The obvious reason is that married love is a union of minds, which stays in the bodily life of the one after the other's death, and it holds the inclination like the tray in a pair of scales. It tips the scales according to the true love involved. But today it is rare to approach more than a few steps toward this love, so the scale of the overriding inclination usually rises to the balance point and from there dips and inclines to the other side—that is, to marriage.

It is the opposite with people whose previous love, in their foregoing marriage, veered off from the real love in marriage. The reason is that veering away from it is a separation of minds. This tendency, too, stays in the bodily life of the one after the other's death, and it enters the will of the one—the will disjoined from the other's will—and makes an inclination toward a new union. The thinking that the will's inclination introduces is in favor of this and it introduces hope of a more united and thus happier relationship.

It is well known that inclinations to remarry spring from the condition of the previous love, and reason sees this, too. For true married love has in it a fear of loss, and after loss, grief, and this grief and that fear are in the most inward parts of the partners' minds. So however much true married love there is in it, that is how much a soul inclines, both in will and in thought—that is, in intention—to be in the person that it was with and was in. Consequently, your mind is held in balance about a second marriage according to the degree of love it enjoyed in the first.

On account of this, the same two people are reunited after death, and they love each other just as they did in the world. But, as said before, that love is rare today, and few lay a finger on it. And those who do not touch it—more so, those who back far off from it—long to join with another woman or another man, after death, as much as they longed for separation from their partner in their past life, which was frigid.

But more about these things is in what follows.

319   (2) *Remarriage after the death of a partner also depends on the state of marriage the partners had lived in.* Here "state of marriage" does not mean the state of love, dealt with in the last article, because the love produces an *inner* inclination toward or away from marriage. But the state of the marriage produces an *outward* inclination toward or away from it.

This condition, with its tendencies, is very involved. For example: (a) If there are babies in the home and a new mother must be provided for them. (b) If more children are desired. (c) If the home is large and furnished with servants of both sexes. (d) If things to be taken care of continually outside the home distract a man's mind from family matters at home, so that without a new wife there is fear of trouble and misfortune. (e) If they need mutual aid and service, as in different businesses and jobs. (f) Besides, it depends on the separated male or female partner's makeup whether they can or cannot live alone or without a partner. (g) Also, the previous marriage either leaves a fear of married life, or it leaves a partiality to it. (h) I have heard that polygamous love, love of the other sex and also lust for defloration and lust for variety lead some people's minds into a desire for marrying again. And that fear of the law and fear for their reputation, if they were to commit adultery, lead some people's minds into it—besides many other things that promote outward inclinations toward marriage.

320   (3) *Nothing stands in the way or is against those who did not have married love, if they marry again.* Those who did not have married love have no spiritual or inner bond but only a worldly or outward bond. And if an inner bond does not hold the outer one together in its order and continuity, the outer one lasts only like a sash with its knot undone, which falls off or blows loose in the wind. The reason is that something natural springs from something spiritual, and in its being is nothing but a construct of spiritual

things put together. So if something natural is separated from the spiritual that produced it and begot it, so to speak, it is no longer held together inwardly but only outwardly by the spiritual part. This goes around it and ties it together, in a general way, but does not bind all of its parts together. For this reason the natural level separated from what is spiritual between two married partners makes no union of minds and therefore none of will, but only a union of some outward feelings that cling to the bodily senses.

There is nothing to hinder or halt such partners if they can remarry, because they did not have the essentials of marriage, so none of the essentials are in them after separation by death. So then they are in full freedom to bind their sensual feelings to any woman who is agreeable and free, in the case of a widower, or in the case of a widow, to any man who is agreeable and free. They only think of marriages on a worldly plane and as conveniences owing to various external necessities and expediencies that can be restored, in case of death, by another person in place of the previous one. And perhaps if their inner thoughts were looked into, as in the spiritual world, no distinction would turn up in them between married relationships and extramarital couplings. For the reason given above, they may get married again and again, because merely worldly intimacies dissolve of themselves after death and drift away. External affections follow the corpse at the time of death and are buried with it, leaving the affections that attach to more inward things.

But note that marriages that join inwardly are not easy to enter on earth, because the Lord cannot provide selections of inwardly similar people there as He can in the heavens, since they are limited in many ways—as, limited to equals in status and condition within the district, community, and town where they live. On earth it is mostly outward things that bind them together, and therefore not inner ones. The inner things come out only after a period of marriage, and they become noticeable only when they spill into outward things.

321   (4) *Those who have lived together in real married love do not want to marry again, unless for reasons not connected with married love.* These are the reasons why those who have lived in real married love do not want to remarry after their partner's death: (a) As to

souls and therefore as to minds they are united, and this uniting is an actual joining of one's soul and mind to the other's, because it is spiritual—a joining that absolutely cannot be dissolved. That a spiritual conjunction is like this has already been shown in various places. (b) They are also united in body by the wife's receiving the propagations of her husband's soul, and thus by his life being put into hers—which turns a virgin into a wife. And, the other way around, they are united by the husband's receiving his wife's married love, which puts the inner parts of his mind, and at the same time the interiors and exteriors of his body, into a state to receive love and to perceive wisdom—which makes a young man into a husband (see no. 198, above, about these things). (c) The sphere of love from the wife and the sphere of intellect from the man flows out all the time, it makes their marriage complete, and it surrounds them with its pleasant breath and unites them (also see no. 223, above). (d) Couples united like this in marriage think and breathe permanence, and their eternal happiness is based on this idea (see no. 216). (e) for all these reasons they are no longer two but one person—that is, one flesh. (f) To spiritual eyes it is plainly clear that they cannot be torn apart by either one's death. (g) This new thing should be added to these observations: that these two are not even separated by the death of one, since the spirit of the deceased husband or wife continues to live with the husband or wife who is not yet deceased. And this continues until the other one's death, when they meet again and reunite themselves and love each other more tenderly than before because they are in the spiritual world.

These things afford the undeniable conclusion that those who have lived in real married love do not want to remarry.

But if they do enter something like a marriage later, it takes place for reasons separate from married love, and these reasons are all external. For example, if there are small children in the home and their care must be seen to, if the home is large and furnished with servants of both sexes, if management of matters outside the home distracts the mind from family matters at home, if mutual help and services are necessary, and other things like that.

322   (5) *The state of marriage of a young man with a virgin is different from the state of marriage of a young man with a widow.* The state of a

marriage means the state of each one's life—the husband's and the wife's—after the wedding, which is to say in marriage. It has to do with what their living together is like then—whether it is a living together of the inner dimensions of souls and minds, which is living together in its principal form, or is only living together of the outer dimensions of souls, senses, and bodies. The state of a young man's marriage with a virgin is precisely the state that initiates a genuine marriage, because between them married love can go forward in its right order, which is from its first warmth to its first blaze, and from there it advances from the first seed in the young husband and from the flower in the virgin wife. And in this way it can sprout, grow, and bear fruit. And they can introduce each other into these things. But if living together was external, the young man was not a young man, nor was the virgin a virgin, except in outward appearance. But between a young man and a widow there is not the same initiation from the beginnings to the marriage nor the same progression in marriage, since a widow has more of her own judgment and decision than a virgin has. So a young man approaches a widow wife with a different outlook than he has for a virgin wife.

But there are many variations and diversities in these matters, so this is only put down in a general way.

323   (6) *And the state of marriage of a widower with a virgin is different from that of a widower with a widow,* for a widower has already been initiated into married life, and the virgin is about to be introduced. But married love perceives and feels its pleasure and joy in initiation for both at once. The young husband and the young wife notice and feel things that are ever new in what goes on by way of initiation. Due to these things they are in a kind of continual initiation and therefore in a lovely process. It happens differently in the married state of a widower with a virgin. The virgin wife has an inner inclination, but it has passed by for the man. But in these matters there are many variations and diversities. The same goes for a marriage between a widower and a widow. So beyond a general notion of them nothing specific can be added.

324   (7) *The variations and diversities of these marriages, as to love and its characteristics, are beyond number.* There is infinite variety in

everything, and diversity is infinite, too. Variations here means variations among things that are of one kind or of one species and also variations among kinds and among species, but diversities means differences between things that are opposite.

This will illustrate our concept of the distinction between variation and diversity: The angelic heaven, which holds together as one unit, has infinite variety. There is no one there absolutely like anyone else, not in souls and minds, not in feelings, perceptions, and the thoughts from them, not in inclinations and the intentions springing from them, not in tone of voice, face, body, gesture, walk, and many other things. And yet, though they are millions and millions, the Lord has arranged them and goes on arranging them into one pattern that has complete unity and harmony. This could not be, except that One leads all the angels, who are generally and particularly so different. These are the things we mean by variations.

But by diversities we mean the opposites of those variations, which are found in hell, for each and every one there is diametrically opposite to those who are in heaven. And the hell composed of them is held together as one unit by variations, one from another, which are totally opposite to the variations in heaven—therefore, by perpetual diversities.

These things show how to understand "infinite variety" and "infinite diversity."

Marriages are the same. There are infinite varieties among those who are in married love and infinite varieties between those who love extramarital sex. And therefore there are infinite diversities between the one group and the other.

These observations lead to this conclusion—that variations and diversities in marriages of whatever type and kind, whether marriage of a young man and a virgin, a young man with a widow, a widower with a virgin, or a widower with a widow, exceed all number. Who can pick infinity apart into numbers?

325   (8) *A widow is in a worse situation than a widower.* The reasons are external and internal. The external are clear to everyone. (a) A widow cannot provide the necessities of life for herself and her household nor spend her money like a man, or as she did before

through a man and with a man. (b) She cannot protect herself and her home as it should be done, because when she was a wife her husband was her protection and like her arm. Even when she was her own protector she relied on her man. (c) On her own she is without advice in the kind of things that have to do with inner wisdom and its experience. (d) A widow is without someone to receive the love that she has as a woman, so she is in a condition foreign to the one that is innate and is brought about by marriage.

These outward reasons, which are worldly, also spring from inner ones that are spiritual, like everything else in the world and in your body (see no. 220, above).

The outward, worldly reasons can be gleaned from the inner, spiritual reasons, which emerge from the marriage of good and truth, and principally from these aspects of it: Good cannot provide nor dispense anything, except through truth. Good cannot protect itself except through truth, so truth is the protector and is like the arm of good. Good without truth is without advice because it has advice, wisdom, and experience through truth. Now, a man is truth by creation and a wife is its good from creation, or similarly a man is intellect by creation and a wife is its love from creation, so clearly the outward or worldly reasons that make a woman's widowhood worse spring from inner or spiritual reasons. These spiritual reasons that are joined with worldly ones are what the Word means by the things it says about widows in many places (they appear in *Apocalypse Revealed*, no. 764).

326   I add to these observations two stories. This is the first:

After the problem about the soul was aired and solved in the school, I saw them filing out, the master teacher in front, after him the elders, with the five young men who had answered among them, and then the others. And as they came out they scattered aside around the building, where there were walks bordered by shrubs. Gathering there, they divided into small groups, each one a gathering of young men chatting about things having to do with wisdom. A wise man from the balcony was in each of the groups.

Seeing them from my lodgings I became in spirit and went out to them in my spirit and approached the master teacher who had recently proposed the problem about the soul.

When he saw me he said, "Who are you? I was surprised when I saw you coming this way on the road. Sometimes you came into my sight, and sometimes you faded out of my sight. In other words, at one point I could see you, and suddenly I couldn't. You're certainly not in our state of life!"

Smiling at that, I answered, "I'm neither a magician nor a Vertumnus [Roman god of the changing seasons], but I am by turns sometimes in your light and sometimes in your shade, so I'm an alien and also a native."

At that the master teacher looked at me and said, "You're saying strange and remarkable things. Tell me who you are."

I said, "I'm in the world you were in and have left, called the natural world. And I'm also in the world you came into and are in, called the spiritual world. This makes it possible for me to be in a state of nature and a spiritual state at the same time—in an earthly state with people of earth and in a spiritual state with you. And when I'm in an earthly state I don't see you, but when in a spiritual state I do. It's a gift of God that I'm like this.

"You, an enlightened man, know that a person in the natural world doesn't see a person in the spiritual world, nor vice versa, so when I put my spirit into my body you didn't see me, but when I put my spirit out of my body you saw me. In the scholarly contests, you taught that you are souls and that souls see souls, because they are human forms. And you know that you didn't see yourselves—that is, your souls—in your bodies when you were in the natural world. This comes from the difference there is between spiritual and natural."

When he heard "difference between spiritual and natural," he said, "What difference? Isn't it like the difference between more and less pure? So what is spiritual but a purer natural?"

I answered, "The difference isn't like that but is like the difference between earlier and later, between which there's no finite ratio. Actually, the earlier is in the later the way a cause is in its effect, and the later is from the earlier as the effect comes from the cause. This is why the one doesn't appear to the other."

To these ideas the master teacher said, "I've studied and ruminated about this difference, but in vain, so far. If only I could fully grasp it!"

"You're not only going to grasp the difference between spiritual and natural," I said, "but you're going to see it, too."

Then I told him this. "You are in a spiritual state when among your associates but in an earthly state with me. For with them you speak a spiritual language that is common among all spirits and angels, but with me you speak my native language. For all spirits and angels speaking with a person speak the person's own language—as, French with a Frenchman, English with an Englishman, Greek with a Greek, Arabic with an Arab, and so on. And so to recognize the difference between spiritual and earthly as far as language goes, do this. Go to your associates, say something there and remember the sounds, and come back with them in your memory, and pronounce them in front of me."

He did it, and he came back to me with his words to them on his lips, and he spoke them and did not understand one of them. They were thoroughly foreign and alien sounds not found in any language in the natural world. This experiment, repeated a few times, clearly showed that everyone in the spiritual world has a spiritual language that has nothing in common with any language in the natural world, and that after death every person picks up that language by himself.

At the same time, he also learned by the experiment that the very sound of spiritual language is so different from the sound of earthly language that a person in nature cannot hear a spiritual sound at all—not even a loud one—nor a spiritual person an earthly sound.

Then I asked the master teacher and the bystanders to go off by themselves and write some sentence on paper and come back out to me with the paper and read it. They did it and came back with the paper in hand. But when they read it they could not understand it at all, since the writing consisted merely of certain letters of the alphabet with strokes above them, each of which stood for some idea on the subject. Since every letter in the alphabet there stands for some idea, it is clear why the Lord is called Alpha and Omega.

When they had gone off again and again, written and returned, they found out that that writing involved and expressed innumerable things that no natural writing can ever express. And someone said that this is because a spiritual person thinks things that are not understandable, and cannot be expressed, to an earthly person, and that these things cannot flow or carry over into any other form of writing or language.

Then, because the bystanders were unwilling to believe that spiritual thought is so far beyond natural thought that it cannot be expressed in worldly terms, I said to them, "Do an experiment. Go into your spiritual community and think about something, and remember it and come back and express it in front of me."

They went in, thought, remembered it, and came out. And when they wanted to express the thing they thought about, they could not. For they found no idea in earthly thought adequate to any idea of spiritual thought, and thus no word to express it. For ideas of thought make the words of speech. Then they went in again and came back again and convinced themselves that spiritual ideas are above the natural level—inexpressible, not to be spoken and incomprehensible to an earthly person. And they said that because spiritual ideas tower so far above worldly ones, spiritual ideas or thoughts, compared to worldly ones, are ideas of ideas, and thoughts of thoughts, and so they express characteristics of characteristics and feelings of feelings. So spiritual thoughts are the elements or beginnings of earthly thoughts. So it was clear from that that spiritual wisdom is wisdom of wisdom, thus it is not to be fully grasped by any wise person in the natural world.

Then they were told from the third heaven that there is a still more inward, or higher, wisdom, called heavenly. Relative to spiritual wisdom it is like spiritual wisdom relative to worldly. And these wisdoms flow down from the Lord's divine wisdom, which is infinite, in the order of the heavens.

327   When these things were done I said to the bystanders, "From these three experimental discoveries you've seen the kind of difference there is between spiritual and worldly, as well as the reason why a spiritual person doesn't see a worldly one, nor a worldly person a spiritual one. And yet they are together in feelings and thoughts and therefore in presence. That's why you sometimes saw me on the way, Master Teacher, and sometimes you didn't."

After this we heard a voice out of a higher heaven, saying to the master teacher, "Come up here." He went up, and came back, and said that before that, like himself, the angels had not known the differences between spiritual and earthly. The reason was that they had never before been around a person who was in both worlds at the same time, to provide some full comparison, and those differences are not found out without a comparison.

328   After this we left, and we talked about this matter again. I said, "The differences only exist because you who are in the spiritual world and therefore are spiritual exist in substance, not in matter, and substance is where material things originate. You are at the beginnings and thus in touch with single things, but we are in touch with the results of beginnings and with compound things. You are in the parts, we are in the assembled parts, and just as the whole can't enter its parts, things of nature, which are material, can't enter spiritual ones, which are substance—just as a ship's cable can't enter or be pulled through the eye of a sewing needle, or as a nerve can't enter or be put into one of the fibers that it is made up of, or a fiber into one of the fibrils it is made up of. This is known in the world, too, so the learned agree that natural doesn't flow into spiritual but spiritual into natural.

"This, then, is the reason why a person in nature can't think things that a spiritual person does, and therefore can't speak them. So Paul said the things he heard out of the third heaven were "inexpressible" [2 Cor. 12:4]. In addition, thinking spiritually is thinking apart from time and space, and thinking in nature is thinking with time and space, so something of time and space clings to every idea in earthly thought, but not to every idea of spiritual thought. The reason is that the spiritual world isn't in space and time like the world of nature but is in something that resembles space and time. And this is how knowing things and perceiving things differ. So you can think of God's essence and omnipresence from eternity—that is, of God before the world's creation—since you think of God's essence from eternity apart from time and of His omnipresence apart from space. Thus you grasp the kind of things that go beyond an earthly person's ideas."

And then I related how I once thought about God's essence and omnipresence from eternity—in other words, about God before the world's creation—and it bothered me that I could not get space and time out of the ideas in my mind. The idea of nature came in instead of God. But I was told, "Take away the ideas of space and time, and you'll see." And I was able to take them away, and I did see. And from that time I could think about God from eternity, and nature not from eternity at all, because God is in all time apart from time and in all space apart from space, but nature is in all time within time and in all space within space. Nature with her time and space had to begin and spring from somewhere, but not so God, who is without time and space. So nature came from God. Nature does not reach back to eternity, but is within time—that is, nature came at the same time as nature's time and space.

329   After the master teacher and the others left me, some boys who had also been at the scholarly contests followed me home, and they stood near me for a while as I was writing there. They saw a moth running on my paper! And they asked in surprise, "What's that little animal that's so fast?"

"It's called a moth," I said, "and I'll tell you some surprising things about it." I said, "In a living creature that small are as many outer parts and inner parts as there are in a camel! There are brains, heart, windpipe, organs of sense, motion, and reproduction, stomach, intestines, and other things. And each one is woven out of fibers, nerves, blood vessels, muscles, tendons, and membranes. And each of *these* is woven out of still finer parts that lie deeply hidden, beyond the sight of any eye."

They said the little creature still looked like just an uncomplicated object to them.

I said, "All the same, there are more things inside it than you can count. I say these things so you'll know that it's the same in every object that seems to be one thing, simple and small to you, and in your actions, feelings, and thoughts as well. I can assure you that every scrap of your thoughts and every drop of your feelings can be separated to infinity. And insofar as your ideas can be divided you are wise. Learn this—that everything gets more and more complicated as you take it apart, and not more and more simple, because division after division gets closer and closer to infinity, where everything is infinite. I'm passing this new idea on to you, which was never heard before."

After I said these things the boys went from me to the master teacher and asked him sometime to suggest in the school some new problem never heard before.

He said, "What?"

They said, "That everything gets more and more complicated as you take it apart, and not more and more simple, because it gets closer and closer to infinity, where everything is infinite."

He promised to propose it and said, "I see this, because I've noticed that one worldly idea is a vessel containing innumerable spiritual ideas. In fact, one spiritual idea is a container of innumerable heavenly ideas. That makes the difference between the celestial wisdom that the angels of the third heaven have, and the spiritual wisdom that the angels of the second heaven have, and between the worldly wisdom that the angels of the lowest heaven, and also men, have."

330   The second story: Once I heard a friendly discussion among men that was about the feminine sex—whether any woman who constantly loves her beauty, that is, who loves herself on account of her looks, can love her man. First they agreed among themselves that women have two kinds of beauty, one kind the natural beauty of their face and body, and the other the spiritual beauty of their love and their manners. They also agreed that these two kinds of beauty are often separated in the natural world and are always together in the spiritual world, for there beauty is the form that love and manners take. So it often happens that deformed women become beautiful after death and beautiful women become disfigured.

While they were discussing this, some wives came and said, "Accept our presence, because knowledge teaches you what you are discussing, but experience teaches it to us. And also, you know so little about the love of wives that it's hardly anything. Do you know that it is the good sense of wives' wisdom to keep their love for their husbands hidden deep in their breasts or within their hearts?"

Then a discussion began, and first the men concluded that every woman wants to be regarded as beautiful in face and beautiful in manners because by birth she is an inclination toward love, and the image of this inclination is beauty. So a woman who does not want to be beautiful is not a woman who wants to love and be loved, so she is not truly a woman.

To this the wives said, "A woman's beauty rests in her delicate tenderness and the exquisite sensation from it. A woman's love for a man and a man's love for a woman comes from that. Maybe you don't understand this."

The men's second conclusion was that before marriage a woman wants to be beautiful for men, but after marriage, if she is chaste, for one man and not for men.

To this the wives said, "After a husband has tasted his wife's natural beauty he no longer sees it, but sees her spiritual beauty and returns her love on account of it. And he recalls her natural beauty, but from a different point of view."

The third conclusion of their discussion was that if a woman wants to be regarded as beautiful after marriage the same as before it, she loves men and not a man, because a woman who loves herself for her beauty always wants her beauty to be tasted. And because her man no longer sees it, as you said, she turns to men who do notice it. Clearly this woman loves the other sex, not one of the other sex.

At this the women held their peace. Still, they murmured, "What woman is there so free of vanity that she doesn't want to be regarded as beautiful by men at the same time as by her one man?"

Some wives from heaven, who were beautiful because they were heavenly affections, heard these things, and they agreed with the men's three conclusions. But they added, "They only love their beauty and the embellishment of it on account of their husbands, and due to them."

331   Indignant that the wives from heaven confirmed the men's three conclusions, the three wives said to the men, "You've asked if a woman who loves herself on account of her beauty loves her man. In turn we'll discuss whether a man who loves himself on account of his intelligence can love his wife. Come and listen."

And they came to their first conclusion. "Every wife loves her man not for his face, but for the intelligence in his duty and behavior. Be aware that a wife joins herself with the man's intelligence, and in this way with the man. So if a man loves himself for his intelligence, he withholds his intelligence from his wife and keeps it to himself. This makes for separation and not union. Besides, for him to love his intelligence is to be wise by himself, and this is foolish, so it's loving his folly."

To this the men said, "Maybe a wife unites herself with a man's potency."

The wives laughed at this, saying, "Potency isn't lacking while a man loves his wife out of intelligence, but it fails if he loves her out of folly. Intelligence is to love only one wife, and this love doesn't lack potency. But folly is to love not a wife but the whole female sex, and potency does desert this love. Do you grasp this?"

The second conclusion was, "We women are born into love of men's intelligence. So if men love their own intelligence, the intelligence can't unite with the real love of it, which a wife has. And if a man's intelligence doesn't unite with the real love of it, which a wife has, the intelligence becomes folly out of contempt, and married love becomes cold. So what woman can unite her love with coldness? And what man can unite the insanity of contempt with a love of intelligence?"

But the men said, "What honor does a man have from his wife if he doesn't set a high value on his intelligence?"

But the wives answered, "From love. Because love honors. Honor can't be separated from love, but love can be separated from honor."

Then they drew this third conclusion. "You seem to love your wives, and you don't see that you love *from* your wives so you love them back. And your intelligence is a receptacle. So if you love your intelligence in yourselves, it makes you the receptacle of your own love. And self-love won't stand for a rival, so it never becomes married love, but as long as it lasts it remains a love of fornication."

At these things the men held their peace. Still, they muttered, "What's married love?"

Some husbands in heaven heard this. They agreed with the wives' three conclusions.

Chapter 15

Polygamy

If the reason why the Christian world has thoroughly condemned polygamous marriages is traced, no one can see it clearly,
however endowed he is with a gift for seeing into things with his
keen abilities, unless he is first taught that there really is married
love, that it is not to be had except between two, and not between
two unless it is from the Lord alone, and that heaven with all its
happiness is inscribed on this love. Unless these ideas come first
and lay the first stone, so to speak, your mind labors in vain to
draw from your intellect any reasons to base and build on—like a
house on its stone or its foundation—any reasons why the Christian
world condemns polygamy.

It is well known that the institution of monogamous marriage
is based on the Word of the Lord that whoever divorces his wife
(except for fornication) and takes another, commits adultery, and
that from the beginning, or the first establishment of marriages, it
was for two to become one flesh, and that people are not to separate
what God has joined together (Matt. 19:3–11). But although the Lord
dictated these words from the Divine law inscribed on marriage, if
intellect cannot altogether support it in some way with its reason, it
certainly can circumvent that Divine law by its usual twists and by
perverse interpretations and carry the law away into dim uncertainty, and from there into a negative affirmation—affirmation
because it also comes from civil law, and negative because it does
not come from people's rational insight. The human mind becomes
involved in this trouble unless it has first been instructed about the
ideas mentioned above. It is important for the intellect to begin its

calculations with these ideas. These ideas are that there really is married love, that it is not to be had except between two, and not between two unless it is from the Lord alone, and that heaven with all its happiness is inscribed on this love.

But these things and more about the condemnation of polygamy by the Christian world will be demonstrated one at a time according to the following topics.

The topics are:

(1) Real married love cannot be had except with one wife, so neither can real married friendship, confidence, potency, and a union of minds such that the two are one flesh.

(2) By the same token, the heavenly blessings, spiritual happiness and earthly joys that are provided from the outset for those who have real married love cannot be had except with one wife.

(3) All these can be had from the Lord alone, and they are given to no one but those who approach Him only and at the same time live according to His teachings.

(4) Consequently real married love with its happiness cannot be had except among those who are from the Christian church.

(5) This is why a Christian is allowed to take only one wife.

(6) If a Christian takes more wives, he commits not just worldly adultery but spiritual adultery, too.

(7) The Israelite nation was allowed to have more wives because they did not have the Christian religion, and therefore real married love was not possible for them.

(8) Mohammedans today are allowed to have more wives because they do not recognize the Lord Jesus Christ as one with Jehovah the Father and thus as God of heaven and earth, and so they cannot receive real married love.

(9) The Mohammedan heaven is outside the Christian heaven, and it is divided into two heavens, a lower one and a higher one, and only the ones who give up concubines and live with one wife and acknowledge our Lord as equal with God the Father, who has power over heaven and earth, are raised into the higher heaven.

(10) Polygamy is lascivious.

(11) For polygamists the chastity, purity, and holiness of marriage are not possible.

(12) Polygamists cannot become spiritual so long as they remain polygamists.

(13) Polygamy is not a sin for those who do it from religion.

(14) Polygamy is not a sin for those who do not know about the Lord.

(15) Even the polygamists among Mohammedans are saved if they acknowledge God and from religion live according to the laws of civil justice.

(16) But none of them can be together with angels in the Christian heavens.

Now comes the explanation of these topics.

333   (1) *Real married love cannot be had except with one wife, so neither can real married friendship, confidence, potency, and a union of minds such that the two are one flesh.* It has been pointed out several times already that the real love of marriage is so rare today that it is generally unknown. That there actually is such a thing, for all that, was pointed out in its own chapter [Chapter 4] and after that at times in later chapters. In any case, who does not know that there is such a love, which rises above all other loves in excellence and pleasantness to the point where all other loves are small in comparison to it? Experience testifies that it goes beyond self-love, love of the world, and even love of life. Have there not always been—and are there not still—men who fall on their knees before the woman they have chosen and asked for as a bride, entreat her as a goddess, and submit to her whims like the lowest servants? This suggests that that love exceeds their self-love. Have there not always been—and are there not still—men who, for the woman they have chosen and asked for as a bride, value riches as nothing—even treasures—and squander them? This suggests that that love exceeds love of the world. Have there not always been— and are there not still—men who think their life worthless before the woman they have chosen and asked for as a bride, and long to die unless she grants their wish? Witness the many fights of rivals, even to death. This suggests that this love exceeds the love of life.

Have there not always been—and are there not still—men who are driven out of their mind on account of a denial from the woman they have chosen and asked for as a bride?

Who cannot reasonably conclude from this beginning of that love in many people that because of what it is, that love rules supreme over every other love, and that the person's soul is in it, then, and promises itself eternal blessings with the one who is chosen and asked for? Who, if he searches diligently everywhere, can see any reason for this except that the man has given up his soul and heart to the one woman? For if a lover in that condition had the chance to choose from the whole feminine sex the worthiest, richest, and most beautiful, wouldn't he drop the choice and cling to his chosen? For his heart belongs to her alone.

These things are said so you'll know that there is such an overtowering married love, and that it is possible only when you love one person of the other sex.

What intellect that keenly inspects the interlinked evidence can fail to deduce from it that if a lover always stays in love with her from his soul or his depths, he will have those eternal blessings that he promised himself before the agreement to marry and promises in agreeing to marry? That he does have them if he approaches the Lord and from Him lives a true religion, was shown above. Who else enters a person's life from above, puts the inner heavenly joys in it, and carries them into the things that follow—and moreover, at the same time, gives steady potency all the while?

The conclusion that there is no such love and cannot be because it is not found in yourself or in this or that person is not valid.

334   Real married love joins the minds and hearts of two together, so it is also united with friendship and through friendship it is united with confidence and makes both of these qualities part of the marriage. So they tower so far above other kinds of friendship and confidence that just as this love is the love of loves, this friendship is the friendship of friendships, and the same goes for this confidence. It also goes for potency, for many reasons. Some of them appear in the second story after this chapter. The potency keeps this love on its course.

It has been shown in its own chapter (nos. 156–83) that the real love of marriage makes one flesh of two partners.

335   (2) *By the same token, the heavenly blessings, spiritual happiness, and earthly joys that are provided from the outset for those who have real married love cannot be had except with one wife.* We say heavenly blessings, spiritual happiness, and earthly joys because the human mind is divided into three levels. The highest is called heavenly, the second spiritual, and the third worldly. The three levels stand open in people who have real married love, and the flow in them follows its course when they are open. The delightful things about this love are most outstanding in the highest region, so they are felt there as blessings. They are less outstanding in the midregion, so there they are felt as happiness, and finally, in the lowest region, as joys. The fact that these delightful things exist, are felt, and are sensed is clear from accounts that describe them.

The reason why all the delightful things are provided from the outset to those who have true married love is that an infinity of all blessings is in the Lord, and He is Divine Love, and love's essence is that it wants to share its good things with another whom it loves. So He created married love when He created mankind and inscribed on mankind the ability to receive and know about the delightful things.

Who has too dull and irrational a makeup to be able to see that there must be some love into which the Lord puts all the blessings, happiness, and joys that ever can be put in?

336   (3) *All these can be had from the Lord alone, and they are given to no one but those who approach Him only and at the same time live according to His teachings.* This has already been pointed out in many places. It should be added that all the blessings, happiness, and joys are not forthcoming except from the Lord, and so He is the only One to approach. Who else is there, when He made all things that were made (John 1:3), when He is God of heaven and earth (Matt. 28:18), and when except through Him, God the Father's likeness was never seen nor His voice heard (John 1:18; 5:37; 14:6–11)? These and many other places in the Word establish that the

marriage of love and wisdom, or good and truth, which is the only source of marriages, comes from Him alone.

It follows that married love, with the delightful things about it, is available only to those who approach Him, and only to those who live by His teachings, because love unites Him with them (John 14:21–24).

337   (4) *Consequently real married love cannot be had except among those who are from the Christian church.* Except among those who are of the Christian religion there is no married love of the kind described in the chapter about it (nos. 57–73) and in the chapters after that—in other words, married love as it is in essence—because that love comes only from the Lord, and the Lord is not known anywhere else, in such a way that He can be approached as God. And besides, married love is in keeping with the state of the religion in a person (no. 130), and a genuine state of religion comes from the Lord alone, so it exists only among those who receive it from Him. These two things are the beginnings, the introductions, and the establishment of that love. This has already been settled by so many clear and convincing reasons that adding anything more would be thoroughly redundant.

The reason why real married love is rare even in the Christian world (nos. 58–59) is that few there do go to the Lord, and among them some that do believe in the church do not live by it. And other reasons are brought out in *Apocalypse Revealed,* where it fully describes the state of the Christian church today.

But the fact remains that real married love is possible only for those in the Christian Church. And polygamy is totally condemned for this reason. It is palpably clear to those who think straight about providence that this is also due to the Lord's Divine Providence.

338   (5) *This is why a Christian is allowed to take only one wife.* This follows as confirmed by the proofs of the preceding articles. It should be added to this that genuine marriage is more deeply etched on the minds of Christians than on the minds of non-Christians who have embraced polygamy, and so the Christians' minds are more receptive of this love than polygamists' minds

are. For this real marriage is etched on the inner reaches of Christians' minds because they recognize the Lord and His Divinity, and their civil laws inscribe it on their outer minds.

339   (6) *If a Christian takes more wives, he commits not just worldly adultery but spiritual adultery, too.* It is according to the Lord's words that a Christian who takes more wives commits earthly adultery. The words are that to divorce a wife is not lawful, because they are created to be one flesh, and he who divorces his wife without just cause and takes another commits adultery (Matt. 19:3–11). The more so for someone who does not send his wife away but keeps her and takes another one besides. This law that the Lord required about marriages has an inward reason from spiritual marriage, for whatever the Lord spoke was spiritual per se— which is what these words mean: "The words that I speak to you are spirit and life" (John 6:63).

The spirit in the words [from Matthew] is that polygamous marriage in the Christian world profanes the marriage of the Lord and the church. Likewise the marriage of good and truth, and on top of that the Word, and with the Word the church. Profanation of these is spiritual adultery.

Apocalypse Revealed (no. 134) establishes that profanation of the church's good and truth from the Word is spiritually analogous to adultery, and so it is spiritual adultery, and the same goes for making good and truth false, though in a lesser degree.

Polygamous marriages profane the marriage of the Lord and the church, because there is a relationship between that marriage and Christian marriages (see nos. 83–102 above). This relationship is lost completely if you add one wife to another, and when it is lost, a human spouse is no longer Christian. Polygamous marriages among Christians profane the marriage of good and truth because marriages on earth derive from this spiritual marriage. And the marriages of Christians are different from the marriages of other people in that husband and wife love each other in the way that good loves truth and truth loves good, and they are one. So if a Christian added another wife to the wife he has, he would tear up that spiritual marriage within himself. Thus he would profane the source of his marriage and in this way commit spiritual adultery.

(Nos. 116–31, above, show that marriages on earth derive from the marriage of good and truth.)

A Christian would profane the Word and the church by a polygamous marriage because the Word, seen for what it is, is a marriage of good and truth, and so is the church, insofar as it is based on the Word (see nos. 128–31 above).

Now, a Christian person knows about the Lord and has the Word and has a religion that is from the Lord through the Word, so more than a non-Christian he has the ability to regenerate and thus become spiritual and also to attain to real married love, for these attributes go together. Because those among the Christians who take more wives commit not only natural adultery but also spiritual adultery at the same time, it results that the damnation of Christian polygamists after death is worse than the damnation of those who only commit adultery on the plane of nature. When I asked about their condition after death, I received the answer that heaven is totally closed for them, and that in hell they look as if they are lying in a warm bath in a tub. They look this way from a distance even though they are standing on their feet and walking around. This comes from an inner insanity. Some of that kind are banished to chasms at the ends of the world.

340   (7) *The Israelite nation was allowed to have more wives because they did not have the Christian religion, and therefore real married love was not possible for them.* There are some people today who have doubts about the institution of monogamous marriages—of one man with one woman—and debate the reason within themselves. They judge that because polygamous marriages were openly allowed for the Israelite nation and their kings, and David and Solomon, polygamous marriages would, in themselves, be all right for Christians. But they do not have a clear understanding of Israelite and Christian peoples, nor about an outer and inner religion, nor about the Lord's changing religion from an outward one to an inner one. So they do not know anything from inner judgment about marriages.

Keep it generally in mind that a person is born worldly to become spiritual, and that so long as he remains worldly, it is as if he is sleeping in the night as far as anything spiritual goes, and at that time he does not even know the difference between the outward, worldly person and the inner, spiritual, person.

We know from the Word that the Israelitish people did not have the Christian religion. They were waiting for a Messiah who would raise them up over all the races and peoples in the world—as they still are waiting. So if they had been told, and if they were told now, that the Messiah's kingdom is over the heavens and therefore *is* over all peoples, they would consider it a joke. This was why they not only did not acknowledge Christ, or the Messiah, our Lord, when He came to the world, but they cruelly removed Him from the world, besides. These things show that that race did not have the Christian religion, as it does not today. And those who do not have the Christian church are worldly inside and out, and polygamy does not hurt them, for it is an attribute of man's worldly side. For such a person does not perceive anything more about the love in marriages than that it is desire. This was the meaning of the Lord's statement that Moses let them send away wives because of the hardness of their hearts but that it was not so from the beginning (Matt. 19:8). He said that Moses allowed it, to show that it was not the Lord who allowed it.

Also, the Lord's teachings and His repeal of rituals that only met the needs of man's worldly side show that He was teaching to the inner spiritual person. His teaching about washing shows that "washing" is the cleansing of the inner parts of the person (Matt. 15:1, 17–20; 23:25–26; Mark 7:14–23). The teaching about adultery shows that it is willful selfishness (Matt. 5:28). The teaching about sending wives away shows that it is unlawful and that polygamy is not in keeping with Divine law (Matt. 19:3–9).

The Lord taught these and other things that have to do with the spiritual person because He alone opens the inner parts of the human mind and makes them spiritual. And He puts these inner things into worldly things so the worldly ones will also take on a spiritual essence—which they do, too, if you approach Him and live by His teachings. In summary the teachings are to believe in Him, and to avoid bad acts because they are the devil's and come from the devil, and also to do good acts because they are the Lord's and are from the Lord, and to do these things as if from yourself and at the same time believe that the Lord does them through you.

The reason why the Lord alone opens the inner spiritual part of a person and why He puts it in the outer earthly part of a person is precisely that every person thinks on the worldly plane and acts on the worldly plane, so he could not notice anything spiritual and take it into his earthly life unless God had taken on a Humanity in nature and made this Divine, too.

These observations establish the truth that the Israelite race were allowed to take more wives because they did not have the Christian religion.

341   (8) *Mohammedans today are allowed to have more wives because they do not recognize the Lord Jesus Christ as one with Jehovah the Father and thus as God of heaven and earth, and so they cannot receive real married love.* Owing to the religion that Mohammed taught, Mohammedans acknowledge Jesus Christ as Son of God and the Greatest Prophet, and that God the Father sent Him into the world to teach people, but not that God the Father and He are one and that His Divinity and His Humanity are one Person, united like soul and body, according to the faith of all Christians from the Athanasian Creed. For this reason Mohammed's followers could not acknowledge our Lord as any God from eternity, but only as a perfect man in the world.

Mohammed thought this way and therefore his disciple followers thought this way, and they knew that God is one and He is the God who created the universe, so they had to bypass Jesus Christ in their worship—the more so because they pronounce Mohammed the greatest prophet. Nor do they know what the Lord taught.

It is for these reasons that the interiors of their minds, which are in themselves spiritual, could not be opened. Only the Lord opens these (seen already, no. 340). The real reason why the Lord opens them when someone acknowledges Him as God of heaven and earth and approaches Him—someone who lives by His teachings—is that no one else is joined with Him, and there is no reception without being joined with Him. The presence of the Lord and unity with Him are available to people. Going to Him makes presence, and living by His teachings makes unity. His presence alone lacks the reception, but His presence together with unity includes reception.

I bring this news about these things back from the spiritual world. There a person becomes present at the thought of him. But no one is united with another except by the feeling of love, and a feeling of love comes from doing what the other person says and likes. This commonplace of the spiritual world takes its source from the Lord. This is how He is present and united.

These things are said to make known why Mohammedans are allowed to take more wives, and that it is because they cannot have the true love in marriage, which is only between one man and one wife, since they do not acknowledge from religion that the Lord is the same as God the Father and thus is the God of heaven and earth.

(No. 130 and other places before that show that the love in marriage is in keeping with the state of religion in anyone.)

342   (9) *The Mohammedan heaven is outside the Christian heaven, and it is divided into two heavens, a lower one and a higher one, and only the ones who give up concubines and live with one wife and acknowledge our Lord as equal with God the Father, who has power over heaven and earth, are raised into the higher heaven.* First, before saying anything particular about these points, it is important to put in something about the Lord's Divine Providence in respect to the source of the Mohammedan religion. The fact that this religion is accepted in more countries than the Christian religion could be a stumbling block to people who consider the Divine Providence and believe, at the same time, that only people who are born Christians can be saved. But the Mohammedan religion is not a stumbling block to those who believe that everything is under Divine Providence. They investigate where Providence is, and they do find it. It is in the fact that the Mohammedan religion recognizes our Lord as the Son of God, the wisest of men, and as the greatest prophet, who came into the world to teach people. But they make the Koran the only book of their religion, and therefore Mohammed, who wrote it, occupies their thoughts, and they follow him with a kind of worship, so they do not think about our Lord very much.

Now to explain in an organized way that the Lord's Divine Providence stimulated that religion to abolish many nations' idolatries, so it will be clearly understood.

First, then, about the source of idolatries. Before that religion there was idol worship throughout the world. The reason was that all the churches before the Lord's advent were symbolic. The Israelite church was also like that. The Tabernacle in it, Aaron's clothes, the sacrifices, everything in the temple at Jerusalem, and the laws as well—were symbolic. And among the ancient people there was knowledge of correspondences, which is also knowledge of symbols—precisely the knowledge of wise men—cultivated especially by the Egyptians. This is where hieroglyphics came from. From knowledge of symbols they knew what all kinds of animals and all kinds of trees, and also what mountains, hills, rivers, springs, and the sun, moon, and stars stood for. Through this knowledge they also had a grasp of spiritual things, inasmuch as the things that were represented—the kind of things that have to do with spiritual wisdom in angels—were the sources of it. Now, because all their worship was symbolic (it consisted of pure correspondences) they held worship on mountains and hills, and also in groves and gardens. And for the same reason they made springs sacred, and in their prayers they turned their faces to the rising sun. And they also sculpted horses, oxen, calves, lambs—even birds, fish, and snakes. They put these in their houses and other places, arranged according to the spiritual things having to do with religion that they corresponded to or symbolized. They also put these things in their temples to call to mind the holy aspects of worship that the images stood for. After a time, when the knowledge of correspondences was forgotten, their descendants began to worship the same sculptures as holy in themselves, not realizing that their ancient ancestors saw nothing holy in them except that they symbolized things by correspondence and for that reason stood for holy things. The idolatries that filled the whole world—Asia with the islands around it, as well as Africa and Europe—sprang from this chain of events.

To root out all those idolatries, it came about in the Lord's Divine Providence that a new religion suited to the spirit of the Middle Eastern people was begun—a religion that would have something of each Testament of the Word in it and would teach that the Lord came into the world and that He is the greatest prophet, the wisest of all, and the son of God. This was done through Mohammed, so the religion has that name.

These things make it clear that the Lord's Divine Providence purposely brought to life this religion suited to the nature of the Middle Eastern people, as was said, to blot out the idolatries of so many nations and provide them some knowledge of the Lord before their coming into the spiritual world—which happens after each person's death. This religion would not have been accepted by so many nations and could not have rooted out their idolatries unless it had been accommodated their ideas—above all, unless polygamy had been allowed. Another reason: the Middle Eastern people, more than Europeans, would have been afflicted with foul adulteries and would have been lost.

343   Mohammedans have a heaven, too, because everyone in the whole world who recognizes God and avoids evils as sins against Him is saved. From Mohammedans themselves I heard that the Mohammedan heaven is divided in two, a lower one and a higher one, and that in the lower heaven, as in the world, they live with more than one woman—wives as well as mistresses—but that those who give up mistresses and live with one wife are raised into the higher heaven. I also heard that it is impossible for them to think that our Lord is God the Father, but that it is possible for them to consider Him an equal and that the rule of heaven and earth is given to Him because He is His Son. So this is the faith among those whom the Lord permits to go up into the higher heaven.

344   Once I had a chance to learn what the warmth of the polyga-mists' married love is like. I spoke with someone who was making an appearance for Mohammed. Mohammed himself is never there, but a substitute takes his place so that new arrivals from the world can see him, in a sense. After I talked with this substitute for a while from a distance, he sent me an ebony spoon and other things as signs that he was Mohammed. And at that same time a way for me to feel the heat of their marital love there opened. And it struck me as like the heat of a bad-smelling public bath. I turned away when I smelled it, and the channel of communication closed.

345   (10) *Polygamy is lascivious.* This is because its love is divided among more than one and is love of the other sex. It is also a superficial love, or love on man's worldly plane, and so it is not the love in marriage, which is the only chaste love.

It is well known that polygamous love is love divided among more than one. And a divided love is not the love in marriage, for you cannot separate this love from one person of the opposite sex. So a divided love is lascivious, and polygamy is lascivious.

Polygamous love is love of the other sex because the only difference is that it is limited to the number of wives that the polygamist can get, and is held to whatever laws are passed for the public good. Also, it allows taking mistresses in addition to wives. And so, because it is love of the other sex, it is a lascivious love. Polygamous love is love on a person's outer plane or the plane of nature because it is etched on that part of a person. And whatever the worldly side of man does from itself is bad. He is only led away from this through being raised into his inner, spiritual person, which the Lord alone does. And the evil residing in the natural plane of a person, regarding a sex, is whoredom, but this destroys society, so something like whoredom—polygamy—is introduced in its place. All the evil that a person is born into from his parents is implanted in his worldly level, but none of it in his spiritual level, because he is born into this by the Lord. On account of the reasons brought out, and also many others, you can see clearly that polygamy is lascivious.

346   (11) *For polygamists the chastity, purity, and holiness of marriage are not possible.* This is in keeping with the things already established above, and especially with the things pointed out in the chapter about the chaste and unchaste—principally from these things in it: That chaste, pure, and holy only apply to monogamous marriages, of one man with one wife (no. 141). That, also, real married love is chastity itself, so all the pleasant things about that love, even the most bodily, are chaste (nos. 143–44). And it is also in keeping with the things that were brought up in the chapter about the real love in marriage, such as these: That the real love in marriage, which is love of one man with one wife, is heavenly, spiritual, holy, and clean from its source and from its correspondence, more than all other loves (nos. 64 ff.). Now, chastity, purity, and holiness are only found in real married love, so consequently they are not found and are not possible in polygamous love.

347   (12) *Polygamists cannot become spiritual so long as they remain polygamists.* To become spiritual is to be elevated out of nature—that is, out of the light and heat of the world into the light and heat

of heaven. Only a person who is elevated is aware of this elevation. Still, a worldly person who is not elevated does not know but what he is. The reason is that, just like a spiritual person, he can raise his intellect into heaven's light and think and speak spiritually. But if his will does not follow his intellect into that height at the same time, he is not elevated at all, for he does not stay up there, but in a moment he abandons himself to his will and takes his stand with it. We say "will" and mean love at the same time, because will is love's container, for what a person loves, he wants. These few remarks may establish that while a polygamist remains a polygamist—or while a worldly person remains worldly, which is the same thing—he cannot become spiritual.

348 (13) *Polygamy is not a sin among those who do it from religion.* Everything that is against religion is thought to be a sin, because it is against God, and, vice versa, everything that is for religion is thought not to be a sin, because it is on God's side. Polygamy was a matter of religion for the children of Israel, and the same today for the Mohammedans, so it could not and cannot be charged to them as a sin. Besides, they stay worldly and do not become spiritual to keep it from being a sin for them. A worldly person cannot see that there is any sin in anything of an accepted religion. Only a spiritual person sees this. This is the reason that even though they recognize our Lord as the Son of God, owing to the Koran, they still do not approach Him, but Mohammed. And all the while they remain worldly, so they do not know that anything bad, or even that anything lascivious, is in polygamy. Also, the Lord says, "If you were blind, you would not have sin. But now you say you see, so your sin remains" (John 9:41). Since polygamy cannot convict them of sin, they have their heaven after death (no. 342), and there they enjoy pleasures in keeping with their lives.

349 (14) *Polygamy is not a sin for those who do not know about the Lord.* The reason is that real married love is from the Lord alone, and the Lord can only give this to those who know about Him, accept Him, believe in Him, and live the life that is from Him. And those whom He cannot give that love to do not know but what love of the other sex and the love in marriage are the same

thing, so polygamy is, too. In addition, polygamists who know nothing of the Lord stay worldly, for only the Lord makes a person spiritual, and what is in line with religion and the laws of society is not charged to a worldly man as a sin. He acts according to his reason, and the worldly person's reason is in a complete fog about the real love in marriage, and this love is spiritual in its excellence. But their reason is taught by experience to generally restrict promiscuous lust for the public and private peace, and leave it to everyone within his household.

This is what polygamy comes from.

350 It is well known that man is born lower than an animal. All the animals are born with knowledge matching the love of their lives. For as soon as they are born, or hatched, they see, hear, walk, know their foods, their mother, their friends and enemies, and not long after, know the other sex and how to love and also rear young. Only people know nothing like that when born, for nothing of knowledge is inborn in them, only the ability and inclination to acquire the things that have to do with knowledge and love. And if they do not get these from others, they stay lower than animals. The story in nos. 132–36 shows that a human is born like this on purpose so that he can attribute nothing to himself but to others and eventually attribute all wisdom, and the love belonging to it, to God alone, and so that because of this he can become an image of God. Consequently, a person who does not find out from others that the Lord came into the world and that He is God, and only learns something about the religious concepts and laws of his land, is not to blame if he thinks no more of married love than of love of the other sex and believes that polygamous love is the only married love. The Lord leads these people in their ignorance and by Divine power carefully keeps them from being charged with any guilt if from religion they avoid evil things as sins, so that they can be saved. For every person is born for heaven and none for hell, and everyone enters heaven thanks to the Lord and enters hell by himself.

351 (15) *Even the polygamists among Mohammedans are saved if they acknowledge God and from religion live according to the laws of civil justice.* Everyone in the entire world who acknowledges God and

lives by laws of civil justice because of religion is saved. Laws of civil justice means rules like the ones in the Commandments, which are not to kill, not to commit adultery, not to steal, not to testify falsely. These rules are the laws of civil justice in all countries on earth, for a country would not survive without them. But some people live according to the laws from fear of the law's penalties, some from civil obedience, and some also from religion. Those who live by them also from religion are saved.

The reason is that then God is in them, and the person whom God is in is saved. Who does not see that before the departure from Egypt, not to kill, not to commit adultery, not to steal, and not to testify falsely were among the Children of Israel's laws because their community or society could not have survived without them? And yet Jehovah God pronounced these same laws on Mount Sinai with a stupendous miracle. But the reason for those pronouncements was to make the laws religious laws, too, and in this way make them not just for the good of society, but also for God, and so that when the people did them from religion, for God, they would be saved.

These things may establish that pagans who acknowledge God and live by laws of civil justice are saved. For it is not their fault that they know nothing about the Lord, consequently nothing about the chastity of marriage with one wife. For it is against Divine Justice for people to be damned when they acknowledge God and on account of religion live the laws of justice—to avoid wrongs because they are against God and do good things because good things are for God.

352 (16) *But none of them can be together with angels in the Christian heavens.* The reason is that in the Christian heavens is the light of heaven, which is Divine truth, and the warmth of heaven, which is Divine love. And these two reveal what good and true things are like, and what bad and untrue things are like. This is why all communication between Christian heavens and Mohammedan heavens is taken away, and the same goes for heavens of non-Christians. If there were communication, no one could have been saved except those in the light of heaven, and at the same time its heat from the Lord. In fact, *they* could not have been saved if the

heavens were united, because this union would weaken all the heavens so much that the angels could not survive. For an unchasteness and lasciviousness that the Christian heaven cannot bear would seep in from the Mohammedans, and a chasteness and purity that the Mohammedan heaven cannot bear would seep in from the Christians. And then Christian angels would become worldly, and thus adulterers from the communication and the union that it brought, or if they remained spiritual, they would always sense a lasciviousness around them that would intercept all the happiness of their life. Something similar would happen in the Mohammedan heaven, for spiritual things from the Christian heaven would always be surrounding and enveloping them and would take away all the joy of their life. And in addition, they would insinuate that polygamy is a sin and thus the Christian influence would be a constant rebuke.

This is the reason why all the heavens are totally separate, so that there is no connection among them except through the influence of the light and heat from the Lord through the sun. He is in the middle of it. This influence enlightens and gives life to everyone according to their reception, and their reception is according to their religion. There is this communication, but no communication of these heavens among each other.

353   I add to these things two stories. This first:

Once I was among angels and listened to them talking. Their conversation was about intelligence and wisdom—that a person does not notice but what both intelligence and wisdom are in himself and thus that what he thinks by intellect and intends by will is from himself, when yet not a shred of it is from the person, except the ability to receive from the Lord the things that have to do with intellect and will. And every person tends toward self-love from birth, so it was provided from creation that, to keep man from being destroyed by self-love and the pride of his own intelligence, that love in a man would be transferred into a wife, and from birth it is implanted in her to love her husband's intelligence and wisdom, and thus her husband. So a wife is always attracting to herself her husband's pride in his own intelligence, quenching it in him and giving it life in herself, and in this way turning it into the love in marriage, and filling it with immeasurable pleasantness.

The Lord provides this so that a man's pride in his own intelligence will not make him such a fool as to think he understands and is wise by himself and not due to the Lord, and in this way eat from the Tree of Knowing Good and Bad, and, because of that, think he is like God and also is a god—as the serpent, who was love of one's own intelligence, said and persuaded. For this, man was thrown out of Paradise after he ate, and the way to the Tree of Life was guarded by angels.

Spiritually, paradise is intelligence. To eat from the Tree of Life, spiritually, is to understand and be wise from the Lord. But to eat from the Tree of Knowing Good and Bad, spiritually, is to understand and be wise on your own.

354   At the end of this conversation the angels went away, and two clergymen came, together with a man who in the world was an ambassador of a kingdom. I reported to them what I heard from the angels.

After they heard it they began to argue about intelligence and wisdom and the practical judgment from it—whether these come from God or from people. It was a heated discussion. At heart, the three believed the same—that these come from the person, because they are in a person, and that the very idea and feeling that it is like this proves it. But the ministers, who had theological zeal at that time, said that not a shred of intelligence and wisdom, and so not a shred of practical judgment, is from a person. And when the ambassador retorted, "Then not anything of thought?" they said, "No, nothing."

But in heaven they could tell that the three had the same belief, so they told the ambassador of a kingdom, "Put on a minister's clothes, and think of yourself as a minister, and then talk."

He put the clothes on and talked, and now he said in a loud voice, "There can't be a shred of intelligence and wisdom, and therefore not a shred of practical judgment except from the Lord," and with his usual eloquence he demonstrated this fully, with rational arguments. It is extraordinary, in the spiritual world, how a spirit thinks he is like whatever the clothing on him is like. The reason is that intellect is everybody's clothing there.

Then the two ministers were told from heaven, "Take off your vestments, and put on the clothes of public servants, and consider yourselves public servants." They did so, and then at once they thought from deep within themselves and spoke in favor of self-intelligence, from arguments that they inwardly cherished. Just then a tree appeared near the path, and they were told, "It is a tree of knowing good and bad. Beware that you don't eat from it." But the three were so infatuated with their own intelligence that they burned with a desire to eat from it and said among themselves, "Why not? Isn't it good fruit?"

They went over and ate. The three at once became best friends, because they had the same belief, and turned together to the road of self-intelligence, which led them toward hell. However, I saw them brought back from there, because they were not ready yet.

355   The second story: Once as I looked around in the world of spirits I saw, in a meadow, men dressed in clothes like the ones people in the world have, so I knew they were recently arrived from the world. I went up and stood beside them to listen to what they were saying to each other. They were talking about heaven, and one of them, who knew something about heaven, said, "There are wonderful things there that no one could ever believe without seeing them, like paradisal gardens, magnificent palaces, built by architecture, because they are built by the art itself, and shining like gold. In front of them are silver columns with heavenly figures on top of them, made from precious stones. And houses, too, of jasper and sapphire with noble porches in front of them, that angels come through. And inside the houses are decorations that neither skill nor voice can describe. As for the angels themselves, there are angels of both sexes. There are young men and husbands, and there are young women and wives—such beautiful young women that beauty like it isn't found in the world. But the wives are still more beautiful. They look like true embodiments of heavenly love, and their husbands heavenly wisdom embodied. And they are all young adults. And what's more, they don't know about any sexual love there other than married love. And what's going to surprise you is that the husbands' ability to enjoy never stops."

When the newly arrived spirits heard that there was no sexual love other than married love and that they always had the ability to enjoy it, they laughed among themselves and said, "You're saying incredible things. There is no ability like that. Maybe you're telling fairy stories."

But then an angel from heaven unexpectedly stood among them and said, "Please hear me. I'm an angel of heaven, and I've lived with my wife a thousand years now and in the same flower of youth over those years as you see me in here. I get it from married love with my wife. And I can assure you that ability has been and is continual for me. I can tell that you think it's impossible for this to be, so I'll talk to you reasonably about this thing according to the light of your intellect. You don't know anything about the primeval state of mankind, which you call a state of innocence. In that state all the inner parts of the mind were open all the way to the Lord, and so they participated in the marriage of love and wisdom, or good and truth. The good that belongs to love and the truth that belongs to wisdom always love each other so they always want to unite. And when the inner parts of the mind are open, that spiritual married love flows in freely with its perpetual effort, and brings that ability.

"A person's soul itself not only has a continual urge to unite, because it's in a marriage of good and truth, but it also has a continual urge to bear fruit and produce its like. When that marriage opens a person's inner dimension all the way from his soul—and inward qualities always look to an end result in order to come to something—from that the continuing urge to bear fruit and produce its likeness, which is in the person's soul, becomes physical. The final work of soul in body for married partners is in the most outward acts of love there, and these depend on your state of soul, so it's clear where they get this constant ability.

"They also have constant fertility, because there radiates from the Lord a universal sphere of generating and producing heavenly things, which have to do with love; spiritual things, which have to do with wisdom; and from them natural things, which are offspring. It fills the whole heaven and the whole earth, and that heavenly sphere fills all people's souls and goes down through their minds into their bodies, clear to the most outward parts of them, and gives the power to reproduce. But this is to be had only for people whose passage from soul, through higher mind and lower mind, into their bodies, to the most outward parts, is open. This happens for those who lay themselves open for the Lord to lead them back to the state of creation's first life.

"I can vouch that for a thousand years now neither ability nor strength nor manhood has ever left me, and that I know absolutely nothing about a lessening of powers, since the universal sphere I mentioned constantly renews them. And then these powers also gladden my soul and do not make it sad, as with those who suffer their loss.

"Besides, the real love in marriage is quite like the warmth of spring. Under its influence everything breathes seeding and fertility. There is no other warmth in our heaven, either. So spring, with its steady impulse, is with the married partners there, and this steady impulse is what that strength comes from.

"But for us in heaven fertility is different than for people on earth. We bear spiritual fruits, which are love and wisdom, or good and truth. From her husband's wisdom, a wife receives in herself a love for that wisdom, and the husband receives the wisdom in himself from his wife's love for it. In fact, a wife is actually formed into the love of her husband's wisdom. This happens through accepting the offsprings of his soul with the delight that arises from the fact that she wants to be the love of her husband's wisdom. This is the way she changes from a virgin to a wife and a likeness. And this is also why love with its deep friendship grows over the years in a wife, and wisdom with its happiness in a husband—and this to eternity.

"This is the condition of angels in heaven."

When the angel had said these things, he looked at the spirits who recently came from the world and said to them, "You know that you loved your partners when you had the vigor of love and that after the pleasure you turned away from them. But you don't know that in heaven we don't love our partners on account of that vigor, but we have the vigor on account of love, and we always have it because we always love our partners. So if you can turn your state of mind right side up, you can grasp this. Doesn't someone who always loves his partner love her with his whole mind and whole body? For love turns your whole mind and your whole body toward what it loves, and it joins the two this way so that it makes them just like one, because it takes place mutually."

He said further, "I'm not going to tell you about married love being implanted in male and female from creation, and their inclination toward being legally joined together, nor about the ability to have offspring in a male, which is the same as the ability to increase wisdom from a love of truth, and that a person is in real married love and its accompanying virtue to the extent that he loves wisdom from the love of wisdom, that is, loves truth on account of good."

356   When he had said this, the angel was silent, and the new arrivals understood from the spirit of his speech that a constant ability to enjoy is possible. This gladdened their souls, so they said, "Oh, what a happy state the angels have! We can tell that you in heaven always stay in youthful condition and therefore in the vigor of youth. But tell us how we can get that vigor, too!"

The angel answered, "Avoid adulteries as hellish things, and go to the Lord, and you'll have that vigor."

They said, "We'll avoid them like that, and we'll go to the Lord."

But the angel answered, "You can't avoid adulteries as hellish evils unless you avoid the other evils the same way, because adulteries are all the evils wrapped together. And you can't go to the Lord unless you avoid them. The Lord doesn't accept them."

After this the angel left, and the new spirits went away disappointed.

Chapter 16

Jealousy

357   Jealousy is discussed here because it, too, has to do with married love. But there is justified jealousy and unjustified jealousy. Couples who love each other have justified jealousy. They have a proper and sensible zeal for keeping their married love from being injured, and from it a righteous grief if it is injured. But unjustified jealousy occurs among those who are naturally suspicious, and who have melancholy minds due to sluggish and bilious blood. And for another thing, some people consider all jealousy a fault. Fornicators do this especially. They even hurl reproaches at righteous jealousy.

Jealousy comes from *zeli typo*, "image of zeal." There are justified and unjustified images or forms of zeal. But the differences will unfold in the topics that now follow, which they do in this order:

(1) Zeal, viewed in itself, is like the fire of love flaring up.

(2) The flaring up or flame of this love, which is zeal, is a spiritual flaring or flame springing from a threat to love and an assault on it.

(3) The zeal a person has is like the love he has, which is to say it is one thing in someone whose love is good and another in someone whose love is bad.

(4) The zeal of a good love and the zeal of a bad love are alike in outward appearance but totally different in inward appearance.

(5) The zeal of a good love harbors love and friendship within it, but the zeal of a bad love harbors hate and revenge within it.

(6) The zeal of married love is called jealousy.

(7) Jealousy is like a fire flaring out against violators of love with a spouse, and it is like a bristling fear for the loss of that love.

(8) Spiritual jealousy is found among monogamists, and worldly jealousy among polygamists.

(9) In those partners who love each other tenderly, jealousy is a justified anguish, from sound reason, lest married love become divided and perish as a result.

(10) Partners who do not love each other have jealousy for many reasons. With some it comes from various mental afflictions.

(11) Some people do not have any jealousy, also for various reasons.

(12) There is also jealousy for mistresses, but it is not the same kind as for wives.

(13) Animals and birds also have jealousy.

(14) Jealousy is different in men and husbands than in women and wives.

Now comes the explanation of these topics.

358   (1) *Zeal, viewed in itself, is like the fire of love flaring up.* You do not know what jealousy is without knowing what zeal is, because jealousy is the zeal of married love. Zeal is like the fire of love flaring out because zeal has to do with love, and love is spiritual heat, and this, in its source, is like fire. The first point, that zeal has to do with love, is well known. Having zeal and acting from zeal means nothing but acting from the force of love. But when zeal comes out, it does not look like love. It looks like an unfriendly enemy threatening and fighting the one who injures love, so it can also be called the defender and protector of love. It is characteristic of every love to erupt in indignation and anger—even rage—when taken away from its pleasures, so if a love, especially a ruling love, is struck, it stirs your soul. And if the blow hurts, it makes an outbreak of anger. These observations should show that zeal is not the highest level of love but is love burning.

One person's love and another's answering love are like allies, but when one person's love rises up against another's, they become like enemies. The reason is that love is the essence of a person's life, so someone who attacks your love attacks your life itself, and then comes a condition of anger breaking out against the attacker, like the condition of any person whom someone else tries to kill. Every love can break out in anger like this—even the most peaceful—as you can see clearly from chickens, geese, and all kinds of birds, which fearlessly jump up and fly at those who bother their chicks or carry off their food. It is well known that some animals are prone to anger, and wild animals to fury, if their pups are threatened or their prey is carried off.

Love is said to flare up like fire because love is nothing other than spiritual heat, rising from the fire of the angelic sun, which is pure love. It is strikingly clear from the warmth of living bodies that love is heat like the heat of a fire. Body heat is from nowhere but people's love. People become warm and are enkindled according to how high their love flares up.

It is clear from these observations that zeal is like the fire of love flaring up.

359   (2) *The flaring up or flame of this love, which is zeal, is a spiritual flaring or flame springing from a threat to love and an assault on it.* It is clear from what was said above that zeal is a spiritual blaze or flame. Since love in the spiritual world is warmth from the sun there, love there actually looks like a flame, from a distance. Heavenly love appears that way among the angels of heaven, and hellish love does among the spirits of hell. But note that that flame does not burn things up like fire in the natural world.

Zeal arises from an attack on love because love is one's vital heat, so when the love of your life is attacked, the heat of your life kindles, takes a stand, and breaks out against the attacker, and in its power and strength, which is like a flame breaking out from a fire, it acts like an enemy to the one that stirred it up. You can see that it is like a flame from eyes that flash, a face that is inflamed, and from the tone of voice and gestures. Love is the heat of life, so it does this to keep from being smothered, together with all its love's eagerness, liveliness, and perception of joy.

360   Now to say how love is set fire and kindles into zeal, like a fire into flame, from an attack on it. Love resides in a person's will. But it is stirred up in your intellect not your will, for it is like

a fire in your will and like a flame in your intellect. Love does not know it is in your will, because it does not sense anything of itself there, nor act on its own there, but it does this in your intellect and in intellectual thought. So when love is attacked, then it rasps on your intellect. This takes place in the form of various reasoning processes. These are like firewood that the fire lights, so they burn. Thus they are like so much kindling or so many inflammable materials that make the spiritual flame—which takes many forms.

361   The exact reason why a person is stirred up by an attack on his love will come clear. In its inner depths the human form is from creation the form of love and wisdom. All the feelings of love, and all the perceptions of wisdom from them, are put together in a person in the most perfect order, so that they form a single purpose together, and thus a unit. These feelings and perceptions are substance, for they act on substances. So, as the human form is put together out of these, clearly, if your love is attacked, that whole form, with each and every thing about it, is also attacked in that instant, or at the same time. And since it is put into everything living by creation to want to stay in the form it has, the general structure expects this of its parts, and the parts of the whole. So when love is attacked, it defends itself through its intellect, and the intellect operates by reasonable and imaginative ways, which it uses to realize the outcome—especially by ways that act in accord with the love that is attacked. If this did not happen, that whole form would be toppled by having its love taken away.

This, then, is why love hardens the substances of its form to resist attacks and, so to speak, raises its crest—so many hackles. In other words, it bristles. The exasperation of love, called zeal, is like that. And so if there is no chance to resist, anxiety and pain arise, because love foresees the smothering of its inner life, together with its joy. But on the other hand, if love is coddled and soothed, that form settles back, softens, and spreads out, and the form's substances become smooth, soothing, mild, and alluring.

362   (3) *The zeal a person has is like the love he has, which is to say it is one thing in someone whose love is good and another in someone whose love is bad.* Since zeal has to do with love, it follows that what zeal is like, love is like. And there are generally two loves—a love of

good and of the truth from it and a love of evil and the falsity that comes from it—so in general you have a zeal for good and the truth from it and a zeal for evil and the falsity from it.

But note that both loves come in infinite varieties. This is strikingly evident from the angels of heaven and from the spirits of hell. They are both the images of their love, in the spiritual world, and yet there is not one angel of heaven quite like another in face, speech, walk, gestures, and behavior, nor one spirit in hell. In fact, there cannot be forever, though they increase to millions of millions. This shows that loves come in infinite varieties, because their forms do. Zeal is the same, because it belongs to love. Obviously one person's zeal cannot be quite like, or the same as, another person's zeal. Broadly speaking, there is the zeal of a good love and the zeal of a bad love.

363　　(4) *The zeal of a good love and the zeal of a bad love are alike in outward appearance but totally different in inward appearance.* Zeal in anyone seems on the surface like wrath and an outbreak of anger, for it is love inflamed and kindled to protect itself against the violator and remove him. The reason why the zeal of a good love and the zeal of a bad love seem outwardly the same is that in both cases love burns when in a state of zeal. But in the good person it only burns in externals, while in a bad person it burns inside as well as outside. And so long as the inner dimensions escape attention, the zeals seem alike to outward appearances. But that they are totally different inwardly will be seen under the next heading.

From all that people say and do from zeal you can see and hear that zeal appears outwardly like wrath and an outbreak of anger. You see it in a preacher, for example, when he harangues from zeal. His tone of voice is loud, ardent, piercing, and harsh, his face glows and sweats, he draws himself up, beats the pulpit, and calls down hellfire on evildoers. And there are many other examples.

364　　To obtain a distinct idea of zeal in good people and zeal in bad people and how these differ, you need to form some idea about the inner things and the outer things in people. Let us do it with an image of these things that is simple because it is for the general populace. Take the image of a nut—an almond—and its kernel. In good people the inner things are like whole and good kernels inside, surrounded by their ordinary, natural shell. But it is totally different in bad people. The inner things in them are in comparison like kernels that are either too bitter to eat, or rotten, or wormy, but their outsides are like their crusts or shells—either like their native shells, or reddish like mussel shells, or dappled like iris stones. This is what their outsides look like. Within them lurk the insides mentioned above. Their zeal is the same.

365   (5) *The zeal of a good love harbors love and friendship within it, but the zeal of a bad love harbors hate and revenge within it.* We said that outwardly zeal seems like wrath and an outbreak of anger, in people with a good love as well as in people with a bad love. But what is inside is different, and the wrath and outbreaks of anger differ inwardly. The differences are: (a) The zeal of a good love is like a heavenly flame that never breaks out against someone else but only defends itself. It defends itself against an evil, as if the evil rushes into a fire and is burned up. But the zeal of a bad love is like the fire of hell, which breaks out of itself and attacks and wants to burn someone else up. (b) The zeal of a good love instantly subsides and mellows when the other one withdraws from his attack, but the zeal of a bad love lasts and does not go out. (c) The reason is that what is inside a person who loves good is in itself mild, gentle, friendly, and kind, so when he becomes violent outwardly, waves his fists, bristles, and acts roughly like this by way of defense, it is still tempered by the goodness of his inward makeup. It is different with bad people. What is inside them is unfriendly, fierce, hard, breathes hate and revenge, and nurses itself on the joy of these qualities. And they still lie hidden like fire in logs under the ashes, even when the trouble has been settled. If these fires do not break out in the world, they do after death.

366   Since zeal seems outwardly the same in good and bad people, and the outward sense of the Word consists of things that correspond, and of appearances, it often says there that Jehovah is angry, burns with wrath, takes revenge, punishes, throws people into hell, and does other things that are outward manifestations

of zeal. This is also why He is called "jealous," in spite of the fact that there is not a shred of wrath, outbursts, or vengeance in Him. In fact, He is mercy, grace, and clemency itself—which is to say, good itself, in which nothing like that can exist. But more about this appears in the book *Heaven and Hell* (nos. 545–50) and in *Apocalypse Revealed* (nos. 494, 498, 525, 714, 806).

367   (6) *The zeal of married love is called jealousy.* Zeal for married love is the zeal of zeals, because that love is the love of loves, and its delights, which the zeal rises for, are the delights of delights, for that love is the head of all loves, as shown above. The reason is that that love imposes the form of love on a wife and the form of wisdom on a husband, and from these forms joined into one, nothing can come out but what savors of wisdom and love together. Since the zeal of married love is the zeal of zeals, it is called by a new name, *zelotypia*—the figure of zeal.

368   (7) *Jealousy is like a fire flaring out against violators of love with a spouse, and it is like a bristling fear for the loss of that love.* We are dealing here with the jealousy of those who are spiritually in love with their spouses. In the next article we deal with the jealousy of those who are in worldly love, and after that with the jealousy of those who are in genuine married love.

Jealousy is varied in those who are spiritually in love, because their love is varied. No love, whether spiritual or worldly, is exactly alike for two people, much less for more.

Jealousy on the spiritual plane, or in spiritual people, is like a fire flaring out against violators of their married love, because the beginnings of love in two people is in the inner reaches of them both, and their love is faithful to its principles from its beginnings clear to its most outward characteristics. Due to these outmost characteristics and the first inner ones, everything mental and bodily in between is intertwined in a lovely way. Being spiritual, spiritual people see union, and the spiritual peace in union and its delights, as the purpose of their marriage. Now, because their souls reject disunion, spiritual jealousy is like a fire stirred up and flashing out against violators. It is like a bristling fear because their spiritual love intends them to be one, so if there is a threat, or if separation seems to be occurring, it creates a bristling fear, as when two joined parts are pulled apart.

I got this description of jealousy from heaven—from those who are spiritually in married love. For there is married love on the worldly level, spiritual married love, and heavenly married love. The next two articles tell about worldly and heavenly people and their jealousy.

369   (8) *Spiritual jealousy is found among monogamists, and worldly jealousy among polygamists.* There is spiritual jealousy among monogamists because only they can receive spiritual married love, as pointed out amply already. We say "there is," but it means that among them it can exist. It has also been established already that it is found in only a few in the Christian world, where there are monogamous marriages, and yet it can occur there. The chapter on polygamy (nos. 345–47) shows that for polygamists married love is on a worldly level. So is jealousy, for this keeps pace with love. Certain firsthand accounts about jealousy among Orientals show what it is like in polygamists. Wives and mistresses are guarded like captives in workhouses, and they are restrained and shut off from all communication with men. No man is allowed to enter the women's apartments or their chambers unless accompanied by a eunuch. And they zealously watch whether any one of them looks at a passerby with a flirtatious eye or face, and if they notice this, the woman is flogged. And if she acts wantonly with any man brought indoors by stealth, or outdoors, she is punished by death.

370   These things certainly illustrate the sort of fire of jealousy that polygamous married love breaks into—wrathful and vindictive—wrathful in gentle people and vindictive in harsh people. This happens because their love is worldly and does not partake of anything spiritual. This follows from things pointed out in the chapter about polygamy—that polygamy is lascivious (no. 345), and that a polygamist is worldly so long as he remains a polygamist and cannot be made spiritual (no. 347).

But the fire of jealousy is another thing in worldly monogamists. Their love does not take fire against the women, but against the violators. It becomes anger against them, but cold towards the women. It is different in polygamists whose jealous fire also flares up in frenzy of revenge. This is also among the reasons why the polygamists' mistresses and wives are mostly set free after death and are assigned to unguarded apartments for women, to produce various things in the line of women's work.

371   (9) *In those partners who love each other tenderly, jealousy is a justified anguish, from sound reason, lest married love become divided and perish as a result.* There is fear and pain in every love—fear that it might be lost and pain if it is lost. The love in marriage is no different, but its fear and pain are called zeal, or jealousy. In married couples who tenderly love each other this zeal is justified and based on sound reason, because it is fear for the loss of eternal happiness—not just your own, but your partner's, too—and at the same time because it is a protection against adultery.

As to the first point, that it is a righteous fear of losing your eternal happiness and your partner's, this follows from everything that has been brought up so far about the genuine love in marriage, and from the fact that the blessedness of a couple's souls, their minds' happiness, their hearts' joys, and their bodies' pleasure come from that love. And because these things are theirs forever, each fears for the other's eternal happiness.

It is obvious that this zeal is a rightful protection against adultery. Therefore it is like a fire flaring up against violation and guarding against it.

These things establish that someone who loves his mate tenderly is jealous as well, but it is right and healthy according to the man's wisdom.

372   We said that inherent in married love is fear of separation and anguish lest love end, and that its zeal is like a fire against violation. Thinking about this one time, I asked some angels with zeal about where jealousy resides. They said that it is in the intellect of a man who receives his partner's love and loves in turn, and that what the jealousy is like depends on his wisdom. They also said that jealousy has something in common with honor, which is also in married love, for whoever loves his partner also honors her.

"The reason why a man's zeal resides in his intellect," they said, "is this. Married love protects itself by intellect just as good does by the truth. In the same way a wife protects through her husband the things they have in common. And this is why zeal is implanted in men, and in women through men and because of men."

I asked, "What part of men's minds does zeal reside in?"

They answered, "In their souls, because it is also a protection against adultery, and this especially destroys married love, so the man's intellect hardens up in peril of violation and becomes like a horn, goring the adulterer."

373   (10) *Partners who do not love each other have jealousy for many reasons. With some it comes from various mental afflictions.* The reasons why partners who do not love each other are also jealous are mainly their reputation for potency, fear that their name and also their wife's name might be sullied, and dread of their household affairs falling to pieces. It is well known that men acquire a reputation from potency—that is, that they want to be admired for it. For as long as they have this reputation their minds are as if buoyed up, and their faces are not downcast among men and women. Also this reputation is associated with courage, so it is attached to military officers more than others.

That it is fear that their name and also their wife's name might be sullied fits together with the previous reason. Besides, living together with a prostitute, and prostitution at home, are a disgrace.

Some are jealous to keep their household affairs from falling to pieces, since it disgraces a husband so much and interrupts shared duties and the household help. But for some people, this jealousy wanes in time and disappears. For some it turns into a mere pretense of love.

374   It is no secret in the world that some people's jealousy is from various mental afflictions, for there are jealous men who constantly think that their wives are unfaithful and believe that they are prostitutes just from hearing or seeing that they talk in a friendly way with men or about men. There are several mental defects that bring on this affliction. Suspicious fantasy takes first

place among them. If cherished very long, this brings your mind into communities of similar spirits whom it can hardly be removed from. It also sets in on your body, which makes the serum, and therefore the blood, sticky, tenacious, thick, slow, and acrid. Lack of potency aggravates it, too, for this makes your mind unable to be raised out of its suspicions. The presence of potency raises it, and its absence depresses it, for it makes your mind droop, crumble, and wither, and then it plunges into this fantasy more and more until it is crazy. And this comes out as a delight in rebukes and in abuse as much as is allowed.

375   Also, in places there are families who suffer the disease of jealousy more than others. They shut wives up, tyrannically keep them from talking with men, guard them from men's sight by windows fitted with shutters to cover them, and terrify them with threats of death if a cherished suspicion finds a pretext, besides other hardships that wives in those places endure from their jealous husbands.

But there are two reasons for this jealousy. One is the captivity and stifling of thoughts in spiritual matters of religion. The other is an inner lust for revenge. As to the first reason, the captivity and stifling of thoughts in spiritual matters of religion, you can conclude what these things do from what was pointed out above— that everyone has married love in keeping with the state of the church in him, and because the church is from the Lord, married love is from the Lord alone (nos. 130–31). And so, when living and deceased people are approached and called upon instead of the Lord, the consequence is that there is not a state of the church that married love can act together with. And all the less when their minds are frightened into worship by threats of a cruel prison. This causes their thoughts together with their speech to be violently imprisoned and stifled. With them stifled, the kind of things that are either against the church, or are fancied to favor the church, pour in. All that comes from all this is a burning for prostitutes and chill for a married partner. From these two things together in one person gushes an uncontrollable fire of jealousy like this.

As to the second reason, which is an inner lust for revenge, this totally thwarts the influence of married love, swallows it up, devours it, and turns its joy, which is heavenly, into the joy of revenge, which is hellish, and its closest target is a wife. It also seems that the malignity of an atmosphere heavy with poisonous vapors of the surrounding regions is a secondary reason.

376   (11) *Some people do not have any jealousy, also for various reasons.* The reasons for no jealousy and ceasing jealousy are several. Those with no jealousy are mainly those who make no more of married love than of fornication and also are not famous, valuing the reputation of their name as a trifle. They are not unlike married pimps. Also without jealousy are those who scorn it from a sense that it disturbs your mind and that it is useless to guard a wife, and she becomes aroused if guarded, so it is better to shut your eyes and not even look through the keyhole in the door, so as not to uncover anything by seeing it. Others scorn it because of malicious talk about the name "jealousy," thinking that a man who is a man has nothing to fear. Others are forced to reject it so as not to ruin their household affairs and so as not to be blamed in public if a wife who is lustful is exposed. Moreover, jealousy fades to nothing in men who give their wives permission because they lack potency, for the purpose of raising children as heirs, and also in some on account of making money, and so on. There are also adulterous marriages where by mutual consent both give permission for sexual intercourse and still meet each other with a friendly face.

377   (12) *There is also jealousy for mistresses, but it is not the same kind as for wives.* Jealousy for wives wells up from the deepest parts of people, but jealousy for mistresses springs from outer things, so these are jealousies of different kinds. Jealousy for wives wells from the deepest parts because that is where the love in marriage resides. It resides there because marriage unites souls and joins minds very deeply, because of its permanent contract settled by the covenant and also by the equal justice that one belongs to the other. Once imposed, this joining and union remains unbreakable, whatever kind of love, warm or cold, comes in later. This is why an incitement to love from a wife chills the whole man, inside and out, but incitement to love from a mistress does not chill a lover

this way. A desire for a reputation of honor attaches to jealousy for a wife, and there is not this ingredient in jealousy for a mistress. But still, both these kinds of jealousy vary according to where the love resides that a wife receives, and that a mistress does, and also according to the discernment of the man receiving it.

378 (13) *Animals and birds also have jealousy.* It is well known that animals such as lions, tigers, bears, and other wild beasts have jealousy when they have young. And also bulls even without young. And most outstandingly roosters, which spar with their rivals to the death for their hens. They have so much jealousy because they are vainglorious lovers, and the pride of that love does not brook an equal. It is clear from their bearing, the motions of their heads, their stride, and their voice that they are vainglorious lovers more than any other genus or species of bird. It was already established that a reputation for honor among men, whether lovers or not, brings on jealousy, heightens it, and sharpens it.

379 (14) *Jealousy is different in men and husbands than in women and wives.* But these differences cannot be given precisely, because jealousy is different in married partners who love each other spiritually, in partners who are merely worldly, in partners whose souls disagree, and in a partner who puts a spouse under his yoke of obedience.

Seen as they are, the jealousies of men and women are different, because they come from different sources. The source of a man's jealousy is in his intellect, but the source of a woman's is in her will, attached to her husband's intellect. So a man's jealousy is like a flame of anger and wrath breaking out, but a woman's is like a fire controlled by varying fear, a varying glance at her husband, a varying regard for her love, and a varying skill in not disclosing it to her husband through jealousy. They differ because wives are loves and men are recipients, and it hurts wives to spread their love among men but not likewise the recipients among women.

But to be sure, it is different with spiritual people. For them the husband's jealousy is transferred to the wife, as the wife's love is transferred to the husband, so it seems the same to both of them—jealousy against the violator's effort. But a wife's jealousy against a violating prostitute is inspired into the man as weeping grief and a prodding of his conscience.

380   I add two stories. The first is this:

I was amazed, once, at a huge crowd of people who gave nature the credit for creation and therefore everything under the sun—and above the sun. When they saw anything, they said from a heartfelt belief, "Isn't this nature's work?" They were asked why they said it was nature's work and why not God's work, when, for all that, they sometimes say, as most people do, that God created nature, so they can equally well say that the things they see are God's work as that they are nature's. But they answered in an almost soundless inner voice, "What is God but nature?"

They all seem so conceited, from their persuasion that nature created the universe, and from taking this insanity for wisdom, that they regard everyone who accepts God's creation of the universe as ants that creep on the ground and wear a highway, and sometimes as butterflies that fly in the air. They say these people's dogmas are dreams, because they see what they don't see, saying, "Who sees God? And who doesn't see nature?"

During my astonishment that there was crowd like that, an angel stood by my side and said to me, "What are you thinking about?"

"About such a crowd," I said, "who think that nature created the universe."

The angel told me, "People like that make up all of hell, and they are called satans and devils there. Satans have confirmed themselves on the side of nature, so they deny God. Devils lived viciously and so they threw all acceptance of God out of their hearts. But I'll take you to the school in the southwestern zone, where there are people like that who are not yet in hell."

He took my hand and led me away. I saw small houses with schools in them, and among them one that was like the headquarters of the rest. It was built of pitch-black stones, overlaid with something like plates of glass, sparkling sort of like gold and silver, like the ones called *glacies Mariae* [sheets of mica], with shells among them here and there, that sparkled the same way.

We went up and knocked, and soon someone opened the door and said, "Welcome," ran to a table, brought four books and said, "These books are the wisdom that many, many in today's kingdoms applaud. Here's the book—the wisdom—that many applaud in France, here's the one they applaud in Germany, this one some applaud in the Netherlands, and this one some applaud in Britain." He went on, "If you want to see something, I'll make these four books shine before your eyes!"

Then he poured out a flood of praise for his own reputation, and soon the books gleamed. But this light instantly vanished before our eyes.

Then we asked, "What are you writing now?"

He answered that he was now extracting and expounding things of deepest wisdom from his treasures, "which, in brief, are these: first, whether nature is due to life, or life to nature; second, whether the center is due to its surroundings, or the surroundings are due to the center; third, about the center and the surroundings of nature and life."

After saying this he sat down on a chair at a table, but we strolled around in his school, which was roomy. He had a candle on the table, because there was no daylight from the sun, but the light of night from the moon. And what surprised me was that the candle seemed to move around the rooms, giving light. But it wasn't trimmed, so it did not give much light. As he wrote, we saw images in various shapes fly from the table onto the walls. In that nocturnal moonlight they seemed like beautiful Indian birds. But in daylight, when we opened a door, they looked like bats, with webbed wings, for they were likenesses of the truth that were turned into falsities by being confirmed. He connected them ingeniously in a series.

After we saw these we went to the table and asked him, "Now what are you writing?"

He said, "About the first one—whether nature is due to life or life to nature," and about this he said that he could establish either thing and make it true, but that something he was afraid of lay hidden inside, so all he dared establish was that nature is due to life—i.e., from life—and not that life is due to nature—i.e., from nature.

We politely asked, "What are you afraid of that lies hidden inside?"

He said it was that the clergy might call him a naturalist, and thus an atheist, and laymen might call him a man of unsound reason, "since ministers and laymen either believe by blind faith or else they see through the sight of the ones who assert a thing."

But then, out of some displeasure due to zeal for the truth, we spoke to him and said, "Friend, you're very much mistaken. Your wisdom, which is ingenuity in writing, misleads you, and the renown of your reputation leads you to confirm what you don't believe. Don't you know that the human mind can be raised beyond things having to do with the five senses—things that in your thought come from the body's senses—and that when raised it sees that things having to do with life are above and things having to do with nature are below? What is life but love and wisdom? And what is nature but a vessel for them where they work their effects or the things they do? Can life and nature be one except as a cause and its instrument? Can light be the same thing as an eye? Sound as an ear? Where are their sensations from, but from life, and their forms, but from nature? What's a human body but an organ of life? Aren't all the things in it formed organically to bring about what love wants and intellect thinks out? Don't the body's organs come from nature and love and thought from life? Aren't they totally distinct from each other? Raise the keen sight of your skill a little higher, and you'll see that feeling and thinking come from life, and that feeling is from love and thinking from wisdom, and both are from life, for, once again, love and wisdom are life. If you raise your ability to understand a little higher still, you'll see that love and wisdom can only come from some source, and that their source is Love Itself and Wisdom Itself, and therefore Life Itself. And these are God, whom nature comes from."

Then we talked with him about the second question, Whether the center is from its surroundings or the surroundings from the center, and we asked him why he was discussing it. He said it was so he could demonstrate something about the center and the surroundings in nature and life—that is, about the source of the center and the surroundings. And when we asked him what his own opinion was, he answered about these things the same as before—that he could demonstrate either side, but for fear of losing his reputation he proved that the surroundings are from the center. "Yet I know that there was something before the sun, and it was everywhere in the universe, and that these things flowed together by themselves—that is, into centers."

But then we spoke to him again out of displeasure from zeal, and we said, "You, friend, are insane." And when he heard this he pulled his chair from the table and looked at us hesitatingly and then pricked up his ears. But he was laughing. But we went on, "What's more insane than to say that the center is from its surroundings (by your center we understand the sun, and by its surroundings we understand the solar system), and therefore to say that the solar system came to be without the sun? Doesn't the sun make nature and all that belongs to it—which depend solely on the heat and light coming from the sun through the atmospheres? Where were these things before?

"But we'll tell where these things came from in the discussion that's coming next. Aren't the atmospheres and everything on the earth like surfaces, and the sun their center? What would they all be without the sun? Could they survive one moment? So what were they before the sun existed? Could they have existed? Isn't continued existence a steady coming-to-be? So, when the continuing existence of everything having to do with nature is due to the sun, it follows that so is its coming into being. Everyone sees this and accepts it from firsthand observation. Doesn't a result continue to be, because of its cause, just as it comes to be because of it? If the surfaces were first and the center afterwards, wouldn't the first thing continue to be because of the later, which is against the laws of order? How can things that come later produce something sooner, or outsides produce insides, or something more gross produce something purer? So how can the surfaces, which make the surroundings, produce the center? Who doesn't see that this is against the laws of nature? We have brought up these proofs for an analysis of the theory by way of settling it that the surroundings come to exist because of the center, and not the other way around, even though anyone who thinks straight sees it without the proofs. You said that the surroundings flowed together into the center by themselves. Then is it accidentally in such wonderful and amazing order that one thing exists on account of another and each and every thing on account of people and their eternal life? Can nature look after such things by some love through some wisdom, and can it make people into angels and angels into a heaven? Consider these things and think, and your notion about nature's coming from nature will collapse."

After this we asked him what he had thought about the third proposition, about the center and surroundings of nature and of life, and what he thought now—whether he believed that the center and surroundings of life are the same as the center and surroundings in nature.

He said he was unsure and that he had thought earlier that the innermost activity of nature was life, and that love and wisdom, which essentially make man's life, are from that life, and that the fire of the sun produces life through heat and light, via the atmospheres, and that now, because of the things he heard about man's eternal life, he was wavering and this uncertainty carried his mind now up, now down. When on the upswing he accepted the center he knew nothing about before, and on the downswing he saw the center he had thought was the only one. And he said that life is from a center he had not known about and nature is from the center that he used to think was the only one. And that both centers had surroundings around them.

To this we said, "Good. Only you also want to consider the center and surroundings of nature from the center and surroundings of life, and not the other way around." And we informed him that above the angelic heaven there is a sun that is pure love—to all appearances a fire like the world's sun—and angels and people have free will and love due to the heat that comes from that sun, and intellect and wisdom due to the light from it. And the things that have to do with life are called spiritual, and the things that come from the world's sun are vessels for life and are called natural. Also, the surroundings of the center of life are called "the spiritual world," which survives due to its sun, and the surroundings in nature are called "the natural world," which survives due to its sun.

"Now, you can't apply space and time to love and wisdom,

but instead, conditions, so the surroundings of the angelic heaven's sun do not spread outwards, but they are in the spread of the natural sun all the same, and they are in the living objects there according to their reception—and reception depends on the things' forms."

But then he asked, "Where does the fire of the world's sun, or nature, come from?"

We answered that it is from the sun of the angelic heaven, which is not fire but Divine Love going out from right near God, who is Love Itself.

This surprised him, so we explained it this way. "In essence, Love is spiritual fire. For this reason fire, in the spiritual sense of the Word, means love. This is why the priests in the churches pray for heavenly fire to fill people's hearts—meaning love. The fire of the Israelites' altar in the Tabernacle and the fire of the candlestick represented nothing other than Divine Love. The heat of blood, or the vital heat of people and animals in general, comes from nowhere but love, which makes their life. This is why a person takes fire, gets hot, and burns when his love is aroused in zeal, ire, or wrath. So from the fact that spiritual heat, which is love, causes natural heat in people to the point where their faces and limbs get hot and inflamed, you can establish that the fire of nature's sun exists from no source other than the fire of the spiritual sun, which is Divine Love.

"Now, the surroundings arise from the center, and not vice versa, as we said above, and the center of life, which is the sun of the angelic heaven, is Divine Love going out from right near God, who is in that sun. And the surroundings of that center, which are called the spiritual world, come from there. And from that sun the world's sun comes to be—and its surroundings, which are called the natural world, come from it. So it is clear that the universe was created by the one God."

After this we went away, and he went with us beyond the yard of his school and talked with us about heaven and hell and Divine care, with a new acuteness of character.

381   The second story: Once as I was looking around in the world of spirits, I saw at a distance a palace surrounded by a crowd, as

if it were besieged. And I saw many others running up, besides. When I saw this, I hurried outside and asked one of the people running up what the matter was there.

He answered, "Three newcomers from the world were carried up to heaven and saw magnificent things there—including young women and wives of amazing beauty. And when they came down from the heaven they went into that palace and told about what they saw—mainly that there were such beauties as their eyes had never seen, and couldn't see without being enlightened by the light of heaven's atmosphere. About themselves, they said that in the world they were orators from the kingdom of France and devoted themselves to works of oratory, and now a desire to hold forth about the source of beauty had come over them. The news got around the neighborhood, so a crowd gathered to hear the discussion."

When I heard this I hurried too, and went in and saw the three men standing among them, dressed in sapphire-colored robes that shone like gold when they moved, due to inwoven gold threads. They stood behind a sort of pulpit, ready to speak. Soon one orator climbed up onto the step behind the pulpit to speak about the source of the feminine sex's beauty, and he spoke these words:

382   "What source of beauty is there other than love? When it floods into young men's eyes and sets them afire, it becomes beauty. So love and beauty are the same thing. For love tints the face of a marriageable young woman from deep within like a flame, with a transparency that is the daybreak and crimson of her life. Who does not know that this flame sends rays into her eyes and from them as a center spreads over her whole face, and it sinks into her breast as well, sets her heart on fire, and in this way has an effect no different from the warmth and light of a fire to someone standing by it. This warmth is love, and this light is love's beauty.

"The whole world agrees that someone is beautiful according to his love. But the masculine sex's love is different from the feminine sex's love. Masculine love is love of becoming wise, and feminine love is love of loving the love of becoming wise in the masculine. So a young man is lovable and beautiful to a young woman in the measure that he has a love of becoming wise, and a young woman is lovable and beautiful to a young man in the measure that she has a love of the young man's wisdom. So just as one's love meets and kisses the other's, their beauties do the same. And so I conclude that love forms beauty in its likeness."

383   After this the second stepped up to disclose the source of beauty through cultivated discourse. He said, "I have heard that love is the source of beauty, but I do not favor the opinion. What man knows what love is? Who has contemplated any abstract image of it in his mind? Who has seen it with his eyes? Say where it is.

"But I claim that wisdom is the source of love—in women a wisdom lying hidden deep within and concealed, in men an open wisdom that stands forth. What makes a person a person except wisdom? Otherwise a person would be a sculpture or a picture. What does a young woman notice in a young man but the condition of his wisdom? And what does a young man notice in a young woman but the condition of her feelings about his wisdom?

"By wisdom I mean genuine morality, because this is the wisdom of life. For this reason, when the hidden wisdom goes up and embraces the open wisdom—which happens inwardly in the spirits of both—they mutually kiss and join together, and this is called love. And then they seem beautiful to each other.

"In a word, wisdom is like light or the gleam of a fire, which touches the eyes, and forms beauty as it touches them."

384   After this the third one stepped up and expressed these ideas. "The source of beauty is not love by itself or wisdom by itself, but it is a combination of love and wisdom—a union of love and wisdom in the young man and a union of wisdom with the love of it in the young woman. For a young woman does not love wisdom in itself but in a young man, and for that reason she sees him as beauty. And when a young man sees this in a young woman, he sees her as beauty. So love forms beauty through wisdom, and wisdom receives it through love.

"It is strikingly clear in heaven that this is so. I saw virgins and wives there, and I studied their beauty, and I saw it was totally different in virgins than in wives. There was just the glow of it in virgins, but in wives there was the brilliance of it. I saw a difference like a diamond sparkling with light and a ruby also flashing fire.

"What is beauty but a joy to your eyesight? Where is the source of this delight but in the play of love and wisdom? From this play your eyesight glows, and the glow glitters from eye to eye and gives forth beauty. What makes the beauty of a face except red and white in a lovely blend? Isn't the red from love and the white from wisdom? For love is red from its fire, and wisdom is white from its light. I saw clearly that these two colors are in the faces of two married partners in heaven—the red of the white in the wife and the white of the red in the husband. And I observed that they beamed on looking at each other."

When the third had said these things, the crowd applauded and shouted, "This is the winner." And at once a flaming light that is also the light of married love filled the house with brightness, and at the same time filled their hearts with delight.

Chapter 17

Married Love's Connection
with Love for Children

385   There are signs showing poignantly that married love and love for children (called parental love) are connected, and there are also signs that can lead to the belief that they are not connected. Love for children is found in partners who love each other from the heart, and it is also found in partners who disagree at heart, and also separated partners—sometimes more tender and stronger in them than in the others.

But it can be established, even so, that love for children is forever connected with married love, on account of the source that it flows down from. Though they differ in the recipients, the loves still remain unseparated—plainly, like the end in view at the outset and the end result, which is the effect. The end in view for married love is to raise up offspring, and the end result, which is the effect, is the raised-up offspring. You can see that the end in view carries over into the effect, is in it just as it was at the beginning and does not desert it, by rationally observing the progress of purposes and causes in their steps toward an effect.

But many people's reasonings only begin at the effects and go on from them to certain conclusions, and not at the causes and from them analytically to the effects, and so on, so reasonable things that belong in the light can only become obscure things in a cloud. This leads to detours from the truth, due to appearances and mistakes. But to show that married love and love for children are connected deep within, even if separated outwardly, it will be demonstrated in this order:

(1) Two general auras radiate from the Lord to keep the universe in its created condition. One of them is an aura of having offspring, and the other is an aura of protecting the offspring.

(2) These two general auras converge with the aura of married love and the aura of love for children.

(3) These two auras influence generally and specifically everything in heaven and everything on earth, from first to last.

(4) The aura of love for children is an aura of protecting and nourishing those who cannot protect and nourish themselves.

(5) This aura affects bad people as well as good and disposes everyone to love, protect, and nourish his offspring on account of his own love.

(6) This aura affects the feminine sex—that is, mothers—especially, and through them it affects the masculine sex, or fathers.

(7) This aura is also an aura of innocence and peace from the Lord.

(8) The aura of innocence influences children, and through them their parents, and affects them.

(9) It also influences the parents' souls and joins itself with the same aura in the children, and it is induced especially through touch.

(10) As children grow less innocent, the affection and closeness diminish, and this goes on until they leave home.

(11) The conscious attitude of parents toward the innocence and peace in their children is that the children understand nothing and can do nothing by themselves but depend on others, especially their father and mother, and this state also keeps receding as children know and can act by themselves and not depend on others.

(12) That aura goes ahead step by step from the purpose through causes into effects and produces cycles. This keeps creation in the condition that was foreseen and provided.

(13) Love for children goes downward, not upward.

(14) The state of wives' love before conception is different than it is from conception until birth.

(15) Love in marriage is connected with love for children in parents for spiritual reasons and therefore for worldly ones.

(16) Love for babies and children is different in spiritual partners than in earthly ones.

(17) In spiritual partners that love is from inner things, or first things, but in earthly partners it is from outer or resultant things.

(18) This is why that love exists in partners who love each other and also in partners who do not love each other at all.

(19) Love for children remains after death, especially in women.

(20) These people bring up children under the Lord's guidance, and the children grow bigger and smarter, as in the world.

(21) There the Lord sees to it that the innocence of their childhood becomes innocence of wisdom and that in this way the children become angels.

Now comes an explanation of these topics.

386   (1) *Two general auras radiate from the Lord to keep the universe in its created condition. One of them is an aura of having offspring, and the other is an aura of protecting the offspring.* The Divinity coming out of the Lord is a "sphere" because it radiates from Him, surrounds Him, fills both worlds, spiritual and natural, and brings about the end results that the Lord determined ahead of time in creation and sees to since creation. Everything that flows out of some object and surrounds and envelops it is a sphere—for example, the sun's aura of heat and light around it, the aura of a person's life around him, the aura of a plant's smell around it, the aura of a magnet's attraction around it, and so on. But the general auras being discussed here are from the Lord and around Him, and they radiate from the spiritual world's sun, which He is within. An aura of heat and light—or an aura of love and wisdom, which is the same thing—radiates from the Lord through that sun to bring about results, which are activities. But the auras are given various names according to the things they do. The Divine aura that sees to preserving the world in its created condition generation after generation is called an aura of having offspring, and the Divine aura that sees to taking care of the offspring at their beginnings and

afterwards in their development is called an aura of protecting offspring. In addition to these two Divine auras there are many other ones that have different names according to the things they do (see no. 222, above). The accomplishing of useful things through these auras is the Divine Providence.

387   (2) *These two general auras converge with the aura of married love and the aura of love for children.* It is obvious that the aura of married love is the same as the aura of having offspring, for having offspring is a purpose, and married love is the intermediate cause of it, and the purpose and cause act as one thing in producing the result, and in the result, because they act together.

It is also clear that the aura of love for children converges with the aura of protecting offspring, because it is a purpose that comes from the original purpose, which was producing offspring, and love for children is the intermediate cause that makes it happen. For purposes go ahead in series, one after the other, and as they go, the end result becomes a purpose, and so on all the way to the finish, where they stand still, or stop. (But more about this appears in the explanation of item 12.)

388   (3) *These two auras influence generally and specifically everything in heaven and everything on earth, from first to last.* We say "generally" and "specifically" because when you say "generally," the specifics that make it up are understood at the same time, because the general thing comes out of the specifics and is made up of them. So it takes its name from them as the whole does from its parts, because with the specifics taken away the general is only a name and is like a surface with nothing inside it. So to attribute the general guidance to God and take the specifics away is empty talk and is like mentioning nothing. The comparison with the general government of kings on earth is not valid. So now we say these two auras have influence generally and specifically.

389   The auras of having offspring and of protecting offspring—or the auras of married love and of love for children—radiate into everything in heaven and into everything in the world, from first to last, because all things that radiate from the Lord—or from the sun that is from Him and that He is in—go together throughout

the created universe, clear to the outermost parts of all the things in it. The reason is that Divine qualities, which are called heavenly and spiritual as they radiate, are outside of space and time. It is well known that nothing related to extent applies to spiritual things, because nothing related to space and time does. Owing to this, whatever radiates from the Lord goes from start to finish instantly. Nos. 222–25, above, show that the aura of married love is universal in this way. The fact that the same goes for the aura of the love for children is clear from the presence of that love in heaven, where there are children from the earth, and from the presence of that love in the world in people, animals and birds, snakes and insects. This love even has its analogue in the vegetable and mineral kingdoms—in the vegetable kingdom in that seeds are protected in shells, like baby blankets, and furthermore in fruit as in a home, and they are nourished with sap as if with milk. It is clear that something similar is in minerals from the matrices and coverings that the precious gems and precious metals are concealed and protected in.

390   The aura of having offspring and the aura of protecting offspring make a unit in an unbroken series because love of having offspring carries over into love for the offspring. You can tell what the love of having offspring is like from its joy. It surmounts and surpasses everything. Men in a position to have offspring have that joy, and women in a position to receive have it extraordinarily. This highest joy, with its love, results in birth, where it fulfills itself.

391   (4) *The aura of love for children is an aura of protecting and nourishing those who cannot protect and nourish themselves.* It said above (no. 386) that accomplishment of useful things by the Lord through the auras radiating from Him is the Divine Providence, and so this is what the aura of protecting and nourishing those who cannot protect and nourish themselves means. For it is part of creation that the things created are to be kept intact, guarded, protected, and sustained. Otherwise the universe would fail. But the Lord could not do this directly in living creatures left in freedom of choice, so He does it indirectly through His love implanted in fathers, mothers, and nurses. They do not know that their love

is love from the Lord in them, because they do not notice the Lord's influence, much less His universal presence. But who does not see that this is not nature's doing, but Divine Providence working in nature, through nature, and that there could not be a universal thing like that except from God through some spiritual sun that is in the center of the universe? And who does not see that its work is instantaneous and present from beginning to end, because it is apart from space and time? But what follows later will tell how living creatures receive that Divine work, which is the Lord's Divine Providence.

Mothers and fathers protect and nourish children because children cannot protect and nourish themselves. This is not the reason for the love but the rational motivation resulting from the love's coming into intellectual perception. For on that motivation alone, without an inspired love to excite it or a law and penalties to compel him, a person would not look after children any more than a statue does.

392   (5) *This aura affects bad people as well as good and disposes everyone to love, protect, and nourish his offspring on account of his own love.* Experience witnesses that love for children, or parental love, is in bad people just as much as in good people, just as it is in fierce and gentle animals. In fact, it is sometimes stronger and more ardent in bad people, as in fierce animals. The reason is that all love coming from the Lord and flowing in is turned, in the recipient, into the love of his life, for no living being feels anything but that he loves by himself, since he does not notice what flows into him. And when he does actually love himself, he makes his love for children his own, for he sees himself in them, so to speak, and them in himself, and himself united with them in this way. This is why that love is more fierce in savage beasts—as in lions and lionesses, male and female bears, leopards and leopardesses, male and female wolves, and others like that—than in horses, deer, goats, and sheep. The reason is that these savage beasts have power over the tame ones, and it gives them an especially dominant self-love, and this love loves itself in its offspring. So, as was said, the love that flows in turns into their own love.

This turning of the inflowing love upside-down into your own love, and the consequent protection and nourishment of offspring and young by bad parents, is due to the Lord's Divine Providence, for otherwise only a few of the human race would survive, and not any of the savage beasts—which are useful, nevertheless.

These observations show that everyone is disposed to love, protect, and nourish his offspring, due to his own love.

393   (6) *This aura affects the feminine sex—that is, mothers—especially, and through them it affects the masculine sex, or fathers.* This comes from the same source mentioned earlier—that women receive the aura of married love and it carries over to men through women, because women are born loves of men's intellect, and intellect is a vessel. It is the same with the love for children because this love arises from the love in marriage.

Everyone knows that mothers have a more tender love for children, and fathers have a less tender love. Love for children is etched on the love of marriage that women are born with. This is clear from the loving and friendly affection that girls have for babies and for dolls that they carry, dress, kiss, and hug to their chest. Boys do not have such affection.

It seems as if mothers get their love for children from nourishing them by their own blood *in utero* and from taking on their life this way, thus from a sympathetic union. Still, this is not the source of this love, since if another baby were substituted after birth for the right one, without the mother's knowing it, she would love it as tenderly as if it were her own. Besides, nurses sometimes love babies more than the mothers do.

From these considerations it follows that this love comes from nowhere but the love of marriage implanted in every woman. Joined to it is a love of conceiving. The joy of this love makes a wife receptive. This is the beginning of the love that comes across to the offspring, fully, with its joy, after birth.

394   (7) *This aura is also an aura of innocence and peace from the Lord.* Innocence and peace are the two innermost things of heaven—innermost because they radiate directly from the Lord. For the Lord is innocence itself and peace itself.

In respect to innocence the Lord is called a Lamb. And in

respect to peace, He says, "I leave you peace. I give you my peace" (John 14:27). And it is also what the "Peace" means with which they were to greet a city or house that they entered, and if it were worthy, peace would come on it, and if not worthy, the peace would return to them (Matt. 10:11–15). And, also, the Lord is called "Prince of peace" (Is. 9:6).

The fact that peace and innocence are the innermost things of heaven is also the reason why innocence is the being of everything good, and peace is the blessing of every joy that has to do with good. (See the book *Heaven and Hell*, concerning the heavenly angels' state of innocence, nos. 276–83, and concerning the state of peace in heaven, nos. 284–90).

395   (8) *The aura of innocence influences children, and through them their parents, and affects them.* It is well known that little children are innocent, but it is not well known that their innocence flows into them from the Lord. It flows in from the Lord because He is Innocence itself, as said already above, and nothing can flow in from where it does not exist, but only from where it originates—which is the essential thing.

But to say a few words about what the innocence of children is like, which affects the parents—it shines out from their faces, from some of their motions, and from their early speech, and it has an effect. Children have innocence because they do not think from deep inside, for they do not yet know what is good and bad and what is true and false to think from, so they have no individual prudence, nor considered plan, and thus no bad intentions. They have no selfhood acquired from self-interest and materialism. They attribute nothing to themselves. Everything they have they attribute to their parents. They are happy with trifles given to them as presents. They do not worry about food and clothing or anything in the future. They do not study the world and want many things from it. They love their parents, their nurses, and the young companions whom they play with innocently. They let themselves be led. They listen and obey. This is the child's innocence that is the reason for the love called parental love.

396   (9) *It also influences the parents' souls and joins itself with the same aura in the children, and it is induced especially through touch.*

The Lord's innocence flows into the angels of the third heaven, where everyone has wisdom's innocence, and it goes through the lower heavens—but only through the innocence of the angels there—and thus it goes into children directly and indirectly. They are almost like sculpted models, but they can still receive life from the Lord through the heavens.

But if the parents did not also receive this influence in their souls and in the innermost parts of their minds, they would be affected by the innocence of the children for nothing. There has to be something equal and similar in another person to provide communication and to get reception, affection, and thus conjunction. Otherwise it would be like a delicate seed falling on flint, or like a lamb thrown to a wolf. This, then, is the way innocence, flowing into the parents' souls, joins together with the innocence of children.

Experience can teach that this rapport happens for parents by way of the body's senses—but mainly through touch. For instance, sight is deeply pleased by looking at them, hearing by their voices, smell by their smell. You can see clearly that communication, and rapport through it, with innocence is mainly made by touch, from the pleasure of carrying them in your arms, of hugging and kissing them, especially in the case of mothers, who delight in their resting their mouth and face on their bosoms, and the touch of their hands there at that same time, and in general from the sucking on their breasts and giving milk. Also from feeling their naked bodies and from the untiring work of diapering them and cleaning them on their laps.

It has already been pointed out several times that between married partners communication of love and its delights is done through the sense of touch. Communication of their minds is also made by touch because hands are a person's most outward parts, and the essential person is in the most outward parts at the same time. Touch also holds together everything in the body and everything in the mind, which is in between, in an unbroken connection. This is why Jesus touched the little children (Matt. 19:13, 15; Mark 10:13, 16), and why He healed the sick by touch, and why those who touched Him were healed. This is also why initiation into the ministry today is done by laying on of hands.

These things show that the parents' innocence and the

children's innocence meet each other through touch—especially of hands—and in this way they join them together the same as kisses do.

397   It is well known that innocence does the same things by touch in animals and birds as it does in people. It does the same things because everything that radiates from the Lord instantly pervades the universe (see nos. 388–90 above). And it goes through stages and continuous transitions, so it comes across not only to animals but even further, to vegetables and minerals (no. 389). It comes across to the earth itself, which is the mother of all vegetables and minerals. For in springtime the earth is ready to receive seed as in a womb, and when it does receive it, it conceives, so to speak, warms the seeds, carries them, births them, nurses them, feeds them, clothes them, raises them, protects them, and in a sense loves the offspring from them, and so forth. If the aura of having offspring goes there, why not to all kinds of animals—even worms? It is an established fact that the bees in any hive have a common mother, just as the earth is common mother to the plants.

398   (10) *As children grow less innocent, the affection and closeness diminish, and this goes on until they leave home.* It is a known fact that love for children, or parental love, leaves the parents as innocence leaves the children until the children leave home, in the case of humans, and in the case of animals and birds until they drive the young from their presence and forget they are their offspring. This makes it evident, clinching the argument, that innocence flowing in on both sides produces the love called parental love.

399   (11) *The conscious attitude of parents toward the innocence and peace in their children is that the children understand nothing and can do nothing by themselves but depend on others, especially their father and mother, and this state also keeps receding as children know and can act by themselves and not depend on others.* The aura of love for babies is an aura of protecting and nourishing those who cannot protect and nourish themselves. This was demonstrated in its own article above (no. 391). It was noted there that this reason is only the visible reason in people, but not the real reason for the love in them. The real, basic reason for their love is innocence from the

Lord, which flows into a person without his knowing it and produces the discernable cause, so that as the first cause makes a
withdrawal from that love, so does the second cause. Or, in other
words, as communication of innocence withdraws, so does the
reason for their conviction. But this happens only in people, so
that they can do what they do rationally and in freedom and
therefore support their grown offspring according to what they
need and can use, on account of rational and also moral law.
Animals without rationality lack this second reason. They have
only the primary reason, which they have by instinct.

400   (12) *The aura of the love of having offspring goes ahead step by step
from the purpose through causes into effects and produces cycles. This
keeps creation in the condition that was foreseen and provided.* All the
processes in the universe go forward from purposes through causes
into effects. In their own right these three things cannot be separated,
although they seem divided in concept. Yet a purpose is nothing
unless you also view the intended effect, nor does either of these
do anything unless a cause is there, upholding, foreseeing, and
uniting. A progression like this is etched on every person in a
general way and in each part. It is just like intention, understanding,
and action. Every purpose in a person has to do with intention,
every cause has to do with understanding, and every effect has to
do with action. Likewise, every purpose has to do with a love,
every causal factor that it works through has to do with wisdom,
and every effect has to do with usefulness. The reason is that love's
vessel is intention, wisdom's vessel is understanding, and the
vessel of usefulness is action. So since the processes in people,
in general and in detail, progress from intention through understanding to action, in the same way they go from love through
wisdom to usefulness—but here wisdom means everything that
has to do with judgment and thinking. The three things are plainly
one in the result. You can tell that they also are one in concepts
before the effect, from the fact that only the doing stands between
them, for, mentally, the purpose comes from an intention and
builds itself a cause in the intellect and expresses itself in an effort,
and the effort is like an action before it happens. This is why a wise
person, and also the Lord, accepts an effort as an act.

What reasonable person cannot see, or accept it when he hears it, that these three things flow out of some first cause and the cause is that love, wisdom, and usefulness continually go out from the Lord, the Creator and Sustainer of the universe, and the three things go out as one? Tell where else they come from, if you can.

401 The aura of having offspring and protecting them has the same progression from purpose through cause into effect. In this case the purpose is the intention to have offspring, or the love of offspring. The intermediate cause that the purpose goes through and ends in is the love in marriage. The series of causes that do it, step by step, is the lovemaking, the conception, and the gestation of the embryo or fetus to be brought forth. The effect is the born offspring itself. But although purpose, cause, and effect go ahead one after the other as three, they still make one thing in love of having offspring and inwardly in the separate causes, and in the effect itself. They are only the working causes—which follow one another in time, because they are in nature. The purpose, or the intention, and the love remain constantly the same, for purposes in nature do go forward through points of time, without time, but they cannot come out and be known before the effect, or the useful accomplishment emerges and becomes something. Before that, the love could love only the process but could not settle and focus itself.

It is well known that cycles have such a process and that creation is kept in the condition foreseen and provided, by means of them. But the progress of the love for children, from its greatest to its least—or to its end, or point where it stops or leaves off—goes in reverse order, because it follows the waning of the innocence in its object, and also because of its cycles.

402 (13) *Love for children goes downward, not upward.* That is, it goes down from one generation to the next, or from sons and daughters to grandsons and granddaughters and does not go upwards from them to fathers and mothers of families. This is known. The reason the love grows as it descends is the love of bearing offspring or producing useful results, and, where the human race is concerned, the reason is the love of increasing the race. But this has its source only in the Lord, since in the growth of the human race He sees to

the preservation of creation and, as the final purpose of this, the angelic heaven, which is from the human race alone. And the heaven of angels is the purpose of purposes and therefore the love of loves for the Lord, so not only is love of having offspring implanted in people's souls, but so is loving the offspring in the following generations. This is why this love is only to be found in people and not in any animal or bird.

In people this love grows as it goes downward because of praise for a good reputation, too. This likewise grows for them as it extends. (A later article, 16, will show that love of reputation and praise accepts into itself love for children, flowing in from the Lord, and makes it like its own.)

403   (14) *The state of wives' love before conception is different than it is from conception until birth.* This is mentioned in order to make it known that love of having offspring, and consequent love for the offspring, are implanted in married love in women, and that these two loves are divided in a woman when the purpose, which is love of having offspring, begins its process.

It is clear from many signs that then parental love carries over from the wife to the husband, and also that then the love of having offspring, which in a woman unites with her love of marriage, is not the same, as was said.

404   (15) *Love in marriage is connected with love for children in parents for spiritual reasons and therefore for worldly ones.* The spiritual reasons are to multiply the human race and to increase the angelic heaven from it, and so that those who will become angels will be born—serving the Lord for useful things in heaven, and also in the world through association with the people on earth. For the Lord does associate angels with every person. They are associated in such a way that if they were removed a person would immediately fall down dead.

The earthly reasons for the connection of the two loves are for those who carry on useful activities in human communities to be born and be incorporated in the communities as members.

Married partners themselves think that these are the worldly and spiritual reasons for love of children and love of marriage, and they sometimes express it, saying that they have enriched heaven with as many angels as they had offspring and that they have distinguished society with as many helpers as they had children.

405   (16) *Love for children is different in spiritual partners than in earthly ones.* Spiritual partners have a love for children that is similar in appearance to the love for children in worldly partners, but it is more inward, so it is more tender, because that love comes out of innocence and from the closer reception of innocence in themselves, and thus from a more powerful perception of it. For spiritual partners partake of innocence to the extent that they are spiritual. But, in fact, after these fathers and mothers have tasted the sweetness of innocence in their babies, they love their children in an altogether different way than worldly fathers and mothers do. Spiritual parents love children for their spiritual intelligence and moral life. In other words, for fear of God and for active piety, or piety that is lived, and at the same time for loving and doing activities that serve society, which is to say, for the virtues and good behavior in them. It is mainly for love of these things that they look after their needs and provide for them. So if they fail to see this kind of thing in them, it draws their souls away from them, and they do things for them only from duty.

In worldly fathers and mothers, to be sure, there is also love for children on account of innocence, but when they receive the innocence it becomes wrapped up in their own love, so they love the children for both of these things at the same time, kissing, hugging, and carrying them, hugging them to their chests, fondling them beyond measure. And they see them as if they had the same heart and soul as themselves. And then, after their state of childhood, up to adolescence and beyond, when innocence is no longer working, they do not love them from any fear of God, and active or living piety, nor for any rational and moral intelligence in them. They take little if any note of their inner feelings or the virtues and good behavior from them, and they notice only the outward virtues that they dote on. They join, fasten, and glue their love to these things, and so they close their eyes to their faults, excusing them and encouraging the children. The reason is that in them, love of their offspring is also self-love, which attaches to its object outwardly and does not enter into it any more than it does into itself.

406   From spiritual and natural parents after death it is plain to see what their love of babies and children is like, for when they arrive in the spiritual world, most fathers remember their children who have died before them, and they appear and recognize each other. Spiritual fathers only look their children over and ask how they are. They rejoice if things are well and grieve if bad. And after a little conversation, instruction, and advice about the moral life of heaven, they separate. And before separating they teach them not to think of them as fathers any longer, because the Lord alone is father to everyone in heaven, according to His words (Matt. 23:9), and they never think of them as children.

But when worldly fathers first realize they are living after death and recall to mind their children who have died before them, and when they are made present in answer to a prayer of longing, they instantly cling together like a bundle of sticks tied together. And then the father keeps delighting in looking at them and talking with them. If the father learns that some of his children are satans, and that they have brought harm to good people, he still keeps them in a cluster around him or in a group in front of him. If he himself sees them bringing harm and doing wicked things, he pays no attention even to that and does not separate one of them from himself. To keep such a destructive herd from lasting, they all have to be sent into hell together, and there the father is locked up under guard in front of his children, and the children are taken separately and each sent to a place suited to their life.

407   I add this remarkable thing to these observations. In the spiritual world I have seen fathers who looked at children brought before their eyes with hate and a kind of rage, and in such a fierce temper that they wanted to kill them if they could. But as soon as they were told, falsely, that these were their own children, the rage and fierceness went away, and they instantly loved them desperately. Those who have been inwardly deceitful in the world and have struck out against the Lord in their souls have this love and hate at the same time.

408   (17) *In spiritual partners that love is from inner things, or first things, but in worldly partners it is from outer or resultant things.* To think and draw conclusions from innermost and first things is to

work from purposes and causes to effects, but to think and draw conclusions from outward or resultant things is to work from effects to causes and purposes. This second process is against order, but the first one is in order, for thinking and reaching conclusions from purposes and causes is thinking from good and true things seen in the mind's higher level to the effects on the lower level. Human reason itself is like this by creation. But thinking and reaching conclusions from effects is surmising causes and purposes from the mind's lower level, where the body's senses are, with their apparent and fallacious qualities. This in itself is nothing but confirming falsities and selfish wants, and after confirming these, seeing and believing that they are the truths of wisdom and the good results of wisdom's love.

It is the same with love of babies and children in spiritual and worldly people. The spiritual love them for the things that come first, thus according to order, but the worldly love them for resultant things, thus against order.

These remarks are brought in just to confirm the last article.

409   (18) *This is why that love exists in partners who love each other and also in partners who do not love each other at all,* thus in worldly ones as well as spiritual. But the one kind have married love, while the other kind do not—only the appearance and pretense of it. Still, love for children and love in marriage work together, because love of marriage is implanted in every woman by creation, and together with it love of having offspring. This love focuses on the created offspring and flows together, and it carries over into men from women, as said above. For this reason, in households where there is not married love between a man and wife, it is in the wife even so, and through it there is some sort of outward conjunction with the man. For this same reason, prostitutes love their offspring, too, because whatever is implanted in souls by creation and looks to reproduction cannot be erased or uprooted.

410   (19) *Love for children remains after death, especially in women.* As soon as children are awakened after death, which happens at once, they are raised into heaven and given to angels of the feminine sex

who loved children in their bodily lives in the world and also feared God. Because they loved all children out of motherly tenderness, they receive them just like their own. The babies there love them spontaneously, just like their mothers. Women there have as many children around them as they want due to spiritual parental love.

The heaven where babies are appears in front, in the forehead area, on the line or radius along which the angels look directly toward the Lord. That heaven is located there because all babies are brought up under the Lord's direct guidance. And the heaven of innocence, which is the third heaven, flows in among them. After this first age is over, children are moved to another heaven, where they are educated.

411   (20) *These people bring up children under the Lord's guidance, and the children grow bigger and smarter, as in the world.* Children in heaven are educated in this way: From their teacher they learn to talk. Their first talk is only the sounds of affection, yet something of elementary thought is in it, which makes a human sound differ from an animal's sound. This talk gradually becomes more distinct as ideas enter their thought from their feelings. All their feelings, which also grow, come from innocence. First the kind of things that are before their eyes and are pleasant are insinuated into them. Since these are of a spiritual origin, heavenly influences flow into them at the same time, which opens the most inward parts of their minds. After these beginnings, the children grow bigger and also look more mature as they understand more. The reason is that spiritual nutrition is precisely intelligence and wisdom. For that reason, what nourishes their minds also nourishes their bodies there. But children in heaven grow up only to the prime of life, stop there, and stay there forever. And when they reach that age they are given in a marriage that the Lord provides. It is celebrated in the heaven where the young man is, and he soon follows his wife into her heaven, or, if they are in the same community, into her house.

So that I would know for certain that infants grow and mature in size the same as in intellect, I had a chance to talk with some while they were children and afterwards when they had grown up, and I saw that they were growing to the same size as young adults in the world.

412   Children are taught mainly by representations adjusted and suitable to their talent. In the world it is almost impossible to believe how beautiful and full of inner wisdom the representations are. I can bring in two representations here, which will give an idea about others.

Once they represented the Lord rising out of the tomb and at the same time the unity of His Humanity with His Divinity. First they brought out the idea of a tomb, but not an idea of the Lord at the same time, except so remotely that you could hardly tell it was the Lord, except as if in the distance, because the idea of a tomb has something of a corpse about it, which they removed in this way. Afterwards they skillfully introduced into the tomb something like an atmosphere that all the same seemed delicately watery. This stood for the spiritual life in baptism—also appropriately remote.

Afterwards I saw a representation by them of the Lord's coming down to those who were bound and going up to heaven with them. And in a childlike way they let down very pliant, very delicate, almost invisible cords to help the Lord go up—always in holy fear not to have anything in the representation border on something with no heavenly quality in it. I also saw other representations that bring them to an acquaintance with truth and at the same time an affection for good as by games suitable for children's minds.

The Lord leads the children to these and similar things by the innocence passing through the third heaven, and so spiritual things are brought into their feelings and from there into their tender thoughts in such a way that the children do not know but what they do and think such things by themselves. This gives their intellect a start.

413   (21) *There the Lord sees to it that the innocence of their childhood becomes innocence of wisdom [and that in this way the children become angels].* Many people may assert that children remain children

and become angels at once after death. But intelligence and wisdom make an angel, so as long as children do not have these, they are among angels, to be sure, but are not angels. But they become angels as soon as they have become intelligent and wise. So children are led forward from the innocence of childhood to the innocence that comes with wisdom—that is, from external innocence to internal innocence. This innocence is the purpose of all their instruction and growth, so when they achieve the innocence that comes with wisdom, the innocence of childhood that has served them as a platform is attached to them. I have seen the quality of childhood's innocence represented by something wooden, almost without life, that comes alive as it absorbs an acquaintance with truth and feelings for good. And later the quality of the innocence that comes with wisdom was represented as a live, naked baby. Angels of the third heaven, who are in a state of innocence from the Lord more than the rest, appear to the eyes of spirits below the heavens as naked babies, and they are more alive than others because they are more wise. The reason is that innocence corresponds to infancy and also to nakedness. So it says that Adam and his wife were naked and did not blush when they were in a state of innocence, but after they lost the state of innocence they blushed at their nakedness and hid themselves (Gen. 2:25; 3:7, 10, 11). In a word, the wiser the angels are, the more innocent they are. You can see something of what the innocence of wisdom is like from the innocence of childhood described above (no. 395), except that in place of the parents mentioned there, take the Lord to be the Father who leads them and to whom they attribute all they receive.

414   I have talked with angels, at various times, about innocence, and they said that innocence is the essence of all good and that good is good so far as innocence is in it. And they said wisdom has to do with life and therefore with good, so wisdom is wisdom so far as it partakes of innocence. The same goes for love, charity, and faith. They said that this is why no one can enter heaven unless he is innocent, and that is what these words of the Lord mean: "Let the children come to Me. Don't keep them away, for the kingdom of the heavens is made up of them. Truly I say to

you, whoever does not receive the kingdom of heaven as a child does, won't go into it" (Mark 10:14,15; Luke 18:16, 17). There and elsewhere in the Word "children" means those in innocence.

The reasons why good is good so far as innocence is in it is that all good is from the Lord, and it is innocence to be led by the Lord.

415 The following story should be added to these remarks.

One morning, woken up from sleep, meditating before I was fully awake in the clear morning light, I saw through the window a sort of lightning flash and soon heard a sort of rolling thunder. And as I was wondering where it came from I heard this from the sky: "Not far from you some people are arguing passionately about God and nature. The flash of light like lightning and the crash in the air like thunder correspond to the fight and clash of arguments, from one side for God and from the other for nature, and the phenomena are from the correspondences."

The reason for this spiritual fight was this. There were some satans in hell who said among themselves, "If only we were allowed to talk with angels of heaven, we'd totally and fully demonstrate that nature is what they call 'the God that everything comes from' and that 'God' is only a word unless you take it to mean nature."

The satans believed this with all their heart and soul, and they were very anxious to talk with angels of heaven, so they were allowed to go up out of the mire and darkness of hell and talk with two angels who now came down from heaven. They were in the world of spirits, which is halfway between heaven and hell.

Seeing the angels there, the satans quickly ran up and shouted in a furious voice, "Are you the angels of heaven with whom we're allowed to get into an argument about God and nature? You're called wise because you accept God, but oh, how simple-minded you are! Who sees God? Who understands what God is? Who accepts that God rules, and can rule, the universe and each and every thing in it? Who but a common lowbrow accepts what he doesn't see and understand? What is more obvious than that nature is the all-in-all? Who sees anything but nature with his eye? Who ever heard anything but nature with his ear? Who ever smelled anything but nature with his nose? Who ever tasted anything but nature with his tongue? Who feels anything but nature with the touch of his hand and body? Aren't our bodily senses the only witnesses of truth? Who can't swear from them that something is so? Aren't your heads in nature? Where does the influence on the thoughts in your heads come from except there? Take nature away, and can you think anything?" And other chaff like that.

After listening to all this, the angels answered, "You talk this way because you are only sense-oriented. In hell they all have the ideas of their thinking immersed in the bodily senses and can't raise their minds above them, so we excuse you. A life of evil and a belief in false notions from it has closed the innermost parts of your minds to the point where there is no such thing for you as rising above sensory things, except in a position removed from evils of life and falsities of belief. For a satan as well as an angel can understand truth when he hears it, but he doesn't retain it, because evil erases truth and substitutes lies. But we notice that you are in a removed position now, so you can understand the truth that we speak. So pay attention to what we say."

They said, "You were in the natural world, and you left there, and now you are in the spiritual world. Did you know anything about life after death until now? Didn't you used to deny it and put yourselves on the same level as animals? Before, did you know anything about heaven and hell or anything about the light and warmth of this world? Or about the fact that you're no longer in nature, but above it? For this world and everything about it is spiritual, and spiritual things are so far above natural that not the tiniest bit of nature can seep into this world. But you thought nature was a god or goddess, so you think the light and warmth of this world is the light and warmth of the natural world, too, when they are not at all, for here the light of nature is darkness, and the heat of nature is cold here. Did you know anything about the sun of this world, where our light and our heat come from? Did you know that this sun is pure love, and the natural world's sun is pure fire, and that the world's sun, which is pure fire, is what nature came out of and is supported by, and that the sun of heaven, which is pure love, is what life itself—which is love with wisdom—came from and is supported by, and so nature, which you make a god or goddess, is completely dead?

"If you have a guard, you can go up into heaven with us, and if we have a guard, we can go down into hell with you. In heaven you'll see magnificent and splendid things, but in hell squalid and unclean things. These differences exist because everyone in heaven worships God, and everyone in hell worships nature. And the magnificent and splendid things in heaven are objectified feelings having to do with good and truth. The squalid and unclean things in hell are objectified selfishness having to do with evil and untruth.

"Infer from these two facts, now, whether God or nature is the all-in-all."

To this the satans answered, "In the state of mind we're in now, we can tell from what we've heard that it's God, but when the pleasure of evil invades our minds, all we see is nature."

The two angels and the two satans stood not far from me, to my right, so I saw and heard them. And I saw around them many spirits who were celebrated as learned in the natural world! I was surprised that those learned people sometimes stood near the angels, sometimes near the satans, and that they favored the ones they were standing near. I was told, "Their changes of position are changes in their states of mind, sometimes favoring one side and sometimes the other, for they are chameleons. And we'll tell you a secret. We've looked down to the earth at the ones celebrated for their learning who, in their discernment, thought about God and nature, and we found six hundred in a thousand for nature and the rest for God. But they were not for God because of understanding, just from hearing the words spoken many times, 'Nature is from God.' Speaking frequently from memory and recollection, and not from thought and intellect at the same time, introduces a kind of faith."

After this the satans were given a guard, and they went up to heaven with the two angels and saw magnificent and splendid things. And then, with enlightenment from the light of heaven there, they admitted that God exists and that nature was created for the service of the life that is in God and from God, and that nature in itself is dead, so nothing acts by itself but is acted upon by life. After seeing and understanding these things they went down, and as they went down their love of evil came back and closed their intellect from above and opened it from underneath. And then a sort of veil, flashing with hellfire, appeared over them. And when their feet touched ground, the ground immediately opened under them, and they sank back to their own kind.

416   After this the two angels, seeing me nearby, said to the people standing around me, "We know that this man has written about God and nature. Let's listen."

They came up and asked for what had been written about God and nature to be read to them, and I read the following things [*Divine Love and Wisdom*, nos. 351–57]:

"Those who believe that Divinity is at work in the small details of nature can reassure themselves in favor of Divinity from all the many things they see in nature, just as well as—in fact, better than—those who confirm themselves in favor of nature. For those who confirm themselves in favor of Divinity heed the wonders that stand out in what vegetables produce as well as what animals do.

"In the products of vegetables: A root goes out from a little seed sown in the ground. Out of the root comes a stem, and, one by one, branches, leaves, flowers, fruit—all the way to new seeds— just as if the seed understood the steps to follow, or the process, for it to renew itself. What reasonable person can think that the sun, which is pure fire, understands this, or that it can put the knowledge of how to do things like that into its heat and light, and then that it can regulate the marvels in these things and intend something useful? When a person whose reason is lifted up sees these things and considers them, he cannot help thinking that they come from the One who is infinite wisdom, which is to say from God. Those who acknowledge Divinity see and think it, too, but those who do not acknowledge do not see and think it, because they do not want to. And they lower their reason to the sensory level, so that all their ideas come out of the light that the bodily senses are in, and they confirm their fallacies by saying, 'Don't you see the sun doing these things by its heat and its light? What is a thing that you don't see? Is it anything?'

"Those who are confirmed for Divinity heed the wonders that

stand out in the products of animals. To mention only eggs here, a chicken lies hidden in each—in its seed or beginning—with all it requires until it hatches, and also during the whole process after it hatches until it becomes a bird, or a flying creature, put together like its parent. And when you consider the way an animal is made, it is such that you cannot help being astounded if you think deeply. For example, in the smallest of them, as in the greatest, in fact, in the invisible ones as in the visible, that is, in tiny insects as in birds or large animals, there are organs of sense that are sight, hearing, smell, taste, and touch, and organs of motion, which are muscles, for they fly and walk. There are also viscera around the heart and lungs, controlled by brains. You know from anyone's description of their anatomy—especially Swammerdam's in his *Book of Nature*—that even insects have these organs.

"Those who attribute everything to nature certainly see things like this, but they only think 'there they are' and say that nature produces them. They say this because they have turned their minds away from thinking about Divinity, and people who have turned away from thinking about Divinity cannot think rationally, much less spiritually, when they see the marvels in nature, but they think sensorily and materialistically, and then they are thinking in nature and from nature, and not above it, just as the people who are in hell do. They only differ from animals in that they have the power of reason—that is, they can understand—and so they can think differently if they want.

"When those who have turned away from thinking about Divinity see wonders in nature and it makes them sense-oriented, they do not consider that eyesight is so gross that it sees many tiny insects as one blur, and yet each of them is organized for sensing and moving, so it is furnished with fibers and vessels, and a little heart, windpipes, tiny viscera, and a brain, and these are woven together from the purest things in nature, and the weavings correspond to some life that makes the tiniest of them act with precision. If eyesight is so gross that many things, with innumerable things in each one, seem to it like a little blur, and those who are sense-oriented still think and judge from sight, it shows how gross their mind has become and therefore what darkness they are in about spiritual things.

417 "Everyone can convince himself about Divinity from what is visible in nature if he wants to, and also, one who thinks about God according to life does convince himself, as when he sees birds in the sky, each species of which knows its food and where it is. It knows its own kind by the sound and look. And it knows which others are friendly and which are unfriendly. They mate, know how to come together, skillfully build nests, lay eggs there, sit on them, know the time of incubation, hatch the young when the time is up, love them tenderly, keep them warm under their wings, offer them food and feed them, until they mature and can do the same things and have a brood to continue the kind. Everyone who wants to think about the Divine influence through the spiritual world into the natural can see it in these things and, if he cares to, can say in his heart, 'Knowledge like that can't radiate into them from the sun through its light rays, because the sun, which nature gets its beginning and essence from, is only fire, and so its light rays are quite dead.' And in this way they can conclude that things like that are from the influence of Divine Wisdom in the lowest level of nature.

418 "Anyone can confirm himself in favor of Divinity by things seen in nature, when he sees caterpillars that enjoy a certain desire to try to achieve a change from their earthbound state to something comparable to a heavenly state, and so they creep into places and put themselves into a kind of womb to be reborn, and there they become chrysalids, aurelias, nymphs, and finally butterflies. And after this metamorphosis they wear the beautiful wings of their species, fly into the air as if into their heaven and happily play there, mate, lay eggs, and provide themselves a posterity, and all the while nourish themselves with delightful sweet food from flowers. What person who confirms himself in favor of Divinity from the things seen in nature fails to see some representation of man's earthly state in them as caterpillars and a representation of a heavenly state in them as butterflies? Those who have confirmed themselves for nature, however, certainly do see those things, but they say they are just natural instincts, because they have banished the heavenly state of man from their minds.

419 "From things seen in nature, anyone can confirm himself in favor of Divinity, when he considers what is known about bees—

that they know how to collect wax and suck honey from plants and flowers, and build cells like little houses and arrange them in the form of a city with streets that they go in and out by. From a distance they smell the flowers and plants that they collect the wax from for their home and the honey for food, and loaded with these they fly back to their hive 'by the compass.' In this way they provide food and lodging for the coming winter just as if they knew about it and foresaw it. And they place a leader over them like a queen, who propagates offspring. And they build her a sort of palace above them, with servants around her. When the time comes for offspring, she goes from cell to cell accompanied by servants and lays eggs, which the crowd of followers seal up to keep the air from injuring them. This provides new progeny. Later, when they are old enough to do the same thing, they are driven from home, and the expelled crowd collects and forms a swarm so as not to break up the group. Then it flies away to find itself a home. And about autumn they bring the useless drones out and take away their wings to keep them from coming back and eating their food, which they expended no labor on. And other things. You can conclude from all this that, for the use they perform for the human race, these bees have a form of kingdom, due to influence from the spiritual world, as among men on earth, and, in fact, among angels in heaven.

"What person with sound reason fails to see that they do not get these things from the natural world? What does the sun that nature comes from have in common with a government that copies, and is the analogue of, the government of heaven?

"From these and similar things in the lower animals, the one who avows and worships nature confirms himself in favor of nature, while the one who avows and worships God confirms himself in favor of God by them, for the spiritual person sees spiritual things in them, and the worldly person sees worldly things in them, so to each his own.

"As for me, things like this have been witnesses to me of the influence of the spiritual in the natural, or the spiritual world in the natural world, thus the Lord's Divine Wisdom. And consider whether you can think analytically of any form of government or any civil law, or any moral virtue, or any spiritual truth unless

Divinity is radiating through the spiritual world by His wisdom. As for me, I cannot and never could, for I have been noticeably and sensibly aware of that influence, steadily, for twenty-five years now. So I say this as a witness.

420   "Can nature have a useful activity as its purpose and put useful activities into series and forms? This is impossible except for one with wisdom, and no one but God, Who has infinite wisdom, can arrange and form a universe this way. Who else can foresee and provide all the things that are food and clothing for people— food from the fruits of the earth and from the animals, and clothing from the same? Among the wonders is the fact that the lowly worms called silkworms clothe and splendidly adorn with silk both women and men from queens and kings to maids and footmen, and that lowly insects called bees freely supply wax for the lights that keep cathedrals and palaces in splendor. These and many other things are outstanding evidence that the Lord does all the things in nature from Himself, through the spiritual world.

421   "I should add to these remarks that people who have confirmed themselves in favor of nature by things seen in the world, to the point of becoming atheists, have been seen in the spiritual world, and in spiritual light their intellect appeared open below but closed above, because in thought they look down to the earth and not up toward heaven. There seemed to be something like a curtain over their sensory level—the lowest level of the intellect. In some it was lit with infernal fire, in some it was black like soot, and in some livid like a corpse. So beware of confirmations in favor of nature, everyone. Confirm yourself in favor of Divinity. There is no lack of material."

422   Certainly others are to be excused for attributing to nature certain things they see because they know nothing about the sun of the spiritual world, where the Lord is, and the influence from there, nor anything about that world and its condition, nor anything, in fact, about its presence among people, so that they could only think that spiritual is a purer natural, and thus that angels are either in space or among the stars, and about the devil, that he is either an evil person or, if he really exists, is in the air or in the depths. And that after death people's souls are either deep in the earth or in some indefinite place until Judgment Day. And other

things like that which imagination has introduced from ignorance of the spiritual world and its sun. This is the reason why those who have believed that nature produces the things you see by something implanted from creation are to be excused. But still, those who have made themselves atheists by confirming themselves in favor of nature are not to be excused, because they could have confirmed themselves in favor of Divinity. Ignorance does indeed excuse, but it does not take away the confirmed falsity, for this falsity clings to evil, and evil to hell.

PART 2

The Foolish Pleasures
of Illicit Love

Chapter 18

Illicit Love and Married Love Are Opposite

423   First to show here at the threshold what "illicit love" means in this chapter. It does not mean extramarital love that comes before marriage or follows it after a partner's death, nor life with a mistress undertaken for legal, upright, and serious reasons. Nor does it mean the mild kinds of adultery nor the serious kinds that a person actually repents of. For these adulteries do not become opposite to the love in marriage, and such extramarital love is not opposite. Later, where each is discussed, it will be seen that these are not opposites.

But here the illicit love opposite to the love in marriage means adulterous love when not regarded as a sin nor as bad, dishonorable, and against reason, but as reasonably permissible. This love of fornication not only makes married love the same as itself, but it debases it, destroys it, and finally vomits it up, too. This chapter deals with this love's opposition to the love in marriage. You can tell it is not about any other because there are later chapters about fornication, living with a mistress, and the different kinds of adultery.

But to make that opposition clear in the sight of reason, it is going to be demonstrated in this order.

(1) Without knowing what married love is you cannot know what illicit love is.

(2) Illicit love is opposite to married love.

(3) Illicit love is opposite to married love as a worldly person per se is opposite to a spiritual person.

(4) Illicit love is opposite to married love just as a "marriage" of evil and lies is opposite to the marriage of good and truth.

(5) So illicit love is opposite to married love just as hell is opposite to heaven.

(6) The filthiness of hell is from illicit love, and the cleanness of heaven is from married love.

(7) The same goes for uncleanness in the church and cleanness there.

(8) Illicit love makes a person more and more not a person and not a man, and married love makes a person more and more a person and a man.

(9) There is an aura of illicit love and an aura of married love.

(10) The aura of illicit love comes up from hell, and the aura of married love comes down from heaven.

(11) These two auras meet each other in both worlds but do not mingle.

(12) There is a balance between these auras, and people are in this balance.

(13) A person can turn to whichever aura he likes, but insofar as he turns to one, he turns away from the other.

(14) Either aura brings delights with it.

(15) The delights of illicit love begin in the body, and they are physical even in the spirit, but the delights of married love begin in the spirit, and they are spiritual even in the body.

(16) Illicit love's delights are foolish pleasures, and married love's delights are sensible joys.

Now comes the explanation of these topics.

424   (1) *Without knowing what married love is you cannot know what illicit love is.* Illicit love means the love of adultery that destroys the love of marriage (as above, no. 423). The fact that you cannot know what this illicit love is like without knowing what married love is like does not need to be demonstrated but only illustrated by comparisons. For instance, who can know what is evil and false without knowing what is good and true? And who knows what is unchaste, dishonest, unsuitable, and ugly without knowing what is chaste, honest, suitable, and beautiful? And who

can recognize folly except someone who is wise, or who knows what wisdom is? And who can correctly pick out dissonances except someone who has learned harmonic progressions through teaching and study? Likewise, who can tell what adultery is like unless he sees what marriage is like? And who can judge illicit love's foul pleasure except someone who first judges married love's clean pleasure?

I have finished "The Sensible Joy of Married Love," so now I can describe, from the knowledge acquired there, the pleasures of illicit love.

425   (2) *Illicit love is opposite to married love.* There is nothing in the universe without its opposite, and opposites are not relative to one another but are opposite. Relative relationships are between the most and the least of the same thing, but opposites come from the opposite of something and these opposites are related to each other among themselves the way relative relationships are, so the relationships themselves are opposed.

It is clear from light, heat, the world's seasons, feelings, perceptions, sensations, and many other things that each and every thing has its opposite. The opposite of light is darkness, the opposite of heat is cold. Opposite periods in the world are day and night and summer and winter. Opposite feelings are joy and grief and happiness and sadness. Opposite perceptions are good and evil, true and false, and opposite sensations are pleasure and displeasure. So with all the evidence you can conclude that the love in marriage has its opposite. This is adultery, as anyone can see if he wishes, from the dictates of sound reason. Tell, if you can, what else is its opposite. In addition, since sound reason can see this strikingly in its light, it made laws called civil laws of justice in favor of marriage and against adultery.

To make it stand out more clearly that they are opposites, let me tell about something I have often seen in the spiritual world. When those who have been confirmed adulterers in the world of nature notice the aura of married love floating out from heaven, either they flee at once into caverns and hide, or if they stand their ground against it, they are provoked to rage and act like furies. This happens because all happy and unhappy things to do with feelings are perceived there—sometimes as clearly as your nose smells an odor—for they do not have a material body that absorbs things like this.

But many in the natural world do not know that illicit love and the love in marriage are opposite, due to physical pleasure, which outwardly seems to rival the pleasure of married love, and those who are only interested in pleasure do not know anything about that opposition. And I can affirm that if you said that each thing has its opposite and concluded that married love has its opposite as well, adulterers would answer that married love has no opposite, because illicit love is not different from it in any sense. It is also clear from this that whoever does not know what married love is like does not know what illicit love is like. And, in addition, it is clear that you cannot find out from illicit love what married love is like, but the former from the latter—nor good from evil, but evil from good. For evil is in darkness, while good is in the light.

426   (3) *Illicit love is opposite to married love as a worldly person per se is opposite to a spiritual person.* It is known in the church that a worldly person and a spiritual are so opposed to each other that one does not want what the other does—in fact, that they fight each other—but so far this has not been explained. So now to tell what distinguishes the spiritual and the worldly and stirs one up against the other. The worldly person is the one everyone is led to be at first when he grows up, which happens through information and finding things out, and through rational intellectual thoughts. But the spiritual person is the one he is led to be through love of doing useful things—the love that is also called charity— so someone is spiritual in the measure that he has this love. And he is worldly in the measure that he does not have it, even if he is talented with insight and has wise judgment.

Just from his natural bent, which is without charity, it becomes clear that this man, called worldly, as distinguished from spiritual, still abandons himself to pleasures and devotes himself to them, however much he raises himself into the light of reason. And whoever is without charity is abandoned to all the kinds of wantonness that belong to illicit love. So when you tell him that this lustful love is opposite to chaste love in marriage and ask him to consult his rational enlightenment, he still just consults that enlightenment in connection with the joy in evil ingrafted in the worldly man by birth. From this he concludes that his reason sees nothing against the sweet, sensuous enticements of his body. After he confirms himself in these, it numbs his reason to all the sweet things attributed to the love in marriage. In fact, he fights against them, as said above, and wins, and like the victor after a slaughter, he destroys married love's camp in himself from outside to inside. This is what the worldly man does because of his illicit love.

This is brought in to make known where the opposition of these two loves comes from. For, as pointed out often before, the love in marriage per se is a spiritual love, and illicit love per se is a worldly love.

427 (4) *Illicit love is opposite to married love as a "marriage" of evil and lies is opposite to the marriage of good and truth.* It was pointed out in its own chapter above (nos. 83– 102) that the source of married love is the marriage of good and truth. Consequently, the source of illicit love is the marriage of what is evil and what is untrue, and so they are opposite just as evil is opposite to good and the falsity of evil is opposite to the good of truth. What are opposites this way are the pleasures of each love—for a love without its pleasures is not anything. The pleasures do not seem to be opposite this way, at all. The reason they do not seem to be opposite is that a bad love's pleasure outwardly counterfeits a good love's pleasure. But inwardly the pleasure of a bad love consists of plain longings for evil. Evil itself is a wound-up mass, or ball, of them. But the pleasure of a good love consists of innumerable good inclinations. Good itself is like a bundle of them tied together. A person just feels the bundle or the ball as one pleasure, and the pleasure of evil counterfeits the pleasure of good outwardly, as was said, so the person feels the pleasure of adultery just as he would the pleasure of marriage. But after death, when everyone takes off the outward parts and the inward ones are exposed,

then it is plain to see that the evil of adultery is a ball of longings for evil and that the good of marriage is a bundle of inclinations toward good—thus that they are totally opposite to each other.

428   Regarding the "marriage" of evil and lies, it is well known that evil loves a lie and wants to unite with it, and that they do join together, too, in the way that good loves a truth and wants to unite with it, and they also join together. This makes it obvious that the spiritual source of adultery is a "marriage" of evil and falsity, just as the spiritual source of marriage is a marriage of good and truth. In the spiritual sense of the Word, therefore, adulteries, fornication, and whoredom mean this "marriage" (see *Apocalypse Revealed*, no. 134). It is on account of this principle that someone who lives in evil and espouses untruth, and someone who lives a lie and takes evil for a bedfellow encourages adultery by being in league with it and commits it as much as he dares and is able to. He encourages it due to evil, by lies, and he commits it due to lies, through evil. And, vice versa, someone who lives in good and espouses truth or who lives in truth and takes good as a bedfellow confirms himself against adultery and for marriage and embraces a blessed married life.

429   (5) *So illicit love is opposite to married love just as hell is opposite to heaven.* Everyone in hell is in a "marriage" of evil and falsity, and everyone in heaven is in a marriage of good and truth. And since a "marriage" of evil and falsity is adultery as well (as shown now above, nos. 427–28), it is also hell. This is why everyone there is involved in illicit love's lust, lasciviousness, and shamelessness, and they flee the chaste and modest aspects of marriage and are horrified (see no. 428, above).

These observations show that these two loves—of illicit sex and of marriage—are opposite to each other just as hell is opposite to heaven and heaven is to hell.

430   (6) *The filthiness of hell is from illicit love, and the cleanness of heaven is from married love.* All hell seethes with obscenities, and their common source is a shameless and obscene love of illicit sex. In hell they take pleasure in things like that.

Who would think that in the spiritual world all of love's delights emerge as various sights to see, various odors to smell, and various forms of birds and animals to look at? In hell the sights that illicit love's lascivious pleasures emerge to be seen as are excrements and filth. The odors they emerge as to smell there are stenches and fumes. And the forms of birds and animals that they emerge in to be seen are pigs, snakes, and birds called *ochim* and *tziim* [birds of night].

But the chaste joys of married love in heaven are the other way around. The sights that they emerge to be seen as are gardens and flowery fields, the odors that they emerge to the smell as are the scents from fruits and the fragrances from flowers, and the animal forms that they emerge to be seen as there are lambs, kids, turtledoves, and birds of paradise.

The pleasures of loves turn into things like that because all the things that come forth in the spiritual world are correspondences. The inner things in people's minds turn into these correspondences when they are externalized before the senses.

But note that there are innumerable varieties of uncleannesses that the wanton acts of fornication turn into when they emerge in their correspondences. And the varieties are according to the genera and species of those acts, which appear in later articles that deal with adulteries and their degrees. But impurities like that do not emerge from the pleasures of the loves of those who have repented, because they have been washed clean of them in the world.

431 (7) *The same goes for uncleanness in the church and cleanness there.* The reason is that the church is the Lord's kingdom on earth, corresponding to His kingdom in the heavens. And, besides, the Lord joins these kingdoms together and makes them one. He also separates those who are there as He separates heaven and hell, and He separates them according to loves. Those who dwell in illicit love's shameless and obscene pleasures associate with their likes from hell, but those who dwell in married love's modest and chaste pleasures the Lord associates with angels from heaven who are the same. When these angels with a person come near confirmed and open adulterers with a person, they notice the heavy odor mentioned above (no. 430) and draw away a little.

Because foul loves correspond to filth and mire, the descendants of Israel were ordered to carry a paddle with them to cover their excrement so that Jehovah God, walking among their tents, would not see the nakedness of the thing and turn away (Deut. 23:13–14). This was ordered because the descendants of Israel's camp represented the church, and those unclean things symbolized the wanton acts of fornication, and "Jehovah God walking among their tents" stood for His presence with angels. They were to cover their excrement because all the places in hell where such a crowd lives are covered and closed—which is also why it says "so . . . [He] would not see the nakedness of the thing."

I have been allowed to see that all the places in hell are closed, and also that when they are opened—which was done when a new demon was going in—it gave off such a stench that the odor turned my stomach. And, remarkably, those stinks are as delightful to them as excrements are to pigs.

These observations show how to understand the idea that uncleanness in the church is from illicit love and cleanness there is from the love in marriage.

432   (8) *Illicit love makes a person more and more not a person and a man not a man, and married love makes a person more and more a person and a man.* Every single one of the things brought to light for reason in the Part 1, about love and the joys of its wisdom, illustrates and establishes that love in marriage makes a person. Such as: (a) Someone who is in real married love becomes more and more spiritual, and the more spiritual anyone is, the more human he is. (b) That he becomes more and more wise, and the wiser anyone is, the more he is a person. (c) That the inner reaches of his mind are opened more and more so that he sees, or intuitively accepts, the Lord, and the more anyone has that vision or acceptance, the more he is a person. (d) That he becomes more and more moral and more a citizen because a spiritual soul of morality and citizenship is in him, and the more anyone is morally a citizen, the more he is a person. (e) Also, he becomes an angel of heaven after death, and an angel is a person in essence and figure, and moreover, true humanity shines in his face, from his speech, and from his manners. These things establish that love in marriage makes a person more and more a person.

From the very opposition of adultery and marriage, dealt with and being dealt with in this chapter, it follows as proved that it is the opposite with adulterers. As: (a) That they are not spiritual but extremely worldly, and the worldly man separate from the spiritual is only human as to his intellect, but not as to his will. He plunges this into his body and physical lusts, and his intellect also goes with it at those times. If he lifts up the reason of his intellect he himself can see that he is only half a person. (b) The chapter about adulteries will prove that adulterers are only wise in their speech and also in their actions when in company with high-ranking dignitaries, with people famous for learning, and with well-mannered people, but alone with themselves they are foolish, considering the divine and holy things of the church to be worthless, and defiling the moralities of life with immodesties and unchasteness. Who does not see that mimics like that are only people in outer form and not people in inward form? (c) My own eyes, by seeing them in hell, have given me clear confirmation that adulterers become more and more inhuman, for there they are demons who, when seen in the light of heaven, have faces sort of like pimples, sort of hunchbacked bodies, sort of scratchy speech, and theatrical gestures.

But note that confirmed and intentional adulterers are like this, not people who are adulterers from lack of consideration. For there are four kinds of adultery, discussed in the chapter about adulteries and their degrees: the ones who are adulterers by the desire of their will are adulterers by intention, those who are adulterers by intellectual persuasion are confirmed adulterers, those who are adulterers by sensual enticement are adulterers by plan, and those without the ability or freedom to consult their intellect are adulterers not by plan. The first two kinds of adulterers are the ones who become more and more inhuman, but the second two kinds become human as they move away from those errors and then become wise.

433   The things brought out in the preceding part, about married love and its joys, also illustrate that married love makes a person more a man. They are: (a) That the ability and strength called manly goes together with wisdom insofar as this is inspired by the spiritual things of the church, so it is inherent in married love. And wisdom opens up this love's course from its fountain in your soul, and in this way it invigorates your intellectual life, which is

masculine life precisely, and also blesses it with permanence.
(b) That this is why angels of heaven have this eternally, as told
from their mouths in the story (nos. 355–56). And from their own
mouths I heard that the most ancient people, in the gold and silver
ages, also had continuous potency, because they prized the loving
of their wives and thoroughly dreaded the loving of harlots (see
the stories, nos. 75–76). I was told from heaven that even in the
natural world this spiritual adequacy will not be missing today in
those who approach the Lord and abhor adulteries as hellish things.

But the opposite befalls intentional and confirmed adulterers
(mentioned above already, at the end of no. 432). It is known, but
not publicized very much, that among them the ability and
strength called manly trails off to nothing, and when it does, a
frigidity toward the other sex begins, and after that follows a
loathing approaching nausea. I have heard (from a distance) from
female seducers, who are outworn passions for sexual love, and
also from brothels in hell, that this is what those adulterers are
like there.

From these things it is clear that illicit love makes a person
more and more not a person and not a man, and that love in
marriage makes a person more and more a person and a man.

434   (9) *There is an aura of illicit love and an aura of married love.* It was
pointed out (nos. 222–25 and 386–97, above) what "auras" means,
and that there are many of them, and that the ones that are auras
of love and wisdom radiate from the Lord and come down into
the world through the angelic heavens and penetrate clear to its
lowest parts. No. 425 shows that there is nothing in the universe
without its opposite. According to this, since there is an aura of
married love, there is also an aura of its opposite, which is called
an aura of illicit love, for those auras are opposite to one another
just as love of adultery is opposite to love of marriage. This opposition was covered in the earlier parts of this chapter.

435   (10) *The aura of illicit love comes up from hell, and the aura of
married love comes down from heaven.* It has been pointed out in the
places cited just above (no. 434) that the aura of married love
comes down from heaven. But the aura of illicit love comes from

hell because this love is from there (no. 429). The aura comes up from there out of the filthy things that the pleasures of adultery of people of either sex there are turned into (concerning them, see nos. 430–31, above).

436   (11) *These two auras meet each other in both worlds but do not mingle.* "Both worlds" means the spiritual world and the natural world. In the spiritual world the two auras meet each other in the world of spirits, because this is halfway between heaven and hell. But in the natural world they meet each other on the rational level in people, which is also halfway between heaven and hell. For the marriage of good and truth flows into this level from above, and a marriage of evil and falsity flows into it from below. The latter flows in through the world, but the former from heaven. On account of this the human rational faculty can turn to either side and receive the influence. If it turns to good, it receives the one from above, and then the person's rational faculty is formed more and more to receive heaven, but if it turns to evil, it receives the influence from below, and then the person's rational faculty is formed more and more to receive hell.

The two auras do not join together, because they are opposites, and toward opposites, opposites only act as enemies. The one attacks the other out of rage, burning with murderous hatred, although the other has no hatred but only a zeal to protect itself. It is clear from these observations that the two auras just meet each other but do not join together. The middle ground that they find is, on the one part, evil not from falsity and falsity not from evil, and on the other part good not from truth and truth not from good. These two can touch, to be sure, but not join together.

437   (12) *There is a balance between these auras, and people are in this balance.* The balance between them is a spiritual balance, because it is between good and bad. A person has freedom of choice on account of this balance. In it and through it a person thinks and wills and consequently speaks and acts as if by himself. His rational mind has the option and choice whether he wants to accept the good or wants to accept the bad—accordingly, whether he wants to incline himself toward love in marriage rationally and in

freedom or wants to incline himself toward illicit love rationally
and in freedom. If he inclines toward the latter, he turns the back
of his head and body to the Lord, if toward the former, he turns
his forehead and breast to the Lord. If he turns to the Lord, the
Lord leads his rationality and freedom, but if he turns away from
the Lord, hell leads his rationality and freedom.

438   (13) *A person can turn to whichever aura he likes, but insofar as he
turns to one, he turns away from the other.* A person is created to do
what he does in freedom according to reason and totally as if by
himself. Without these two things he would not be a person, but
an animal, for he would not accept anything flowing into him
from heaven and take it to himself as his own, so nothing of
eternal life could be etched on him. For it has to be etched on him
as his own in order to be his own. And there is no freedom in one
direction unless there is the same freedom in the other as well, the
same as there is no weighing unless the scales can tilt both ways,
so it is the same unless a person has freedom rationally to accept
evil too—to turn from right to left and from left to right. Similarly, he must have freedom to turn to the aura of hell, which is
the aura of adultery, the same as to the aura of heaven, which is
the aura of marriage.

439   (14) *Either aura brings delights with it.* That is, the aura of illicit
love that rises from hell furnishes pleasures for the person receiving it as much as the aura of married love does that comes down
from heaven. The reason is that the lowest plane, where the pleasures of either love rest, and where they fulfill and complete
themselves—the plane that makes them appear in its feelings—is
the same. This is why illicit lovemaking and the lovemaking in
marriage seem alike superficially, although they are totally unlike
inwardly. You cannot tell from any sensation of the differences
that therefore they are unlike on the surface as well, for only
those who are in real married love feel the unlikeness from the
differences. Indeed, you can tell bad things by what is good but
not good things by what is bad, as the nose cannot tell a sweet
smell when a foul smell besets it.

I have heard from angels that they can tell what is lascivious from what is not lascivious in their extremities just as one can tell a fire of dung or burning horn, by its bad smell, from a fire of spice or burning cinnamon-wood, by its sweet smell—and this is due to the difference in the inner joys that invade the superficial ones and kindle them.

440   (15) *The delights of illicit love begin in the body, and they are physical even in the spirit, but the delights of married love begin in the spirit, and they are spiritual even in the body.* The delights of illicit love begin in the body because the sexual heat of the body is their start. They tinge the spirit, or are physical even in spirit, because the spirit, not the body, senses the things that take place in the body. It is the same with this sense as with the others. For example, it is not the eye that sees and tells the differences in objects, but the spirit, and it is not the ear that hears and notices the harmonies in the measures of a song and how the sounds of speech fit together, but the spirit. And spirit senses everything according to the level of its wisdom. A spirit that is not raised above the body's sensory matters and clings to them notices only the pleasures that flow into it from the body and from the world through the body's senses. It seizes on these, is charmed by them, and makes them its own.

Now, because illicit love's beginnings are only the sexual heat and itches of flesh, in spirit they are obviously smutty attractions that arouse and kindle according to how they rise and fall and come and go.

By class the physical passions per se are nothing other than globs of desires for evil and falsity. This is where the truth in the church comes from, that the flesh lusts against the spirit—that is, against the spiritual person. So accordingly, the pleasures of the body, as far as illicit love's pleasures go, are nothing but the boiling over of sensuality. They become gushes of immodesty in spirit.

441   But the pleasures of married love have nothing in common with illicit love's foul pleasures. Of course, these pleasures are in the flesh of every person, but they are separated and moved away as the person's spirit is raised above the sensualities of his body and, from above, sees their appearances and deceits below.

Likewise, it then perceives physical pleasures first as seeming pleasures and deceptive pleasures and then as lustful and lascivious ones to be avoided, and gradually as destructive and harmful to the soul, and it finally perceives them as unpleasant, repulsive, and sickening. And in the degree that it sees and feels those pleasures that way, it perceives the pleasures of married love as harmless and chaste, and finally as delightful and blessed.

The pleasures of married love also become spiritual in the body because after illicit love's pleasures are removed, as mentioned above already, the spirit enters the body free of them and chaste, and it fills your breast with its blessed delights, and from your breast fills that love's physical parts. So then the spirit acts in complete unity with these and they with the spirit.

442   (16) *Illicit love's delights are foolish pleasures, and married love's delights are sensible joys.* Illicit love's delights are foolish pleasures because only worldly people have that love, and a worldly person is foolish in spiritual matters. For he is against them, so he embraces only worldly, sensory, and bodily pleasures.

We say "worldly, sensory, and bodily pleasures" because worldly people fall into three separate levels. People who are worldly on the highest level are those who have a reasonable view of follies and still are carried away by their pleasure like skiffs by the current of a river. Those who see and judge only from bodily senses and disdain the rational arguments against appearances and deceits and reject them as worthless are worldly on a lower level. People who are worldly on the lowest level are those who are carried away by the enticing tides of their bodies, without judgment. These are the ones called the bodily worldly, the ones mentioned before them are called sensually worldly, but the first are called worldly. Illicit love, its insanities, and its pleasures have the same levels in them.

443   Married love's delights are the joys of wisdom because only spiritual people enjoy that love, and a spiritual person is in a state of wisdom, so he embraces only delights that harmonize with spiritual wisdom. A comparison with houses will clarify what illicit love's delights are like and what married love's delights are

like. Illicit love's delights compare to a house with walls that glow red outside like seashells, or glow from the false gold color of reflecting stones called selenite, but in the rooms inside the walls there is in fact filth and rubbish of every kind. But the delights of married love can be compared to a house whose walls seem to sparkle with pure gold, and the rooms inside shine as if filled with many kinds of precious treasures.

444a   The following story is added to these remarks.

After I finished my thoughts about love in marriage and had laid out my thoughts about illicit love, two angels were suddenly standing by me, and they said, "We noticed and understood what you were thinking about before, but the things you're thinking about now go right by us and we don't grasp them. Drop them, because they are nothing."

But I answered, "This love that I'm thinking about now isn't nothing, because there is such a thing."

But they said, "How can there be such a thing as any love that doesn't come from creation? Love in marriage comes from creation, doesn't it? Isn't this the love between two who can become one? How can there be a love that divides and separates? What young man can love a young woman other than the one who loves him in return? Doesn't one's love recognize and accept the other's love when they meet, and don't they join themselves together spontaneously? Who can love no love? Only married love is mutual and reciprocal, isn't it? If not returned, doesn't it retreat and become nothing?"

When I heard this I asked the two angels what community in heaven they were from, and they said, "We are from a heaven of innocence. We came into this heavenly world as children and were brought up under the Lord's guidance. And when I grew up and my wife, who is here with me, was a marriageable girl, we made a commitment and promised and were joined in a virgin marriage. And the only love we have known is true wedded and married love, so when your meditations about a strange love clearly opposite to our love were communicated to us, we didn't understand it at all. So we came down to find out why you are thinking about incomprehensible things. So tell us how there can be a love that not only doesn't come from creation but is even opposite to creation. We regard things opposite to creation as objects without reality."

When they said that, I was glad at heart that I had been allowed to talk with angels so innocent that they did not know what fornication is at all. So I opened my mouth and taught, saying, "Don't you know that there is good and bad, and that good is from creation, but not bad, and while bad per se is not nothing, still it has nothing to do with good? There is good from creation and also good in the greatest degree and in the least degree. And at the point where this least degree becomes nothing, bad emerges on the other side. So there is no relation or progression of good to bad, but a relation and progression of good to greater and less good and of bad to greater and less bad, for they are opposites in all respects. And since good and bad are opposites, there is a midpoint, and a balance there, where bad acts against good. But it does not prevail, so it continues in the effort. Every person is brought up in this balance. Since it is a balance between good and bad, or between heaven and hell, which is the same thing, it is a spiritual equilibrium that produces freedom for those who are in it. In keeping with this balance the Lord draws everyone to himself, and the person who follows in freedom He leads out of bad into good, and thus into heaven.

"It is the same with love—especially with married love, and with illicit love. The one is good, but the other is bad. Every person who hears the Lord's voice and follows in freedom the Lord leads into married love and into all its delights and blessings. But anyone who does not hear and does not follow leads his own self into illicit love and at first into its delights—but afterwards into displeasures and finally into unhappiness."

When I had said these things, the two angels asked, "How could evil come into existence when nothing but good had existed from creation? To exist, something must have its beginning. Good could not be the source of evil, because evil has nothing to do with good, for it is the negative of good and destructive of it. Yet there is such a thing, and it is detectable, so it isn't nothing but is something. So tell what this something comes from after being nothing."

To this I answered, "This mystery can't be solved except by knowing that no one is good except God alone and that there is no good that is good in itself, except from God. So someone who looks to God and wants to be led by God participates in good, but someone who turns away from God and wants to be led by himself does not participate in good, for the good he does is either on account of himself or on account of the world, so it is either for gain or is feigned or hypocritical. These facts make it clear that man himself is the origin of evil. Not that this origin was put into man by creation, but he put it into himself by turning away from God to himself.

"The source of evil was not in Adam and his wife, but when the serpent said, 'On the day you eat from the tree of knowing good and evil ... you will be like God' (Gen. 3:5), and then, because they turned away from God and turned to themselves as to a god, they made the source of evil in themselves. To 'eat from the tree' referred to thinking that you know about good and evil and are wise by yourself and not from God."

But then the two angels asked, "How could people turn away from God and turn to themselves, when people can want, think, and therefore do nothing, except by God? Why did God permit this?"

But I answered, "People were created in such a way that everything they want, think, and do seems to them to be in themselves and therefore from themselves. A person without this appearance would not be a person, for he wouldn't be able to take anything of good and truth—or love and wisdom—to himself, keep it, and make it as if his own. Consequently, without this sort of living appearance a person would not have a way to join with God, and so he wouldn't have eternal life. However, if from this appearance he leads himself to think that he wants, thinks, and therefore does good by himself and not due to the Lord—even though it *is* by himself to all appearances—he turns good into bad in himself and in this way makes the source of evil in himself. This was Adam's sin.

"But I'll place the question in a little clearer light. The Lord looks at every person in the forehead, and the look goes through to the back of his skull. Your cerebrum is in your forehead, and your cerebellum is in the back of your head. Your cerebellum is devoted to love and its good, and your cerebrum is devoted to wisdom and its truth. So someone who turns his face to the Lord receives wisdom from Him and, through this, love. But someone who looks backward, away from the Lord, receives love and not wisdom, and love without wisdom is love from man and not from the Lord. This love joins itself to untruths, so it does not accept the Lord but accepts itself as god and secretly confirms this with the ability to understand and perceive implanted in it from creation as if from itself. So this love is the source of evil.

"It can be demonstrated before your eyes that this is so. I'll call some evil spirit here who turns away from God, and I'll speak to him from behind—or to the back of his head—and you'll see that the things said will turn into their opposites."

I called one like that. He came, and I spoke behind him, saying, "Do you know anything about hell, damnation, and the torment there?" And soon, when he turned around to me I asked, "What did you hear?"

He answered, "I heard these things, 'Do you know anything about heaven, salvation, and the happiness there?'" And then when these things were said behind his back, he said he heard what I said before.

Then these things were said behind his back: "Do you know that those who are in hell are insane because of untruths?" And when I asked what he heard, he said, "I heard, 'Do you know that those who are in heaven are wise because of truths?'" And when these words were said behind his back, he said that he heard, "Do you know that those in hell are insane because of untruths?"

And so on. From these things it was clearly evident that when a mind turns itself away from the Lord, it turns toward itself and then understands things backwards.

"This is the reason why, as you know, it is not lawful in this spiritual world to stand behind another person and speak to him, for this inspires into him a love that his own intelligence favors and obeys for its own enjoyment. But this is from the person and not from God, so it is a love for evil or falsity.

"Besides this I can report something else like it to you, namely, that at different times I have heard good things and true things sink from heaven into hell, and there they were gradually turned into opposites—good into bad and truth into falsity. The reason for this is the same, without doubt—that everyone in hell turns away from the Lord."

After hearing these things the two angels thanked me and said, "Since you are thinking and writing about a love opposite to our married love, and the opposite of that love saddens our minds, we are leaving."

And as they said, "Peace to you," I asked them not to tell their brothers and sisters in heaven anything about this love, because it would hurt their innocence.

I can affirm for certain that people who die as children grow up in heaven, and when they reach the stature of eighteen-year-old youths and fifteen-year-old girls in the world, they stay there, and then the Lord provides them marriages. Also that before as well as after marriage they simply do not know what illicit sex is or that there can be such a thing.

Chapter 19

Fornication

444b   Fornication means an adolescent's, or a young man's, wantonness with a loose woman before marriage. But wantonness with a woman who is not loose, that is, with a virgin or with someone else's wife is not fornication. With a virgin it is violation, and with someone else's wife it is adultery. A rational person can see how these two activities differ from fornication only if he observes sexual love in all its levels and diversities—both its chaste qualities on the one hand and its unchaste qualities on the other—and divides each part into genera and species, and contrasts them in this way. There is no other way the difference between more and less chaste and between more and less unchaste can emerge as a concept for a person. Without these distinctions all reference is lost, and along with it insight in matters of judgment, and your intellect is wrapped in such shadow that it does not know how to tell fornication from adultery, still less the mild aspects of fornication from the serious ones—and the same for adultery. Thus it mixes the evils together and makes one stew from different evils and one pie from different types of good.

So for sexual love to be clearly recognized as to the part of it that tends and moves toward the illicit love that is totally opposite to married love, it is useful to throw light on its beginning, which is fornication. This is done in this order:

(1) Fornication is related to love for the other sex.
(2) It begins when a growing boy starts to think and act from his own understanding and his voice starts to become manly.
(3) Fornication belongs to the worldly side of a person.

(4) Fornication is a desire, but not a desire for adultery.

(5) In some people, love for the other sex cannot quite be kept from escaping into fornication—not without harm.

(6) This is why brothels are tolerated in populous communities.

(7) A desire for fornication is a small matter in the degree that it has married love in view and prefers it.

(8) A desire for fornication is serious in the degree that it has adultery in view.

(9) A desire for fornication is more serious as it shades off towards a desire for promiscuity and a desire for defloration.

(10) The aura of a desire for fornication, the way it is at its beginning, is in the middle between illicit love's aura and married love's aura, and it provides a balance.

(11) Watch out that the love in marriage is not lost due to disorderly and immoderate fornications.

(12) Because the marriage relationship of one man with one wife is the precious treasure of human life and the Christian religion's treasury.

(13) This marriage relationship can be protected in those who cannot enter marriage for various reasons and who cannot hold their passions back because of their sex drive, if their unsettled love of the other sex is confined to one mistress.

(14) Having a mistress is better than indulging roving passions, if only it is not done with more than one, nor with a virgin or not yet sexually active woman, nor with a married woman, and if it is kept separate from the love in marriage.

Now comes the explanation of these remarks.

445   (1) *Fornication is related to love for the other sex.* We say that fornication is related to love for the other sex because fornication is not love for the other sex but comes from it. Love for the other sex is like a spring that married love and illicit love can both be drawn from. They can be drawn from it both with and without fornication, because love for the other sex is in every person, and it either comes out or does not come out. If it comes out before marriage, with a loose woman, it is called fornication; if not until with a wife, it is called marriage; if with another woman, after

marriage, it is called adultery. For, as was said, love for the other sex is like a spring that chaste love can bubble out of as well as unchaste love, and the following articles will show the caution and good sense that will bring chaste married love out through fornication and the recklessness that will bring out unchaste or illicit love through it.

Who can assume that someone who has fornicated cannot be far more chaste than that when married?

446   (2) *Love of the other sex, which fornication comes from, begins when a growing boy starts to think and act from his own understanding and his voice starts to become manly.* This is brought up in order to make the beginning of love for the other sex, and therefore of fornication, known—which is when the intellect begins to be rational on its own, or to look around from its own rationality and foresee what things are profitable and useful. Things remembered from parents and teachers serve as a basis for this.

A change takes place in the mind at that time. Before, it only thought from things committed to memory, thinking about them and obeying them, then by reasoning about them. Then, with love leading, it arranges things fixed in the memory into a new order and undertakes a life of its own consistent with this order, thinks more and more according to its own reason and wills from its own freedom.

It is well known that love for the other sex accompanies the entrance of your own intellect and advances in keeping with its vigor—a sign that this love ascends as intellect ascends and declines as it declines. By "ascend" understand ascend to wisdom, and by "decline" decline to folly. Wisdom is to manage love for the other sex, and folly is to let it run wild. If set free in fornication, which is a beginning of its activity, it should be governed on the principles of respectability and morality that are implanted in memory and from that in reason, and later implanted in reason and from that in memory.

The reason why your voice begins to become manly at the same time that your own intellect begins is that intellect thinks, and it speaks from thought—a sign that intellect makes the man and also his manliness, so that as intellect is elevated it makes the person a man and also a manly man (see nos. 432–33, above).

447   (3) *Fornication belongs to the worldly side of a person,* just like love for the other sex, which is called fornication if it becomes active before marriage. Every person is born physical, develops the senses, then becomes worldly and gradually rational, and if he does not stop there he becomes spiritual. It proceeds in this way to form plateaus on which higher things can rest, as a palace rests on its foundations. The lowest level, with what is built on it, can also be compared to soil where excellent seeds can be sown when it is prepared.

Concerning love for the other sex specifically, it is also physical at first, for it starts out in the body. Then it develops in the senses, for it is delightful to the five senses. Afterwards it becomes worldly, just like the same love in animals, because love for the other sex is roving. But man is born to become spiritual, so this love later becomes rational on a worldly plane and from being rational on a worldly plane, it becomes spiritual, and finally it becomes spiritual on the worldly plane. And then this love, having become spiritual, influences and acts on rational love, and through this on sensory love, and finally through this on the love in body and flesh. And because this is its lowest plane it acts on it spiritually and rationally and sensorially all at once. It follows this same pattern of influence and acts this way when a person is thinking about it, but simultaneously when he is occupied on the outermost level.

Fornication belongs to the worldly side of a person because it comes right out of a worldly love of the other sex. Also, it can be rational on a worldly plane, but not spiritual, because love for the other sex cannot become spiritual until it becomes marital. And love of the other sex turns from worldly to spiritual when a person moves away from roving passion and devotes himself to one partner whose soul he unites his soul to.

448   (4) *Fornication is a desire, but not a desire for adultery.* The reasons why fornication is a desire are: (a) It comes from the worldly side of a person, and there is selfishness and lust in everything

that comes from that, for the worldly side of a person is nothing but a home and a container of self-interests and passions, since everything blameworthy inherited from your parents settles there. (b) A fornicator has a roving and promiscuous eye for the other sex and is not looking for one person of the other sex yet, and so long as he is in that condition, passion prompts him to do what he does. But as he inclines toward one and loves to join his life together with her life, lust becomes a chaste affection, and passion becomes human love.

449   Anyone can observe from common sense that a desire for fornication is not a desire for adultery. What law or judge charges a fornicator with the same offense as an adulterer? The reason you discover this from common sense is that fornication is not opposite to married love the way adultery is. Love for marriage can be stored away deep within fornication as something spiritual can be in something worldly. In fact, the spiritual does indeed develop out of the worldly. And when spirituality develops, worldliness surrounds it like the bark on wood and the sheath of a sword and also serves the spiritual thing as protection against violence.

It is clear from these observations that the worldly love that is for the other sex comes before the spiritual love that is for one person of the other sex. But though fornication comes from a worldly love for the other sex, it can be wiped clean, too, provided that you look to the love in marriage, want it, and seek it, as the best thing.

It is totally different with the lustful and obscene love of adultery—which the previous chapter, about illicit love and married love being opposite, pointed out is opposite to the love in marriage and the destroyer of it. So if for various reasons an intentional or confirmed adulterer gets into a marriage bed, things turn upside-down. Worldliness with its lewd and obscene qualities lies within, and a spiritual appearance veils it outwardly. From these observations reason can see that the lust of controlled fornication compares to the lust of adultery as early warmth compares to the midwinter cold in arctic regions.

450   (5) *In some people, love for the other sex cannot quite be kept from escaping into fornication—not without harm.* There is no point in

listing the bad effects that too much restraint of love for the other sex can cause and bring about in those who have to live with sexual arousal due to excessive potency. Certain physical afflictions in them spring from it, and moodiness, not to mention strange, unmentionable offenses.

It is different for those who have little enough sex drive to resist the pressures of what it wants. The same goes for those who are free to begin a legitimate bedroom relationship at a young age without loss of worldly goods—in a virgin marriage, that is. Since this happens for children in heaven when they reach an age to marry, they do not know what fornication is there. But the situation is not the same on earth, where people cannot marry until their youth is past. This happens to many under governments where it takes a long time to be entitled to work, to obtain the means to support a home and family, and then at last to seek a suitable wife.

451   (6) *This is why brothels are tolerated in populous communities.* This is mentioned to reinforce the previous article. It is well known that kings, magistrates, and therefore judges, prosecutors, and the people, tolerate brothels in London, Amsterdam, Paris, Vienna, Venice, Naples, and also Rome, as well as in many other places. The things noted above are among the reasons why.

452   (7) *Fornication is a small matter in the degree that it has married love in view and prefers it.* There are degrees of badness just as there are degrees of goodness, so any evil is slighter or more grave the same as any good thing is better or best. It is the same with fornication—which is an evil because it is a desire and belongs to the still unpurified worldly person. But every person can be purified, so the evil becomes a smaller evil in the degree that he is approaching a purified state, because in that degree it is wiped away—in the degree that fornication approaches married love, which is the purified state of love for the other sex. The next article will show that the evil of fornication is more serious in the degree that it approaches adulterous love.

Fornication is a small matter so far as it looks toward married love, because then it is looking from the unchaste state it is in, toward a chaste state. And in the degree that the person prefers this state he is in it, too, so far as his mind goes, and in the degree that he not only prefers it but loves it more, he is also in it as to his will, thus as to his inner person. Then if he persists in fornication just as much, it is something unavoidable for reasons that he is examining in himself.

Two considerations cause fornication to be a small thing in those who prefer the state of marriage and love it more. The first is that married life is their purpose, intention, or goal. The second is that within themselves they keep the evil separate from the good. Concerning the first consideration—that married life is their purpose, intention, or goal—it is because a person is the kind of person he is in his purpose, intention, or goal, and this is also what he is like in the eyes of the Lord and in the eyes of the angels. In fact, this is how he is viewed in the eyes of wise people in the world. For intention is the soul of every act and causes convictions and pardons in the world, and is attributed to you after death. Concerning the second consideration—that those who prefer married love to the lust of fornication keep the bad separate from the good, or the unchaste from the chaste—those who separate these two in concept and intention before they are in a good or chaste life are still separated and purified of the evil of their lusts when they enter a married state. The article that follows next will show that this does not happen to those who look to adultery in fornication.

453   (8) *A desire for fornication is serious in the degree that it has adultery in view.* All those who do not think adultery is a sin and think the same thing of marriages as of adulteries, with "allowed" and "forbidden" the only difference, have adultery in view in their desire for fornication. Also, they make one evil out of all evils and mix them together like filth with edible food in one dish, and like dregs mixed with wine in one drink, and they eat and drink that way. This is like what they do with love for the other sex, fornication, keeping a mistress, mild, serious, and most serious adultery— even with violation and defloration. Besides this they not only stir all these together but also mix them in with marriages and defile the marriages with the same notion. But after roving encounters with the other sex, those who do not even find any difference

between these acts and marriages encounter coldness, distaste, and nausea, first for their spouse, then for other partners, and finally for the whole other sex. It is self-evident that there is no good or chaste purpose, intent, or goal in them to excuse them, nor any separation of good from bad or chaste from unchaste to purify them, as in those who look forward from fornication to married love and prefer it (mentioned in the last article, no. 452).

I am allowed to confirm these things by this news from heaven. I have met many who outwardly lived like others in the world—dressing smartly, dining in style, doing business for profit like others, seeing plays, joking about love affairs as if out of lust, and other things like that—and yet the angels attributed these things to some as sinful evils, and to some as not evils. And they pronounced the one group guilty and the others innocent. On being questioned why it was this way, even though both groups did the same things, the angels answered that all are viewed as to their purpose, intention, or goal and separated on the basis of these things. So they excuse or condemn those whom the goals excuse or condemn, since everyone in heaven has a good goal, and everyone in hell a bad one. And this and nothing else is the meaning of the Lord's words, "Do not judge, so you will not be judged" (Matt. 7:1).

454   (9) *A desire for fornication is more serious as it shades off towards a desire for promiscuity and a desire for defloration.* The reason is that these two things reinforce adultery and thus make it worse. For there is mild, serious, and very serious adultery, and the details are weighed according to their opposing, and therefore destroying, married love.

Articles about it to come later will show that desire for promiscuity and desire for defloration established by actual behavior ruin the love in marriage and sink it as if to the bottom of the sea.

455   (10) *The aura of a desire for fornication, the way it is at its beginning, is in the middle between illicit love's aura and married love's aura, and it provides a balance.* The two auras of illicit love and married love were discussed in an earlier chapter, and it showed that illicit love's aura comes up out of hell and married love's aura

comes down from heaven (no. 435), that the two auras meet in both worlds but do not mingle (no. 436), that the two auras are in balance and people are in this balance (no. 437), that a person can turn toward the aura he chooses, but so far as he turns toward one he turns away from the other (no. 438), and what is meant by auras (no. 434 and the places cited there).

The aura of a desire for fornication is in between these two auras and makes the balance, because while a person is in this aura he can turn to the aura of married love—that is, to this love—and also to the aura of adulterous love—that is, to a love of it. But if he turns toward married love he turns toward heaven. If toward adulterous love he turns toward hell. Either choice is at the judgment, pleasure, and will of the person, so that he can act freely according to reason and not by instinct—therefore, so he can be a human and take the influence on himself, not a beast that takes nothing to itself.

The heading says "desire for fornication the way it is at its beginning" because it is in the intermediate state then. Who does not know that at first whatever a person does comes from selfishness because it comes from the person's worldly side? And who does not know that he is not blamed for that selfishness when he changes from worldly to spiritual? It is the same with the desire for fornication, once the person's love turns into married love.

456   (11) *Watch out that the love in marriage is not lost due to immoderate and disorderly fornications.* The immoderate and disorderly fornications by which the love in marriage is lost means fornications that not only sap your strength but also take all the happiness out of the love in marriage. From free and unrestrained fornications spring not only diseases and resultant weaknesses, but also impurities and immodesties that keep the love in marriage from being noticed and felt in its cleanness and chastity, thus in its sweetness and in the bloom of its delight—not to mention physical and mental injuries, as well as forbidden enticements that not only deprive married love of its happy pleasures but take it away besides and turn it into coldness and thus into loathing.

Grecian orgies are that kind of fornications. They twist married play into tragic scenes. For immoderate and disorderly fornications are like fires that rise up from your lowest parts and inflame your body, parch its fibers, foul your blood, and corrupt the rational parts of your mind. For they break out like a fire from the basement into the house and burn it all up.

Parents should be careful not to let this happen, because an adolescent boy excited by desire cannot yet put limits on himself by reason.

457 (12) *Because the marriage relationship of one man with one wife is the precious treasure of human life and the Christian religion's treasury.* These are the two things that have been demonstrated generally and in detail in the whole preceding part about the sensible joy of married love. It is the precious treasure of human life because a person's life is just the same as that love in him. It makes his innermost life, for it is the life of wisdom living together with its love and of love living together with its wisdom, and so it is the life of the delights of each of these. In a word, a person is a living soul through this love. This is why the marriage relationship of one man with one wife is called the precious treasure of human life.

These things mentioned above confirm it: With one wife real married friendship, confidence, and potency are possible, because a union of minds is possible (nos. 333–34). In marriage and from it are the heavenly blessings, spiritual pleasures, and worldly happiness provided from the beginning for those who are in real married love (no. 335). It is the basic love of all heavenly, spiritual and, therefore, worldly loves, and all joys and all kinds of happiness from first to last are gathered together in that love (nos. 65–69). And in "The Sensible Joy of Married Love," which is the first part of this book, it is fully shown that viewed in its source it is wisdom playing with love.

458 This love is the Christian religion's treasury because this religion becomes one with this love and they live together. For it was pointed out that no others come into that love or can be in it, except those who approach the Lord and do the true and good things of His church (nos. 70–71). That love is from the Lord only and is found only among those who are of the Christian religion (nos. 131, 335, 336). Married love is in keeping with the condition of the church, because it is in keeping with the state of wisdom in a

person (no. 130). In the whole chapter about its correspondence with the marriage of the Lord and the church (nos. 116–31), and in the chapter about the source of that love from the marriage of good and truth (nos. 83–102), it is established that these things are so.

459   (13) *This marriage relationship can be protected in those who cannot enter marriage for various reasons and who cannot hold their passions back because of their sex drive, if their love of the other sex is confined to one mistress.* Reason sees and experience teaches that those who are salacious cannot hold in their immoderate and disorderly passions. So, to curb this excess and disorder and hold it to some moderation and order in those who have to live with their sex drive and for many reasons cannot rush quickly into marriage, the only refuge and asylum, so to speak, seems to be taking a mistress—as the French say, *maitresse.* It is a well known fact that in countries with regulations many cannot marry until their youth is past, because they have to win positions first and obtain the means to keep a house and family, and only then court a suitable wife. And yet, few can keep the spring of their potency turned off and saved for a wife in the years leading up to this. It *is* best to save it, but if the runaway energy of the desire prevents this, you look for a middle path to keep marriage love from dying in the meantime. These points argue that having a mistress is the way: (a) It curbs and limits disorderly promiscuous sexual relationships and in this way brings about a stricter condition, which is more like marriage. (b) The fire of love—burning and sort of consuming at the outset—is settled and tamed, and thus the wantonness of lecheries, which is foul, is tempered by something analogous to marriage. (c) It keeps one from throwing away sexual energy and becoming weak, as through roving and unlimited carousing. (d) Bodily diseases and mental ills are avoided by it as well. (e) At the same time, it guards against adulteries, which are affairs with wives, and debaucheries, which are violations of virgins, not to mention unmentionable offenses. For a boy in adolescence does not think that adulteries and debaucheries are any different from fornications—that is, he thinks that the one is the same as the other—nor does he know from reason how to resist enticements from those of the other sex who have studiously applied

themselves to the art of prostitution. But he can learn and see the differences in having a mistress, which is more orderly and healthier fornication. (f) There is not an approach, through having a mistress, to the four kinds of lust that are in the highest degree destructive of married love—which are lust for defloration, lust for promiscuity, lust for rape, and lust for seducing innocent ones, discussed in what follows.

But these things are not said to those who can control the heat of passion, nor to those who can enter the married state as soon as they grow up, and can offer to their wife the first fruits of their manhood, and lay them before her.

460   (14) *Having a mistress is better than indulging roving passions, if only it is not done with more than one, nor with a virgin or not yet sexually active woman, nor with a married woman, and if it is kept separate from the love in marriage.* When and for whom having a mistress is better than indulging wandering lusts was already pointed out just above. (a) Having a mistress should not be done with more than one woman because with more than one, something polygamous is in it, which puts a person in a merely worldly state, and puts him into such a sensual state that he can hardly be raised into the spiritual state where married love has to be (see nos. 338–39). (b) It should not be done with a virgin or woman not yet sexually active because the love of marriage in women is partner to their virginity. This is where that love gets its chastity, purity, and holiness. So for a woman to promise it and to give it up to any man is to give a token that she is going to love him forever. Because of this a young woman cannot hazard it through any reasonable agreement except with the security of a marriage covenant. And it is the crown of her reputation. So to take it away without a marriage covenant and later abandon her is to make a harlot of some virgin who could be a bride and chaste wife, or to defraud some man, and either thing is destructive. Because of this, someone who joins a virgin to himself as a mistress may in fact live with her and in this way introduce her to the friendship of love, but always with a firm intention that she be, or become, his wife if she does not commit adultery. (c) It is obvious that a married woman should not be a mistress, because that is adultery.

(d) Love with a mistress should be kept separate from married love, because the two loves are different and therefore should not be mixed. For love with a mistress is an unchaste, worldly, and external love, but married love is chaste, spiritual, and internal. Love with a mistress keeps the two souls apart and joins only the sensory parts of their bodies. But married love unites souls—and from the union of souls the sensual parts of bodies, too—until from two they become like one, which is one flesh. (e) Love with a mistress only enters your intellect and the things that depend on intellect, but married love enters your will and the things that depend on will, therefore each and every thing in the person. So if love with a mistress becomes married love, the man has no right to withdraw without a violation of married union. And if he does go away, and takes another, married love is lost in the break. Note that love with a mistress is kept separate from married love by not promising the mistress marriage nor leading her to hope for marriage at all.

Still, it is better for the torch of sexual love to be first lighted with a wife.

461   The following story is added to these remarks.

I once spoke with a newly arrived spirit who had thought a lot about heaven and hell when he was in the world. ("Newly arrived spirits" means people newly deceased, who are called spirits because they are people's spirits.) As soon as he entered the spiritual world he began to think about heaven and hell in the same way as before and found himself happy when thinking about heaven and sad when thinking about hell. When he realized he was in the spiritual world, he asked at once where heaven and hell are, what they both are, and what they are like.

They told him, "Heaven is above your head, and hell is under your feet, for you're now in the world of spirits, which is halfway between heaven and hell. But what heaven and hell are and what they are like we can't describe in a few words."

He had a burning desire to know, then, so he threw himself on his knees and devoutly prayed to God to be instructed.

And an angel appeared at his right! The angel stood him up and said, "You prayed to be instructed about heaven and hell.

Ask around and find out what is delightful, and you'll know."
The angel ascended after saying this.

Then the newly arrived spirit said to himself, "What *is* this?
'Ask around and find out what is delightful, and you'll know
what heaven and hell are and what they are like'!"

But leaving that place he wandered around and asked the
people he met, "Please tell me what is delightful, if you will."

And some said, "What kind of question is that? Who doesn't
know what's delightful? Isn't it joy and gladness? Delight is delight.
One pleasure is like another. We don't know the difference."

Others said that delight is mental laughter. "For when your
mind laughs your face is cheerful, your voice chuckles, your gestures play, and the whole person is delighted."

But others said, "What's delightful is just to feast and eat fine
foods, and drink, and get drunk on noble wine, and then chat
about different things—mainly the games of Venus and Cupid."

When he heard this, the newly arrived spirit, peeved, said to
himself, "These answers are common and uncultivated. These
delights are not heaven or hell. I wish I'd meet some wise people."

He went away and asked, "Where are some wise people?"

And then an angelic spirit saw him and said, "I notice that
you are burning with a desire to know what the general idea of
heaven and the general idea of hell is. It's delight, so I'll take you
up a hill where people who explore results gather every day, and
people who investigate the reasons, and people who investigate
the purposes. There are three groups. The ones who explore
results are called spirits of facts, and abstractly, facts. The ones
who investigate the reasons are called spirits of intelligence, and
abstractly, intelligences. And the ones who investigate the
purposes are called spirits of wisdom, and abstractly, wisdoms.
Right above them, in heaven, are angels who view the reasons
from the purposes and the results from the reasons. The three
groups get enlightenment from these angels."

Then he took the newly arrived spirit's hand and led him up
the hill to the group made up of those who explore purposes and
are called wisdoms.

"Pardon my coming up to you," he said. "The reason is that
from childhood I've thought about heaven and hell, and I just

arrived in this world, and then some people joined me and said that here heaven is above my head and hell is under my feet. But they didn't say what heaven and hell are and what they are like. So my constant thought about them made me so anxious I prayed to God. And there stood an angel, and he said, 'Ask around and find out what is delightful, and you'll know.' I asked, but so far in vain. So I beg of you, teach me what is delightful."

To this the wise men answered, "Delight is all of life for everyone in heaven and all of life for everyone in hell. For the ones in heaven it is delight in good and truth, but for the ones in hell it is delight in the bad and the false. For all delight has to do with love, and love is the essential thing in a person's life. So a person is a person according to his kind of delight just as he is a person according to what kind of love he has.

"Love in action gives a feeling of delight. In heaven it acts with wisdom, in hell it acts with folly. Either way, it produces delight in the ones under its influence. But the heavens and the hells have opposite delights, because they have opposite loves— the heavens have the love of doing well, and its delight, but the hells have the love of doing ill, and its delight. So if you know what is delightful, you know what heaven and hell are, and what they are like.

"But ask around some more and find out what is delightful from those who investigate the reasons and are called intelligences. They are to the right from here."

He left, went over to them and told why he came, and he asked them to teach him what is delightful.

Happy to be asked, they said, "It is true that someone who knows what delight is knows what heaven and hell are and what they are like. Will, which is what makes the person the person, is not moved even a jot except by delight. For will, per se, is nothing but the disposition and the performance of some love—some delight— because what makes you will is something pleasant, agreeable, and delightful. And will moves your intellect to think, so thought hasn't a single idea except from the influence of will's delight.

"This is so, because the Lord puts all the souls and all the minds of angels, spirits, and men into action by His influence. He puts them into action by the influence of love and wisdom. And this influence is the very activity that all delight comes from—which is called blessed, blissful, and happy in its source and delight, pleasantness, and pleasure in its outcome. In a general sense it is called 'good.'

"But the spirits of hell turn everything about themselves upside down, so they also turn good into evil and truth into a lie. The delight remains, for without the delight remaining they have no will nor feeling, and thus no life.

"These observations make it clear what the delight of hell is, what it is like, and where it comes from, and what the delight of heaven is, is like, and comes from."

After hearing these things he was led to the third group, where there were the ones who explored results and are called facts. They said, "Go down into the lower land, and go up into the higher land. In the one you will observe and feel the delights of the spirits of hell, and in the other the delights of the angels of heaven."

But then the ground opened up at a distance from them, and three devils came up through the opening! They seemed afire with the delights of their love. Those who were with the newly arrived spirit could tell that the three came up from hell providentially, so they said to them, "Don't come closer, but from the place where you are, tell something about your delights."

They said, "Everyone, you understand, whether good or bad, has his delights. The good have the delights of their good, and the bad have the delights of their evil."

"What is your delight?" they asked.

They said that it was delight in whoring, stealing, cheating, and blaspheming.

Then they asked, "What are those delights like?"

They said, "To others they smell like the bad smells from excrement and like the stenches from corpses and like the fumes from stagnant urine."

They were asked, "Are they delightful to you?"

They said, "They are very delightful!"

"Then you are like the filthy animals that spend their time in things like that," they said.

They answered, "If we are, we are. But things like that are delightful to our noses."

They were asked, "What else?"

"Everyone is allowed to enjoy his delight, even the most filthy, as they call it, so long as he doesn't bother good spirits and angels," they said. "But on account of our delights we can't help bothering them, so we're thrown into penitentiaries, where we suffer dreadfully. The withholding and denial of our delights there is what they call the torment of hell. And it is inner pain, too."

"Why do you infest good people?" they were asked.

They said they couldn't help it. A kind of rage sets in when they see an angel and feel the Divine aura around him.

"So you are indeed like wild animals," they said.

And when they saw the newly arrived spirit with angels, a rage soon came over the devils, which seemed like the fire of hatred. So they were thrown back into hell to keep them from doing harm.

After this the angels appeared who see the reasons from the purposes and results from the reasons. They were in the heaven above the three groups. They appeared in brilliant light, circling down in spiral curves. They brought a round wreath of flowers, and put it on the newly arrived spirit's head, and then a voice came to him from up there, "This laurel is given to you because you have thought about heaven and hell from childhood."

Chapter 20

Having a Concubine

462   The previous chapter, about fornication, also dealt with having a mistress—which means a bachelor's joining with a woman by agreement. Here, however, having a concubine means a married man's joining with a woman, likewise by agreement. People who do not distinguish the types use these two terms indiscriminately, as if they had the same meaning and therefore stood for the same thing. But there are two types, and the term *mistress* suits the first because a mistress is a loose woman, and the term *concubine* suits the other because a concubine is a secondary bed partner. So to mark the difference, having a mistress refers to having an agreement with a woman before marriage, and having a concubine, refers to the same thing after marriage.

Discussion of having a concubine is in order here because the nature of marriage, on the one hand, and the nature of adultery, on the other, is being disclosed point by point. That marriage and adultery are opposite was first stated in the chapter about their opposition. How different they are, and in what way, can only be learned through the relationships that fall somewhere between marriage and adultery—one of which is having a concubine. But there are two types of this, which should be carefully distinguished from each other, so this discussion is broken down into its parts, like the former ones, as follows:

(1) There are two types of concubinage, which are very different—one that occurs while a man is with a wife, the other when he is separated from his wife.

(2) Having a concubine while with a wife is totally impermissible for Christians, and is abhorrent.

(3) It is polygamy, which is condemned in the Christian world, and ought to be.

(4) It is an illicit relationship that destroys the marriage relationship, which is the precious treasure of Christian life.

(5) Having a concubine when separated from a wife is permissible when done for legitimate, just, and truly important reasons.

(6) The legitimate reasons for divorce, when the wife is nevertheless kept in the house, are legitimate reasons for this type of concubinage.

(7) The justified reasons for separation from bed are the justified reasons for this type of concubinage.

(8) There are serious reasons for this type of concubinage, some valid and some specious.

(9) The serious reasons that are valid are the just ones.

(10) But the serious reasons that are specious are the ones that are not just but yet appear to be just.

(11) Those who have a concubine this way for legitimate, just, and really important reasons may have love for marriage at the same time.

(12) While this concubinage continues, sexual union with a wife is not permissible.

Now comes the explanation of these topics.

463   (1) *There are two types of concubinage, which are very different— one that occurs while a man is with a wife, the other when he is separated from his wife.* There are two types of concubinage that are very different from each other. One kind is adding a bedmate and living with her, together with a wife, at the same time. The other kind is taking a woman as a bed partner in place of a wife after legitimate and just separation from her. Those who examine the matter closely and carefully can see that these two types of concubinage are far apart, like dirty and clean linen, but those who look in confusion and carelessly cannot see it. Indeed, those who have love of marriage can, but not those who love adultery. These people are in the dark about all the things that come from

love of the other sex, but the others are in the light of day about them. But even those who are adulterers can see these things and their differences when they hear about them from others—though not on their own—for an adulterer has the same ability to lift up his intellect as a chaste partner does. But after an adulterer has accepted the differences, from others, he still blots them out when he sinks his intellect into his foul pleasures. For chaste and unchaste and healthy and unhealthy cannot be the same, but intellect can tell them apart by separating them.

In the spiritual world I once asked people who did not consider adultery a sin whether they saw any difference between fornication, having a mistress, the two types of concubinage, and the degrees of adultery. They said that one thing is just like another. I asked if the same goes for marriage, and they looked around to see if any member of the clergy was there, and when there was not, they said that it is the same, per se. The ones who considered adultery a sin, in their thoughts, were different. They said that in their inner ideas, which come from perception, they saw the difference, but so far they had not taken the trouble to separate the acts and tell them apart. This I can affirm—that the angels of heaven can tell the differences down to the smallest detail.

So, to make it clear that there are two opposite types of concubinage—one that destroys the love in marriage and another that does not—the type that is condemned will be described first, and then the other type, which is not condemned.

464 (2) *Having a concubine while with a wife is totally impermissible for Christians, and is abhorrent.* It is impermissible because it is against the marriage covenant, and it is abhorrent because it is against religion, and what is against both of these at once is against the Lord. So as soon as someone adds a concubine to a wife, without a valid, serious reason, it shuts him out of heaven, and the angels no longer count him among Christians. And from that time he scorns things that have to do with church and religion, and then he does not lift his face up above nature but turns to nature as a deity that favors his desire and whose influence gives his soul life from then on. The inner reason for this abandoning of faith will come out in what follows.

The man himself does not know that this way of having a concubine is abhorrent, because with heaven closed off spiritual folly comes on. But the chaste wife sees right through it, because she is married love, and it makes this love sick. Therefore, after this many of them also give up joining sexually with their husbands. It would taint their chastity by the infection of the lust that clings to the men from the prostitutes.

465   (3) *It is polygamy, which is condemned in the Christian world, and ought to be.* Everyone can see, even without much perception, that having a concubine at the same time or in connection with a wife is polygamy, even though it is not identified as such because it is not established by any law and given the name that way, for the woman serves as a wife and marriage-bed partner.

The chapter on polygamy has shown that polygamy is condemned by the Christian world, and ought to be—mainly by these articles there: It is not lawful for a Christian to take more than one wife (no. 338). And if a Christian takes more than one, he commits not only worldly adultery but also spiritual adultery (no. 339). The Israelite nation were allowed to do it because the Christian church was not among them (no. 340).

These points make it clear that it is foul polygamy to add a concubine to a wife and share your bed with both.

466   (4) *It is an illicit relationship that destroys the marriage relationship, which is the precious treasure of Christian life.* Arguments that are convincing to a wise person's reason will show that this illicit act is more opposed to the love in marriage than the ordinary illicit act called simple adultery, and that it is a deprivation of every ability and inclination toward the married life that is in Christians by birth.

As to the first point—that having a concubine at the same time as a wife, or together with a wife, is an illicit act more opposed to the love in marriage than the ordinary illicit act called simple adultery—it can be seen from these facts. Ordinary illicit sex, or simple adultery, does not have a love like married love in it, for it is only a physical blaze that soon cools and sometimes does not leave behind it a trace of love for the woman. So this flaring wantonness takes away from married love only in some small way, if it is not done by plan or from conviction, and if the adulterer comes to his senses. Illicit polygamy is different. There is a love in it patterned after the love in marriage, because it does not die down, scatter, and go away at all like ordinary simple adultery after it flares up, but it stays, renews itself, and settles in, detracting from love for the wife to that extent and bringing on coldness toward the wife instead. For then a man finds the prostitute he is sleeping with attractive because his options are not restricted and he can get away from her if he wants to. This independence is inborn in a worldly person, and it bolsters his love by pleasing. And besides, there is a closer attachment to a concubine by enticements than to a wife. And, vice versa, he finds his wife unattractive on account of his obligation to live with her imposed by the lifetime covenant, which seems the more restricting for the freedom he has with the other. It stands to reason that love for a wife grows cold and she herself worthless in the degree that love for a prostitute grows warm and she becomes precious.

As to the second point—that having a concubine at the same time as a wife, or together with a wife, deprives a man of every ability and inclination toward married life, which is inborn in Christians—it can be seen from these facts. As pointed out already above, however much the love for a mate is transferred to a concubine, to that extent love for the mate is torn away, suffered through, and emptied out. This happens by closing off the inner reaches of the man's worldly mind and unclosing its lower levels. This can be established by the fact that in Christians the inclination to love one person of the other sex is seated deep within, and this seat can be closed off but not rooted out. An inclination to love one person of the other sex, and also an ability to receive that love, is implanted in Christians at birth because that love comes only from the Lord and is made a matter of religion, and in Christianity the Lord's Divinity is accepted and worshiped, and the religion is from His Word. This is the source of its being implanted, and also transplanted from one generation into another.

It was said that this Christian marriage relationship dies as the result of polygamous fornication. This means that in a polygamous Christian it is closed off and intercepted but can still be revived in his descendants—the way the resemblance of a grand-father, or of *his* grandfather, returns in a grandson, or great-grandson. This is why that marriage relationship is called the jewel of Christian life and the precious treasure of human life and the treasury of the Christian religion (nos. 457–58 above).

It is very clear that the marriage relationship is destroyed in a Christian who practices polygamous fornication, from the fact that he cannot love a concubine and a wife equally, like a Moham-medan, but fails to love his wife or cools off toward her in the measure that he loves his concubine or warms up to her. And, more detestably, in the same measure he at heart identifies the Lord as just a man of this world and as the son of Mary but not the Son of God as well. And in the same measure he also devalu-ates religion.

But note well that this happens to those who add a concubine to a wife and join sexually with both—definitely not those who for legitimate, just, and truly important reasons separate from a wife and disconnect themselves from her physical love, and make an arrangement with a kept woman.

This type of concubinage comes next.

467   (5) *Having a concubine when separated from a wife is permissible when done for legitimate, just, and truly important reasons.* The rea-sons meant by "legitimate," "just," and "truly important" will be given in their place. A mention of the reasons is put here at the beginning just to distinguish this type of concubinage—which the following articles deal with—from the former type of concubinage.

468   (6) *The legitimate reasons for divorce, when the wife is neverthe-less kept in the house, are legitimate reasons for this type of concubinage.* Divorce means abolishing a marriage contract, and full separation on account of it, and afterwards complete freedom to take another wife. The only reason for this total separation or divorce is illicit sex, according to the Lord's instructions (Matt. 19:9). And in the same category are open obscenities. They remove modesty and fill and infest the home with a shameful bawdiness, producing sexual immodesties that your whole mind is dissolved in. Add to these ill-willed desertion that involves illicit sex and makes the

wife commit adultery and be rejected for it (Matt. 5:32). These three reasons are legitimate reasons for divorce—the first and third in the eyes of a public judge and the second in the man's own judgment—so they are also legitimate reasons to have a concubine, in case the adulterous wife is kept on in the home.

The reason why illicit sex is the only cause of divorce is that it is diametrically opposed to the life of married love and destroys it until it is exterminated (see no. 255 above).

469   Many men still keep an adulterous wife on in their homes. The reasons are: (a) The man is afraid to sue his wife, charge her with adultery, and in this way publicize the offense openly. For if visual evidence or the equal of visual evidence did not bring a conviction, in groups of men he would be smothered in abuse quietly, and in groups of women, openly. (b) He also fears the clever pleas of his prostituted wife, and also the court's protection of her, and the resulting dishonor to his name. (c) Besides all that, there are the conveniences of life at home that argue against her separation from the home, such as if they have children, whom even an adulteress has a mother's love for; if they have mutual duties that stand in the way, keep them together, and cannot be broken off; if the wife has inheritance and assistance from relatives and friends, and there is hope of a fortune from them; if he had cherished the friendly relations with her in the beginning; and if, after she became a prostitute, she knows how to cleverly soothe the man with flattering wit and pretended friendliness so as not to be blamed.

Other things, too, are in themselves legitimate reasons for divorce, so they are also legitimate reasons for having a concubine, since the reasons for keeping her on in the home do not take away the reason for divorce when she has committed adultery. Who but a scoundrel can keep the vows of the marriage bed in view and share a pillow with a prostitute? If it does happen here and there, that demonstrates nothing.

470   (7) *The justified reasons for separation from bed are the justified reasons for this type of concubinage.* There are legitimate reasons for separation, and there are just reasons. Legitimate reasons are decided by judges, and just ones are decided by the man alone. Both

the legitimate and the just reasons for separation from bed and from home were summed up earlier (nos. 252–53). Some of them are bodily defects—sicknesses that infect the body so much that contagion could be fatal. In this category are malignant and infectious fevers, leprosy, venereal diseases, and cancers. Then there are ailments that depress the whole body so much that there is no associating together, and they give off very harmful fumes and dangerous vapors, either from the body's surface or from inside it, particularly from the stomach and lungs. On the body's surface are malignant pocks, warts, pimples, wasting scurvy, poison scabs—especially if they make the face ugly. From the stomach is constant foul, rank, and smelly belching. From the lungs is foul and putrid breath given off by tumors, ulcers, or abscesses, or by corrupt blood or serum.

Besides these there are also other diseases of various names, like lipothymy, which is total weakening of the body and lack of energy; paralysis, which is a loosening and relaxing of the membranes and ligaments needed for motion; epilepsy; permanent feebleness from a stroke; certain chronic ills; the iliac passion; hernia; as well as other ills that pathology teaches.

There are mental defects that are justifiable reason for separation from bed and home, like mania, frenzy, insanity, simpleness and foolishness in actions, loss of memory, and other defects like that.

Reason does not need a judge to see that these reasons are justified reasons for having a concubine, because they are justified reasons for separation.

471   (8) *There are serious reasons for this type of concubinage, some valid and some specious.* Besides the just reasons that are justified reasons to separate and therefore justified reasons to have a concubine, there are also important reasons that depend on the judgment and justice of the man himself, so they are noted here, too. But the judgments of justice can be abused, and made to appear just by rationalization, so these reasons are divided into the valid ones and the specious ones and discussed separately.

472   (9) *The serious reasons that are valid are the just ones.* To recognize these reasons only requires listing a few that are truly

important—like no love for children and rejection of them on account of it, intemperance, drunkenness, uncleanness, shamelessness, eagerness to spill household secrets, quarreling, beating, getting revenge, being malicious, stealing, cheating, inner differences that cause bad feelings, demanding fulfillment of the marriage obligations, which makes a man as cold as a stone, addiction to magic and sorcery, extreme impiety, and other things like that.

473   There are also milder reasons that are valid, important reasons, and they separate a spouse from bed, though not from the home—such as the end of childbearing in a wife, due to advancing age, and a resulting impatience with sexual love, and refusing it, while the man's sex drive continues. And other things like that, which rational judgment sees the justice of, and which do not wound the conscience.

474   (10) *But the serious reasons that are specious are the ones that are not just but yet appear to be just.* You can tell these from the real, important reasons listed above. They can seem just, if not duly examined, and yet are unjust—reasons like the time of abstinence required after birth, a wife's temporary afflictions, the waste of sperm on that and other accounts, the polygamy permitted the Israelites, and other similar reasons with no basis in justice. Men fabricate them after they become cold when unchaste passions have taken away their married love and made fools of them with the notion that married love is illicit love. When these men take up with a concubine, they make these counterfeit and false reasons valid and genuine to save face. And they usually spread rumors about their wives, which their social friends sympathetically support and celebrate.

475   (11) *Those who have a concubine this way for legitimate, just, and really important reasons may have love for marriage at the same time.* Saying that they can have love for marriage at the same time means that they can keep this love hidden away within themselves, for this love does not die out in the one whom it is in, but is inactive.

Here are the reasons why married love stays on in those who prefer marriage to having a concubine and go into concubinage for the reasons noted above. This type of concubinage does not oppose married love, it is not a parting of the ways, for it only covers it up, and this covering comes off for them after death.

(a) This kind of concubinage does not oppose the love in marriage, according to what was pointed out above—that this kind of concubinage is permissible when done for legitimate, right, and important, real reasons (nos. 467–73). (b) This kind of concubinage is not a parting of the ways with the love in marriage, because when legitimate, or just, or important valid reasons come between, persuade, and force it, married love is not taken away from the marriage but only interrupted, and love that is interrupted and not taken away remains in the one under its influence. It is the same as with someone who holds a job that he loves and is kept away from it by company, by shows, or by travel, yet his love for the job is not lost. And it is the same as with someone who loves fine wine. When he drinks inferior wine, he does not lose his eager taste for the fine wine. (c) This kind of concubinage only covers married love up, because love for a concubine is worldly and married love is spiritual, and a worldly love covers a spiritual one when it interrupts it. The lover does not know that this is so, because a spiritual love is not felt per se, but through the worldly plane, and it seems like a delight with a blessing from heaven in it. But a worldly love per se is felt as just the delight. (d) This covering comes off after death, because then the person changes from worldly to spiritual, and instead of a material body he enjoys one made of substance. In it natural delight is intensified by spiritual. I have heard that this is so by consulting with certain ones in the spiritual world—even a king who had a concubine for important, valid reasons in the natural world.

476   (12) *While this concubinage continues, sexual union with a wife is not permissible.* The reason is that then married love, which per se is spiritual, chaste, pure, and holy, becomes worldly, is degraded, decays, and is lost in this way. So for this love to be kept safe, having a concubine for important, valid reasons (nos. 472–73) has to be done with one woman, and not with two at once.

477   The following story is added to these articles.
I heard a young spirit, recently from the world, boasting about

illicit affairs and wanting to win compliments for being more masculine than others, and among his arrogant boasts he poured out these words. "What's more dismal than to jail your love and live alone with one woman? And what's more delightful than to set love free? Who doesn't get tired of one woman and get excited by many women? What's sweeter than promiscuous freedoms, variety, deflorations, deceiving husbands, and the hypocrisies of an affair? Don't the things you get by cunning, tricks, and secrecy give deep-down satisfaction to your mind?"

When the bystanders heard that, they said, "Don't talk that way. You don't know where you are, and with whom. You just got here. Hell is under your feet, and heaven is over your head. You're in the world halfway between the two now, called the world of spirits. All the people who leave the world come and are gathered here and are examined to find out what they are like, and are prepared—the bad ones for hell and the good for heaven. Maybe you still remember from ministers in the world that fornicators and harlots are thrown down into hell and that chaste married people are taken up into heaven."

The newcomer laughed at these admonitions, saying, "What is heaven, and what is hell? Isn't heaven where someone is free, and isn't someone who is allowed to love as many women as he wants, free? And isn't hell where someone is a slave? And isn't a person who has to stick to one woman a slave?"

But an angel looking down out of heaven heard that, interrupted his speech to keep him from going any further in profaning marriage, and said, "Come up here, and I'll show you in real life what heaven is and what hell is, and what it is like for confirmed fornicators," and pointed out the way.

He went up. When he was let in, he was first led into a paradisal garden, where there were fruit trees and flowers that filled the mind with the joys of life due to their beauty, pleasantness, and fragrance. He admired them greatly when he saw them. But he was using his outward sight that he had used in the world when he saw things like that, and in that sight he was rational. In his inner vision, however, where fornication had the leading role and occupied every bit of his thought, he was not rational. So his outer vision was closed and his inner opened. When it was, he said, "What do I see now? It's straw and dry wood, isn't it? And now what do I notice? It's a bad smell, isn't it? Where are the paradisal things now?"

The angel said, "They are nearby and present, but they don't appear before your inner vision, which is a fornicator's, so here it turns heavenly things into hellish ones and only sees their opposites. Every person has an inner mind and an outer mind, thus inner vision and outer vision. In evil people the inner mind is foolish and the outer one is wise, and in good people the inner mind is wise, and on account of this the outer one is, too. And in the spiritual world a person sees objects according to the way his mind is."

After this, by a power given to him, the angel closed the young man's inner sight and opened his outer sight and led him through gates toward the center of population, and he saw magnificent palaces of alabaster, marble, and various precious stones with colonnades by them, and columns all around topped and covered with marvelous decorations and ornaments. When he saw it he was amazed and said, "What am I seeing? I see splendors of splendor and the very state of the art of architecture!"

And then the angel again closed his outer vision and opened his inner vision, which was evil because horribly given to fornication. When that happened he cried out, saying, "Now what am I seeing? Where am I? Where are the palaces and splendors now? I see rubble, debris, and gaping holes!"

He was soon returned to his outer vision and taken into one of the palaces, and he saw the decorations on the doors, windows, walls, and ceilings—especially the furniture that had heavenly designs on it and around it made of gold and precious stones. One could not describe it with any words or draw it with any art, for it was beyond spoken ideas and beyond the concepts of the arts. When he saw these he cried out again, saying, "These are splendor itself, which eyes have never seen!" But then his inner vision was opened, and his outer vision was closed, as before, and he was asked what he saw now.

"Just walls," he answered, "here of rushes, there of straw, and there of matchwood."

But he was brought into his outer state of mind once more,

and young women were brought who were beauties because they were the images of heavenly feelings, and they talked to him in the gentle voice of their feelings. And then his face changed because of what he saw and heard, and he shifted back by himself from his outside to his inside—which was a fornicator's. This inside could not bear anything that had to do with heavenly love and, vice versa, nothing having to do with heavenly love could bear what was inside, so they disappeared for each other—the young women from the man's sight and the man from the young women's sight.

After this the angel informed him why the conditions of the things he saw had changed back and forth. "I can tell," he said, "that you were two-sided in the world you came from—one person on the inside and another on the outside—a civil, moral, and reasonable person on the outside but neither civil nor moral nor reasonable on the inside, because you were a fornicator and an adulterer. That kind of people can see heavenly things when they go up into heaven, so long as they stick to their outer personalities there. But when the things inside them are opened up, they see hellish things in place of the heavenly ones. But you need to know that here everyone's outside is gradually closed off and what is inside is opened up. People are made ready for heaven or for hell in this way. The evil of illicit sex pollutes the insides of your mind more than any other evil, so you can't help being carried down to the filths of your love, and these are in hell, where the caverns stink of excrements.

"Who can't reason out that in the spiritual world anything unchaste and lascivious is impure and unclean, so that nothing fouls and pollutes a person more and brings something hellish into him? So be careful not to brag about your love affairs any more—that they make you more masculine than others. I'm warning you that you're going to be so impotent that you'll hardly know where your manhood is. That is what happens to people who boast about the potency of illicit sex."

When he heard this he went down and returned to the world of spirits and his former companions. And he talked modestly and chastely with them. But not for long.

Chapter 21

Adultery: Its Types and Levels

478   No one who forms an opinion about adultery just from outward factors can tell that there is anything bad in it, because in outward appearances it is like marriage. When you mention inward factors to people who judge by outward factors, and tell them that the outward factors get their good or evil from the inward ones, they say to themselves, "What inward factors? Who sees them? This is going beyond the range of anyone's understanding, isn't it?" They are like people who take every pretense of good for genuine good intention, and who judge a person's wisdom by the elegance of his talk, or who estimate the man himself by his fine clothes and his driving an expensive carriage, not by his inner character—which has to do with discernment based on affection for good. It is just the same as judging the fruit of a tree, or anything edible, from just its look and feel, instead of judging its worth by taste and knowledge. This is what everyone unwilling to notice the inner dimensions of a person does.

This is why so many people today have the insanity to see nothing bad in adulteries, and in fact put them together in the same bed with marriages—that is, make them just alike—and only because of an appearance of outward similarity.

The following evidence from experience clearly demonstrates that this is true. Angels once called together several hundred people from the European world, who were very talented, learned, and wise. The angels asked them about the difference between marriages and adulteries, and urged them to call on their intellectual powers. After consultation all but ten answered that public law makes the only difference, for the sake of some benefit that people can recognize, to be sure, but that is served through jurisprudence.

Then they were asked if they saw anything good in marriage and anything evil in adultery.

They answered, "No measurable evil and good."

Asked if they saw any sin there, they said, "Where? It's the same act, isn't it?"

The angels were amazed at this answer and cried out, "Oh, what gross times!"

The wise hundreds turned to each other when they heard that, and laughing among themselves they said, "This is grossness? Is there any wisdom that can convince us that loving someone else's wife deserves eternal damnation?"

But the first chapter of this part—about illicit love and married love being opposite—demonstrated that adultery is a spiritual evil and therefore a moral and civil evil, and diametrically against the wisdom of reason. Also that adulterous love is from hell and returns there, and married love is from heaven and returns there.

But every evil, like every good, has its spread and its height—its types go according to its spread and its levels according to its height—so for adulteries to be known in both dimensions, they are going to be examined first in their types and then in their levels—which is done in this order:

(1) There are three types of adultery—simple, double, and triple.

(2) Simple adultery is adultery of an unmarried man with another's wife, or an unmarried woman with another's husband.

(3) Double adultery is adultery of a husband with another's wife, or the other way around.

(4) Triple adultery is adultery with blood relations.

(5) There are four levels of adultery. Accusation, guilt, and (after death) blame for them depends on the level of the adultery.

(6) Adulteries of the first level are adulteries from ignorance, committed by people who do not yet, or cannot, consult their intellect and in this way curb them.

(7) The adulteries committed by these people are mild.

(8) Adulteries of the second level are adulteries of passion, done by people who can indeed consult their intellect, but not at the time, because of the circumstances.

(9) People are to blame for these adulteries precisely as their intellect does or does not favor them afterwards.

(10) Adulteries of the third level are rationalized adulteries committed by people who intellectually demonstrate that adulteries are not sinful wrongs.

(11) The adulteries committed by these people are serious, and the people are to blame for them according to their being confirmed.

(12) Adulteries of the fourth level are intentional adulteries committed by people who represent them as lawful, acceptable, and not even worth intellectual consideration.

(13) The adulteries that these people commit are the most serious and are attributed to them as purposeful evils, and they adhere as guilt.

(14) Adulteries of the third and fourth level are sinful wrongs to the extent, and in the way, that intellect and will are involved in them, whether actually committed or not.

(15) Adulteries by willful purpose and adulteries by intellectual conviction make people worldly, sense-oriented, and physical-minded.

(16) So much so that these people finally reject everything having to do with the church and religion.

(17) They still flourish in human rationality like anyone else.

(18) But they use that rationality in outward activities yet abuse it inwardly.

Now comes the explanation of these topics.

479   (1) *There are three types of adultery—simple, double, and triple.* The Creator of the universe divided each and every thing that He created into general types, and each type into different varieties, and He subdivided each variety and each particular kind the same way, and so on, so that infinity would be represented in the continual variety of qualities. Thus the Creator of the universe divided the good things and the truths that go with them and similarly the

bad things and the falsities that go with them, once they had sprung up.

Things brought to light in the book *Heaven and Hell* (published in London in 1758) may establish that He divided each and every thing in the spiritual world into types, varieties, and particular kinds, and that He gathered all good and true things together in heaven and all evil and false things in hell and arranged the latter diametrically opposite to the former.

The fate of people after death—heaven is for the good and hell is for the bad—tells us that in the natural world He has divided and does divide the good and true things and the evil and false things in people, and thus the people themselves.

Now, since all things having to do with good and all things having to do with evil are divided into kinds, species, and so forth, by the same token marriages are divided into them, and similarly the opposite of marriages, which are adulteries.

480   (2) *Simple adultery is adultery of an unmarried man with another's wife, or an unmarried woman with another's husband.* Adultery here and in what follows means the illicit love that is opposite to marriage. It is opposite because it violates the life covenant settled between the partners, mangles their love, pollutes it, and shuts off the union begun at the time of engagement and confirmed in the beginning of the marriage. For the married love of a man with one wife unites their souls after the agreement and covenant. Adultery does not dissolve this union, because it cannot be dissolved, but closes it off just like someone stopping up a spring where it bubbles out, thus stopping its stream, and filling the cistern with contaminated, smelly waters. In the same way, adultery plasters up and closes off the love in marriage, whose source is a union of souls. When this is plugged up, adulterous love rises up from below. As it grows it makes the former love physical, and this rises up against married love and destroys it. This is where the opposition of adultery and marriage comes from.

481   To make known, once again, how dull this age is in that its wise people do not see anything sinful in adultery (as angels disclosed already in no. 478 above), I am adding this account.

There were certain spirits who used to infest me with unusual skill due to practice in their bodily life, and they did it with
quite a gentle, almost wave-like influence, like the usual influence
of good spirits. But I noticed cunning and things like that in them,
to entice and deceive.

I finally talked with one of them who, I was told, had been
the leader of an army when he lived in the world. I could tell that
there were dirty ideas in his thinking, so I spoke with him in
spiritual language with symbols. It expresses ideas fully, and many
at a time.

He said he thought nothing of adultery in his bodily life in
the former world.

But I was able to tell him that adulteries are against divine
law, even if they do not seem that way—in fact, seem lawful—to
people like that, on account of the pleasure they take and their
conviction due to the pleasure. Also that you can know it from
this—that marriage is the nursery of the human race and thus
also the kingdom of heaven's nursery and is therefore not to be
violated, but held sacred. And also from this—that the love in
marriage comes down from the Lord through heaven, and that
love for each other, which is the mainstay of heaven, derives from
that love as a parent (which he should have known, being in the
spiritual world and in a position to notice). And you can tell from
this—that when adulterers merely approach heavenly communities
they notice their own heavy odor and fling themselves away from
there toward hell. At the least he might know that violating marriages is against divine laws, against the civil laws of all countries,
also against the genuine light of reason, and thus against the law
of nations, because it is against both divine and human order,
besides many other things.

But he answered that he had not thought about things like
that in his former life. He wanted to argue about whether it was so.

But he was told that there is no room for arguments about
the truth, because arguments defend the pleasures of flesh against
the pleasures of spirit, and he knew nothing about what spiritual
pleasures are like. And he was told that he should think about the
things that he had been told, first, because they were true. Or
think from the principle, which is well known in the world, that

no one should do to someone else what he doesn't want someone else to do to him. And if someone deceived in this way his own wife whom he loved (as you do in the beginning of every marriage), then, while in a state of rage about it, would not he himself also have denounced adulteries if he spoke his mind? And besides, because he has an aggressive nature, he would protest against it more than others, would he not, to the point of damning it to hell? And, because he was the leader of an army with active troops available, he would either have done away with the adulterer or thrown the adulteress out of his house to keep it from being a reproach to him.

482   (3) *Double adultery is adultery of a husband with another's wife, or the other way around.* This adultery is called double because two commit it. Each of them violates the marriage vow, so it is twice as serious as the former kind.

It said above (no. 480) that the married love of one man with one wife joins their souls after the agreement and vow, and that this union is married love itself in its origin, and that adultery closes this and stops it up like the bubbling and flow of a spring. It is clear that the two people's souls join when love for the other sex is restricted to one woman or one man of the other sex—which happens when the young woman totally pledges herself to the young man and, vice versa, the young man totally pledges himself to the young woman—because the lives of each join together, and so their souls do, because these are the origins of life. This union of souls is possible only in monogamous marriages, or marriage of one man with one wife, but not in polygamous marriages, or marriage of one man with more than one woman, because in these, love is split up, and in the others it is united.

Married love is spiritual, holy, and pure in this highest temple for the reason that every person's soul is heavenly by its origin, so it receives influence directly from the Lord, for it receives from Him a marriage of love and wisdom, or of good and truth, and this influence makes a person a person and distinguishes him from the animals. From this union of souls, married love, which is in its spiritual holiness and purity in this union, flows down into the life of your whole body and fills it with blessed pleasures as long as its stream stays open—which happens in those whom the Lord makes spiritual. From the Lord's words that it is lawful to put away a wife and take another only because of adultery (Matt. 19:4–9), it is clear that only adultery closes and stops up this seat, source, or spring of married love and its stream, and also from these words there, that he who takes the divorced wife commits adultery (v. 9). So when that pure, holy spring is stopped up, as said above, it becomes packed with foulness, like a precious stone packed in dung, or a loaf of bread full of vomit—things which are totally opposite to the purity and holiness of that spring, or married love. From this opposition comes marital coldness, and in keeping with this, a lascivious pleasure in illicit love, which willingly destroys itself.

This is an evil of sin because the holiness is covered up, so its flow into your body is thwarted, and a profane thing comes in place of it, whose flow into your body is opened. This changes a person from heavenly to hellish.

483   I add to these observations some things from the spiritual world that are worth recording.

I heard there that some married men take pleasure in fornicating with inexperienced women, or virgins, some with women who are not virgins, or prostitutes, some with married women, or wives, some with women from the nobility, and some with women who are not highborn. I have been convinced that this is so by many people from different countries, in that world.

While I was thinking about the variety of these passions I asked if there are any who get all their pleasure with other people's wives and none with unmarried women. So, to show me that there are, many people from a certain kingdom were brought to me. They were obliged to speak according to their lusts. They said that for them the only delight and joy was, and is, to commit adultery with other people's wives, and that they seek beautiful ones for themselves and bribe them with rewards sized according to their wealth, and they usually agree on the price with the woman alone.

I asked why they did not hire unmarried women.

They said that to them this is low-class, that it is cheap in itself, and there is no pleasure in it.

I asked if the wives go back to their husbands afterwards and live with them.

They answered that either they do not, or else they return cold, because they have been made into prostitutes.

Next I asked in all seriousness if they had ever thought, or thought now, that this is double adultery, because they do it while they have wives, and that adultery like that wipes out all spiritual good in a person.

But most of those who were present laughed at these words, saying, "What is spiritual good?"

But I held my ground, saying, "What is more detestable than to mix your soul with a husband's soul, in his wife? Don't you know that a man's soul is in his semen?"

At this they turned away and muttered, "What does it hurt there?"

I finally said, "Even if you're not afraid of Divine laws, aren't you afraid of the civil laws?"

They answered, "No, we're only afraid of certain people in the preaching profession, but in their company we conceal it— and if we can't, we treat them right."

Later I saw them separated into groups and some of the groups driven into hell.

484   (4) *Triple adultery is adultery with blood relations.* This adultery is called triple because it is three times as serious as the first two kinds. The blood relations, or "vestiges of your body," that are not to be approached are listed in Leviticus 18:6–17. There are inner and outward reasons why these adulteries are three times as serious as the first two mentioned. The inward reasons come from their corresponding to a violation of the spiritual marriage, which is the marriage of the Lord and the church, and of good and truth from that. The outward reasons are for the sake of protection against man's becoming an animal. But here there is no room to go ahead and explain these reasons.

485   (5) *There are four levels of adultery. Accusation, guilt, and (after death) blame for them depends on the level of the adultery.* These levels are not types, but they apply to each of the types and make the difference in them between more or less evil or good—here whether an adultery of any kind should be considered mild or

serious because of circumstances and contingencies. It is well known that circumstances and contingencies make a difference in everything.

Yet the person considers them one way by his rational lights, a judge another way by law, and the Lord another way by the person's state of mind. This is why I said "accusation, guilt, and (after death) blame." For people make accusations of them by their rational lights, a judge condemns them by the law, and the Lord lays blame for them according to the person's state of mind.

Without any explanation, these three things can be seen to be very different, for by rational convictions according to circumstances and contingencies, a person can excuse someone whom a judge sitting in judgment cannot excuse under the law. And also a judge can excuse someone who, after death, is condemned. The reason is that the judge gives a sentence according to what was done, but after death each one is judged according to the intentions of his will and therefore his understanding of it, and according to his intellectual convictions and therefore his will. A judge does not see either of these things. And yet both kinds of judgment are just—one for the good of civil society, the other for the good of heavenly society.

486   (6) *Adulteries of the first level are adulteries from ignorance, committed by people who do not yet, or cannot, consult their intellect and in this way curb them.* All evils, and therefore adultery too, per se have to do with the inner and outer person at the same time. The inner intends them, and the outer does them. So whatever the inner person is like in things done by the outer, that is what the deeds are like, in themselves. But the inner person and his intention does not appear to people's eyes, so in court everyone is judged by deeds and words according to established law and its requirements. A judge should also consider the inner intent of the law.

But examples make it clear. If a growing boy, who does not yet know that adultery is more evil than fornication, happens to commit adultery, if a very simpleminded person does it, if someone deprived of clear judgment by disease does it, or someone who has temporary insanity, as some do, and at the time is in a state that the truly insane are in, and also if it is done in wild drunkenness, and so on, clearly the inner person, or mind, is not present in the outer at that time, much more than in someone irrational. Anybody who is rational discusses these people's adulteries according to those circumstances. Yet the same person, sitting as a judge, still blames and punishes them by law. But after death the adulteries are blamed on them on the basis of the presence, quality, and skill of the intellect in the people's intent.

487   (7) *The adulteries committed by these people are mild.* This stands from what was said above (no. 486) without more explanation, for obviously the nature of every act—of everything generally—depends on the circumstances, and these make it mild or serious. But adulteries on this level are mild when they are committed. And they also remain mild insofar as a man or woman abstains from them over the course of life afterwards for the reasons that they are evils against God or evils against one's neighbor or evils against the civic good or, for these reasons, they are evils against reason. On the other hand, these also count as more serious adulteries if the people do not abstain from them for one of the reasons mentioned. This is so by Divine law (Ezek. 18:21, 22, 24, and elsewhere). But a person cannot forgive or condemn or accuse someone of them and judge them as mild or serious on the basis of these circumstances, because they do not appear to his eyes—in fact are not for him to judge. So this means that they are accused and blamed in this way after death.

488   (8) *Adulteries of the second level are adulteries of passion, committed by people who can indeed consult their intellect, but not at the time, because of the circumstances.* In the beginning there are two things that struggle with each other in a person who changes from worldly to spiritual, which are commonly called spirit and flesh. Married love belongs to spirit and adulterous love belongs to flesh, so there is also a struggle between these. If married love wins it masters and subdues the adulterous love, which is done by removing it. But if it happens that bodily passion is excited to surge beyond what one's spirit can hold back by reason, it creates an inverted situation, and the surge of passion swamps the spirit with such enticements that it is no longer in control of its reason,

and therefore of its judgment. This is the meaning of second-degree adultery done by people who can indeed consult their intellect, but not at the moment, because of the circumstances.

But examples are illustrative—for instance, if a whorish wife captures a man's mind by cunning, enticing him into a bedroom and exciting him until control of his judgment escapes, and more so if at the same time she threatens him with shame if he does not. Equally, if some whorish wife is good at trickery or excites the man with aphrodisiacs to the point where the enthusiasm of his body takes away his intellect's freedom to think. Similarly, if a man leads someone else's wife on by pleasing enticements until her aroused desire is no longer under her control. And other cases like that.

Reason agrees and assents that these contingencies and others like them soften the seriousness of adultery and swing the assignment of blame for it onto the milder side for the seduced man or woman.

Next, the blame for this degree of adultery.

489   (9) *People are to blame for these adulteries precisely as their intellect does or does not favor them afterwards.* A person takes on evils and makes them his own to the extent that he intellectually favors them. Favor is agreement, and agreement puts him in a frame of mind to love them. It is this way with adulteries that were originally committed without consent, and that come to be relished. It is the opposite if they are not relished afterwards. The reason is that evils, or adulteries, committed with the intellect blind are committed due to the body's desire. These come close to being like the instincts that animals have. In a person, intellect is indeed present when he does evils, but with inactive or dead force, not with active or living force. From these observations the concept emerges by itself that acts like that are only blamed on a person in the measure that he does or does not relish them afterwards.

Attributing here means blame after death and a judgment from it—which is done in keeping with the state of the person's spirit—but it does not mean an accusation by a person before a judge. This is not done in keeping with the state of his spirit, but his body, in the act. If these states were not different things, whoever is acquitted in the world would be absolved after death, and whoever is condemned there would be damned, and therefore there would be no hope of salvation for him.

490   (10) *Adulteries of the third level are rationalized adulteries committed by people who intellectually demonstrate that adulteries are not sinful wrongs.* Everyone knows that there is will and intellect, for in speech we say "I want this" and "I understand this." Yet we do not distinguish between them, but make one the same as the other. The reason is that everyone reflects only on things that have to do with thought due to intellect and not on things that have to do with love due to will, for these do not appear in the open like intellectual matters. And yet someone who does not differentiate between will and intellect cannot distinguish between evil and good and therefore can certainly not know anything about the guilt of a sin. But who does not know that good and truth are two separate things, like love and wisdom? And who cannot conclude from that, when he is in rational light, that in a person there are two faculties that receive good and truth differently and assign them to themselves, and that one faculty is will and the other intellect? For that reason, what your will receives and in turn puts forth is called good, and what your intellect receives is called truth. For what will loves and does is called good, and what intellect notices and thinks is called truth.

Now the first part of this book dealt with the marriage of good and truth, and there many things were mentioned about will and intellect and the various attributes and qualities of each. (Even those who have not thought about any difference between intellect and will, I may say, could grasp those statements, for human reason is such that it understands truths due to their light, even if it has not seen the difference before.) Therefore, to make the difference between intellect and will more clearly noticeable, I bring out some things here for the purpose of making known what adulteries of reason or intellect are like, and afterwards what adulteries of will are like.

These items will serve to give an idea about them. (a) Will alone does not act by itself, but whatever it does it does through intellect. (b) And on the other hand, intellect alone does not act by itself, but whatever it does it does due to will. (c) Will flows into intellect, but not intellect into will, but intellect teaches what is good and bad and consults will to choose between these two and do will's pleasure. (d) After this a double connection is formed— one where will acts from the inside and intellect from the outside, the other where intellect acts from inside and will from outside.

This is how reason's adulteries, dealt with here, are distinguished from will's adulteries, dealt with later. They are distinguished because one is worse than the other, for reason's adulteries are less serious than will's adulteries. The reason is that in reason's adultery intellect acts from inside and will from outside, but in will's adultery will acts from inside and intellect from outside, and will is the person himself, intellect the person due to will. And what acts within rules over what acts from outside.

491   (11) *The adulteries committed by these people are serious according to their being confirmed.* Only intellect confirms, and when it confirms it wins your will over, draws it up around itself, and thus makes it obedient. Confirmations are made through arguments that the mind summons either from its higher reaches or from its lower reaches. If from the higher reaches, which are in touch with heaven, it confirms marriages and condemns adulteries, but if from its lower reaches, which are in touch with the world, it confirms adulteries and makes little of marriages.

Anyone can confirm bad just the same as good, and likewise falsity and truth, and confirming evil seems more pleasant than confirming good, and confirming falsity more brilliant that confirming truth. The reason is that confirmation of evil and falsity draws its conclusions from the joys, pleasures, appearances, and fallacies of the bodily senses, but confirmation of good and true things draws its reasons from an area above the sensory qualities of the body.

Now, since you can confirm bad and false things just the same as good and true ones, and since intellect gets your will on its side when it makes its confirmation, and will together with intellect makes up your mind, as a result the makeup of a human mind is in keeping with the confirmations. It is turned toward heaven if its confirmations are pro-marriage, but turned toward hell if they are pro-adultery. And whatever the form of a person's mind is like, his spirit is like, so that is what the person is like.

From these observations it is now established that adulteries of this degree are laid to your account according to your confirmations of them.

492   (12) *Adulteries of the fourth level are intentional adulteries committed by people who represent them as lawful, acceptable, and not even worth intellectual consideration.* The source of these adulteries distinguishes them from the previous ones. These adulteries originate in the distorted will inborn in a person—in other words, in a bad heredity—which the person blindly obeys after his judgment is formed, forming no opinion about whether they are evils or not. So we say that he does not think that they require intellectual consideration.

However, adulteries called rationalized adulteries originate in a distorted intellect, and they are done by those who confirm that adulteries are not sinful evils. In these people intellect takes the lead; in the others, will does. In the natural world these two distinctions do not appear to a person at all, but they are obvious to angels in the spiritual world. In that world everyone is generally sorted out by the evils that originally spring from will or from intellect and are accepted and taken to oneself. In hell people are also separated according to those evils. There the ones who are intellectually evil live in front and are called satans, but the ones who are evil in will live in back and are called devils. The Word speaks of satans and devils on account of this general difference. In those evil spirits—including adulterers—called satans, intellect takes the lead, and in the ones called devils, will takes the lead.

But the difference can be explained so as to be seen intellectually only if the differences between will and intellect are already known, and the way will forms your mind through intellect and intellect forms it through will is explained. A knowledge of these things would provide light for reason to see the differences mentioned above, but the job would take a whole sheet of paper.

493   (13) *The adulteries that these people commit are the most serious and are attributed to them as purposeful evils, and they adhere as guilt.*

They are the most serious and worse than the former ones because will takes the lead in them, but intellect leads in the former, and a person's life has to do with his will essentially and his intellect in the form his will takes. The reason is that will acts in unison with love, and love is the essence of a person's life. Will takes form in intellect through things that agree with it. So intellect in its own right is nothing other than the form that will takes. And since love has to do with will, and wisdom with intellect, wisdom is nothing other than a form that love takes. Similarly, truth is nothing other than a form that good takes.

What flows from this very essence of a person's life—that is, from his will, or love—is mainly called a concept, but what flows from the form of his life—that is, from intellect and its thought— is called the application. Also, guilt mainly applies to your will. This is why they say that the guilt for someone's evil is from heredity but the evil is from the person. So adulteries of this fourth degree are blameworthy as purposeful evils and are beset with guilt.

494   (14) *Adulteries of the third and fourth level are sinful wrongs to the extent, and in the way, that intellect and will are involved in them, whether actually committed or not.* Rationalized, or intellectual, adulteries, which are of the third degree, and adulteries of will, which are of the fourth degree, are more serious, and consequently are sinful wrongs, according to the kind of intellect and will in them. You can see this from the discussion of them above (nos. 490–93). This is because a person is a person by reason of his will and intellect, for not only all the things he does in his mind but also all the things he does in his body come from will and intellect. Who does not know that a body does not act on its own initiative, but will acts through a body, and that a mouth does not speak by itself, but thought speaks through the mouth? So if will were removed, action would stop at once, and if thought were removed, your vocal speech would stop at once. It is quite evident from this that adulteries that are actually committed are serious according to how much and what kind of intellect and will is involved in them.

The Lord's words establish that they are serious in the same way when not actually committed:

The ancients said, "Do not commit adultery." But I tell you that whoever looks at someone else's woman in a longing way has already committed adultery with her in her heart. (Matt. 5:27–28)

To commit adultery in your heart is to commit it in your will.

There are many motives that make an adulterer not an adulterer in act, and yet in will and intellect, for there are those who abstain from adulteries as far as the act goes for fear of civil law and its penalties, for fear of damage to their reputation and dignities due to it, for fear of diseases from adulteries, for fear of trouble at home from the wife resulting in unquiet life, for fear of vengeance by the husband or in-laws and by the same token for fear of a beating by the servants, because of poverty or stinginess, because of weakness stemming from disease, burn-out, age, or impotency, and the shame of it. If someone restrains himself from actually committing adultery for these reasons and others like them, and yet is for them in will and intellect, he is still an adulterer. For he believes no less that they are not sins, and in his spirit he does not make them unlawful before God, and so he commits them in spirit though not physically before the world. So after death when he becomes a spirit he openly speaks in favor of them.

495   (15) *Adulteries by willful purpose and adulteries by intellectual conviction make people worldly, sense-oriented, and physical-minded.* A person is a person and is different from an animal in that his mind is in three separate regions—the same number as the heavens—and in that it can be raised from the lowest region into the higher one, and also from that into the highest, and thus become an angel of one of the heavens, even the third one. For that purpose a person has the ability to raise his intellect all the way there. But if the love of his will is not raised at the same time he does not become spiritual but stays worldly. Nonetheless he retains his ability to raise his intellect.

The reason why he retains it is so he can be reformed, for

you are reformed through understanding. This happens through thinking about good and truth and through rational intuition from it. If he rationally pays attention to those thoughts and lives by them, then the love of his will is raised at the same time, and in that degree his humanity is completed and he becomes more and more human.

It works out differently if he does not live by the thoughts about good and truth. Then the love of his will stays worldly, and his intellect becomes spiritual off and on, for it raises itself like an eagle, by turns, and looks down at what belongs to his love below. When it sees this it flies down to it and joins itself to it. And so if bodily desires are its love, it comes down to them from its height and enjoys itself with the pleasures of them. And again, with an eye to public opinion, intellect soars again in order to be thought wise, and so up and down by turns, as was just said.

Adulterers of the third and fourth level—the ones who have made themselves adulterers by willful purpose and intellectual confirmation—are quite worldly and become more and more sense-oriented and physical. This is because they have immersed the love of their will and at the same time their intellect in foul things having to do with their illicit love and have enjoyed them the way unclean birds and animals enjoy as delicacies and dainties things that are rotten and filthy. For the fumes rising up from their flesh fill their mind's dwelling place with their dense odors and make their will find nothing more fine and dainty. These are the ones who become physically-minded spirits after death, and the unclean hellish and ecclesiastical things mentioned above (nos. 430–31) well up from them.

496   The worldly person has three levels. People who love only the world, setting their hearts on wealth, belong to the first level. These are appropriately called the worldly. Those who love only sensual pleasures, setting their hearts on all kinds of luxuries and pleasures, belong to the second level. They are appropriately called sensual. Those who love only themselves, setting their hearts on seeking status, belong to the third level. These are appropriately called physical, because they submerge in their bodies everything that has to do with their desire and therefore their intellect, and they see themselves reflected in others, and strictly speaking love

only what is their own. But the sensual ones sink everything related to their inclinations and therefore their intellect in the charms and deceits of the senses, indulging only in these things. The worldly, however, sink everything having to do with their inclinations and therefore their intellect in the world, grubbing for wealth with greed and cheating, and seeing no use in it or from it except having it.

The adulteries named above turn people degenerate on these levels, one on one level, another on another, each in keeping with the satisfying pleasure that gives him his character.

497   (16) *So much so that these people finally reject everything having to do with the church and religion.* Adulterers on purpose and by confirmation reject everything that has to do with the church and religion because married love and adulterous love are opposites (no. 425), and married love acts at one with the church and religion (no. 130 and everywhere else in the Part 1). So adulterous love acts at one with things that are against the church, because it is opposite.

These adulterers cast away from themselves everything having to do with the church and its religion because married love and adulterous love are opposites just as the marriage of good and truth is opposite to a marriage of evil and falsity (nos. 427–28), and a marriage of good and truth is the church, but a marriage of evil and falsity is antichurch.

These adulterers cast away from themselves everything that has to do with the church and religion because married love and adulterous love are opposites like heaven and hell (no. 429), and love for everything having to do with the church is in heaven, but hatred against everything having to do with the church is in hell.

These adulterers also cast away from themselves everything that has to do with the church and religion because their pleasures start in the flesh and are fleshly even in spirit (nos. 440–41), and flesh is against spirit—that is, spiritual things of the church. This is why the pleasures of illicit love are called foolish pleasures.

If you want proof, please go to those who you know are adulterers like that and privately ask them what they think about God, church, and eternal life, and you shall hear. Naturally, the reason is that just as married love opens the inner reaches of your mind and thus raises them above the sensory aspects of your body, all the way to the light and heat of heaven, adulterous love, on the other hand, closes the inner reaches of your mind and, as far as your will goes, drags your mind itself down into your body until it is taken over by all the desires of your body's flesh. And the deeper it drags your mind down, the farther it takes it from heaven.

498   (17) *They still flourish in human rationality like anyone else.* The worldly, sense-oriented, and physical person is just as reasonable intellectually as a spiritual person. This has been demonstrated to me by satans and devils rising up from hell, with permission, and talking with angelic spirits in the world of spirits. (These things are mentioned here and there in the stories.) But the will's love makes the person, and it draws intellect into agreement, so that kind of people are rational only in a state where they are removed from their will's love. But when they return to this love they are less reasonable than wild animals. And in any case, a person without the ability to raise his intellect above his will's love would not be a person but an animal, for an animal does not enjoy that ability. He consequently would not be able to choose anything and do what is good by choice, so he could not be reformed and led to heaven and live forever.

For this reason adulterers on purpose and by confirmation are as fully gifted as others in understanding, or rationality, even though they are quite worldly, sense-oriented, and physical. But they do not enjoy this rationality when involved in the sensuality of adultery and think and talk about it from that standpoint. The reason is that then their flesh is acting on their spirit and not their spirit in their flesh. But note that after death they finally become stupid. Not that the ability to be wise is taken from them, but they do not want to be wise, since it displeases them.

499   (18) *But they use that rationality in outward activities, yet abuse it inwardly.* They are in their outer role when they speak in public or in a group but in their inner role when at home by themselves. Try it, if you want. Take someone like that—someone of the order called Jesuit, for example—and have him talk in a group or teach

in church about God, holy matters of the church, and about heaven and hell, and he will sound like a more rational zealot than anyone else. He might even move you to sighs and tears over salvation. But take him home, praise him above the other orders, call him the father of wisdom, and make yourself a friend until he opens his heart, and you will hear what he will pronounce about God, holy church matters, and heaven and hell then, namely, that these things are fantasies and sleights so they are traps for souls—bonds with which they seize and tie the great and small, the rich and poor, and hold them in their power.

These observations are enough to show what it means that worldly people—even the physically-minded—flourish in rationality like anyone else and that they use rationality in outward activities but abuse it inwardly. Consequently one is not to be judged by any of the wisdom he speaks, except together with the wisdom of his life.

500   I add the following story to these remarks.

Once in the world of spirits I heard a big uproar. Thousands were gathered together shouting, "They ought to be punished! They ought to be punished!"

I went closer and asked, "What's this?"

Someone separate from the huge crowd said to me, "They're in a burning rage against three ministers going around denouncing adulterers everywhere, saying that adulterers have no knowledge of God and that to them heaven is closed and hell open. And that in hell adulterers are filthy devils, because from a distance there they look like pigs rolling in manure. And the angels of heaven detest them."

"Where are those ministers," I asked, "and why such an outcry over that?"

He answered, "The three ministers are among them, guarded by bodyguards, and it's a crowd who think adulteries aren't sins and say that adulterers acknowledge God as much as those who stick with their wives. They're all from the Christian world, and some angels visited to see how many there believed adulteries are sins. They didn't find a hundred in a thousand.

"And," he told me, "here's what the other nine hundred say

about adulteries. 'Who doesn't know that the joy of adultery overtops the joy of marriage? That adulterers are always hot, so they have a more lively, industrious, and active life than those who live with only one woman? And that love with a married partner cools, on the other hand, sometimes to the point where at last hardly one word of speech and companionship survives? It's different with prostitutes. The deadliness of life with a wife, coming from lack of potency, is remade and brought back to life by illicit sex. Isn't something that remakes and revives worth more than something that deadens? What's marriage but licensed sexual love? Who knows the difference? Can love be forced? And yet love with a wife is forced by the vows and laws. Isn't love with a spouse sexual love? And so common that the birds and animals have it? What's married love but sexual love? And sexual love is free with every woman.

"'The civil laws are against adulteries because the lawmakers thought it would be for the public good, and yet the lawmakers themselves, and the judges, sometimes commit adultery and say to each other, "He who is without sin can cast the first stone." Only simpleminded and religious people think adulteries are sins, not intelligent people who, like us, look at them in natural light. Aren't children born of adulteries the same as children of marriages? Aren't illegitimates just as fit and useful for duty and employment as legitimates? Besides, it provides families for people who are otherwise without children. Isn't this a benefit and not an injury? What does it hurt a wife to accept several suitors? And what does it hurt the man? It's a worthless and imaginary opinion that this shames a man. That adultery is against the laws and statutes of the church is due to the ecclesiastical order, on account of power. But what do theological and spiritual things have to do with a purely physical and fleshly pleasure? There are priests and monks like that, aren't there? Does it keep them from accepting and worshiping God?

"'So why do those three preach that adulterers don't accept God? We won't allow such blasphemies. They'll have to be judged and punished.'"

Then I saw them call judges. They asked them to sentence the three to punishment.

But the judges said, "That is not a job for us, since it has to do with accepting God and with sin, so it's a matter of salvation and damnation. These things are judged from heaven. But we'll advise you how you can find out if the three ministers have preached true things. We judges know of three places where things like this are investigated and disclosed in a remarkable way. In one place a road to heaven is visible to everyone, but when they enter heaven they find out what they themselves are like as far as accepting God goes. There's a second place where a road to heaven is also visible, but no one can get on the road except those who have heaven in themselves. And there's a third place where there's a road to hell, and people who love hellish things get on that road willingly because it makes them happy. We judges send to those places everyone that wants us to pass judgment about heaven and hell."

When they heard this the crowd said, "Let's go to those places."

On the way to the first place, where a road to heaven is visible to everyone, it suddenly became dark. So some of them lit torches and carried them in front. The judges with them said, "This happens to everyone on the way to the first place, but the flames of the little torches get dimmer as they come close, and at the place they go out, due to the light of heaven falling on it. This is a sign that they're there. The reason is that heaven is closed to them at first and opened later."

They arrived at the place, and when the torches went out by themselves, they saw a road stretching up into the sky at an angle. The ones who were in a burning rage against the ministers got on the road—the ones who were purposeful adulterers among the first, and after them the confirmed adulterers. On the way up, the ones in front shouted, "Come on!" and the ones following shouted, "Hurry up!" and pushed forward.

In a little while, when they were all inside a community of heaven, a chasm appeared between them and the angels, and the light of heaven, above the chasm, exposed the inner reaches of their minds by flowing into their eyes, so they had to say exactly what they were thinking inside. And then angels questioned them, whether they acknowledged that God exists.

The first, who were adulterers by willful purpose, answered,

"What is God?" They looked around at each other and said, "Has any of you seen Him?"

The second group, who were intellectually confirmed adulterers, said, "Everything is part of nature, isn't it? What's above nature, besides the sun?"

And the angels said to them, "Get away from us. Now you yourselves can tell that you have no acknowledgement of God. When you go back down, the inner parts of your minds will close, and the outer parts will open, and then you'll be able to speak against the things inside and say that God exists. Believe it—as soon as a person becomes an actual adulterer heaven is closed to him. When heaven is closed, God is not acknowledged. Listen to the reason why. All the filth of hell comes from adulteries, and in heaven this stinks like putrid filth in the streets."

When they heard this they turned and went down along three roads. And when they were down below, the first and second groups, talking among themselves, said, "The ministers got the better of us there, but we know we can talk about God as well as they can. And when we say that He exists, don't we acknowledge Him? The inner and outer parts of your mind that the angels told about are something they dreamed up. But let's go to the second place the judges described, where a road to heaven is open to those who have heaven in them—which is those who are about to go to heaven."

When they came near there a voice went out from heaven, "Shut the gates! There are adulterers around here!" The gates were closed at once, and guards with nightsticks in their hands drove them away.

The bodyguards released from custody the three ministers that the disturbance was against, and they brought them into heaven. And as soon as the gates were opened for the ministers the joy of marriage breathed out of heaven on the rebels—which almost took their breath away, because it was chaste and pure.

So, for fear of passing out from suffocation, they hurried to the third place, where the judges said the road to hell started. And then the joy of adultery breathed from it, which revived the purposeful adulterers and the confirmed adulterers so much that they went down fairly dancing and plunged into the filth there like pigs.

Chapter 22

Lust for Defloration

501   The lusts that the next four chapters deal with are not just lusts for adultery, but worse, because they are only there on account of adulteries, since they are taken up after adulteries become loathsome—like lust for defloration, to be dealt with first, which cannot begin in someone before that stage, and, similarly, lust for variety, lust for rape, and lust for seducing innocent women, which are dealt with afterwards. They are called lusts because you make them your own according to how much and in what way you lust for them.

    The following topics in a series will clarify what specifically applies to lust for defloration, to make the point clearly that it is a shameful act.

    (1) A virgin's, or inexperienced woman's, condition before marriage and after marriage.

    (2) Virginity is the crown of chastity and a token of married love.

    (3) Defloration without the goal of marriage is the shameful act of a thief.

    (4) After death the fate of those who in their own minds establish that lust for defloration is not a sinful evil is serious.

    An explanation of these topics follows.

502   (1) *A virgin's, or inexperienced woman's, condition before marriage and after marriage.* Wives in the spiritual world showed me clearly, by the example of women there who left the natural world in childhood and were brought up in heaven, what a virgin's state is

like before she is taught the many things that have to do with the beginning of marriage. They said that when they reached a marriageable state they began to love married life by seeing married partners, but only so as to be called wives and to have friendly and trusting companionship with one man, and also have their own rights, away from the obedience of home. And they said they thought about marriage only for the happiness of shared friendship and trust with a male partner, and absolutely not for the allurement of any passion. And after their wedding that virginal state was changed into a new one that they had known nothing about before. And they said this state is a state of expansion of everything in their bodily life, from first to last, to receive what their husband gives them and unite their life with it, to become his love and wife. And they said this state was started by the moment of defloration and after that the flame of love burned only for their husband, and the delights of this expansion felt heavenly. And because a woman was led into this state by her husband, and because it came from him and so it is his in her, she certainly could not help loving him alone.

These remarks make it clear what a virgin's state is like before marriage and after marriage, in heaven. It is no secret that virgins and wives on earth who are married as virgins are the same. What virgin can know that new state before she is in it? Ask, and you'll hear. It is different with those who learn about allurement before marriage.

503   (2) *Virginity is the crown of chastity and a token of married love.* Virginity is called the crown of chastity because virginity crowns the chastity of marriage and is a sign of chastity as well. This is why a wife wears a crown on her head at a wedding. It is also a sign of marriage's holiness. For after a bride gives and consecrates to the bridegroom, then a husband, the bloom of her virginity, she gives and consecrates herself to him, and the husband gives himself to his bride, in turn.

Virginity is also called a token of married love, because it is in the agreement, and the agreement is that married love is to join them into one person, or into one flesh. Before the wedding even the men themselves regard a bride's virginity as the crown of her chastity and a token of married love and as precisely the delicacy where the joy of that love is to begin and last forever. These facts and the preceding ones establish that after her hymen is taken and her virginity tasted a virgin becomes a wife, and if not a wife, a prostitute. For the new state that she is led into then is a state of love for her man, and if not for her man it is a state of sexual desire.

504   (3) *Defloration without the goal of marriage is the shameful act of a thief.* Some adulterers have desire to deflower virgins and therefore also girls at an innocent age. Virgins are enticed into things like that either by the persuasion of madams or gifts from men, or promises of marriage, and the men abandon them after the defloration and search for more and more others. Add to this that they are not interested in past victims but ever new ones, and this desire grows to be the height of their physical pleasure. And they add to these things this villainy—that by different crafty tricks they entice virgins that are about to be married, or are just married, to bestow on them the firstfruits of marriage, which they disgracefully defile in this way. I have also heard that when that lust fails, together with its potency, they glory in their number of virginities as so many golden fleeces of Jason.

This shameful act, violation, remains inrooted and thus engrafted after death, because it is begun at a vigorous age and is reinforced later by boasting. The dimensions of this shameful act emerge from what was said above—that virginity is the crown of chastity, a token of married love to come, and that the virgin who bestows it on a man bestows her soul and life on him. Also, the friendship of marriage and its trust are founded on it. And also, the woman deflowered by someone like that loses her modesty, after this entrance to married love has been broken through, and becomes a harlot. The ravisher is also the cause of this.

If these thieves themselves, after enacting these sexual excesses and profanations of chastity, turn their minds to marriage, they have in mind only the virginity of their married partner-to-be. After they have tried it they loathe bed and bedroom—the whole feminine sex, in fact, except girls.

And, clearly, Divine justice pursues such people because they are violators of marriage with contempt for the feminine sex, and in this way they are spiritual thieves.

505 (4) *After death the fate of those who in their own minds establish that lust for defloration is not a sinful evil is serious.* Here is what happens to them. When they have gone through the first period in the world of spirits—it is a period of modesty and morality, because it is spent in company with angelic spirits—they are brought from their external life into their inner life and then they have the same lusts that enticed them in the world, to see what level the lusts were on, so that if the lusts were on a lesser level the people can be taken away from them after being introduced to them, and be full of shame. But the ones who enjoyed this wicked passion to the extent that they found outstanding joy in it and took pride in these thefts as in rich spoils, will not let themselves be led away from it. So they are released in freedom, and right away they go around looking for brothels, and when these are pointed out to them, in they go. The brothels are at the sides of hell. But when they find only prostitutes there, they go away and ask where there are virgins. And then they are led to prostitutes who by illusion can represent themselves as outstandingly beautiful, with the blushing charm of girls, and pass themselves off as virgins. The men burn for them the same as in the world. So they bargain with these women. But when they are about to go through with the bargain, heaven takes away the illusion, and then those "virgins" appear in all their ugliness—deformed and dark. Still, the men are compelled to stay with them for a short time. These prostitutes are called sirens.

But if the men do not allow themselves to be led away from that insane passion by enchantments like these, they are driven down into a hell on the border between south and west, under the hell of the more cunning prostitutes and are gathered together with their kind. I was even able to see the spirits in that hell, and I was told that there are many there of noble lineage and from wealthy families. But since they were what they were in the world, all memory of lineage and self-respect due to wealth is taken away from them, and they are convinced that they were vile slaves and for that reason not worthy of any respect. Among themselves they do look like humans, but to others who are allowed to look in there they look like apes, with a savage face instead of a seductive one and a frightful expression instead of a suave face. They walk with their groins tucked in, which bends them with their upper part leaning forward as if they are about to fall. And they stink. They loathe the other sex and turn away from females that they see, because they have no desire. This is how they look close up, but from a distance they look like lap dogs, or favorite puppies. And there is also something like barking heard in their voices.

Chapter 23

Lust for Variety

506   The lust for variety dealt with here does not mean the lust for fornication that was treated in its own chapter. Although that lust is apt to be promiscuous and wandering, it still does not lead to a lust for variety except when it goes beyond limits and the fornicator keeps score and eagerly boasts of it. This attitude initiates the present lust. But only a series of statements can show what it is like as it develops. Here is the series:

(1) Lust for variety means a totally unrestricted lust for illicit sex.
(2) This lust is a love, and at the same time a loathing, for the other sex.
(3) This lust totally eliminates the love of marriage in people.
(4) Their fate after death is miserable, since they lack the innermost quality of life.

An explanation of these topics follows.

507   (1) *Lust for variety means a totally unrestricted lust for illicit sex.* This lust steals into people who have loosened the restraints of modesty in adolescence and who did not lack plenty of prostitutes, and, especially, money to be spent in quest of them. They planted and rooted this lust in themselves by disorderly and unlimited fornications, by shameless thinking about love of the feminine sex and by arguments that adulteries are not bad things, and certainly not sins. This lust in them grows as it goes on, until they desire all the women in the world, and until they want crowds of them, and a new one every day.

This lust banishes itself from the general love of the other sex implanted in every person, and totally from love of one member of the other sex—which is married love—and it injects itself into the outer parts of the heart as the delight of a love that is separate from those other loves and yet comes from them. So it becomes rooted in their skin so completely that it stays in their sense of touch after their potency fails.

They make nothing of adulteries, so they think of the whole feminine sex just the way they think of a common prostitute and think of marriage the way they think of common prostitution, so in this way they mix immodesty up with modesty, and they go crazy with the mixture.

These observations make it clear what lust for variety means here—a totally unrestrained lust for illicit sex.

508   (2) *This lust is a love, and at the same time a loathing, for the other sex.* For them this is love for the other sex, because the other sex provides the variety, and it is a loathing for the other sex, because after one taste they abandon a woman and lust for others. This repulsive lust burns for the new woman and, after the heat, grows cold toward her. Coldness is loathing.

Here is how to illustrate that this lust is love for the other sex and loathing at the same time. On the left put a crowd of women they have already enjoyed and on the right a crowd they have not enjoyed. They will view one group with loathing but the other with love, won't they? Yet both groups are members of the feminine sex.

509   (3) *This lust totally eliminates the love of marriage in people.* This is because this lust is totally opposite to married love—so opposite, in fact, that it does not just tear married love up but practically grinds it into dust and thus annihilates it. For married love is directed to one person of the other sex, but this lust does not linger on one woman but in an hour or a day turns as frigid toward her as it was ardent before. Coldness is loathing, so living together and dalliance under compulsion piles up the loathing *ad nauseam*, so that married love is eaten away to the point where there is none of it left.

These observations will show that this lust is the extermination of married love. Married love forms the innermost thing in a person's life, so this lust is the extermination of his life, and it finally becomes only skin-deep, through gradual blockages and closings of the inner parts of his mind, so it becomes just an enticement, though the faculty of understanding, or rationality, remains.

510 (4) *Their fate after death is miserable, since they lack the innermost quality of life.* The excellence of any man's life is in keeping with his love of marriage, because this links up with the life of his wife and is heightened by the association. But in these people not a scrap of the love for marriage is left, and therefore nothing of innermost life, so their lot after death is miserable. After going through a period of time existing in their outward personalities, in which they speak rationally and act civil, they are transferred into their inner qualities, and then they have the same lust as in the world and take the same pleasures in it. For after death everyone is placed in the same state of life that he has adopted as his own, so that he can be led out of it. No one can be led out of his evil without first being led into it. Otherwise the evil would conceal itself and pollute the deeper parts of his mind, spread like a disease, and then break down the bars and ruin the outward parts belonging to his body.

For this purpose brothels are opened to them, at the side of hell. They get a chance to try all their lusts with harlots there. But this is allowed with one a day and is forbidden with more than one on the same day, under penalty. Later, when the lust proves to have been so ingrained in them that they cannot be led out of it, they are taken to a certain place just above the hell that will receive them, and they seem to themselves as if they are passing out, and to others they seem to be sinking, faceup. And the ground actually does open under their backs, and they are swallowed up and sink into a hell where the likes of them are. So they are gathered to their own.

I was allowed to see them there, and to talk with them, too. To each other they look like people, which appearance they are granted so as not to terrify their associates. But from a distance they appear with expressionless white faces as if made of just skin, and this is because there is no spiritual life in them, which everyone has according to the principles of marriage implanted in him. Their speech is dry, parched, and sad. When they are hungry they moan, and their moans sound like a strange-sounding murmur. They have torn clothes, and pants pulled up over their stomachs, around their chests, because they have no groins, but their ankles start at the bottom of their stomachs. The reason is that people's waists correspond to the love in marriage, and they do not have this. They said that they loathe the other sex because they have no potency. They can still argue among themselves about various things, as if with reason, but they argue on the basis of the tricks the senses play, because they are skin-deep people.

This hell is in the western quarter, towards the north.

From a long distance these same people look like neither people nor monsters but like snowmen.

But note that this happens to the ones who have been steeped in that lust to such a degree that they have torn to pieces the human principle of marriage in themselves and have annihilated it.

Chapter 24

Lust for Rape

511   Lust for rape does not mean lust for defloration. Lust for defloration is lust to violate virginity, not the virgins, when it is done with consent. But the lust for rape this chapter is about is turned off by consent and is excited by a protest. It is a burning desire to violate any women who flatly refuse and violently resist—virgins, widows, or wives. Rapists are like thieves and pirates who delight in plunder and spoils, not gifts and honest gains. And they are like criminals who stare at unlawful and forbidden things greedily and despise things that are permissible and lawful.

     These rapists are totally turned off by consent and are set afire by resistance. If they notice that it is surface resistance, the flame of their lust goes out at once, like a fire with water thrown on it.

     It is well known that wives do not submit willingly to their husbands' will when it comes to the physical acts of love, and that they prudently resist them like violations, in order to take away from their husbands the coldness that comes from something that is routine and always allowed, and also from a notion about these things being lascivious. Though these protests do inflame, they are not the cause of the present lust but are only what starts it up. The cause of it is that after married love, and also illicit love, are worn out from use, rapists like to be set afire by complete resistance in order to recover.

     This lust, begun in this way, then grows, and as it grows it scorns and breaks all limits of love for the other sex, exterminates itself, and changes from a wanton physical and fleshly love into one like cartilage and bone. And then, due to the membrane on bone, which is acutely sensitive, it becomes violent.

But yet this lust is rare, because it only occurs in those who have entered marriage and then indulged in illicit sex until it has worn them out.

Besides this worldly cause of this lust there is also a spiritual cause. Something will be said about it in what follows.

512   This is what happens to rapists after death. At that time they willingly separate themselves from people who practice a limited love of the other sex, and certainly from those with married love— that is, from heaven. Then they are sent to very clever prostitutes who can characterize and portray the part of chastity itself not only by persuasion but by completely theatrical acting. These prostitutes can tell very well who has that lust. They talk in the rapists' presence about chastity and how precious it is, and when a rapist approaches and touches them they flare up and flee as if in terror to their room where a bed and mattress are, close the door after themselves, but not all the way, and lie down. In this way they use their skill to inflame the rapist with an unbridled passion to burst through the door, rush in, and assault them. When he does this the prostitute gets up and begins to fight the rapist with her fists and nails, tearing his face, ripping his clothes, screaming in a frantic voice to the other prostitutes for help, as if to the servants, and opening the window and shouting, "Thief! Robber! Murderer!" When the rapist is in the act she laments and weeps, and after the rape she throws herself down, wails, and cries, "Unspeakable!" And then in a hostile tone she threatens that she will find a way to ruin him unless he atones for the rape with a big payment.

When they are engaged in this theatrical sex they look, from a distance, like cats, which fight, charge, and wail before mating in practically the same way.

After a few brothel fights like this rapists are taken away and moved to a cave, where they are forced to do some job. But they stink because they have shattered the principle of marriage, which is the precious treasure of human life, so they are sent away to the borders of a western region. There they look, at a certain distance, emaciated as if made of bones with just skin stretched over them, but from far away they look like panthers.

When I had a chance to see them closer up I was surprised that some of them had books in their hands and were reading. I was told that this is because in the world they talked a lot about spiritual matters having to do with the church, and yet they completely defiled them by their adulteries, and this is how their lust corresponds to violation of spiritual marriage.

But note that few people are in the grip of this lust. Certainly women do resist now and then because it is not proper for them to be public about their love, and their resistance does excite, but this excitement certainly does not come from any lust for rape.

Chapter 25

Lust for Seducing
Innocent Women

513   Lust for seducing innocent women is not a lust for defloration nor a lust for rape but is distinct and unique in its own right. It is found especially in crafty men. Women who seem innocent to them are ones that consider the evil of fornication a great sin so that they are devoted to chastity and piety both at once. Seducers are inflamed for these women. In countries with the Catholic religion they are the virgins in monasteries. Because these men think them the most pious, innocent women of all, they consider them the sweets and delicacies of their lust. They are crafty, so in order to seduce these women or others, they first study out strategies, and after they steep their talents in the strategies they apply them as if it came naturally, without any shame to hold them back. Their strategies are especially pretenses of innocence, love, chastity, and piety.

        By these arts and other tricks they gain the women's deep friendship and from that their love, and they change it from a spiritual love into a worldly one by persuasion and pretense of various kinds, and then into a physical one with their body, by enticements. And then they have possession of them when they want. After doing all this their hearts are happy, and they joke about the women they have violated.

514   What happens to these seducers after death is sad, because the seduction is not just ungodly but malicious as well. They go through an initial period, involved in superficial things, with more elegant manners and more smooth-talking speech than others. Then they are reduced to the second period of their life, which

involves their inner qualities. In this period their lust is set at liberty and begins its role. Only then are they led to women who have taken the vow of chastity. Among these women they are tested to see how malicious their desire is, so that they will not be judged without clear proof. When they notice these women's chastity their trickery goes into action, and they ply their skills. But it is useless, so they leave the women.

Then they are brought to women of an innocent nature. When they try to deceive these women the same way, the women have a power that heavily penalizes them, for they induce a heavy numbness on their hands and feet, as well as their necks, and finally make them feel that they are passing out. While they are going through this, the women escape from them.

After all this a path opens for them to a certain gathering of harlots who have learned how to imitate innocence skillfully. First these harlots joke at them among themselves and then let themselves be seduced, after various promises.

After a few scenes like these, the third period sets in—a period of judgment. Then the guilty ones sink down and are gathered to their likes in a hell that is in a northern region. From a distance there they look like weasels. But if they have been preoccupied with deceit, they are taken from here down to the hell of frauds, which is in a western region below and behind. Here they resemble, from a distance, various kinds of snakes, and the most deceitful look like vipers. But within the hell itself, which I had an opportunity to look into, they looked ghastly to me, with chalky faces.

They are nothing but selfish desires, so they are not fond of talking, and if they do talk they only mumble and murmur various things that no one understands but the companions next to them. But as soon as they sit or stand they make themselves invisible and fly around the cavern like ghosts, for then they are in fantasies, and fantasy seems to fly. After flying they alight, and then, surprisingly, they do not recognize one another. The reason for this is that they are preoccupied with trickery, and trickery does not believe anyone else and sneaks away.

When these people detect anything having to do with married love they escape into caves and hide. They have no love of the other sex and are impotency itself. They are called spirits of hell.

Chapter 26

How Illicit Sex Corresponds to Profanation of Spiritual Marriage

515   I could say something first about what correspondence is, but it is not the subject of this book. But what correspondence is, is found briefly summarized above (nos. 76 and 342), and *Apocalypse Revealed*, from start to finish, fully explains that there is correspondence between the worldly sense and the spiritual sense of the Word. *The Doctrine for the New Jerusalem Concerning the Sacred Scriptures* shows that there is a worldly sense and a spiritual sense in the Word and correspondence between these senses (specifically in nos. 5–26 there).

516   Spiritual marriage means the marriage of the Lord and the church (see nos. 116–31, above) and therefore also marriage of good and truth (also mentioned above, nos. 83–102), and because this is a marriage of the Lord and the church and therefore a marriage of good and truth, it is in each and every thing in the Word. It is violation of this that violation of spiritual marriage means here, for the church is from the Word, and the Word is the Lord. The Lord is the Word, because He is the Divine Good and Divine Truth in it. You can see it fully established in *Doctrine for the New Jerusalem Concerning the Sacred Scriptures* (nos. 80–90) that the Word is that marriage.

517   So, since violation of spiritual marriage is violation of the Word, it is clear that this violation is adulteration of good and falsification of truth. For spiritual marriage is marriage of good and truth, as was said. Consequently, adulterating the good and falsifying the

truth of the Word violates that marriage. Who does this violence, and how, will be fairly clear from the remarks that follow.

518   Where the marriage of the Lord and the Church (nos. 116 ff.) and the marriage of good and truth (nos. 83 ff.) were dealt with it showed that that marriage corresponds to marriages on earth. As a consequence of this, violation of that marriage corresponds to illicit sex and adultery. It is obvious from the Word itself that this is so, in that the illicit sexual acts and adulteries there stand for falsifications of truth and adulterations of good, as is easy to see in the many passages brought together from the Word in *Apocalypse Revealed*, no. 134.

519   Those in the Christian church who adulterate the good things and the truths of the Word violate it. And those who separate truth from good and good from truth do this. So do the ones who take apparent truths, and falsities, for real truths and confirm them, and also people who know the truths of instruction from the Word and live evilly, and others like that. These violations of the Word and church correspond to the levels of adultery prohibited in Leviticus 18.

520   The worldly and the spiritual levels in any person are united like soul and body, for without the spiritual influence that gives life to the part of him in nature he is not a person. Consequently, someone who is in spiritual marriage is also in a happy earthly marriage and vice versa; someone who is involved in spiritual adultery is also involved in earthly adultery, and the other way around. Now, everyone in hell is in a marriage of the evil and the false, and this is spiritual adultery itself. And everyone who is in heaven is in a marriage of good and truth, and this is marriage itself. Therefore all of hell is called adultery, and all of heaven is called marriage.

521   The following story will be added to these remarks.

My eyes were opened, and I saw a dark forest and a crowd of satyrs in it. The satyrs had hairy chests, some had feet like calves, some like panthers, and some like wolves, and they had the claws of wild animals on their feet in place of toes. They were running around like wild beasts and shouting, "Where are the women?" And then prostitutes appeared, who were waiting for them. They, too, were deformed in various ways. The satyrs ran up and grabbed them and dragged them into a cave deep under ground in the forest. On the ground around the cave lay a huge snake wound in a coil. It breathed its venom into the cave. In the branches of the trees above the snake eerie night birds were croaking and screeching. But the satyrs and prostitutes did not see these creatures because they were the embodiments of their lascivious acts, so that was their normal appearance from a distance.

Afterwards they came out of the cave and went into a small shack that was a brothel, and then they talked among themselves apart from the prostitutes. I listened in—for you can hear conversation from a distance in the spiritual world, as if you were right there, for space there only seems to have extent. They were talking about marriages, nature, and religion.

The ones that seemed to have feet like calves talked about marriages and said, "What are marriages but licensed adulteries? And what is sweeter than the hypocrisies of illicit sex and of deceiving husbands?" The others clapped their hands, laughing at these words.

The satyrs that seemed to have feet like panthers talked about nature and said, "What is there besides nature? What difference is there between man and beast except that a person can put words together and an animal puts sounds together? With nature at work, don't both have life from heat and intellect from light?" At this the others shouted, "Ah! You're talking sense!"

The ones that seemed to have feet like wolves talked about religion, saying, "What is God or Divinity but the most inner workings of nature? What is religion but an invention to capture and shackle the common people?" The others shouted "Bravo!" at this.

A few moments later they came spilling out, and as they did they saw me at a distance watching them. They ran out of the woods, provoked by this, and rushed up to me with threatening looks. They said, "Why do you stand there listening to what we're whispering?"

"Why not?" I answered. "What's to stop me? It was talk," and I repeated what I had heard from them. This settled their temper because they were afraid it might get around, and then they began to speak humbly and act virtuous. I could tell from this that they were not your common people but of more worthy birth. And then I told them how I saw them looking like satyrs in the woods—twenty like calf satyrs, six like panther satyrs, and four like wolf satyrs. There were thirty of them.

This surprised them, because to themselves they didn't look like anything but people there—the way they saw themselves here with me.

I explained that they looked that way from a distance due to lust for illicit sex and that this satyr form is the image of far-gone adultery and not the form of a person. "This is the reason," I said. "Every evil desire produces its likeness in some form, not visible to the one himself but to those standing at a distance." I said, "So you'll believe this, send some of you into the woods while you stay here and watch."

They did it and sent two, and near the brothel shack they saw them just like satyrs. When the satyrs came back they greeted them and said, "Oh, did you look funny!"

While they were laughing I joked about different things with them and told how I had even seen adulterers look like pigs. Then I thought of the myth about Ulysses and Circe—how she sprinkled Ulysses' companions and servants with witch's herbs, touched them with a magic wand, and changed them into swine, or maybe into adulterers, because no art can turn anyone into a pig.

After they finished laughing at this and similar stories I asked if they knew what countries they came from in the world.

They said, "Several," and named Italy, Poland, Germany, England, and Sweden.

I asked if they had seen anyone from the Netherlands among them, and they said, "Not one."

After this I turned the conversation to serious matters again and asked, "Did you ever think that adultery is a sin?"

"What's a sin?" they said. "We don't know what it is."

I asked, "Do you ever recall that adultery is against the seventh commandment of the Decalogue?"

They answered, "What's the Decalogue? Isn't it a catechism? What do we men have to do with that childish little tablet?"

I asked if they had ever thought about hell at all.

They answered, "Who has come up from there to tell about it?"

I asked if they had any idea about life after death while in the world.

"That it's no different than for animals," they said, "and maybe like the 'ghosts' that dissipate if dead bodies exhale them."

I went on to ask if they had heard anything from ministers about these questions.

They answered that they only paid attention to the ministers' tone of voice and not what they were discussing. "And what is it?"

Stunned by these answers I said to them, "Turn your faces and eyes to the middle of the woods, where the cave is that you were in."

They turned and saw the huge snake coiled around it, breathing venom into it and also the eerie birds in the branches over it, and I asked, "What do you see?"

But they were terrified and did not answer.

I said, "Didn't you see something horrible? Be advised that this is a representation of adultery in the shameful act of its lust."

Then, all at once, an angel was standing there. He was a minister, and he opened up a hell in a western region where people like that are finally gathered together. He said, "Look there." They saw a swamp like fire, and in it they recognized some of their friends from earth, who invited them to join them.

After seeing and hearing these things they turned away and rushed out of my sight, away from the woods. But I watched where they went. They pretended to go away, but in roundabout ways they were returning to the woods.

522   After this I went back home. A day later, remembering those sad events, I looked toward that woods, and it had disappeared. In its place was a sandy field with a swamp in it, where there were some red snakes. But weeks later when I again looked there, I saw to the right side of it a plowed field and some farmers in it. And again, weeks later, I saw the field sprouting, and surrounded with trees. Then I heard a voice from the sky, "Go to your room, close the door, and turn to the work you began about the Apocalypse. Follow through and finish it in less than two years."

Chapter 27

Bearing the Guilt for Illicit Love
and
Receiving Credit for Married Love

523   The Lord says, "Do not judge, so you will not be judged" (Matt. 7:1). In no way can this be taken to be judgment of anyone's moral and civil life in the world, but judgment of someone's spiritual and heavenly life. Who does not see that if judging the moral life of people we live with in the world were not allowed, society would collapse? What would society be without public justice and without each person's own judgment of another? But judging what the inner mind, or soul in him is like, that is, what his spiritual condition is like and therefore what happens to him after death—judging this is not allowed, because the Lord alone knows it. Nor does the Lord reveal this until after death, so that everyone can do in freedom what he does, and in this way good or bad can be from him and thus in him—which lets him live in himself and be his own person to eternity.

The things inside your mind, hidden in the world, are revealed after death, because this is in the interest of the community that the person enters at that time and is useful to it, for everyone there is spiritual. That these things are revealed at that time is clear from these words of the Lord:

Nothing is covered that will not be unveiled nor hidden that will not be known. So whatever you have spoken in the dark shall be heard in the light, and what you have whispered in someone's ear in the closets will be shouted from the house-tops. (Luke 12:2–3)

A general judgment is all right, like this: "If you are inwardly as you appear outwardly, you'll be saved," or, "you'll be damned." But a particular judgment is not allowable, such as, "You are inwardly such-and-such, so you'll be saved," or, "you'll be damned."

The subject here is *imputation,* which means judgment of a person's spiritual life, or the inner reaches of his soul. What person knows who is at heart a fornicator and who is at heart a spouse? Yet it is the thoughts of the heart, which are the intentions of choice, that judge every person.

But these subjects will be developed in this order:

(1) After death everyone is held responsible for the bad he is dedicated to. Likewise the good.
(2) It is impossible to consign the good of one person to another.
(3) If *imputation* means consigning one person's good to another, it is a meaningless word.
(4) Everyone's evil is imputed to him in keeping with what his desire is like and in keeping with what his intellect is like. Likewise his good.
(5) It is in this way that illicit love is held against someone.
(6) The same goes for married love.

An explanation of these topics follows.

524   (1) *After death everyone is held responsible for the bad he is dedicated to. Likewise the good.* To make this reasonably clear, it will be examined point by point, like this: (a) Everyone has his own particular life. (b) Everyone's life stays with him after death. (c) Then the evil of a bad person's life is imputed to him, and the good of a good person's life is imputed to him.

(a) It is well known that everyone has his own particular life—that is, separate from anyone else's—for there is constant variety and no two things are the same. This gives each person his own selfhood. This is strikingly clear from people's faces. No one's face is absolutely the same as another person's, nor can it be

502 ⋄ Chapter 27

to eternity. The reason is that there are no identical minds, and faces come from minds. Due to this, a face, as they say, is an image of the mind, and your mind takes its origin and form from your life. If a person did not have his own life, as he has his own mind and his own face, he could not have any life after death separate from another's. Indeed, there would be no heaven, for heaven is made up of more people all the time. Its form is only from varieties of souls and minds arranged in such an order that they make one thing, and they make one thing on account of the One whose life is in each and every one there, like a soul in a person. If this were not so, heaven would be scattered, because its form would be dissolved. The One that each and every one's life is from, and on account of whom the form holds together, is the Lord. Every form generally is made up of various things, and it takes its character from the way they are harmoniously coordinated and arranged into the one form. The human form is like this. This is why a person, made up of so many members, tissues, and organs, feels nothing but unity in himself and about himself.

(b) It is well known in the church that everyone's life stays with him after death, because of the Word, and because of these passages in it. "The Son of man is going to come, and then He will reward each person according to his works" (Matt. 16:27). "I saw the books opened, and everyone was judged according to his works" (Rev. 20:12–13). "On the day of judgment God rewards everyone according to his works" (Rom. 2:6; 2 Cor. 5:10). The works that everyone is rewarded according to are his life, because his life does them, and they are in keeping with his life.

Because I have had the opportunity to be together with angels for many years, and to talk with arrivals from the world, I can testify for certain that each person is examined there as to what kind of life he had, and that the life he put together in the world stays with him forever. I have talked with people who lived ages ago, whose lives I knew about from histories, and I recognized the likeness from description. And I have heard from angels that no one's life can be changed after death, because it is structured according to the person's love and what he has done on account of it, and if it were changed its structure would be mangled, which can never be done. In addition, I have heard from angels that a change in structure is possible only in a material body and not at all possible in a spiritual body, after the material one is cast off.

(c) Then the evil of a bad person's life is imputed to him, and the good of a good person's life is imputed to him. The imputation of evil is not a complaint, prosecution, guilty verdict, and sentencing as in the world, but the evil itself accomplishes this. For evil people separate themselves from the good people of their own free will, since they cannot be together. The delights of an evil love are repulsed by the delights of a good love, and each person gives off his delights, like the odors from every plant in the world, because the delights are not absorbed and hidden by a material body as before, but they flow freely from the people's loves into the spiritual air. And since evil is perceived by its odor there, this is what accuses, prosecutes, gives a guilty verdict, and sentences— not before any judge but before anyone who is living a life of good. This is what imputation means. Besides, an evil person chooses the friends he lives with in his kind of joy, and because he turns his back on the enjoyment of good, he joins his own kind in hell, of his own free will.

Imputation of good happens the same way. This happens to those who acknowledged in the world that all the good in them is from the Lord and none from themselves. When they are ready they are launched on the inner joys of good, and then a path to heaven is opened for them, to a community where the joys are the same kind as theirs. The Lord does this.

525   (2) *It is impossible to consign the good of one person to another.* The evidence of this can also be seen one thing at a time, like this: (a) Every human is born with evil. (b) The Lord leads him into good through rebirth. (c) This is done through a life according to His teachings. (d) So the good implanted this way cannot be consigned to someone else.

(a) It is well known in the church that every person is born with evil. They say that this evil is inherited from Adam, but it is from your parents. You get your disposition, which is your inclination, from them. Reason and experience persuade that this is so, for similarities to parents in face, talents, and behavior come out in their near and distant descendants. Many people know families by this and form opinions about their minds. So the evils that the parents themselves have built up and implanted in their children by passing them on are the ones that people are born with. People think that Adam's sin is etched on the whole human race because few look into any evil in themselves and come to know it by that means. Therefore they suppose that it is so deeply hidden that only God sees it.

(b) The Lord leads a person into good through rebirth. It is clear from the Lord's words in John 3:3, 5 that there is regeneration and that you cannot march into heaven without being remade. It can be no secret in the Christian world that rebirth is purification from evils and thus a renewal of life, for reason sees this, too, when it accepts that everyone is born with evil and that evil cannot be washed away and wiped off with soap and water like dirt, but must be cleansed with repentance.

(c) The Lord leads a person into good by life according to His teachings. There are five teachings about rebirth (seen above, no. 82). Among them are: avoid bad acts because they are the devil's and are from the devil, and do good acts because they are God's and are from God, and approach the Lord so that He can lead people to the doing of those things. Anyone can consider in his own mind and decide if man has good from anywhere else. And if he does not have good, he does not have salvation.

(d) When this good is implanted it cannot be consigned to someone else. Consigning means transferring one person's good to another. It follows from the things said above that by rebirth a person is totally renewed in spirit, and this happens through a life according to the Lord's teachings. Who cannot see that this new beginning can only be done with time and in time, hardly different from the way a tree roots and grows from a seed and becomes a full-grown tree? People who see rebirth any other way know nothing about the human condition, and nothing about bad and good—that these two are totally opposite and that good can be implanted only so far as evil is removed. Nor do they know that so long as someone is preoccupied with evil he has his back turned to any good that is good in its own right. So if someone's good were transferred to anyone preoccupied with evil, it would be like tossing a sheep to a wolf or tying a pearl to a pig's nose. From all this it is clear that transferring good is impossible.

526   (3) *If imputation means consigning one person's good to another,
it is a meaningless word.* It shows above (no. 524) that the evil anyone is preoccupied with is attributed to him after death, and likewise the good. This establishes what imputation means. But if
imputation means transferring good into anyone who is preoccupied with evil, it is a meaningless word because it is impossible,
as was also pointed out already (no. 525).

People in the world can consign merit in a way—can do
kindness to children for their parents' sake or to the friends of
some client as a favor. Yet the good of the kindness cannot be
inscribed on people's souls but only attached outwardly. Something like this cannot be granted to people as far as their spiritual
life goes. As was shown above, this has to be implanted. If it is not
implanted through a life of following the Lord's teachings mentioned above, a person remains preoccupied with the evil he was
born with. Before this is done no good can get to him, and if it does
strike him it bounces off and recoils like a rubber ball hitting a
rock, or it is swallowed up like a diamond thrown into a swamp.

A person who is not reformed in his spirit is like a panther
or an owl and is comparable to briars and nettles, but a reborn
person is like a sheep or doves and is comparable to an olive tree
and a vine. Please think, if you will, how a panther-man can be
changed to a sheep-man, or an owl into a dove, or briars into an
olive tree, or nettles into a vine, by some kind of imputation, if
that means consignment. For the change to take place, would not
the wildness of the panther and the owl, or the harmfulness of the
briars and nettles, first have to be removed and the truly human
and truly harmless implanted that way? In John (15:1–7) the Lord
teaches how this is done.

527   (4) *Everyone's evil is imputed to him in keeping with what his
desire is like and in keeping with what his intellect is like. Likewise his
good.* It is well known that there are two things that make a person's
life—will and intellect—and that all the things a person does come
from his will and his intellect, and that without these active forces
a person would not have action or speech different from a machine.
This makes it clear that what a person is like in his will and
intellect is what he is like. And also, a person's actions in their
own right are like the desire of his will, which produces the act,

and a person's speech, in its own right, is like the intellect of his thought, which produces it. So two or more people can act and speak alike and still be acting and speaking differently—one from a vicious desire and thought and another from an upright desire and thought.

These observations establish what the "acts" or "works" that anyone is judged by mean—his intent and his comprehension. So "evil actions" means actions of an evil will, whatever they may seem like outwardly. And "good works" means works of a good will, even though they might seem the same outwardly as the works of an evil person.

All the things that are done from a person's inner desire are done on purpose, since that desire plans to do what its intention carries out. And all the things he does from his intellect he does from confirmation, since intellect confirms. These observations can establish that good or bad is credited to anyone according to what kind of intention is behind the acts, and according to what kind of understanding is behind them.

Let us confirm these things. In the spiritual world I have encountered many people who lived like others in the natural world, dressing splendidly, eating in style, doing profitable business like others, seeing plays, joking about love affairs as if with pleasure, and other things just like that, and yet angels condemned these things as sinful evils in some of them and did not condemn them as sins in others. They pronounced the first group guilty and the other innocent. To the question why it was like that, even though both did the same things, the angels answered that they size everyone up by his plan, intention, and aim and separate people according to those things, and so they excuse or condemn those whose aim excuses or condemns, since everyone in heaven has a good end in view and everyone in hell has a bad end in view.

528   This is added: In the church they say that no one can fulfill the law—all the less because someone who breaks one commandment of the Decalogue breaks them all. But this catch phrase is not what it sounds like, because, you see, someone who acts against one commandment on purpose and in confirmation acts against the others, since to act on purpose and in confirmation is to fully deny that it is a sin, and whoever denies that it is a sin thinks

nothing of it if he acts against the other commandments. Who does not know that being an adulterer does not make a person a murderer, a thief, and a false witness—or want to be. But someone who is a confirmed adulterer on purpose makes nothing of anything related to religion, thus not murder, not theft, not false witness, and he keeps from doing them not because they are sins but because he is afraid of the law and fears for his reputation. (Nos. 490–93, above, and the two stories, nos. 500 and 521–22, show that confirmed adulterers who commit adultery on purpose count the holy things of the church and religion as nothing.) It is the same if someone acts against one of the other commandments of the Decalogue on purpose or in confirmation. He acts against the rest as well, because he does not consider anything a sin.

529   It is just the same with those who are preoccupied with good from the Lord. If they willingly and with understanding, or, on purpose and with confirmation, keep from doing one bad thing because it is a sin, they keep from doing them all—the more so if they keep from more than one. For as soon as someone purposely and in confirmation keeps from committing some evil because it is a sin, the Lord keeps him to the intention of abstaining from the others. So if he does evil because of ignorance or as a result of being overcome by some bodily drive, it is not held against him even so, because he did not plan it on his own nor confirm it in himself. A person acquires this resolution if he examines himself once or twice a year and repents of the evil that he discovers in himself. It is different with a person who never examines himself.

    These observations make it obvious who is not blamed for sin and who is.

530   (5) *It is in this way that illicit love is held against someone*—namely, not according to the things done, as they appear outwardly before people—in fact, not as they appear before a judge—but as they appear inwardly before the Lord and by Him before angels, that is, according to what kind of desire and understanding the person put into them. In the world, there are different circumstances that soften and excuse crimes and also that make them more serious and more blameworthy. And yet accusations after death are not made according to the outward circumstances of

the act but according to inner mental circumstances. And these are viewed according to the condition of the church in each person. Take, for example, a person who is ungodly in his will and intellect, who does not fear God and has no love for his neighbor, and therefore has no reverence for anything holy related to the church. After death he becomes guilty of all the crimes he did on earth, and no remembrance is made of his good acts, since his heart, which his actions sprang from like a fountain, was turned away from heaven and turned toward hell, and actions flow out from the place where someone's heart lives.

To clarify this, I shall tell something unknown. Heaven is divided into countless communities. So is hell, opposite it. And the mind of every person is actually living in a community that suits his desire and therefore his intellect. What he wants to do and thinks about is like what the people there do. If his mind is in some community in heaven, he wills and thinks like the angels there. If it is in some community in hell, he wills and thinks like the spirits there. But so long as a person lives in the world his mind moves from one community to another according to changes in the feelings of his will and the thoughts of his mind from them. But after death his wanderings are all brought together, and from the whole collection he is assigned a place—if evil, in hell, if good, in heaven. Now, because everyone in hell has an evil will, everyone there is regarded in the light of that, and because everyone in heaven has a good will, everyone in heaven is regarded in the light of that. So imputations after death are made in keeping with what each one's intention and understanding are like.

It is this way with extramarital loves, whether they are plain fornications, or keeping a mistress, or having a concubine, or adulteries, because these are attributed to each one not according to the acts, but according to the state of his mind in the acts. For the acts go to the grave with the body, but the mind rises again.

531   (6) *Married love is attributed to each this way.* There are marriages in which married love does not appear, and yet it is there, and there are marriages in which married love appears to be and yet is not. There are many reasons why, to be found out partly

from the discussions of real married love (nos. 57–73), of the reasons for coldness and separations (nos. 234–60), and of the reasons for pretenses of love and friendship in marriages (nos. 271–92). But outward appearances demonstrate nothing in fixing blame or merit. The only thing that counts is the principle of marriage that is settled in anyone's desire and protected, whatever married condition the person is in. That principle of marriage is like the balance in which that love is weighed. For the marriage principle of one man with one wife is the precious treasure of human life and the treasury of the Christian religion (as shown above, nos. 457–58). And because it is like this, that love can be found in one marriage and at the same time not in another. And that love can lie too deeply hidden for the person himself to notice it at all. And also, it can be inscribed as his life goes on. The reason is that that love goes in step with religion, and religion is the marriage of the Lord and the church, so it initiates and implants that love. So married love is attributed to someone after death according to the rational life of his spirit. And one whom that love is implanted in is provided a marriage in heaven after death, whatever kind of marriage he had in the world.

This conclusion now comes out of these points: You cannot decide from appearances of marriage, nor from appearances of illicit sex, whether someone has married love or not. Therefore "do not judge, so you will not be judged" (Matt. 7:1).

532   I add to this a story.

In spirit I was once whisked up into the angelic heaven and into one of its communities, and then some of the wise people there came up to me and said, "What's new from the earth?"

"This is new," I told them. "The Lord has revealed unknown things that surpass the mysteries revealed from the beginning of the church until now!"

"What are they?" they asked.

I said that they are these: (a) That in all the things in the Word, including its details, there is a spiritual meaning that corresponds to the earthly meaning, and that through this meaning a person in the church is joined to the Lord and is in companionship with angels, and that the holiness of the Word resides in this spiritual content. (b) That the correspondences that the spiritual content of the Word consists of have been disclosed.

The angels asked, "Didn't the world's inhabitants know about the correspondences before this?"

"Not a thing," I said. "They've lain hidden for several thousand years now—certainly since the time of Job. And among the people who lived at that time and before it, knowledge of correspondences was the knowledge of knowledges. It gave them wisdom, because from it they had a grasp of things having to do with heaven and therefore with the church. But that knowledge turned into idolatry, so it was wiped out, thanks to the Lord's Divine Providence, and lost, so no one has seen a trace of it. And yet the Lord has now disclosed it to make a connection with Him for people in the church, and companionship with angels. This is done through the Word, where everything, including the details, are correspondences."

The angels were very much delighted that the Lord saw fit to reveal this great unknown fact, so deeply hidden through so many thousands of years, and they said, "This is for the purpose of reviving the Christian church, which is based on the Word and is now at its end, so it can be revived by the Lord through heaven."

They asked if this knowledge discloses today what baptism and the Holy Supper—which there have been so many different opinions about till now—stand for.

I answered that it is disclosed.

I went on to say: (c) "At this day the Lord has revealed the facts about life after death."

The angels said, "What about life after death? Who doesn't know that a person lives after death?"

"They know," I said, "and they don't know. They say it's not the person but his soul, and that it lives as a spirit, and they foster a notion of a spirit like a wind or atmosphere, and that the person does not live until after the Last Judgment Day. And they think that then the parts of the body they left behind in the world will be gathered again and put back together into a body, even though eaten by worms, mice, and fish, and that this is the way people are to be resurrected."

The angels said, "What is this? Who doesn't know that a person lives after death as a person, with the only difference that he lives as a spiritual person, and that a spiritual person sees a spiritual person just the way a material person sees a material person? And that they know not one difference, except that they are in a more perfect condition?"

The angels asked, (d) "What do they know about our world and about heaven and hell?"

I said, "They know nothing, but at this day the Lord has disclosed what the world where angels and spirits live is like—that is, what heaven is like and what hell is like. Also that angels and spirits are associated with people. As well as many remarkable things about them."

The angels were glad that the Lord was pleased to disclose things like that to keep people from being in doubt about their immortality any longer due to ignorance.

I told them further, (e) "The Lord has revealed at this day that there is a different Sun in your world than in ours, and that your world's Sun is pure love and our world's sun is mere fire. And that therefore everything that radiates from your Sun, because it is pure love, brings something of life, and everything that radiates from ours, because it is mere fire, brings nothing of life. And that this is where the difference between spiritual and natural comes from—a difference unknown till now, which has also been disclosed. This tells where the light that lights human intellect is from and where the heat that kindles the human will with love is from. And besides, (f) it is disclosed that there are three levels of life, so there are three heavens, and the human mind is divided into three levels, and so a person corresponds to the three heavens."

The angels said, "Didn't they know this before?"

I answered that they know about levels between more and less but nothing about the levels between what comes before and after in order.

The angels asked (g) if more things than those have been revealed.

"Many," I said, "about the Last Judgment, about the Lord—that He is God of heaven and earth, that God is one person and essence with the Divine Trinity in it, and that He is the Lord—

also about the New Church established by Him, and about the teachings of that church, about the holiness of Sacred Scripture. Also that the Book of Revelation has been explained, of which not one tiny verse could have been revealed except by the Lord. Moreover, about the inhabitants of the planets and the earths in the universe. Also many noteworthy and amazing things from the spiritual world. By all this many things that have to do with wisdom have been disclosed from heaven."

533   Hearing these things made the angels very glad, but they noticed sadness in me and asked, "What's making you sad?"

I said, "Those unknown things the Lord has revealed at this day are considered on earth to be worthless, even though they are more important, and are worth more, than the things everyone knew before."

The angels were amazed at this and asked the Lord to let them look down into the world. They looked down and saw total darkness there! And they were told to write the unknown things on a paper and drop the paper onto Earth, and they would see an omen. It was done, and the paper with the unknown things written on it dropped from heaven, and on the way it shined like a star in the spiritual world, but when it fell into the natural world the light was diffused, and as it fell it was gradually lost in the darkness. And when the angels dropped it into groups where there were scholars and learned people, some of them clerics and laymen, you could hear many of them muttering these words, "What's this? Is it anything? What does it matter if we know these things or not? They're someone's bright idea, aren't they?" And it seemed as if some of them took the paper, folded it, and rolled it in their fingers to rub out the writing. And it seemed as if some wanted to tear it up, and some seemed to want to stamp on it with their feet. But the Lord kept them from that outrage, and the angels were told to bring it back and guard it. This experience made the angels sad, and they were thinking, "How long will this last?" So someone said, "Until a time and times and half a time" (Rev. 12:14).

534   After this I discussed with the angels something else the Lord revealed in the world.

"What is it?" they said.

I said, "It has to do with the real love in marriage and its celestial joy."

The angels said, "Who doesn't know that the joy of married love surpasses the joy of all other loves? And who can't see that all blessings, happiness, and enjoyments that the Lord could ever bestow are gathered in that love, and that real married love is what receives them? It can receive them and feel them fully."

I answered that they do not know this, because they have not approached the Lord and lived according to His teachings, avoiding evils as sins and doing good things. And the real love in marriage, with its joys, is only from the Lord and is given to those who live by His teachings—that is, it is given to those who are received into the Lord's new church, which is what is meant by the "New Jerusalem" in the Book of Revelation.

I added to this that I am doubtful that they want to believe, in the world today, that this love is a spiritual love in its own right and therefore comes from religion, because they foster a notion about it that is purely physical.

Then they said to me, "Write about it and complete the revelation, and then we'll drop the book written about it down from heaven, and we'll see if they accept the things that are in it. And we'll also see if they want to acknowledge that this love is in keeping with the religion in a person—spiritual in spiritual people, worldly in worldly people, and purely physical in adulterers."

535   After this I heard a hostile murmur from those below and with it these words, "Do miracles and we'll believe."

I asked, "Aren't these things miracles?"

The answer was, "They are not."

"So what are miracles?" I asked.

"Disclose and reveal the future and we'll have faith."

But I answered, "Heaven does not grant things like that, because to the extent that a person knows the future his reason and intellect, together with his prudence and wisdom, fall idle, go numb, and collapse." And again I asked, "What other miracles shall I do?"

They shouted, "Do miracles like the ones Moses did in Egypt."

To this I answered, "Maybe you'll harden your heart to them like Pharaoh and the Egyptians."

The answer was, "No, we won't."

But again I said, "Promise me you aren't going to dance around a golden calf and worship it as the descendants of Jacob did within a month after they saw all Mount Sinai on fire and heard Jehovah Himself speaking from the fire—in other words, after a miracle that was the greatest of all." (The spiritual meaning of a golden calf is physical pleasure.)

The response from below was, "We won't be like the descendants of Jacob."

But then I heard this spoken to them from heaven. "If you do not believe Moses and the Prophets, that is, the Word of the Lord, you'll not believe on account of miracles any more than the descendants of Jacob in the desert, nor any more than they believed when they saw with their own eyes the miracles the Lord did when He was in the world."